P9-CQM-654

THE
ANIMALS'
WHO'S WHO

THE ANIMALS' WHO'S WHO

1,146 CELEBRATED ANIMALS IN HISTORY,
POPULAR CULTURE, LITERATURE, AND LORE

RUTHVEN TREMAIN

ROUTLEDGE & KEGAN PAUL
London, Melbourne and Henley

for Tucky and Jerry

First published in 1982
by Routledge & Kegan Paul Ltd
39 Store Street, London WC1E 7DD,
296 Beaconsfield Parade, Middle Park,
Melbourne, 3206, Australia, and
Broadway House, Newtown Road,
Henley-on-Thames, Oxon RG9 1EN

Manufactured in the United States of America
Copyright © 1982 Ruthven Tremain
No part of this book may be reproduced
in any form without permission from the publisher,
except for the quotation of brief passages in criticism.

ISBN 0-7100-9449-3

With gratitude for permission to reprint excerpts from copyrighted works of the
following authors:

Hilaire Belloc: "Jack and His Pony, Tom" and "Tom and His Pony, Jack" from
Complete Verse. Copyright 1931, renewed 1959 by Eleanor Jebb Belloc, Elizabeth
Belloc, and Hilary Belloc. Reprinted by permission of Alfred A. Knopf, Inc.,
New York, and Gerald Duckworth & Company Ltd., London.

Ludwig Bemelmans: *Madeline's Rescue.* Copyright 1951, 1953 by Ludwig Bemelmans. Copyright renewed 1979, 1981 by Madeleine Bemelmans and Barbara B. Marciano. Reprinted by permission of Viking Penguin Inc.

Thornton Burgess: *The Adventures of Reddy Fox.* Copyright 1913, 1941 by Thornton Burgess; *The Adventures of Peter Cotton-Tail.* Copyright 1914, 1942 by Thornton Burgess; *The Adventures of Grandfather Frog.* Copyright 1915, 1943 by Thornton Burgess; *The Adventures of Buster Bear.* Copyright 1916, 1944 by Thornton Burgess. By permission of Little, Brown and Company.

G. K. Chesterton: "The Oracle of the Dog" from *The Incredulity of Father Brown.* Copyright 1928 by Dodd, Mead and Company, Inc. Copyright renewed 1953 by Oliver Chesterton; "The Ballad of the White Horse" from *The Collected Poems of G. K. Chesterton.* Copyright 1932 by Dodd, Mead and Company, Inc. Copyright renewed 1959 by Oliver Chesterton. Reprinted by permission of Miss D. E. Collins.

Text from GARFIELD by Jim Davis. © 1978 United Feature Syndicate, Inc.

T. S. Eliot: "Bustopher Jones: The Cat About Town," "Gus: The Theatre Cat," "Macavity: The Mystery Cat" from *Old Possum's Book of Practical Cats.* Copyright 1939 by T. S. Eliot. Copyright renewed 1967 by Esme Valerie Eliot. Reprinted by permission of Harcourt Brace Jovanovich Inc., New York, and Faber and Faber Ltd., London.

Paul Gallico: *The Abandoned.* Copyright 1950 by Paul Gallico. Reprinted by permission of Random House, New York.

David Garnett: *Lady into Fox.* Copyright 1923 by Alfred A. Knopf, Inc. Reprinted by permission of the Executors of the Author's Literary Estate and Chatto and Windus Ltd., London.

Jean Giraudoux: *The Madwoman of Chaillot.* Copyright 1947 by Maurice Valency under the title *La Folle de Chaillot* by Jean Giraudoux. English version by Maurice Valency. Reprinted by permission of International Creative Management on behalf of Maurice Valency and the Estate of Jean Giraudoux.

Graham Greene: "Great Dog of Weimar" from *Collected Essays.* Copyright 1951 by Graham Greene. Copyright renewed 1979 by Graham Greene. Reprinted by permission of Viking Penguin Inc., New York, and The Bodley Head, London.

Joel Chandler Harris: *Uncle Remus: His Songs and His Sayings.* Copyright © 1921 Esther La Rose Harris, 1967 Meredith Press. Reprinted by permission of Hawthorn Properties (Elsevier-Dutton Publishing Co., Inc.).

George Herriman: *Krazy Kat.* Copyright © 1969 by King Features Syndicate, Inc., Nostalgia Press, Inc., and Grosset & Dunlap, Inc. Reprinted by permission of King Features.

James Joyce: *Ulysses.* Copyright 1914, 1918 by Margaret Caroline Anderson and renewed 1942, 1946 by Nora Joseph Joyce. Reprinted by permission of Random House, Inc., New York; The Bodley Head, London; and The Society of Authors, London, as literary representative of the Estate of James Joyce.

Walt Kelly: *Ten Ever-Lovin' Blue-Eyed Years With Pogo.* Copyright © 1959 by Walt Kelly; *Pogo: We Have Met The Enemy and He Is Us.* Copyright © 1972 by Walt Kelly; *Pogo's Bats and the Belles Free.* Copyright © 1976 by the Estate of Walt Kelly, Selby Kelly, executrix. Reprinted by permission of Simon & Schuster, a Division of Gulf & Western Corporation.

Munro Leaf: *The Story of Ferdinand,* illustrated by Robert Lawson. Copyright 1936 by Munro Leaf and Robert Lawson. Copyright renewed 1964 by Munro Leaf and John W. Boyd. Reprinted by permission of Viking Penguin Inc., New York, and Curtis Brown Ltd., London, on behalf of the Estate of Munro Leaf.

C. S. Lewis: *The Lion, the Witch and the Wardrobe.* Copyright 1950 by the Trustees of the Estate of C. S. Lewis, renewed 1978 by Arthur Owen Barfield; *Prince Caspian.* Copyright 1951 by the Trustees of the Estate of C. S. Lewis, renewed 1979 by Arthur Owen Barfield; *The Horse and His Boy.* Copyright 1954 by the Trustees of the Estate of C. S. Lewis. Reprinted with permission of Macmillan Publishing Co., Inc., New York, and William Collins Sons & Co. Ltd., London; *The Magician's Nephew.* Copyright 1955 by C. S. Lewis ; and *The Last Battle.* Copyright 1956 by C. S. Lewis. Reprinted with permission of Macmillan Publishing Co., Inc., New York, and The Bodley Head, London.

Hugh Lofting: *The Story of Doctor Dolittle.* Copyright 1948, by Josephine Lofting, Copyright 1920, by Hugh Lofting. All rights reserved. Reprinted by permission of Christopher Lofting.

Amy Lowell: "To Winky" from *The Complete Poetical Works of Amy Lowell.* Copyright © 1955 by Houghton Mifflin Company. Reprinted by permission of the publisher.

Russell Maloney: "Inflexible Logic," first printed in *The New Yorker,* from *A Subtreasury of American Humor,* E. B. White and Katharine S. White, editors. Copyright 1941, by E. B. White and Katharine S. White. Reprinted by permission of Coward-McCann & Geoghegan, Inc.

Don Marquis: *The Lives and Times of Archy and Mehitabel.* Copyright 1933 by Doubleday & Company, Inc. Reprinted by permission of Doubleday & Company, Inc.

A. A. Milne: *Winnie-the-Pooh.* Copyright 1926, by E. P. Dutton & Co., Inc. Renewal, 1954, by A. A. Milne; *The House at Pooh Corner.* Copyright 1928, by E. P. Dutton & Co., Inc. Renewal, 1956, by A. A. Milne. Reprinted by permission of the publisher, E. P. Dutton, Inc., New York, Methuen Children's Books Ltd., London, and The Canadian Publishers, McClelland and Stewart Limited, Toronto.

Christopher Morley: The poem "In Honor of Taffy Topaz" from *Chimneysmoke.* Copyright 1921, by J. B. Lippincott Company. Renewed, 1949 by Christopher Morley. Reprinted by permission of Harper & Row, Publishers, Inc.

Beatrix Potter: *The Tailor of Gloucester.* Copyright 1903, 1931 by Frederick Warne & Co.; *The Tale of Benjamin Bunny.* Copyright 1904, 1932 by Frederick Warne & Co.; *The Tale of Mrs. Tiggy-Winkle.* Copyright 1905, 1933 by Frederick Warne & Co.; *The Tale of Tom Kitten.* Copyright 1907, 1935 by Frederick Warne & Co.; *The Roly-Poly Pudding.* Copyright 1908, 1936 by Frederick Warne & Co.; *The Tale of the Flopsy Bunnies.* Copyright 1909, 1937 by Frederick Warne & Co.; *Ginger and Pickles.* Copyright 1909, 1937 by Frederick Warne & Co.; *The Tale of Mrs. Tittlemouse.* Copyright 1910, 1938 by Frederick Warne & Co.; *The Tale of Timmy Tiptoes*. Copyright 1911, 1939 by Frederick Warne & Co.; *The Tale of Mr. Tod.* Copyright 1912, 1940 by Frederick Warne & Co.; *The Tale of Pigling Bland.* Copyright 1913, 1941 by Frederick Warne & Co.; *Apply Dappley Nursery Rhymes.* Copyright 1917, 1945 by Frederick Warne & Co.; *Cecily Parsley's Nursery Rhymes.* Copyright 1922, 1950 by Frederick Warne & Co.; *The Tale of Little Pig Robinson.* Copyright 1930, 1958 by Frederick Warne & Co.; *The Tale of Tuppenny* from *A History of the Writings of Beatrix Potter* by Leslie Linder. Copyright 1971 by Frederick Warne & Co. Reprinted by permission of Frederick Warne & Co.

Damon Runyon: "Lillian" from *Guys and Dolls.* Copyright 1929, 1930, 1931 by Damon Runyon. Copyright renewed 1957, 1958, 1959 by Damon Runyon, Jr., and Mary Runyon McCann, as children of the author. Reprinted by special permission of American Play Company, Inc., and Anthony Lyons of The Chase Manhattan Bank, N. A.

Saki (H. H. Munro): "The Brogue," "Esme," "Sredni Vashtar," and "Tobermory" from *The Complete Short Stories of Saki.* Copyright 1930 by The Viking Press, Inc. Copyright renewed 1958 by The Viking Press, Inc. Reprinted by permission of Viking Penguin Inc.

Pierre Salinger: *With Kennedy.* Copyright © 1966 by Pierre Salinger. Reprinted by permission of Doubleday & Company, Inc.

Felix Salten: *Bambi*, translated by Whittaker Chambers. Copyright 1928; copyright renewed © 1956 by Simon & Schuster, a division of Gulf & Western Corporation. Reprinted by permission of Simon & Schuster, New York, Jonathan Cape Ltd., London, and the Executors of the Felix Salten Estate.

Dorothy L. Sayers: The short story "The Cyprian Cat." Copyright 1940 Dorothy L. Sayers. Copyright renewed 1967 Anthony Fleming; The poem "War Cat" from *A Quorum of Cats.* Copyright 1963 Dodd, Mead and Company, Inc. Reprinted by kind permission of David Higham Associates, London; The poem "For Timothy, in the Coinherence" from *A Matter of Eternity.* Copyright © 1973 by William B. Eerdmans Publishing Company. Reprinted by permission of William B. Eerdmans Publishing Company.

Charles M. Schulz: *Snoopy and the Red Baron.* Copyright © 1966 by United Feature Syndicate, Inc.

Dr. Seuss (Theodor Seuss Geisel): *Thidwick, the Big-Hearted Moose.* Copyright 1948 by Dr. Seuss. Reprinted by permission of Random House, Inc., New York, and William Collins Sons & Co. Ltd., London.

Isaac Bashevis Singer: "Zlateh the Goat" from *Zlateh the Goat and Other Stories.* Copyright 1966 by Isaac Bashevis Singer. Reprinted by permission of Harper & Row, Publishers, Inc.

Dodie Smith: *The Hundred and One Dalmatians.* Copyright © 1956 by Dodie Smith. Reprinted by permission of Viking Penguin Inc., New York, and William Heinemann Ltd., London.

James Thurber: "The Dog That Bit People." Copyright © 1933, 1961, James

Thurber. From *My Life and Hard Times*, published by Harper & Row; "An Introduction." Copyright © 1943, 1971, James Thurber. From *The Fireside Book of Dog Stories*, published by Simon & Schuster; "And So to Medve." Copyright © 1955, James Thurber. From *Thurber's Dogs*, published by Simon & Schuster; "The Cat in the Lifeboat." Copyright © 1956, James Thurber. From *Further Fables for Our Time*, published by Simon & Schuster. Reprinted by permission of Helen Thurber.

Eve Titus: *Anatole*. Copyright © 1956 by Eve Titus and Paul Galdone; *Basil of Baker Street*. Copyright © 1958 by Eve Titus and Paul Galdone. Used with the permission of McGraw-Hill Book Company.

Brandon Walsh and Darrell McClure: "Little Annie Rooney." © King Features Syndicate.

E. B. White: "Obituary" from *Quo Vadimus*. Copyright 1932, © 1960 by E. B. White; *Stuart Little*. Copyright 1945, © 1973 by E. B. White; *Charlotte's Web*. Copyright 1952, © 1980 by E. B. White. Reprinted by permission of Harper & Row, Publishers, Inc., New York, and Hamish Hamilton Limited, London.

P. G. Wodehouse: "Jeeves and the Dog McIntosh" from *Very Good, Jeeves*. Copyright 1930 by P. G. Wodehouse; "The Story of Webster" from *Mulliner Nights*. Copyright 1933 by P. G. Wodehouse; "Pig-hoo-o-o-o-ey!" from *Blandings Castle*. Copyright 1935 by P. G. Wodehouse. Reprinted by permission of the author's estate and the author's agents, Scott Meredith Literary Agency, Inc., 845 Third Avenue, New York, New York 10022.

William Butler Yeats: "The Cat and the Moon" from *Collected Poems*. Copyright 1919 by Macmillan Publishing Co., Inc., renewed 1947 by Bertha Georgie Yeats. Reprinted with permission of Macmillan Publishing Co., Inc., New York, and of Michael and Anne Yeats and Macmillan London Limited.

With gratitude for permission to reprint the following copyrighted illustrations:

Two drawings from *Ten Ever-Lovin' Blue-Eyed Years with Pogo* by Walt Kelly. Copyright © 1959 by Walt Kelly. Reprinted by permission of Simon & Schuster, a Division of Gulf & Western Corporation.

Photograph of Joe Camp's BENJI © 1982 Mulberry Square Productions, Inc. Courtesy of Mulberry Square Productions.

An illustration by Harrison Cady from *The Adventures of Unc' Billy Possum* by Thornton Burgess. Copyright 1914 by Little, Brown and Company. Copyright 1942 by Thornton Burgess. By permission of Little, Brown and Company.

Two illustrations by Arthur Burdette Frost from the book *Uncle Remus: His Songs and His Sayings* by Joel Chandler Harris. Copyright © 1921 Esther La Rose Harris, 1967 Meredith Press. Reprinted by permission of Hawthorn Properties (Elsevier-Dutton Publishing Co., Inc.).

Two illustrations by Ernest H. Shepard from *Winnie-the-Pooh* by A. A. Milne. Copyright 1926, by E. P. Dutton & Co., Inc. Renewal, 1954, by A. A. Milne. Copyright under the Berne Convention. One illustration by Ernest H. Shepard from *The House at Pooh Corner* by A. A. Milne. Copyright 1928, by E. P. Dutton & Co., Inc. Renewal, 1956, by A. A. Milne. Copyright under the Berne Convention. Reprinted by permission of the publisher, E. P. Dutton, Inc., New York, The Canadian Publishers, McClelland and Stewart Limited, Toronto, and Curtis Brown Ltd., London, on behalf of the Estate of E. H. Shepard.

A still photograph from the MGM release "LASSIE COME HOME" © 1943 Loew's Inc. Copyright renewed 1970 by Metro-Goldwyn-Mayer Inc. Reproduced by permission of MGM.

A copyrighted photograph of Lucy, the Margate Elephant, a representation of which serves as the service mark and registered trademark of The Save Lucy Committee, Inc., Margate, New Jersey. Reprinted by permission of The Save Lucy Committee, Inc.

An illustration by George Herriman from the book *The Lives and Times of Archy and Mehitabel* by Don Marquis. Copyright 1933 by Doubleday & Company, Inc. Reprinted by permission of Doubleday & Company, Inc.

Illustration by Garth Williams from the book *The Rescuers* by Margery Sharp. Illustration copyright © 1959 by Garth Williams. Reproduced by permission of Garth Williams. All rights reserved.

One illustration from each of the following books by Beatrix Potter: *The Tale of Benjamin Bunny.* Copyright 1904, 1932 by Frederick Warne & Co.; *The Tale of Mrs. Tiggy-Winkle.* Copyright 1905, 1933 by Frederick Warne & Co.; *The Tale of Mr. Jeremy Fisher.* Copyright 1906, 1934 by Frederick Warne & Co.; *The Roly-Poly Pudding.* Copyright 1908, 1936 by Frederick Warne & Co. Reproduced by permission of Frederick Warne & Co. All rights reserved.

A still photograph from the MGM cartoon "TOM AND JERRY" © 1940 Loew's Incorporated. Copyright renewed 1967 by Metro-Goldwyn-Mayer Inc. Reproduced by permission of MGM.

Part of an illustration from *Yertle the Turtle and Other Stories* by Dr. Seuss. Copyright © 1958 by Dr. Seuss. Reprinted by permission of Random House, Inc., New York, and William Collins Sons & Co. Ltd., London.

CONTENTS

PREFACE

This directory of animals covers eight thousand years, from the ancient Egyptian zoomorphic cat-god Ra to the anthropomorphic alligator Albert, who smoked cigars and ran political campaigns in a twentieth-century comic strip; from Alexander the Great's durable horse Bucephalus to Nim Chimpsky, a chimpanzee who learned sign language in the 1970s. The animal attributes of the entries vary, from the real Custer Wolf, a hunted predator in South Dakota, to the Teddy Bear, who is more comforting than ursine; from the Lion of Lucerne, a solemn symbol in stone, to Morris, a live cat on television who "says" he is finicky.

With so many possibilities, the question of who should be in this Who's Who had to be settled first, and with a deep bow to birds, fish, insects, and mythical monsters like the half-man, half-bull Minotaur, I decided to confine the entries to named quadrupeds, real or imagined, of known species. Since rules invite exceptions, a few odd creatures appear, like Cerberus, the multiheaded dog with a snake's tail—but he was mostly dog, just as the winged Pegasus was mostly horse. Eight-legged Sleipnir was all horse, only more so. He and Moby Dick and three more aquatic mammals are the only non-quadrupeds. Any collection of famous animals would be incomplete without Moby Dick.

The four-footed rule comes from dictionary definitions of the word "animal": first, a living being capable of spontaneous movement, as distinguished from a plant; second, any one of the lower animals, as distinguished from man; the next, a mammal—or a quadruped—as distinguished from a bird, insect, etc. Although this last definition does exclude some entertaining winged characters, several of them—Donald Duck, Tweety Pie, archy the cockroach, for example—are mentioned, although not as separate entries. And with the roster not restricted to mammals, worthies such as Old Rip, Brer Tarrypin, and Kermit the frog can be celebrated.

As for the entry titles, some animals are notable by association and are listed that way; for example, Cowper's Hares and Actaeon's Hounds, who had names, are better known collectively. Although the name of Paul Revere's horse has been forgotten, she is part of history. It does not matter that Thales' Mule and Froude's Cat are anonymous. They are memorable, and this Who's Who allows identification by apostrophe. But most nameless creatures—the wolf who suckled Romulus and Remus, Mary's little lamb, the camel whose back was broken by a straw, and the like—are excluded because there is little more to say about them.

A few words about what is here: There are more dogs than any other species. Horses are next, then cats. These three account for half the entries. Apes are a distant fourth, followed by cows, calves, and bulls, then hares and rabbits. Approximately eighty species are represented, among them, the anteater and the Tasmanian devil. More than a fourth of the animals described actually existed. Nearly half of the entries are found in literature, including children's books. For some reason, perhaps the ease of making the sound, more names begin with B than with any other letter.

The choice of animals had to be subjective. Every distinguished Standardbred, every animated cartoon character, every ostensible animal in children's books, every zoo star, and so forth could not be included. I sought a fair sample, favoring the most prominent, popular, interesting, bizarre, entertaining. In literature, it seemed obvious that Thornton Burgess, Rudyard Kipling, Jean de La Fontaine, and Beatrix Potter should be generously represented; I may have neglected certain writers. In some categories, a single sample should suffice—for dairy cows, the peerless Beecher Arlinda Ellen; for "talking" dogs, Lola. Deserving animals have undoubtedly been overlooked and I shall welcome their names. Like any Who's Who, this one may someday be revised.

Finding the animals who are included was a treasure hunt, and many people suggested favorites from their childhood. A college senior shyly admitted that he had always liked Curious George; a

40-year-old father spoke of Freddy the detective; a 60-year-old friend said that, as a child, she *was* Old Mr. Benjamin Bunny; and an 85-year-old neighbor recalled his father reading aloud Seton's story of Lobo. I remembered seeing Buddy when Morris Frank came to my school to talk about The Seeing Eye.

Barbara Ninde Byfield, Anne and Joseph Carroll, Polly Rowles, and Peggy and David Van Dyck gave me a lot of help with the entire project, especially with the works of P. G. Wodehouse, James Joyce, and Colette, and with performing animals and the history of the Thoroughbred. I thank them all.

My little dog may have inspired insights during the long preparation of this book. He certainly stimulated the respect and affection that I have for animals, and amused me, as so many of them do. I was also fortunate to receive comments on the manuscript from Jacques Barzun, Sallie Moore, Thomas Powers, and my patient editor, Laurie Graham Schieffelin, who trusted me with her idea—an animals' Who's Who. To them, my heartfelt gratitude. They have contributed to what qualities the book has. The flaws are mine.

Note: A name appearing in the text in small capitals, e.g., MICKEY MOUSE, indicates that a main entry for that name may be found at the appropriate alphabetical location. When two or more animals have the same name, the names are numbered chronologically, e.g., BADGER (1), BADGER (2).

ABDUL

AARDY, born September 24, 1967, at the Crandon Park Zoo in Miami, was the first aardvark born in captivity in the Western Hemisphere. She was 22½ inches long and weighed 4 pounds, 2 ounces. Since the mother would have nothing to do with the wrinkled baby, Aardy was raised by a veterinarian and fed a formula that included strained beef.

The sole member of the Tubulidentata order of mammals, the aardvark (*Orycteropus afer*) is a nocturnal animal whose natural habitat is Africa, in open areas south of the Sahara, where it burrows for termites. Its name comes from the Dutch words for earth, *aard*, and pig, *vark*. It has the ears of a donkey, a tail like a kangaroo's, and a long snout with a tip like a pig's. Its skin is completely covered with black fur, or partly with bristles and partly with nothing. As a zoo official said, "Once you have seen an aardvark, you are not likely to forget it."

ABDUL, a Greek burro, was used by James Simpson Kirkpatrick, an Australian stretcher-bearer in World War I, to carry the wounded after the disastrous Gallipoli landing in 1915. Day after day, Kirkpatrick, who became known as the "Good Samaritan of Gallipoli," set one soldier after another astride Abdul to be carried down the dangerous "Shrapnel Gully" to aid stations on the Turkish beach. Kirkpatrick was killed, but the little donkey kept going. Abdul was later adopted by the 6th Mountain Battery and taken to India. "The Man with the Donkey," a statue by Wallace Anderson of Kirkpatrick supporting a wounded Anzac on Abdul's back, was placed in the Shrine of Remembrance at Melbourne, Australia. In 1964, the statue was reproduced on three postage stamps commemorating the fiftieth anniversary of the Gallipoli landing.

ABLE and BAKER, a 6-pound rhesus monkey and an 11-ounce squirrel monkey, both female, were the first animals to survive being rocketed into space by the United States. They were sent aloft in the nose cone of a Jupiter rocket at Cape Canaveral, Florida, on May 28, 1959. An

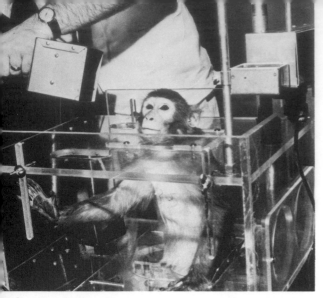

ABLE   BAKER

hour and a half later, after reaching an altitude of 300 miles and a speed of 10,000 mph, they splashed down near Antigua, 1,071 miles downrange. In earlier rocket tests by the U.S., monkeys and mice had reached the upper atmosphere but had perished in flight. Able and Baker endured thirty-eight times the pull of gravity during reentry, and were recovered in apparently good condition, but Able died a few days later, presumably from an anesthetic. "Miss Baker, America's first lady of space," as NASA calls her, settled into a comfortable life at the Alabama Space and Rocket Center in Huntsville. In 1979, the mayor of Huntsville proclaimed her twenty-second birthday, June 29, "Monkeynaut Baker Day"; she has become the oldest squirrel monkey in captivity.

ABU AL-ABBAS, an elephant, was presented to Charlemagne in A.D. 802 by Harun al-Rashid, the Caliph of Bagdad made famous in *The Arabian Nights*. Delighted with the beast, the emperor quartered him at the capital, Aix-la-Chapelle (Aachen), and each spring took him along with an escort of camels on tours of the empire. In 810, Charlemagne expected his Danish foes to panic at the sight of the elephant but Abu al-Abbas died during the journey.

ABUHERRIRA'S CAT was one of four animals admitted to the Moslem paradise in "The Favored Beasts," a poem by Johann von Goethe (1749–1832):

> Abuherrira's Cat, too, here
> Purrs round his master blest,
> For holy must the beast appear
> The Prophet hath caress'd.

A companion of Mohammed, Abū Huraira was a humorous man who was so fond of cats that he was called "the father of the little cat."

ACHELOUS, a river-god in Greek mythology, turned himself into a bull to fight Hercules because they were both in love with the same girl, Deianira. Hercules, who had considerable experience in subduing large animals, threw Achelous to the ground, broke off one of his horns, and gave the horn to the nymphs, who kept it

[2]

full of flowers. He also married Deianira. Although the Greeks believed that the original Horn of Plenty, or Cornucopia, came from AMALTHEA the goat, the Romans said it belonged to Achelous.

ACTAEON, a young hunter in Greek mythology, happened into a grotto at the moment when the goddess Artemis had disrobed to step into its pool. Incensed at being seen naked and having no arrows handy, she splashed water at him, changing him into a stag. The blameless Actaeon, who had never known fear, found his own hounds chasing him. He ran for his life but was not swift enough: they tore him to pieces.

ACTAEON'S HOUNDS were named: Alce (*strength*), Amarynthos, Asbolos (*soot-color*), Banos, Boreas, Canache (*ringwood*), Chediatros, Cisseta, Coran (*crop-eared*), Cyllo (*halt*), Cyllopotes (*zigzagger*), Cyprios, Draco (*the dragon*), Dromas (*the courser*), Dromios (*seize-'em*), Echnobas, Eudromos (*good runner*), Harpale (*voracious*), Harpeia (*tear-'em*), Ichnobate (*tracker*), Labros (*furious*), Lacena (*lioness*), Lachne (*glossy*), Lacon, Ladon, LELAPS (*hurricane*), Lampos (*shining one*), Leucos (*gray*), Lycisca, Lyncea, Machimos (*boxer*), Melampe (*black*), Melanchete (*black-coated*), Melanea (*black*), Menelea, Molossos, Napa (*sired by a wolf*), Nebrophonos (*fawn-killer*), Ocydroma (*swift runner*), Oresitrophos (*mountain-bred*), Oribasos (*mountain-ranger*), Pachytos (*thick-skinned*), Pamphagos (*ravenous*), Pomenis (*leader*), Pterelas (*winged*), Stricta (*spot*), Theridamas (*beast-tamer*), Theron (*savage-faced*), Thoös (*swift*), and Uranis (*heavenly one*). (See ACTAEON.)

ADHA, the slit-eared, was the swiftest of Mohammed's camels.

AGRIPPINA sat on the desk as Agnes Repplier wrote in *Essays in Idleness* (1893), "I have long known that cats are the most contemptuous of creatures, and that Agrippina is the most contemptuous of cats." With a toss of the head to dog owners—"It is better to be beautiful than to fetch and carry"—Repplier produced a portrait, filled with allusions to the literature about cats, of her "droll" companion. Agrippina disdained food that was not in her own blue and white china, perched on the windowsill to taunt the terrier next door, and leaped out of the room if she was laughed at. "But when Agrippina has breakfasted, and washed, and sits in the sunlight blinking at me with affectionate contempt, I feel soothed by her absolute and unqualified enjoyment."

AIRAVATA, in one legend of Hindu mythology, was the first elephant to emerge from an eggshell in Brahma's right hand after the bird-god Garuda burst from the egg. Seven more male elephants followed; then eight females came out of the half shell in Brahma's left hand. These eight couples, the ancestors of all elephants, became the caryatids of the world, supporting it at the four cardinal points and the four between.

In another myth, Airavata was a milk-white elephant who rose from the Churning of the Ocean and was used as a mount by Indra, the king of the gods. Originally, elephants had wings and since white elephants symbolized clouds, the source of rain and fertility, they are still regarded as lucky. One day, a number of winged elephants perched on a branch of a tree to listen to a wise teacher. The bough broke under their weight, several students were killed, and the sage cursed the elephants. They lost their wings and from then on, elephants were doomed to stay on the ground.

AKELA, "the great gray Lone Wolf" in Rudyard Kipling's *Jungle Books* (1894, 1895), was the leader of the Seeonee Wolf Pack until he failed to kill a buck and was deposed; but he was not too feeble to help the boy Mowgli ambush the tiger SHERE KHAN. When Mowgli laid the tiger's hide on the Council Rock, where the Lone Wolf had presided, the pack howled for Akela to lead them again. He turned white as he aged, his ribs showed, and "he walked as though he had been made of wood." When two hundred dholes, vicious red hunting dogs, attacked the wolves, the all-but-toothless Akela fought to the death, with a final cry to his pack, "Good hunting!"

ALBERT, the cigar-chomping alligator in Walt Kelly's comic strip *Pogo*, preferred to win. When POGO the possum cleared the board at checkers twice, Albert dared him to beat four aces. When an opponent in a poetry contest said he was going home to work on his iambic pentameter, the alligator raged, "By tunkit, if you uses any machinery, I'll declare a foul!" Albert was vain, too. Donning an "impenatrabobble" disguise of wig, beard, funny hat, and glasses, he exclaimed, "Dog my cats! A handsome man looks good in anything!"

Kelly created Albert in 1943 for *Bumbazine and Albert the Alligator*, a comic book strip about a little boy who lived in the Okefenokee swamp. After Pogo replaced the boy, it was called *Albert and Pogo*, until

ALBERT

it was moved to a newspaper in 1948. National syndication followed a year later, and *Pogo* soon became one of the most popular comic strips of all time.

ALCIBIADES' DOG, a large, handsome animal, had a luxuriant tail as "his principal ornament," wrote Plutarch (A.D. ca. 26–120) in the *Parallel Lives*. Alcibiades was a willful Athenian general and playboy who behaved so outrageously that he had to leave the city. When he was finally welcomed back to Athens in 407 B.C., ten years later, he bought the dog, who fought off robbers trying to seize his gold collar but is best remembered for what was done to him. Alcibiades had the dog's tail docked and laughed at the public reaction: "Just what I wanted has happened. I wished the Athenians to talk about this, that they might not say something worse of me."

ALEXANDER, a little pig in Beatrix Potter's *The Tale of Pigling Bland* (1913), was "hopelessly volatile," clowning around on the way to market with his brother PIGLING BLAND. When a policeman stopped them, Alexander could not find his license to go to market and had to be taken home. Placed in the neighborhood, he did "fairly well when he had settled down."

ALGERNON, in "Flowers for Algernon" (1959) by Daniel Keyes, was the white laboratory mouse whose intelligence was so enhanced by psychosurgery that doctors were encouraged to try the procedure on Charlie Gordon, a mentally retarded 32-year-old. The operation was a success and Charlie became a genius. In the next few months, however, Algernon became erratic, regressed to his primitive intellectual state, and, finally, died. Before his own decline, Charlie was able to complete a report he had begun on "The Algernon-Gordon Effect," the deterioration of artificially induced intelligence.

Keyes' short story was the basis for a television drama and a novel. The motion picture version, *Charly*, appeared in 1968. *Charlie and Algernon*, the third musical based on the story, had its premiere in Washington, D.C., in March 1980, and featured a live mouse.

ALGONQUIN, an Icelandic calico pony, belonged to young Archibald Roosevelt during the period his father, Theodore, was President of the United States (1901–09). The boy often rode the pony to school. On the White House grounds, Algonquin liked to sneak up behind one of the children and start nudging him across the lawn. The pony had another trick that he performed with Skip, a little black mongrel President Roosevelt had brought back from a hunting trip. As Algonquin cantered around, Skip would leap on his back, and the pony would make a big show of snorting and shaking his head, trying to dislodge the dog. When Archie came down with measles, his brother Quentin was responsible for a White House first and, presumably, last. He smuggled Algonquin into the building and then took him up in the elevator, to cheer up poor Archie, confined to his bedroom upstairs.

ALIBORON, an ass, appeared in one of Jean de La Fontaine's *Fables* (1668), "The Thieves and the Ass." While two thieves scuffled over whether to keep or sell Aliboron, a third grabbed him. The three were fighting over the ass when a fourth thief turned up to settle matters. He seized Aliboron.

Nearly three centuries after the fable appeared, a painting by Boronali titled *Sunset over the Adriatic* was exhibited in Paris and was very well received. It was, in fact, done by a donkey. Some clever fellows in Montmartre, including the writer Roland Dorgelès, had tied a brush to its tail. The "painter's" name is an anagram for Aliboron.

ALIDORO, a swift mastiff sent by the police in *Pinocchio* (1883) by Carlo Collodi (Lorenzini), chased Pinocchio into the ocean. But the dog could not swim, and the puppet dragged him back to the beach by the tail. Alidoro returned the favor by rescuing Pinocchio when, coated with flour, he was about to be fried like a fish. Once safely away, Alidoro gave his paw, Pinocchio shook it, and they departed friends.

ALLAN F-1, a Standardbred foaled in Kentucky in 1886, was inclined to pace when he should have trotted and raced so badly that one owner after another sold him. Nor was he valued at stud: one owner traded him for a mule, another for a jackass. The handsome black stallion was more than 15 years old when James R. Brantley bought him for $110 and bred him to good walking mares in Tennessee. There had been Tennessee Walking Horses long before Allan was foaled, but his ability to transmit the loose-gaited quality that made him a failure at the track contributed so much to the breed that, in 1938, the Tennessee Walking Horse Breeder's Association of America designated him and his son Roan Allen F-38 "foundation sires."

ALVIN THE CHIPMUNK was created in September 1958 by singer-songwriter David Seville (born Ross Bagdaserian), who wanted to simulate little animal voices for a novelty recording of his song, "Christmas, Don't Be Late." He sang each harmonizing part in a little voice taped at half speed. Played back at full speed, the voices sounded most like chipmunks, he decided. Seville sang an introduction in his normal voice, gave the name "Alvin" to the testy chipmunk who bickered with him, and produced a hit record. Seven million copies were sold, and "The Chipmunk Song," as it was soon called, won two Grammy awards from the National Academy of Recording Artists and Sciences. Alvin did a reprise in 1959 with "Alvin's Harmonica," and was seen in an animated television series in the 1960s. His sound can easily be duplicated by playing a 33 rpm recording of a male vocalist at 78 rpm.

AMALTHEA, a female goat in Greek mythology, nursed the infant Zeus while he was in hiding from his father, Cronus. When one of her horns broke off, Zeus made it the Horn of Plenty, or Cornucopia, inexhaustibly full of fruit and grains and flowers. Amalthea was later placed in the sky as the sign of Capricorn. In another version of the same legend, she was the nymph who owned the goat.

ANATOLE, the mouse-hero of a series of picture books by Eve Titus, illustrated by Paul Galdone, was introduced in *Anatole* (1956). Stung by a remark that mice were a disgrace to France, Anatole began commuting by bicycle from his village near Paris to the Duval Cheese Factory, where, as self-appointed cheese-taster, he placed typed and claw-written recommendations on the various cheeses. His advice proved so profitable that he was hired, sight unseen, and from then on Anatole was hailed as "the mouse of action, the mouse of honor, the mouse *magnifique*."

ANDY PANDA, created by Walter Lantz for *Life Begins for Andy Panda* (1939), starred in animated cartoons for ten years. The panda was a nice little fellow who often served as a foil to Woody Woodpecker, the memorable character introduced in *Knock Knock* (1940).

ANNA MARIA, in *The Roly-Poly Pudding* (1908) by Beatrix Potter, was a skinny old rat whose fat husband, SAMUEL WHISKERS, sat around taking snuff and giving her orders. Anna Maria would argue shrilly and then do what he told her to.

ANUBIS, the god of the dead in ancient Egyptian mythology, was a jackal, or a man with a jackal's head. He helped Osiris judge the dead by weighing their hearts against the feather of truth and right. When Osiris was cut into many pieces and Isis reassembled them, Anubis, who was also the patron of embalming, helped her create the first mummy.

APIS (or HAP), the sacred bull of Memphis, was worshiped in ancient Egypt as the incarnation of the gods Ptah and

APIS

Osiris and was believed to be the offspring of a virgin cow impregnated by lightning or a moonbeam. Selected for consecration at birth, the black bull was recognized by certain markings, such as a white triangle on his forehead. Apis' every movement on the grounds of his temple was interpreted as some sort of omen. Whoever inhaled his breath was said to receive the ability to prophesy. Sacrifices were made to him and his birthdays were celebrated. But if he lived past 25, he was drowned, and after mourning ceremonies, the search was begun for a new Apis. In 1851, archaeologists discovered a sepulcher at Sakkara that contained the mummified remains of sixty-four sacred bulls.

APOLLINARIS, BEELZEBUB, BLATHER-SKITE, and ZOROASTER were four cats who belonged to Mark Twain (Samuel Clemens; 1835–1910). In a letter to *St. Nicholas*, a magazine for children, he explained that he named them that way, "not in an unfriendly spirit, but merely to practise the children in large and difficult styles of pronunciation." Two other cats had easier names, Sour Mash and Buffalo Bill.

APPLEY DAPPLY, in *Appley Dapply's Nursery Rhymes* (1917) by Beatrix Potter, was a sharp-eyed, little brown mouse, who lived in a cupboard full of "charming" things like pies.

ARGOS, in the *Odyssey* of Homer (eighth century B.C.), was a dog that Odysseus had bred and trained but had not had time to enjoy before he departed for the Trojan War. Twenty years later Odysseus returned

[7]

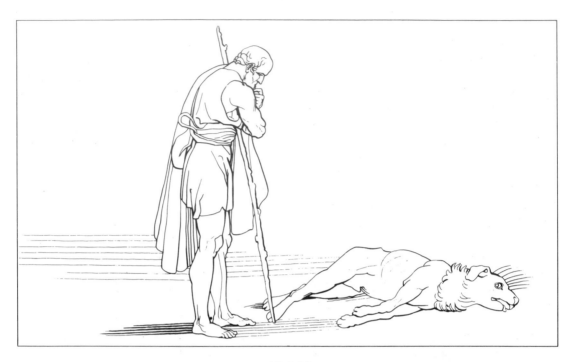

ARGOS

to his palace at Ithaca, disguised as a beggar to protect himself from the suitors surrounding his wife, Penelope. Accompanied by the swineherd Eumaeus, Odysseus entered the courtyard; at the sound of his voice, Argos, lying on a dung heap, raised his head and pricked up his ears. When he saw it was his master, the tick-infested old dog laid his ears back and wagged his tail, too weak to crawl forward. Not daring to show that he recognized his dog, Odysseus furtively brushed away a tear, while Eumaeus told him that the hound had been a marvelous hunter but was neglected now because his master had been gone so long. The two men walked on, and at that moment Argos died.

ARION, in Greek mythology, was the first horse given to man. When Demeter, search-ing for Persephone, was lustfully pursued by Poseidon, she transformed herself into a mare and tried to hide among the herds of Oncius in Arcadia, but Poseidon changed into a stallion and mated with her. The result was Arion, a wild horse of fabulous speed, who belonged to Heracles and then to Adrastus. In the war of the Seven against Thebes, Adrastus was the only one of the Seven to survive, because Arion galloped away with him.

ARISTIDES, a small chestnut colt de-scended from ECLIPSE, won the first Kentucky Derby at Churchill Downs in Louisville on May 17, 1875. Since his owner, Price McGrath, expected his other horse, Chesapeake, to win, Aristides was entered merely to wear out the opposition with his early speed. From the start of the race, however, Chesapeake was never in contention, while Aristides took the lead and held it. Nearing the final turn, the other horses started gaining on him and his jockey appeared to be easing up, expecting Chesapeake to take over the lead. McGrath, standing at the top of the stretch, waved and shouted at the jockey to urge the horse on. The jockey started whipping, Aristides picked up speed, and two challengers faded. It was the first of many Derbies where "the wrong horse" won.

ARKLE, the greatest steeplechaser to date, was foaled in Ireland in 1957 and won the Cheltenham Gold Cup in England three years in a row, the last time at odds of 9 to 100. He was a fast, fluid jumper and when he made a mistake, "found an extra leg" to right it. His greatest talent was accelerating in the stretch. One overtaken rider declared that Arkle went by "as if I were a double-decker bus." The big bay gelding won several races carrying 35 pounds more than any rival and completely dominated British steeplechasing until his thirty-fifth and final race in December 1966, when a small fracture put him out of contention and into a plaster cast.

THE ARMY MULE, mascot of the United States Military Academy football team, made its unofficial debut in 1899 at the Army–Navy game in Philadelphia because an officer at the Quartermaster Depot wanted something to oppose the Navy Goat (see BILL XXII). A white mule who had been pulling an ice wagon was groomed and outfitted with leggings, collar, blanket, and colored streamers. According to West Point legend, when the mascots met, the mule kicked "the astonished goat" toward the Navy stands. Army won, 17–5. In 1936, Mr. Jackson became the first official Army mascot; his most famous successor was TROTTER.

ARNOLD ZIFFEL, the pig on the television series "Green Acres" (1965–71), was a small Chester White from Indiana, whose appearances with the elegant Eva Gabor provided an amusing beauty-and-the-beast combination. Trained by Frank Inn, Arnold played the piano, took letters out of a mailbox, pulled a little wagon, sipped soda through a straw, and performed several other feats. The public loved him. Fan clubs sprouted around the country and a group of sixth graders in Hilliard, Ohio, wrote to the pig, promising that they would stop eating pork chops. In 1968 and 1969, Arnold Ziffel won the American Humane Association's Patsy Award for performing animals but then he outgrew his part by putting on too much weight. He was succeeded by Arnold II, who lasted a year and a half until he, too, had to be replaced.

ARTHUR, the playful elephant in a sailor suit with a red pompon on his hat, is a cousin of BABAR, the King of the Elephants, and the little brother of Queen CELESTE in the Babar books by Jean de Brunhoff.

ARTIO, a bear-goddess, was worshiped by the Helvetii, a Celtic people who inhabited the western part of Switzerland 2,000 years ago. In 1832, a statue of Artio was dug up in Bern. The city, founded in 1191, had been named for—and is still famous for—its bears. One appears on the earliest known town seal, made in 1224; since 1513, live bears have been kept in Bern's bear pit.

ARUNDEL was the great horse who belonged to the legendary Sir Bevis of Hampton, whose adventures in the twelfth century were related in a fourteenth-century English verse romance as well as in French and Italian tales. At a race in England, two knights managed to get a head start of "a large halfe mile and more," but Bevis had only to spur Arundel to overtake them halfway to the finish. Then King Edgar's son wanted to buy the horse. Bevis refused to sell, the prince went to the stable to try to steal the horse, and Arundel killed him with a kick in the head. So great was the king's anger that Bevis fled into exile.

ARVAK and ALSVID (EARLY WAKER and ALL SWIFT) are the horses who pull the sun across the sky in Norse mythology. Long ago, the gods took pity on them and put bellows under their yokes to keep them cool. The sun has to travel fast because she is pursued by the wolf SKOLL, who eventually catches her.

ASLAN, the wondrous Great Lion in the seven Chronicles of Narnia by C. S. Lewis (1898–1963), created the distant world called Narnia, gave its animals the power of speech, and transported English children through time and space to help the Narnian people resist evil forces. The lion manifested himself in a stern, disembodied voice, or materialized to guide his friends. In *The Horse and His Boy* (1954), Aslan clawed a girl's back to inflict the same pain she had caused a servant because she needed to know what it felt like. In *The Lion, the Witch and the Wardrobe* (1950), he saved a boy by submitting to be shorn, muzzled, and apparently killed. But Aslan was restored, golden mane and all, by "a

deeper magic." The lion destroyed evil-ridden Narnia in *The Last Battle* (1956), then guided the survivors to the next world.

ASTA, in Dashiell Hammett's detective story *The Thin Man* (1934), was a schnauzer bitch who liked to punch Nick Charles in the belly with her front feet. In the movie *The Thin Man* (1934), starring William Powell and Myrna Loy, Asta was a sprightly wirehaired fox terrier played by a male named Skippy. His grandson took the part in the fifth sequel, *The Song of the Thin Man* (1947). "The Thin Man" television series began in 1957 and its Asta, also a wirehair, won two Patsy Awards for performing animals, presented by the American Humane Association.

ATAIR, ANTARES, RIGEL, and ALDEBARAN were the Arabian horses who pulled Ben Hur's chariot in Lew Wallace's novel *Ben Hur* (1880), the story of a Jew captured by Romans during the time of Christ. In the great chariot race against Messala the Roman and three others, Ben Hur stayed second behind Messala for five laps, then cracked his whip for the first time at the final turn of the sixth and last lap. "Instantly not one, but the four as one, answered with a leap that landed them alongside the Roman's car." The axle point of Ben Hur's inner wheel caught and broke the outer wheel of Messala's chariot, wrecking the chariot. The Arabian horses opened the lead down the homestretch, running "like the long leaping of lions in harness; but for the lumbering chariot, it seemed the four were flying."

Ben Hur, one of the best-selling novels of all time, was dramatized on Broadway in 1900, and the most recent of three movie versions was filmed in Rome in 1959. In the spectacular chariot race, Charlton Heston as Ben Hur drove four Lippizaners who had been trained to rear and jump as a team to clear two wrecked chariots. Yakima Canutt, a former stunt man, directed the actual race and crashes, stunt men drove the nine chariots, and not a single horse was injured.

ATHOS, an infirm dog in James Joyce's *Ulysses* (1922), belonged to Leopold Bloom's father, Rudolph. Rudolph was a sick old man who committed suicide and in the letter he left, he wrote, "Be kind to Athos, Leopold, . . . my dear son." On the way to the cemetery after another funeral, Bloom recalled that the dog "took it to heart, pined away. Quiet brute. Old men's dogs usually are."

ATOSSA, the Persian cat that Matthew Arnold recalled in his elegy to his canary, "Poor Matthias" (1882), would sit for hours beside Matthias' cage. The "foolish bird" would flutter and chirp but Atossa never stirred:

> —Cruel, but composed and bland,
> Dumb, inscrutable and grand,
> So Tiberius might have sat,
> Had Tiberius been a cat.

AUDHUMLA, the cow of Norse mythology, was formed from the frost that melted on a misty, frozen plain when the world was created. She and the giant Ymir were the world's first living inhabitants. Ymir was nourished by Audhumla's milk, and from his body sprang more giants. Audhumla began licking the salt that was in the ice. As she licked, golden hair appeared, then a head—and Buri, first manlike being,

emerged. He produced his own son, Borr, who married the daughter of a giant. Their offspring were the three gods Odin, Vili, and Ve, who killed Ymir. From then until the end of the world, the race of gods and the race of giants were in mortal conflict.

AUNT PETTITOES, the old sow in Beatrix Potter's *The Tale of Pigling Bland* (1913), decided that eight pigs at home were too many. Keeping one for housework, she sent five away and groomed two, ALEXANDER and PIGLING BLAND, to go to market. Wiping her eyes and their noses with a big handkerchief, she instructed them on their behavior, then handed each one "eight conversation peppermints with appropriate moral sentiments in screws of paper."

AUNTS DORCAS and PORCAS, two Devonshire sows in *The Tale of Little Pig Robinson* (1930) by Beatrix Potter, "led prosperous uneventful lives, and their end was bacon." ROBINSON was their nephew. His adventures began when the aunts sent him to town on errands because they were too fat to go through the stiles.

AZAZEL, in one interpretation of the word, was the scapegoat on the Day of Atonement. In a ritual described in Leviticus 16, the high priest would cast lots over two male goats to select one to be sacrificed to Yahweh (the Lord) and the other, the scapegoat, to be sent into the wilderness, symbolically laden with the sins of the people. In other accounts, he was led to a rocky precipice and pushed over. The word "Azazel" has also been interpreted as "a rugged cliff," the place where the goat was taken, or as the name of the demon in the desert to whom he was sent.

BABAR, the urbane King of the Elephants, was introduced in France in *The Story of Babar* (1931), written and illustrated by Jean de Brunhoff, and based on a story that his wife, Cecile, had made up to amuse their sons. In the book, young Babar, whose mother had been killed by a hunter, fled to the city and was raised by an elegant old lady who saw to it that he dressed well and learned to drive a car. When Babar returned to the forest, the elephants were so impressed by his worldly ways that they crowned him King. His bride, CELESTE, was then crowned Queen.

De Brunhoff wrote six more Babar stories before he died in 1937. His son Laurent resumed the saga with *Babar and That Rascal Arthur* (1946) and has continued to produce books about the well-dressed elephant, his family, and their adventures. The stories have been translated into twelve languages, and a piano composition by Francis Poulenc to accompany a recital of *The Story of Babar* had its premiere in 1951. To celebrate the elephant's fiftieth birthday, three stories by Jean de Brunhoff

and three by his son were reprinted in *Babar's Anniversary Album* (1981), with an appreciation of their work by Maurice Sendak.

BABE, the legendary Paul Bunyan's Big Blue Ox, was seven ax handles wide between the eyes and heavier than the combined weight of all the fish that got away. He could pull anything that had two ends to it. When the Wisconsin River had a log jam that was 200 feet high at the head and backed up a mile, Paul put Babe at the head of the jam and shot him in the rear end with a Savage .303 rifle. That felt like flies to Babe, so he started switching his tail. The way it twirled around and around made the river flow backwards, and the jam was broken.

Paul Bunyan and Babe were created by loggers telling tall tales around campfires. The first published stories, in the *Detroit News* on July 24, 1910, were written by James MacGillivray, a former lumberjack turned reporter. Folklorists collected more yarns and such writers as Carl Sandburg retold them. There are large statues of Paul in at least four states; a park in California has a 30-foot-high statue of Babe; and Bayfield, Wisconsin, is the home of the "Mystic Knights of the Blue Ox."

BABIECA was the Cid's swift horse in *The Poem of the Cid* (ca. 1140), a celebration of the exploits of the real Cid, Rodrigo Díaz de Bivar (d. 1099). In the poem, which is the national epic of Spain, Babieca was the King of Seville's horse until the Cid won him in battle. Knowing nothing about him, the Cid mounted Babieca for the first time to ride out of Valencia to greet his wife and daughters on their return from imprisonment by King Alfonso. The horse galloped so fast that everyone marveled and from then on, Babieca was famous throughout Spain. Twice, armies of 50,000 Moors attacked Valencia and twice, the Christians led by the Cid on his splendidly caparisoned horse put them to flight. The second time, the Cid chased King Búcar of Morocco 7 miles to offer peace with surrender. Búcar refused and galloped away. He had a good horse but Babieca overtook them at the edge of the sea and the Cid killed the king.

BABY was a pet leopard in the movie *Bringing Up Baby* (1938), in which a shy paleontologist (Cary Grant) was so rattled by a dizzy rich girl (Katharine Hepburn) that he lost the animal and a dinosaur bone. He and the girl thought they had recovered Baby when they captured a wild leopard who had escaped from the circus, but after considerable confusion, the leopards were sorted out, the bone was retrieved from a dog, and the young couple were married. Hepburn's biographer Charles Higham re-

ported in *Kate* (1975) that the actress was fearless (as was Grant) about working with Nissa, the half-tame leopard in the film, even when she had to pat and shove the beast. At the trainer's suggestion, however, Hepburn wore a lot of perfume, which soothed the leopard, and also put resin on her shoes lest a sudden slip frighten Nissa into violence.

BADGER (1), one of the animal people, or spirits, in American Indian mythology, was a trickster character to the Micmacs in the northeastern United States. In the creation myths of the Hopis and other Pueblo tribes, he was the first animal to climb up to earth through a hole in the sky of the world below. They also believed that he was a healer. The Zunis valued Badger's medicine, especially during childbirth. A woman in labor would either wear a badger paw, called Badger Old Woman, or it would be placed near her—because a badger digs himself out so quickly.

BADGER (2), in Kenneth Grahame's *The Wind in the Willows* (1908), shunned society in the winter but when RAT and MOLE pounded on his door, he welcomed them with food, gossip, and clean sheets that smelled of lavender. Of his home, Badger said, "There's no security, no peace and tranquility, except underground." With the arrival of summer, he emerged to try to control the restless TOAD, who subsequently escaped. When Toad returned, Badger took charge of recapturing Toad Hall from invading weasels and ferrets, then decreed that Toad give a celebration banquet, but no speeches. The speeches would be full of "gas," said Badger "in his common way." From then on, mother weasels in the Wild Wood made their babies behave by threatening that "the terrible grey Badger" would get them—"a base libel on Badger who, though he cared little about Society, was rather fond of children."

BAGHEERA, the black panther in Rudyard Kipling's *Jungle Books* (1894, 1895), kept SHERE KHAN the tiger from claiming the baby Mowgli and watched over Mowgli as he grew up with the Wolf Pack. Once, when Mowgli got into mischief, Bagheera gave him "half a dozen love-taps from a panther's point of view," a severe beating for a 7-year-old, then carried the boy home. Punishment in the jungle was to settle scores, with "no nagging afterward." The Pack turned against Mowgli when he was about 11 years old, leaving Shere Khan free to attack him, but the boy was prepared. Bagheera had told him to bring fire from the village to the Pack meeting at the Council Rock. Mowgli beat the tiger over the head with a flaming branch and vowed to return to the Rock with Shere Khan's hide. When he did so a few months later, "Bagheera scratched himself all over with pure delight at the way in which Mowgli had managed his war."

BALAAM'S ASS is one of two talking animals in the Old Testament; the other is the serpent in the garden of Eden. The ass appears in Numbers 22:21–35, carrying Balaam, a Midianite seer or magician, toward the city of Moab, where the king wanted him to curse the Israelites. On the way, the angel of the Lord appeared in their path, visible only to the ass. She turned aside. Balaam hit her. She turned aside again, wedging Balaam's foot against

BALAAM'S ASS

a wall. He hit her again. She lay down and Balaam hit her a third time. At that point, the Lord gave her the power of speech and she said, "What have I done to you that you have struck me these three times?" Balaam said he was ready to kill her for making sport of him. She replied, "Am I not your ass on which you have ridden all your life long to this day? Was I ever accustomed to do so to you?" Then the angel became visible to Balaam, telling him that if the ass had not turned away, he, not the ass, would have been killed. The journey was resumed and when Balaam reached the Israelites, he blessed them instead of cursing them.

BALIUS, one of Achilles' immortal horses: see XANTHUS AND BALIUS.

BALOO, the brown bear in Rudyard Kipling's *Jungle Books* (1894, 1895), was allowed to attend the wolves' Pack Council because he taught the Law of the Jungle to their cubs. He was the first to speak in favor of the wolves' keeping the baby Mowgli and became his teacher when the boy grew older. If Mowgli faltered, the stern bear would cuff him. BAGHEERA the panther objected once and Baloo replied, "Better he should be bruised from head to foot by me who love him than that he should come to harm through ignorance." But the bear forgot to warn the boy about the gray apes who were the outcasts of the jungle. They seized Mowgli and carried him off as a prisoner. Baloo was mortified. "Put dead bats on my head! Give me black bones to eat!" he cried. "I am most miserable of bears." Then he lumbered off to help rescue the boy.

BALTO

BALTO, a black, long-haired malamute, was the leader of Gunnar Kasson's dog team, which reached diphtheria-plagued Nome, Alaska, at 5:36 A.M. on February 2, 1925, with antitoxin serum to bring the epidemic under control. Since the weather had made flying impossible, a series of sled teams had had to rush the serum 655 miles overland and along the coast, with Kasson making the final 60-mile run. Struggling through a blizzard with 80 mph winds at temperatures down to —50° F., Kasson often could not see where he was, let alone guess, but Balto somehow scented the trail through the snow and kept going. They crossed bare ice over frozen lagoons, broken ice that cut the dogs' feet like glass, and drifts of soft snow that kept toppling the sled. When they finally struggled into Nome, Kasson slumped in the snow and began pulling ice splinters out of Balto's bleeding paws. "I've been mushing Alaska since 1904," he said. "This was the toughest I've ever had on the trails. But Balto, he brought us through." Since December 16, 1925, generations of New York City children have been "mushing" Central Park astride a statue of Balto placed there on that date.

BAMBI, a newborn fawn, tottered to his feet at the beginning of Felix Salten's story of life in the woods, *Bambi* (1928). He grew to understand the sounds and the scents around him, and to fear the hunters. As a young stag, he fought two others to win FALINE for his mate. Bambi was still a fawn, calling for his mother, when he first saw the majestic stag known as THE OLD PRINCE, who rebuked him for not being able to stay by himself. From then on, Bambi was in awe of the aloof old stag, seeking him out to learn about survival in the forest. The greatest—and the hardest—lesson of all was: "You must live alone."

BANDOOLA, a Burmese elephant born in 1897 who became a powerful tusker in the teak trade, was one of the elephants who continued to extract desperately needed timber in the Kabaw Valley after the Japanese invaded Burma in 1942. When the final evacuation of Burma was ordered in March 1944, Lt. Col. John H. Williams, a former forest manager in charge of the work, had to move 45 elephants, 8 calves, and 198 people (including 64 women and children) 100 miles west over trackless mountains more than 5,000 feet high. In *Elephant Bill* (1950) and *Bandoola* (1955), Williams described how Bandoola led them past the crucial point of the journey. With his rider sitting on his head to direct his feet, Bandoola had to climb steps cut into a sandstone mountain in an ascent so steep that he appeared to be standing on his hind legs. After two hours, he reached a narrow ledge along the mountain's cliff face. As he traversed the ledge, the other elephants followed. At the end of the nineteen-day "Hannibal trek," Bandoola led the procession to a tea plantation near Silchar, carrying eight sick children in a pannier on his back.

BARGE, in James Thurber's "An Introduction" from *The Fireside Book of Dog Stories* (1943), was an ordinary sort of dog who lived with a family in Columbus, Ohio. When some neighborhood fellows lured him into a saloon and gave him a saucer of beer, Barge liked it. Pretty soon, he was drinking whisky, bumping into things, and staying out on the town, completely neglecting his watchdog duties. One night, burglars broke into his home and stole the cut glass and the best silver. Around noon the next day, Barge tottered home, saw the ransacked house, and "realized that he was not only a ne'er-do-well but a wrongo." Sacred trusts had been violated, "but there was still a spark of doghood left in him." Barge ran upstairs, jumped out the window, and killed himself.

BARRY, the famous rescue dog, was born in 1800 and trained at the hospice in the Swiss Alps near the Great St. Bernard Pass, 8,100 feet above sea level. St. Bernard of Menthon had founded the hospice in 1049 to help people crossing the pass. By the eighteenth century, the monks were using their mastiffs, originally kept as watchdogs, to scent a traveler lost or injured in the snow, dig him out, and hug him to restore body heat. (There was no little keg of brandy. Sir Edwin Landseer invented that in 1820 for his painting *Alpine Mastiffs Reanimating a Traveller*.) The breed, usually called *barihund* because the dogs looked like bears, was officially named St. Bernard in 1862 at a dog show in England. Barry, the supreme example of the breed, saved more than forty people. One was a child whose mother managed to strap him to the dog's back before she died. In 1812, after rescuing a young man who thought he was being attacked and had slashed the dog with his knife, Barry was retired. He died two years later.

BASIL, the mouse detective in a series of mysteries by Eve Titus, studied at the feet of Sherlock Holmes, lived in his cellar, and, with the help of a "clever little tailor," dressed like him. In *Basil of Baker Street* (1958), the mouse used a microscope and the *Mouse's Atlas of England* to locate twin white mice who had been abducted. To rescue them, he disguised himself as a sea captain and his biographer, Dr. Dawson, as his first mate. Hailed as the world's greatest detective by his housekeeper, Basil demurred, "The second greatest, Mrs. Judson. Mr. Sherlock Holmes, of course, ranks first."

BASKET, a white royal poodle, was bought by Gertrude Stein in 1928. Alice B. Toklas, who lived with Stein, had wanted one ever since reading Henry James's *The Princess Casamassima* (1886) and chose the name because the puppy looked as though "he should carry a basket of flowers in his mouth." Basket never did carry a basket of flowers but Stein taught him a trick that reflected her disenchantment with Ernest Hemingway. Flapping a handkerchief in front of the dog's nose, she would command, "Play Hemingway! Be Fierce!" and Basket would jump up and bark. She referred to the poodle several times in *How to Write* (1931)—"What is a sentence for if I am I then my little dog knows me"— and later said that the rhythmic sound of his lapping up water inspired the statement in the same book: "A sentence is not emotional a paragraph is." When Basket died in 1938, Pablo Picasso urged Stein to get an Afghan hound but she bought a white royal poodle puppy and named him Basket II, declaring, "Le roi est mort vive le roi is a normal attitude of mind."

BAST, also called Bastet, Pasht, or Ubasti, was an Egyptian goddess of matrimony

BAST

and feminine sensuality who was originally represented as a cat, then as a cat-headed woman bearing a sistrum, a ceremonial rattle. Lavish festivals in her honor were held each year at Bubastis, and cats were venerated throughout ancient Egypt.

BATAILLE, the old pit pony in Emile Zola's *Germinal* (1885), was a fat white horse whose ten years underground in the coal mine had made him so cunning that he could count his tours. After the regulation number, he would balk and have to be led back to the stable. When the new pony, TROMPETTE, was lowered down the shaft, Bataille sniffed him and, perhaps finding the long-forgotten smell of fresh air and grass, neighed with a glad sound that seemed also to carry a sob. In the tunnels, Bataille would perk up at the sight of the newcomer, snort a greeting, and lick him with "the affectionate pity of an old philosopher anxious to console . . . by imparting . . . his own resignation and patience." But Trompette died, and not long after that, the mine flooded. Crazed with fear, Bataille galloped wildly through the tunnels, trying to escape the rushing water, until he was wedged between rocks in a narrow gallery where, with a long, terrible cry, he died.

BA-TOU, a 20-month-old wildcat from Chad who liked to play and purr and have her tummy scratched like any domestic cat, was kept as a pet for a short time by the French novelist Colette. "A spoiled dog is a calculating liar, a cat is deceitful and secretive," Colette remarked in *La Maison de Claudine* (1922). "Bâ-Tou hid nothing." But after Colette saw her licking the neck of the household puppy, Bâ-Tou, "innocent of everything except being a wildcat," was sent to a zoo in Rome.

BAYARD, a bright bay with a white star on his forehead, was Rinaldo's marvelous horse in Carolingian legend. His intelligence was almost human, his speed outstripped the winds, and no sword could penetrate his skin. When Rinaldo first saw him, Bayard fought viciously under a spell that could be broken only if he was thrown to the ground. The horse's foot got caught in the branches of an oak and Rinaldo threw him down. Immediately gentled, Bayard became Rinaldo's faithful steed, until he was stolen and sold to Charlemagne, who gave the horse to his worthless son Charlot. Rinaldo recovered Bayard but then had to give him back. Charlot promptly had the horse thrown off a bridge into the river. Bayard surfaced, saw Rinaldo, and swam to him. Thrown into the water a second time, weighted with millstones, the horse rose to the surface, sighted Rinaldo, and again struggled toward him. Before the horse was dumped for the third time, Charlot ordered Rinaldo to stay out of sight. Bayard surfaced, looked for his master, and then, unable to see him, sank to the bottom. It is said, however, that the horse still gallops over the hills of the Ardennes on St. John's Eve (Midsummer Eve, June 24).

BEAU, wrote William Cowper (1731–1800) in "The Dog and the Water Lily," was "my spaniel, prettiest of his race." When Cowper gave up trying to snag a water lily with his cane, the dog "puzzling set his puppy brains / To comprehend the case," and plunged into the river to fetch the flower. "On a Spaniel Called Beau Killing a Young Bird" was a rebuke for disobeying orders since Beau had no need to kill for food:

> My dog! What remedy remains,
> Since, teach you all I can,
> I see you, after all my pains,
> So much resemble man!

"Beau's Reply" concludes:

> If killing birds be such a crime,
> (Which I can hardly see)

What think you, Sir, of killing Time
With verse address'd to me?

BEAUREGARD BUGLEBOY, the prideful
hound in Walt Kelly's comic strip *Pogo*,
kept reminding his fellow creatures in the
Okefenokee Swamp that he was man's
best friend. When one of them told him
that man's best friend cannot be human,
Beauregard was appalled. "A Hudibrastic
humblement! Me, the noble dog, not
human?—Gulp," he gulped. (See ALBERT
and POGO.)

BEAUTIFUL JOE, the mongrel in *Beautiful
Joe* (1893) by Marshall Saunders, was
given his name by a family in Maine who
rescued him after his brutal owner hacked
off his ears and tail. Like BLACK BEAUTY's,
Beautiful Joe's story is told in the first
person, and although the dog lives con-
tentedly ever after, the incidents he reports
form a catalog of cruelties to animals. The
humane treatment of animals was a concern
of Laura Morris, his owner, who is quoted
on the subject at length. According to
Saunders, Laura was drawn from life, most
of the events in the book actually happened, and there was a real dog named
Beautiful Joe, who had been mutilated in
the manner described.

BEECHER ARLINDA ELLEN, a 1,750-
pound Holstein cow at Harold Beecher's
dairy farm in Richmond, Indiana, set a
world record for milk production in one
year when she produced 55,660 pounds of
milk—five times the national average—in
1975. The next year, she became the first
cow in history to produce over 100,000
pounds (11,765 gallons) of milk in two
successive lactations. Hailed as the perfect
commercial cow, Ellen is the result of years
of genetic restructuring of American dairy
cattle to make them larger, to produce more
beef and more milk.

Holsteins comprise 90 percent of the
nation's herd because their milk has less
butter fat. They have been bred for higher,
less injury-prone udders and longer,
stronger legs to endure milking machines
and concrete barns. Around the age of 7,
after a couple of year-long milkings, most
cows are slaughtered, but not Ellen. She
bore eight sons, was milked through 1978,
and in 1980, at the age of 12, became
pregnant again. Since Ellen was too valuable to risk losing in childbirth, her
fertilized egg was implanted in another
cow.

BEHEMOTH, the legendary creature described in Job 40:15-24, "eats grass like an
ox. . . . His bones are tubes of bronze,
his limbs like bars of iron." As the intensive
plural of the Hebrew *b'hemah* (beast),
"behemoth" meant a colossal beast, and
probably referred to the hippopotamus, the
largest land animal in the Middle East,
although some scholars think it was an
elephant. In Hebrew lore, only one Behemoth was created lest he propagate. He
alone consumed the food on a thousand
mountains in one day and emptied the
River Jordan in a single swallow. At the
end of the world, he slaughtered the sea-
monster Leviathan with his tail even as he
was killed by Leviathan's fins. In Arabian
tradition, Behemoth became Bahamut, an
infinitely large fish on which stood a bull
supporting a great ruby underlying the
world.

BEIFFROR (or BROIEFORT), a black
Arabian horse, was won in battle by Ogier
the Dane, a 7-foot-tall paladin in Caroling-

ian legend. When Ogier was imprisoned for demanding the life of Charlemagne's son Charlot, who had killed his own little son, Beiffror was given to an abbot. The abbot's flapping robes spooked the horse and, accustomed to the great weight of Ogier in armor, Beiffror bounded swiftly up a mountain to a convent, where he dumped his new owner on the ground in front of all the nuns.

The mortified abbot condemned Beiffror to hauling heavy stones for a chapel that was under construction. After seven years of hard labor, the listless, half-starved horse was taken back to Ogier. No other horse was strong enough to carry the Dane, who had been freed so he could accept a challenge to single combat with Bruhier, the leader of the invading Saracens. At the sight of his master, Beiffror raised his head, neighed, and pawed the ground. Ogier mounted him, and the horse frisked about like a colt. The fight, on the plain of St. Denis, was long and close. Finally, a mighty blow from Bruhier that just missed the Dane struck Beiffror, who fell dead. Ogier fought on and beheaded his enemy.

BELAUD, a silver gray cat and "lethal foe of rats," belonged to Joachim du Bellay (ca. 1524–60), the French poet whose eulogy to his "chief treasure, love, and joy" recalls:

> Ah me—what pleasant fun
> 'Twas to watch my Belaud run
> Swiftly for a ball of thread. . . .
> Belaud never mischief did,
> Nor worse crime than but to seize
> And bear off a scrap of cheese
> Or a linnet eat whose song
> Vexed him.

BELKA and STRELKA were the first animals to survive orbital flight. The two female Samoyed huskies were launched in Sputnik V by the Soviet Union on August 19, 1960, and in twenty-five hours, they completed just over seventeen orbits. Both dogs later produced genetically normal litters, and one of Strelka's puppies, Pushinka, was given to Mrs. John F. Kennedy, America's First Lady.

BELLIN, the ram in the twelfth-century beast epic *Reynard the Fox,* was one of the complainants against Reynard, until the fox flattered him into going along on a pilgrimage to Rome. Accompanied by Cuwart the hare, they stopped first at Reynard's house. Leaving Bellin outside, the fox took Cuwart in with him. The next day, Reynard made excuses for the hare, then hung a sack around Bellin's neck, saying it contained two letters he had promised to write to the king. The fox added that the king would be very impressed if Bellin said he had written them himself. The ram hurried happily back to the king to claim full credit for the contents of the sack. The clerk opened it, pulled out Cuwart's head, and Bellin lost his high office and his life. The king gave the ram and all his descendants to Bruin the bear and Isegrim the wolf, "that you may freely bite and eat them."

BEN, the Alaskan brown bear in Walt Morey's *Gentle Ben* (1965), had been captured as a cub and kept chained, half-starved, in a shed for five years. When his only friend, 13-year-old Mark Anderson, tried to turn him loose on the tundra, the half-grown bear just kept following the boy and had to be shown how to roll away rocks to get at grubs. When Ben was full-grown, he wound up on an island full of brown bears; with his great size, he fought for and won supremacy. In time, Mark and his family moved to the island and a hunter arrived, intending to shoot Ben. When the hunter became pinned, helpless, under a large rock, Ben was still tame enough to respond to Mark's urging that he push the rock. Ben freed the hunter and saved his own life as well.

BENJAMIN, the old donkey in George Orwell's *Animal Farm* (1946), made no comment on the animals' rebellion against Mr. Jones or the dispute between the pig leaders, SNOWBALL and NAPOLEON (2), beyond a cryptic "Donkeys live a long time." Old Benjamin did, becoming even more morose and taciturn as the years passed.

BENJAMIN BUNNY, the cousin of PETER RABBIT (1) in Beatrix Potter's stories, married Peter's sister FLOPSY in *The Tale of the Flopsy Bunnies* (1909). They were "very improvident and cheerful." When Benjamin took his bunnies foraging in Mr. Mc-Gregor's trash heap, Mr. McGregor bagged the bunnies but THOMASINA TITTLEMOUSE rescued them. In *The Tale of Mr. Tod* (1912), the babies were stolen and Benjamin wailed to his cousin, "Seven, Cousin Peter, and all of them twins!" Again, they were rescued.

BENJI, a mutt who became a star, was a puppy when trainer Frank Inn adopted him

JOE CAMP'S BENJI © MCMLXXXII MULBERRY SQUARE PRODUCTIONS, INC.

from the Burbank, California, animal shelter in 1960. The shaggy little dog—an apparent mixture of cocker spaniel, poodle, and schnauzer—appeared as Higgins in the television series "Petticoat Junction" (1963–70). He was then chosen for the title role in *Benji* (1974), a highly successful movie about a dog who rescued two kidnapped children. When the film's sequel, *For the Love of Benji*, went into production, Higgins-Benji was seventeen, too old to perform, but Inn had foresightedly been breeding him. One female pup looked and acted enough like old Benji to replace him and has since carried on, as the allegedly male Benji II, in television specials, personal appearances, and another movie, *Oh Heavenly Dog* (1980).

BERGANZA, the sophisticated talking dog in Miguel Cervantes' "Colloquy of the Dogs" from the *Novelas exemplares* (1613), told the story of his life to his fellow watchdog, CIPION. Raised at a slaughterhouse in Seville, Berganza fled to the country to tend sheep. He found not a grain of truth to the pastoral novels so popular at the time—there were no charms of Arcady, and the sweetly singing shepherds were dirty, raucous thieves. Berganza ingratiated himself with a rich merchant whose sons took the dog to school as a pet. "I spent my student days free from hunger or the itch, which is a way of saying how good it was." Expelled for distracting the students, he drifted from one master to another. A drummer trained him to do tricks, and Berganza eventually joined a theatrical troupe. "In less than a month I was a great comedian and player of dumb roles." But he tired of the life and, seeing Cipión carrying a lantern for a watchman, he presented himself to the watchman, who at once chose him as Cipión's companion.

THE BERJUM CATS, in Booth Tarkington's *Gentle Julia* (1922), were a pair of pedigreed Persians sent to Julia Atwater, who told her niece that they were "entirely different from ordinary cats; they're very fine and queer." Kitty Silver, the maid, called them "Berjum cats," and did not like being asked to clean them up after their train ride in a crate. "I ain't no cat-washerwoman!" she moaned.

BERNARD, the pantry mouse in Margery Sharp's *The Rescuers* (1959), launched the rescue of a Norwegian poet imprisoned in the Black Castle by persuading the dainty white mouse, MISS BIANCA, to recruit a mouse in Norway to speak the prisoner's language. Miss Bianca returned with NILS, and the three of them proceeded to the castle, where they hid in the only mouse hole. Bernard covered their scent by pulling a cigar butt in front of the hole to fool the dreaded cat MAMELOUK. Eventually, the mice got into the dungeon and plucky Bernard scampered up the sleeping jailer's body to reach the keys and free the poet. When the Prisoner's Aid Society decorated the mice, Bernard, with "the most generous nature possible," allowed that the newest award, "The Nils and Miss Bianca Medal," would sound awkward if it also included his name. The modest hero reappeared in subsequent Miss Bianca books as her devoted "right-hand mouse."

BERTRAND, a monkey, appeared in two of the *Fables* of Jean de La Fontaine (1621–95). In "The Monkey and the Cat," Bertrand flattered the cat RATON (1) into stealing the chestnuts on the fire by saying it was the cat's day for a coup, since God had not equipped monkeys with paws for pulling them out. As fast as Raton drew out the chestnuts, the monkey ate them—until the maid arrived and the animals departed.

In "The Miser and the Monkey," Bertrand lived by the sea with a man who delighted in stacking his coins and counting them. The monkey liked to steal a coin and toss it out the window. Left alone one day, Bertrand began pitching coin after coin into the ocean and only the sound of his master's key in the door kept him from getting rid of the entire hoard.

BEVIS (1), a "red-roan charger," was Lord Marmion's steed in the battle at Flodden Field in 1513 in Sir Walter Scott's *Marmion* (1808). In the melee:

> . . . fast as shaft can fly,
> Bloodshot his eyes, his nostrils spread,
> The loose rein dangling from his head,
> Housing and saddle bloody red,
> Lord Marmion's horse rushed by.

Marmion had been mortally wounded.

BEVIS (2), Sir Henry Lee's "faithful mastiff" in *Woodstock* (1826) by Sir Walter Scott, had saved his master in the past, and "regularly followed him to church." In the dog's old age, "to lie by Sir Henry's feet in the summer or by the fire in winter, to raise his head to look on him, to lick his withered hand or his shrivelled cheek from time to time, seemed now all that Bevis lived for." The prototype for "the gallant hound, one of the handsomest and most active of the ancient Highland deerhounds," was Scott's own dog, MAIDA.

BEVO X, a Texas longhorn steer, became the tenth mascot of the football team of the University of Texas at Austin in 1976. One of his predecessors was dismissed for being a Hereford instead of a longhorn, and two others were dismissed for being bad-tempered. The longhorn mascot tradition began in 1916, when Bevo I appeared during the Texas–A&M game at Austin. Texas won, but the steer's fate was ignominious. Bevo was branded by some disgruntled Aggie fans and was later served as steak at a Texas–A&M football banquet.

BIG RED, a $7,000 Irish setter formally named Champion Sylvester's Boy in *Big Red* (1945) by Jim Kjelgaard, was raised in the Wintapi wilderness by 17-year-old Danny Pickett because the owner, who intended to show and breed the dog, respected the boy's ability. The setter was lamed helping Danny fight off a wolverine, then suffered from jealousy over the attention given a champion bitch brought in to be bred. When Old Majesty, a notorious killer bear, mauled Danny's father and killed his hounds, the boy tracked the bear into the mountains with Big Red's help. On the second night, Old Majesty charged them. Even after Danny pumped bullets into him, the bear kept coming. Big Red then leaped on Old Majesty, a diversion that saved the boy's life but injured the setter so badly he could never be shown again. His value at stud, however, was established. By the time Danny got him home, Big Red's first litter had been whelped.

BIGWIG, in *Watership Down* (1972) by Richard Adams, was the courageous older rabbit who accepted a subordinate role in the migration led by HAZEL. When Bigwig helped several does escape from GENERAL WOUNDWORT's warren, he was badly hurt but was full of fight again by the time Woundwort attacked Watership Down. In the peaceful times that followed, Bigwig devoted himself to training the new young bucks, who respectfully addressed the battle-scarred veteran as Sir.

BILL XXII, the twenty-sixth goat mascot of the football team of the United States Naval Academy, was acquired in 1979. The first Navy Goat, "El Cid," appeared at the fourth Army–Navy game in 1893, and another non-Bill, "Three-to-Nothing Jack Dalton," named for a football player, celebrated Navy's victory over Army in 1910 by butting a policeman.

BILLY was the first horse that Philip Astley bought when he resigned from the 15th Light Dragoons in 1766 to open a riding school and give equestrian shows on a field near Westminster Bridge. He bought the little pony with the bright and impudent eyes as a wedding present for his bride, but Billy was so trainable that he became Astley's favorite performing horse. In one trick, Billy would take the kettle off the stove and set the table for a tea party. In 1768, Astley developed the riding ring and soon added acrobats, a clown, a rope walker, and a band—two pipers and a drum. Astley's show, with various acts performing in the ring, was the first modern circus.

BILLY-GOAT GRUFF was the name of each of the three goats in an old Scandi-

BILL XXII

navian folk story about an ugly troll who lived under a bridge and ate everybody who tried to cross it. The youngest Billy-Goat Gruff was the first to start over the bridge to the meadow on the other side. When the troll popped up to threaten him, little Gruff begged to be allowed to pass because a bigger and fatter goat was coming. The troll let him go. The second Gruff said the same thing and got away with it, too. The third and biggest Billy-Goat Gruff stomped onto the bridge, but was just as frightened as the others. The troll roared that he would gobble him up. The oldest Gruff bellowed back that he would do the same thing, then charged, and butted the troll right into the river. The troll never came up. The bridge was safe, and all three Billy-Goats Gruff grew fat in the meadow.

BILLY MINK, in the Thornton Burgess nature books, was a great traveler with wide experience whose warnings about Farmer Brown's boy and his traps were ignored in *The Adventures of Jerry Musk-rat* (1914)—until JERRY MUSKRAT had a painful escape from a trap. Then Billy, who was small and quick and had sharp eyes, was assigned to follow Farmer Brown's boy to locate the traps, the animals sprang them, and they all feasted on the bait.

BILLY WHISKERS was the irrepressible goat with a "pie-crust temper" and an appetite for roses—from gardens or ladies' hats—in a series of books by Frances Trego Montgomery, starting with *Billy Whiskers* (1902). Billy did what he pleased. He butted his way past boys, dogs, and men; he chewed through restraining ropes; when he was put in a shed, he knocked it down. He became a fire patrol's mascot after crash-

BILLY WHISKERS

ing into a burning building to save a baby, but he soon ran off to "marry" a pretty Nanny goat. Then he became a circus performer and "behaved like a lamb" until he was put in a cage. Billy escaped, found his way back to Nanny, and was proud to learn that her kids were his.

BINGO, a black and white dog, and Jack the sailor boy have appeared on Cracker Jack packages since 1919. The model for Jack was Robert Rueckheim, whose grandfather, F. W. Rueckheim, with his brother Louis, founded a popcorn business in Chicago in 1873. In 1893, they introduced a confection of popcorn, peanuts, and molasses at the World Columbian Exposition in Chicago; in 1896, the Cracker Jack name was trademarked. As for Bingo, he was young Robert's dog.

Cracker Jack

AMERICA'S FAMOUS CONFECTION

"THE MORE YOU EAT-
THE MORE YOU WANT"

REG. U. S. PAT. OFF.

BINGO

about 14 years old, one cab was so over-loaded that he collapsed. Then his luck changed. A farmer bought him, restored his health, and sold him to three genteel ladies with whom he lived happily ever after.

Black Beauty's "autobiography" became a children's classic, translated into many languages, but it was also a dissertation on the mistreatment of horses. The first to recognize its propaganda value was George T. Angell, the founder of the Massachusetts Society for the Prevention of Cruelty to Animals, who published 200,000 copies of the book in 1890. Sewell, crippled by a childhood injury, was 57 years old and seriously ill when she finished writing *Black Beauty*, her only book, as a plea for the proper care of horses. She sold the manuscript for a few pounds and had the joy of knowing it was a success before she died a year later. Ironically, when the hearse arrived for her funeral, the horses' heads were held high by check-reins. Her mother had them removed at once.

BLACKBERRY, the clever and practical rabbit in *Watership Down* (1972) by Richard Adams, was unimpressed by the tradition that buck rabbits did not dig holes. He and his companions were bucks. They needed holes. Therefore, they would dig them.

BLACK BEAUTY, in Anna Sewell's *Black Beauty* (1877), was foaled on an English farm. A grandson of a Thoroughbred, he had a pleasant life as a saddle and carriage horse until a drunken rider forced him to gallop over stones with one shoe gone. Black Beauty fell, injuring both knees. Sold and resold to a series of owners, he wound up in London pulling cabs. When he was

BLACK BESS, a mare, was used by Dick Turpin the highwayman for his legendary ride from London to York (180 miles). According to Harrison Ainsworth in his "historical" novel *Rookwood* (1834), the real Richard Turpin, hanged in 1739 for horse-stealing, made no such ride, but his fictitious counterpart is still remembered for it.

BLACK COMET, in *Misty of Chincoteague* (1947) by Marguerite Henry, was the pony from the mainland who had won the race on Chincoteague Island's Pony Penning Day three years in a row when PHANTOM (1), the wild mare from Assateague Island, successfully challenged him.

BLACK DIAMOND, an American bison, was the model for the reverse of the Buffalo nickel designed by James Earle Fraser and first minted in 1913. (The Indian head on the obverse is a composite of three different Indians.) The bison's image was not universally applauded. In William Bridges' *Gathering of Animals* (1974), an "unconventional" history of the New York Zoological Society, Dr. William Temple Hornaday, the society's first director, is quoted as saying that the "dejected" buffalo's head "droops as if it has lost all hope in the world, and even the sculptor was not able to raise it." Similar criticism came from the American Numismatic Society, but the Secretary of the Bison Society countered that the need to compress the animal into such a small space was what made it look droopy. The sculptor had his own complaint. In a statement exhibited at the National Cowboy Hall of Fame in Oklahoma City, Fraser said that the contrary animal "refused point blank to permit me to get side views of him, and stubbornly showed his front face most of the time." Fraser also spread confusion by saying that his model lived at the Bronx Zoo. Black Diamond was, in fact, at the Central Park Menagerie, where he died in 1915 at the age of 22. His head was mounted and his hide made into a lap robe. And in 1938, the Buffalo nickel was replaced by the Jefferson nickel.

BLACK DIAMOND

BLACK JACK was the riderless horse following the artillery caisson bearing the coffin of President John F. Kennedy on November 25, 1963, from the Capitol to St. Matthew's Church for the funeral and then to Arlington National Cemetery. A sheathed sword strapped to the saddle and boots reversed in the stirrups were symbols that a leader had fallen and would ride no more. In startling contrast to the somber cortege, the spirited Black Jack appeared restless and hard to handle, although the 16-year-old dark chestnut gelding had served for ten years as Number One of twenty horses kept at Fort Myers for military ceremonies. The young soldier leading him said later that the cold weather and unusually large crowds were probably what made Black Jack so frisky.

The tradition of the riderless horse traces back to the ancient Mongols. When a warrior was killed, his caparisoned horse would be led to the burial and then sacrificed. The Mongols believed that the horse's spirit would go through the gate of the sky to serve his master in the afterworld.

[27]

THE BLACK STALLION, the fabulous wild horse from Arabia in a series of books by Walter Farley, first appeared in *The Black Stallion* (1941), blindfolded, screaming, and rearing on his hind legs as men forced him aboard a ship in a small Arabian port. A storm off Spain's Cape Finisterre sank the ship. The only survivors were the horse and Alec Ramsay, a young American boy who clung to the halter rope as the powerful stallion swam to a small island. They were there alone for three weeks. The stallion, too big to be pure Arabian, ran wild at first. Then, as the resourceful boy helped him find food, the Black let Alec touch him and finally, mount him. The unbroken horse galloped along the beach at tremendous speed, but gradually submitted to the boy's control. After they were rescued, Alec managed to take the stallion home to Flushing, New York, give him clandestine workouts at Belmont Racetrack, and ride the strong and scarcely tamed horse in a match race with two Thoroughbreds. A movie version of the book, also called *The Black Stallion*, appeared in 1979.

BLANCA, a small white wolf in the predatory pack led by her mate LOBO, became Lobo's downfall. Ernest Thompson Seton, who caught both wolves in 1894, wrote in *Wild Animals I Have Known* (1898) that one night, Blanca and another wolf slaughtered 250 sheep, "apparently for the fun of it" because they did not touch the carcasses. When Blanca began foraging ahead of the pack, Seton killed her and used her remains to decoy Lobo to traps from which he could not escape.

BLANCHARD, in Carolingian legend, was Charlemagne's favorite charger. When Ogier the Dane agreed to represent the emperor in single combat with Bruhier, the sultan of Arabia, Charlemagne offered Ogier all the best horses in his stables, except Blanchard.

BLANCHETTE, in *Lettres de mon moulin* (1866) by Alphonse Daudet, was a young goat that Monsieur Seguin bought after losing six previous goats to a wolf on the mountain. She was docile at first, "letting herself be milked without budging, and never putting her foot in the bowl!" Then she grew bored with the meadow where she was tethered and begged Seguin to let her go to the mountain. If a wolf attacked her, she would butt him, she said. Seguin locked her in the stable. Blanchette crashed through the window, went up the mountain, frolicked in the flowers, and romped with a herd of chamois. At dusk, even though a wolf began to howl, she ignored Seguin's horn summoning her back to the tether. The wolf appeared, "smacking his lips in advance." Seguin had told her about one old goat that had fought all night only to be eaten in the morning, and Blanchette hoped to last that long. Head down, horns forward, she repelled the wolf more than ten times until dawn when, sighing, "At last," she fell to the ground. The wolf ate her.

BLANCO, a white collie, was a gift that President Lyndon Johnson (1963–69) accepted from a little girl in Illinois to represent the scores of dogs that had been offered to him as gifts. The beautiful, overbred collie learned to give his paw to shake hands, which delighted the President, but had to be kept on tranquilizers because he enjoyed biting other White House dogs and people. When Johnson left office, he was finally persuaded to give Blanco away.

BLAZE, a bull mastiff, caused three servicemen to be bumped from an Air Transport Command flight in Memphis in January 1945, because their travel priorities were not as high as his. One of the President's sons, Lt. Col. Elliott Roosevelt, had brought the dog from England and left it with his family in Washington, asking that it be shipped to his wife in Los Angeles when there was an empty transport headed that way. One of the stranded servicemen, a sailor heading for California on emergency leave, hitchhiked to Dallas, lost his papers, and was held for two days by M.P.s before he could resume his trip home. The press found out about it and had a field day. Editorials deplored the whole business, Republican senators made up dog jokes, and a Senate subcommittee was appointed to look into the matter. It turned out that, unknown to the Roosevelts, an overzealous ATC officer had given the crated dog the "A" priority usually reserved for VIPs or vitally important cargo.

In the fall of 1945, Blaze was back east, at Hyde Park, where he and the late President's Scotty, FALA, got into a terrible fight. Fala, outweighed by about 100 pounds, was hurt badly; Blaze was ordered destroyed.

BLEMIE, a Dalmatian that Eugene O'Neill bought while he and his third wife, Carlotta, lived in France from 1929 to 1931, became their surrogate child, fitted out with collar, leash, and coat by Hermès. Many years later Carlotta recalled how, during evenings in front of the fire, Blemie would sit first by her, then by Gene, in order not to hurt anyone's feelings. By December 1940, Blemie had become so infirm that they knew he would not live much longer. To console Carlottta about their imminent loss, O'Neill wrote *The Last Will and Testament of Silverdeen Emblem O'Neill,* a tender little essay that could have been, in part, the playwright's own epitaph:

> It is time I said good-by, before I become too sick a burden on myself and on those who love me. It will be a sorrow to leave them, but not a sorrow to die. . . . What may come after death, who knows? I would like to believe with those of my fellow Dalmatians who are Mohammedans, that there is a Paradise where one is always young and full-bladdered; where all the day one dillies and dallies with an amorous multitude of houris, beautifully spotted. . . . But peace, at least, is certain. Peace and long rest for weary old heart and head and limbs, and eternal sleep in the earth I have loved so well. Perhaps, after all, this is best.

BLIND TOM, a blind gelding, pulled flatcars for the Union Pacific when it began laying track westward from Omaha in the spring of 1866 to form the first transcontinental rail line by linking up with the Central Pacific, whose track was being laid eastward. According to Robert West Howard's *The Horse in America* (1965), Blind Tom was said to have hauled every rail of the 1,100-mile track, from the advancing work train "Hell on Wheels," to the ironmen ahead who clamped them into position. "Where's Blind Tom today?" became their expression for "How much track did we lay yesterday?" On May 10, 1869, the two lines met at Promontory Point, Utah, and the golden spike was driven into the last tie. An unofficial guest of honor at the ceremony was Blind Tom, led there by a crew of Union Pacific ironmen.

BLONDI, the Alsatian bitch that Martin Bormann gave to Adolf Hitler, was taken along when the Führer went to the Ukraine in the summer of 1942 to direct the Russian offensive. After General Jodl provoked him into a tantrum, Hitler isolated himself in his bunker and dined only with Blondi for the rest of his stay. Back in Germany, he often began his morning by playing with the dog, making her jump hoops, leap over a 6-foot wall, and climb a ladder. When she reached the top, she would beg. At Berchtesgaden, Blondi was banished from social gatherings after fighting with Eva Braun's two Scotties, but Hitler did show her off on the eve of his fifty-fourth birthday in 1943. He put her through her tricks and then she "sang." The more he praised her, the louder Blondi howled.

On April 28, 1945, with the war lost and the Allies' approach imminent, Hitler and his entourage were in a concrete bunker beneath the Reich Chancellery in Berlin. Near midnight, he married Eva Braun, wrote his will, and issued orders to armies that no longer existed. The next evening, he handed out phials of cyanimide to his inner circle. Someone wondered if the poison would work. Hitler summoned a doctor to give some to Blondi. It worked. On April 30, Braun took the poison, and it is generally believed that Hitler shot himself. Their remains were never found.

BLUEBELL, the comedian among the rabbits in Richard Adams' *Watership Down* (1972), returned from digging one day to be asked if his holes were concealed. He had brought one with him to show, he said. No one could see it. So there.

BOATSWAIN, Lord Byron's favorite dog, was a Newfoundland who went into a fit and died in front of his master in 1808. For Boatswain's tomb at Newstead Abbey, the 20-year-old poet composed an epitaph in verse to:

> . . . the poor dog, in life the firmest friend,
> The first to welcome, the foremost to defend. . . .

But Byron did not write the more frequently quoted prose introduction describing Boatswain as one

> Who possessed Beauty without Vanity,
> Strength without Indolence,
> Courage without Ferocity,
> And all the virtues of Man, without his Vices.

According to Leslie A. Marchand's *Byron* (1957), the poet's friend John Cam Hobhouse thought the epitaph was silly and contributed the introduction as a joke.

BOB, Emily Arundell's wire-haired terrier in *Poirot Loses a Client** (1937) by Agatha Christie, liked to send his ball bouncing down the stairs to anyone who would throw it back up. When Miss Arundell fell downstairs one night, it was assumed that she had tripped on his ball. Although she was not badly hurt, she died two weeks later. Two months after that, detective Hercule Poirot received her distraught letter about "the incident of the dog's ball," and went to her house. It had been put up for sale but Bob greeted him with lively barks, then sat at attention by the drawer where his ball was usually kept. After observing the dog's habits and the behavior of Miss Arundell's disinherited

* Original title: *Dumb Witness.*

relatives, Poirot identified both the cause of her death and the perpetrator. As thanks, he was presented with the dog. The model for Bob was Christie's own terrier, Peter, to whom the book was dedicated.

BOBBY COON, in *The Adventures of Bobby Coon* (1918) by Thornton Burgess, broke his leg when the tree he lived in was chopped down. But he had enough fight left to sink his teeth into the nose of Bowser the Hound, who came sniffing. Farmer Brown's boy took the raccoon home to splint the leg, then carried him back after it mended because the boy had understood Bobby's longing looks toward the forest. Bobby could not comprehend the boy's words of farewell but, realizing he was free, declared himself the happiest coon in the world.

BODGER, the old bull terrier in the trio of pets making their way home through the Canadian wilderness in *The Incredible Journey* (1961) by Sheila Burnford, could not catch prey because his eyesight was poor, but with his wagging tail and hideous grin he twice charmed people into feeding him. He also used an old fighting trick of his breed to rescue Luath (4), the Labrador retriever, from a collie. Bodger sprang at the collie's throat, drew blood, then circled the bigger dog faster and faster, knocking him down. The collie fled. (See also Tao.)

BONES, the raffish dog in "A Yellow Dog," a story by Bret Harte (1836–1902), belonged to nobody and everybody in Rattlers Ridge, where he was credited with such tricks as signaling the contents of a poker hand. He was then called a liar for claiming to be a poker shark. An incompetent hunter, he retrieved a duck who had not

BOBBY COON

been shot and drove a bear into camp instead of away from it. The dog favored drunkards, "barking his delight" as they stumbled along, but his "ultimate and somewhat monotonous reformation" occurred when the prettiest girl in the county arrived on the first stagecoach. Bones was besotted. He followed her home. The girl's father, the local judge, invited the fellows from camp to come see the dog and they did, in "store clothes." "Bones not only *forgot*, but absolutely *cut us!*"

BONZO, a chimpanzee, was the star of *Bedtime for Bonzo* (1951), a movie about raising a chimpanzee like a human baby to prove that environment determines character. The film was entertaining enough to justify a sequel, *Bonzo Goes to College* (1952), but it remains noteworthy mainly because Bonzo's co-star was Ronald Reagan.

BOO-BOO, in Hanna-Barbera Productions television cartoons, is a conformist little bear who believes in abiding by the rules of Jellystone National Park and serves as the conscience for his free-spirited pal YOGI BEAR.

BOOTS, the narrator of Rudyard Kipling's *Thy Servant a Dog* (1930), and Slippers are black Aberdeen terriers (Scotties) who live in the country with their "Gods," Master-Missus and Smallest, the baby. The terriers chase the kitchen cat, make friends with Ravager, an old, one-eyed hound, and let the baby hold onto their noses and ears when he tries to walk. When Smallest gets his own pony seven years later, the three dogs and a lame fox stage a play hunt for the boy. "We was proper pack." When Ravager dies of old age, Boots grieves for his true friend, who "never minded of my short legs or because I were stoopid."

BORAK (or BURAQ), in Muslim tradition, was the white animal that the angel Gabriel brought to Mohammed to ride on his night journey, the *mi'raj*, to the seven heavens. Variously described as a horse, an ass, and a mule, Borak had wings and could cover in one stride the distance he could see; he has also been pictured as a mare with a woman's head and a peacock's tail. Borak, whose name means "lightning," was one of the animals admitted to Paradise.

BOSY, in "The Dog of the World" from *The World of Bemelmans* (1955) by Ludwig Bemelmans, was a Bouvier des Flandres that Bemelmans bought in France. Saying, "You don't want an average dog," his friend Armand persuaded him to have Bosy trained by a retired clown who had had a famous dog act in the circus. The next time Bemelmans saw Bosy, a year later, the dog was big, "very mannerly, respecting flower beds, . . . and sitting at attention when told to." When the old clown said the house was on fire and a little girl upstairs must be rescued, Bosy climbed a ladder, entered a window, and backed down with a large doll in his mouth. Reproached for forgetting someone, the dog then fetched a real cat out of the building. The clown was congratulated and paid; then, as he counted his money, he began to weep at the prospect of losing Bosy, "the only friend I have in this world!" Bemelmans was ready to give him the dog but at Armand's request for a refund, the clown commanded Bosy to go to his "new master." Bosy did.

BOUDEWIN (BALDWIN), the ass in the twelfth-century beast epic *Reynard the Fox*, belonged to a rich man who also owned a hound. While the ass worked hard and ate thistles and nettles, the dog played with his master, jumping up and licking his face, and was fed bones and meat from the table. Boudewin wanted the same love and friendship. Seeing his lord approach, the ass sprang up to plant his forefeet on the man's shoulders and tried to kiss him on the mouth. The master's cries for help brought servants who beat Boudewin, then sent him back to the stable and his thistles and nettles. An ass is an ass, said REYNARD, yet many have risen in the world. What a pity, he declared.

BOUNCE, a Great Dane, belonged to the English poet Alexander Pope (1688–1744). Having made many enemies with his insulting mock-epic about other poets, the "Dunciad" (1728), Pope started taking the huge dog, "my only friend," and a couple of pistols along for protection on the solitary walks he liked to take, despite his weak, deformed body. He had other friends, of course, and one of them, John Gay, noted the value of Bounce's offspring in his poem "Bounce to Fop, An Epistle from a Dog at Twickenham to a Dog at Court":

None but a peer of wit and grace
Can hope a puppy of my race.

The Prince of Wales received one of Bounce's puppies with a couplet by Pope inscribed on its collar:

I am his Highness' dog at Kew.
Pray tell me, sir, whose dog are you?

BOWSER THE HOUND, Farmer Brown's dog in the Thornton Burgess nature books, was the terror of the other animals. In a typical story, *The Adventures of Grandfather Frog* (1915), Bowser found GRANDFATHER FROG in the long grass and turned him over on his back. The frog made a little hop. Bowser flipped him again, making a game of it, flipping and dancing around and barking at the terrified frog. Grandfather Frog finally had the sense to lie perfectly still. "I guess I frightened him to death," Bowser said to himself. "I didn't mean to do that. I just wanted to have some fun with him," and he trotted away in search of more excitement.

BOXER and CLOVER, the cart-horses in George Orwell's *Animal Farm* (1946), accepted the leadership of NAPOLEON (2), the despotic boar, but were troubled by the violence and terror that followed the animals' rebellion. To keep going at the hardest job on the farm, hauling stones, faithful Boxer kept chanting to himself, "Napoleon is always right" and "I will work harder," until he collapsed.

BOY, Prince Rupert's large white poodle, and Rupert's companion during three years' imprisonment at Linz, is generally believed to be the first poodle seen in England. He was taken there when Rupert was released in 1642 and summoned to aid his uncle, King Charles I, in the Civil War. The puritanical Roundheads were convinced that the dog possessed supernatural powers and in one of their pamphlets appealed to America: "For it is impossible to destroy him, until the Colonies of New England come in to help us; they know how to order these Dog-Witches better far than we." On July 2, 1644, Boy was killed at the battle of Marston Moor.

BOZO, a female grizzly bear, played Ben, a male grizzly, in *The Life and Times of Grizzly Adams* (1974), a film based partly on the life of James Capen Adams, a hunter who had trapped a grizzly in the Sierra Nevada range around 1855. The film generated a television series with the same title in 1977 in which Bozo also starred, again with Dan Haggerty, the animal trainer who played Adams. The grizzly bear (*Ursus horribilis*) is a dangerous animal but Bozo was so tractable and so fond of Haggerty that she was the first grizzly who could work without restraints. In one improvised scene, she pulled off a blanket to wake him up, chased him, let him chase her, then rolled on her back to have her stomach scratched. Lloyd Beebe, her owner, had found Bozo in a circus, and although her background was not known, she seemed to have been raised as a pet, which doubtless accounted for her docility.

BRAN was the dog who belonged to the legendary hero known as Finn Mac Cool in Ireland and Fingal in Scotland. As a young dog, Bran helped his master kill a sea serpent by leaping down its throat and tearing out its heart and liver. Bran grew into a giant brute of great strength. A mass of rock near Dunolly Castle in Ireland is still called Bran's Pillars because the dog was chained there while Finn Mac Cool fought the chief of the Black Danes. In both the Irish and Scottish legends, the site of Bran's death is called Craig an Bran. The dog plunged into a lake from a crag so named in the forest of Clare in Ireland. After another dog killed Bran in a fight on the border of Glen Loth in Scotland, Fingal marked Bran's grave with a pile of stones.

THE BRAZEN BULL OF PHALARIS was invented by Perillus of Athens as a new form of punishment to be used by Phalaris, the tyrant of Agrigentum, in Sicily, ca. 570–554 B.C. The hollow brass bull had a door on its flank through which the victim was inserted to be roasted alive. From outside, his screams sounded like the bellowing of a bull. Perillus himself is said to have been the first victim because Phalaris ordered him to demonstrate the device. Eventually, after a popular uprising, the tyrant, too, was put to death in the bull.

BREE, a talking horse, taught the boy Shasta to saddle and ride him so that he could return to Narnia, the place of his birth, in *The Horse and His Boy* (1954), the fifth Chronicle of Narnia by C. S. Lewis. Stolen from Narnia as a foal and trained by his captors as a war horse, Bree was surprised to learn upon returning that the Narnians had too much respect for talking horses to ride them. He liked to roll on the grass and wondered if that was acceptable. *"Do Talking Horses roll? Supposing they don't?"* he groaned. "I can't bear to give it up." He did not have to and lived a long, contented life.

BRER BEAR, in the Uncle Remus stories by Joel Chandler Harris (1848–1908), was ambling along after robbing a bee tree one day when he saw BRER RABBIT dangling from a sapling. The rabbit had been trapped, but he said that he was making a dollar a minute keeping the crows out of BRER FOX's peanut patch. The bear believed him. They changed places and Brer Rabbit fetched Brer Fox, telling him to hit the thief on the mouth every time Brer Bear tried to explain.

BRER FOX, in Joel Chandler Harris' Uncle Remus stories, never could get even with BRER RABBIT, who, at various times, nailed his tail to the roof, spat tobacco juice in his eye, and saddled and rode him like a horse. In his best scheme, the fox made a Tar Baby and rolled on the ground laughing when the rabbit got stuck to it. But Brer Rabbit outfoxed him again and got away. When the animals took to studying how to catch up with the rabbit and his tricks, all Brer Fox could say was that Brer Rabbit had more luck than smartness.

BRER RABBIT was the trickster hero of the Uncle Remus stories by Joel Chandler Harris, who, as a boy on a Georgia plantation, had heard the animal legends passed down by slaves (see ZOMO). In a series of books starting with *Uncle Remus, His Songs and Sayings* (1880), and *Nights*

BRER RABBIT

BRER TARRYPIN

with Uncle Remus (1883), Harris retold the stories, many of them about Brer Rabbit, "sassy ez a jaybird," outwitting the bigger animals. The rabbit cajoled Miss Cow into butting a persimmon tree until one of her horns went through it, then brought his old woman and all his children to milk her dry. When his four feet and head got stuck to BRER FOX's Tar Baby, Brer Rabbit said the fox could "bobbycue," hang, drown, or skin him but "fer de Lord's sake, don't fling me in dat briarpatch." So Brer Fox flung him in the briarpatch, and pretty soon he heard Brer Rabbit calling from way up on a hill, "Bred en bawn in a briar-patch, Brer Fox— bred en bawn in a briar-patch!"

BRER TARRYPIN, a turtle, was one "creetur" in the Uncle Remus stories by Joel Chandler Harris (1848–1908) who got the best of BRER RABBIT. When the two of them argued about who could run faster, the turtle announced that he had $50 that said he could. The rabbit put up his $50 and the race was arranged, a 5-mile heat with a post marking each mile. Brer Rabbit said he'd run on the big road; Brer Tarrypin said he'd go through the woods. He had a wife and three children who looked just like him, and as Brer Rabbit reached each post, a Tarrypin was crawling out of the woods toward it. At the last one, Brer Tarrypin himself was already there.

BRER WOLF, in Joel Chandler Harris' Uncle Remus stories, suspected that BRER RABBIT was in cahoots with a witch because he was so lucky. After overhearing Miss Rabbit say that she had left her old man's money purse at home and that it had something in it that Brer Rabbit would not take anything for, Brer Wolf raced to the rabbits' house. One of the "forty leb'm" babies woke up when he opened the door, but he hushed the little Rab, grabbed the purse off the mantel, and fled. Finding a big rabbit's foot in the purse, Brer Wolf galloped home with the assurance of a man who had discovered a gold mine. For a month, he had all the luck. He got fat; Brer Rabbit got lean. He ran fast; "Brer Rabbit lope heavy like ole Sis Cow." Then the rabbit got his purse back.

BRIGADORE was the "loftie steed" that Sir Guyon lost and found in Edmund Spenser's *Faerie Queene*. In book II, canto III (1590), Braggadocchio stole the horse; in book V, canto III (1596), he pretended he was a knight and took Brigadore to a tournament. There Sir Guyon claimed his steed, saying that Brigadore had a black, horseshoe-shaped mark in his mouth. Two men seized the horse to look. Brigadore broke the ribs of one, bit the shoulder of the other, and kept his mouth shut—until Guyon spoke to him. Then the horse let everyone see the mark in his mouth, and, in his joy at being called by name, broke free to follow Guyon:

> . . . with gladfull glee,
> And friskt, and flong aloft, and louted
>   low on knee.

BRIGHAM was "the best buffalo horse that ever made a track," according to William F. ("Buffalo Bill") Cody in *The Life of Buffalo Bill* (1879). The horse helped him win $500 from Billy Comstock, a noted scout and buffalo hunter, in their eight-hour buffalo-killing match witnessed by about 100 people who had come from St. Louis on an excursion train. After lunch and a great deal of champagne, Cody decided to show off by riding without saddle or bridle, assuring a "fair lady" who expressed alarm, "Old Brigham knows as well as I what I am doing, and sometimes a great deal better." At the end of the afternoon, the slaughter score was Cody 69—Comstock 46, and Buffalo Bill was declared "champion buffalo hunter of the plains."

BRIGHTY, an independent little burro known as the "hermit of Bright Angel Creek," was a familiar sight around the Grand Canyon for thirty years after he was first noticed grazing on the Kaibab Plateau in 1892. If caught, he would struggle free, but he was friendly, and while the suspension bridge was being built over the Colorado River, he willingly packed supplies for the engineers. They, in turn, gave him the honor of being the first to cross the bridge when it was completed. He then hauled water for the National Park Service on the North Rim for six years, until two fugitives wintering there sacrificed him for meat. Marguerite Henry immortalized the burro in *Brighty of the Grand Canyon* (1953); the book was made into a movie; and a bronze statue of Brighty was placed at the visitors center in the canyon. In 1980, the statue was put in storage, replaced by an exhibit describing the damage done to the area by the growing population of wild burros.

BRIGLIADORO, in Carolingian legend, was Orlando's famous charger. Orlando (known as Roland in the French epic) temporarily lost the horse after rescuing a weeping damsel in the woods. While he slept that night, she stole his sword and rode away on Brigliadoro. Another time, the horse was taken to Africa by Agramant, one of the Saracen kings. Brigliadoro was recovered when Orlando and his friends slew the Saracens.

THE BROGUE, in "The Brogue" from *Beasts and Super-Beasts* (1914) by Saki (H. H. Munro), was a brown gelding that the Mullet family had been trying to sell for four years. As a hunter, he had "personally created most of the gaps . . . in banks and hedges for many miles round." As a hack, he suffered from "swerving sickness," brought on by such objects as pigs, perambulators, and "gates painted too aggressively white." Mr. Penricarde, a rich new neighbor who bought him and proposed to one of the Mullet daughters, could not be dissuaded from riding the horse. On the first try, the sight of a green gate that had been white "a year or two ago" impelled the Brogue to make "a violent curtsey, a back-pedal, and swerve," but Mr. Penricarde suffered only minor damage and gave the horse to his fiancée as a wedding present.

BRONZOMARTE, in the *Adventures of Sir Launcelot Greaves* by Tobias George Smollett (1721–71), was Sir Launcelot's horse. Smollett's Sir Launcelot was a sort of Don Quixote who wandered around England on his mettlesome sorrel during the reign of King George II, seeking to right wrongs and to reform society.

THE BROWN BULL OF COOLEY, according to legend, had such magic powers that four Irish kings invaded Ulster in the hope of possessing him, but Cuchulainn, Ulster's legendary first-century A.D. champion, defended the bull and the kingdom singlehanded.

BROWN EYES, a Jersey cow, is Buster Keaton's true love in the silent film *Go West* (1925). Keaton, the incompetent new hand on an Arizona cattle ranch, becomes her Androcles by pulling a stone out of her sore foot. From then on, she follows him like a dog. When Keaton gets his foot stuck in a gopher hole, she saves his life by blocking a charging bull. Keaton saves her from a huge longhorn steer by disguising her with a pair of antlers from the ranch house. The herd is eventually shipped to Los Angeles to be sold, but breaks loose to stampede through the streets. Riding Brown Eyes like a pony, Keaton rounds up the cattle and drives them to the stockyard. In the final scene, the grateful owner drives off in his touring car, with his daughter beside him and Keaton in the back seat with his reward, Brown Eyes.

BROWNIE (1), Charlie Chaplin's co-star in the film *A Dog's Life*: see SCRAPS.

BROWNIE (2), an Irish setter bitch, was the only being T. H. White could love without reserve, and her death was the greatest tragedy of his life. White, best known as the author of *The Once and Future King* (1958), was a loner with few close friends and no interest in women. He was given the dog in 1933 after she took to sleeping on his bed at an inn whose proprietor raised Irish setters, but it wasn't until nearly four years later, while he was nursing her through distemper, that it dawned on him that he loved her. They were living in Ireland when she died in 1944, probably of old age. White was away for the day in Dublin. Tormented by guilt that he had not been with her, he grieved in his journal, "She was a sprite who danced before me through 12 perfect years of love. . . . It means that I died last night. All that was me is dead." After a week of visiting Brownie's grave twice a day, White went back to Dublin for a nine-day drunk, then bought another Irish setter, a puppy bitch he named Killie. When she died in 1958, he wrote, "I did not love her like Brownie. Dear Brownie, you were and still are the most loved thing in my life."

BRUIN, the bear in the twelfth-century beast epic *Reynard the Fox*, was sent to summon REYNARD to the court and was warned that the fox was tricky. Bruin said he could handle him, but as soon as Reynard mentioned honey, he vowed, "As long as I live, I shall be to you a true friend." The fox told him the honey was in the cleft of a felled oak that the carpenter had wedged open. The bear stuck in his head and front paws, Reynard knocked out the wedges, and Bruin was stuck. In pulling himself free, he ripped off his ears, skinned his head and paws, and was blinded by the blood in his eyes. The carpenter and his neighbors began beating him, but Bruin managed to swim across the river and, by sliding on his tail, make his painful way back to the court.

BUCEPHALUS, a blaze-faced black stallion who was bought by Philip of Macedon ca. 346 B.C., appeared to be unmanageable but Philip's son, Alexander, then about ten years old, bet the price of the horse that he could tame him. Having noticed that Bucephalus shied at his own shadow, the boy, later known as Alexander the Great, turned him to face the sun, soothed him, then leaped aboard and galloped off. From then on, Bucephalus had no other rider and

was later trained to kneel in full harness for easier mounting when his master wore armor. Alexander, a slight man, used him sparingly. In the rout of the Persian emperor Darius III at Gaugamela in 331 B.C., Alexander kept his 25-year-old horse fresh for the climax of the battle. Bucephalus was 30 years old and had traveled 11,000 miles in eight and a half years when Alexander reached India in 326 B.C. During the final battle against Rajah Porus at the Jhelum River, the horse died, of wounds or exhaustion, and Alexander founded the town of Bucephala near the site in his honor.

Having worn golden horns in battle because his name meant "ox-head," Bucephalus lived on in legend as the first unicorn in the Western world. To link themselves with Alexander, his successors minted coins showing horned horses. In Balasham (northern Afghanistan) in the thirteenth century, Marco Polo heard that the rulers there had owned a breed of horses who were "all foaled with a particular mark on the forehead" because they were descended from Bucephalus. The line ended, he was told, when the last stallion was killed in a royal family squabble.

BUCHIS, a black bull shown with two feathers and the disk of the sun between his horns, was worshiped by the people of Hermonthis in ancient Egypt as the representative of their chief gods.

BUCK, in Jack London's *The Call of the Wild* (1903), was a family dog, part Saint Bernard and part Scotch shepherd, who was stolen to be sold as a sled dog for men participating in the gold rush in Alaska, where both men and dogs lived by "the law of club and fang." Rescued by John

Thornton, a prospector, Buck proved his devotion with a show of strength that won an enormous bet for the man. Harnessed to a sled bearing ½ ton of flour, the 150-pound dog jerked the runners free of the snow and pulled the load 100 yards. In the wilderness with Thornton and his partners, Buck was irresistibly drawn by a howl from the forest to stalk a wolf one night, and to run with him for several hours. The dog's bond with men ended when Yeehat Indians slaughtered all the prospectors. After killing several of the Indians, Buck joined the timber wolves and became their leader, dreaded by the Yeehats as a terrible "Ghost Dog."

BUDDY, the first Seeing Eye dog, was a German shepherd bitch born in Switzerland at the kennels where Dorothy Harrison Eustis was developing the breed for police and rescue work. Mrs. Eustis' article in the *Saturday Evening Post* in November 1927 about dogs being trained in Germany to help blinded war veterans prompted an inquiry from Morris Frank, a young blind man in Tennessee, and she invited him to Switzerland to learn to work with a guide dog who would be trained for him. The dog chosen was known as Kiss but Frank renamed her Buddy. Frank spent five weeks there, winning her affection by taking complete care of her and learning to be guided by holding onto her harness strap. On one walk, she dragged him up an embankment to get clear of a pair of runaway horses. The day they went alone to the village for him to get a haircut, he burst out laughing that he was "free at last!" Reporters were skeptical when Frank and the dog disembarked in New York in June 1928, until

BUDDY
Buddy and Morris Frank

she led him through heavy traffic, across the street in front of the pier.

The independence that Buddy gave Frank generated so much public interest that Mrs. Eustis soon arrived to arrange the training of guide dogs in the United States. In January 1929, she founded The

Seeing Eye Inc.* Buddy spent the rest of her life touring the country with Frank on behalf of the nonprofit organization. Over the years she pulled him away from an open elevator shaft, woke him when she smelled fire in their hotel, and, with Frank clutching her tail, towed him to shore when he tired during a swim. She also snitched canapes at receptions, nipped an inquisitive terrier, and occasionally responded to an ovation from an audience by barking back.

BUGLE ANN, a great foxhound, had a trumpet cry that soared above the baying of the other hounds in *The Voice of Bugle Ann* (1935), a story by MacKinlay Kantor set in Missouri in the 1930s. Springfield Davis, Bugle Ann's 82-year-old owner, had waited most of his life to have a dog like her and was in no hurry to breed her. When she disappeared one night, he tracked her to the fenced property of a man named Terry, who threatened him with a shotgun. Davis killed him. Months after the old man went to jail, the voice of Bugle Ann rang across the valley, and people believed her ghost was leading a spectral pack of great hounds of the past. Davis was 86 when he was pardoned and sent home. By then, the dog's remains had been found but, incredibly, the high, clear baying of Bugle Ann was heard again. A friend revealed her fate—and the one puppy who had inherited her great voice.

BUGS BUNNY, the bucktoothed, carrot-chomping star of Warner Brothers animated cartoons, was developed from a crazy rabbit first seen in *Porky's Hare Hunt*

* The name is from Proverbs 20:12: "The hearing ear, and the seeing eye, the Lord hath made even both of them."

(1938). Remodeled and billed as Bugs Bunny in *A Wild Hare* (1940), he had the opening line, "What's up, Doc?" It became his trademark. Mel Blanc, who also created voices for PORKY PIG and SYLVESTER (1), gave Bugs's wisecracks a Brooklyn twang, and for more than twenty years the resourceful rabbit made fools of his adversaries. Elmer Fudd, a dim fellow who usually went after him with a shotgun, never could catch him. The rabbit won an Oscar for *Knighty Knight Bugs* (1958); he has appeared in comic books and strips since 1941; and the first of several Bugs Bunny television shows was aired in 1960. More recently, the entire antic Warner Brothers menagerie reappeared in two feature-length films compiled by former directors—Chuck Jones's *The Bugs Bunny/ Road Runner Movie* (1979) and Fritz Freleng's *Looney Looney Looney Bugs Bunny Movie* (1981).

BULLE ROCK, sired in England by THE DARLEY ARABIAN, was the first Thoroughbred imported to America. Samuel Gist, a tobacco planter in Virginia, imported the 21-year-old horse for stud service in 1730.

BULLET, a German shepherd billed as Roy Rogers' "wonder dog," made his debut in Rogers' movie *Spoilers of the Plains* (1951) and continued on television in *The Roy Rogers Show* (1951–64). Besides accompanying the horse TRIGGER in chase scenes, Bullet did various stunts, but an attack dog was imported for fights. Retired at the end of the series, Bullet died at Rogers' ranch and, like Trigger and Dale Evans' horse, Buttermilk, is now on display, stuffed and mounted, at the Roy Rogers–Dale Evans Museum in Victorville, California.

BULL'S-EYE, in Charles Dickens' *Oliver Twist* (1839), was a "white shaggy dog, with his face scratched and torn in twenty different places," and he was as mean as his master, Bill Sikes. When Sikes kicked him and tried to hit him with a poker, the snapping, growling dog grabbed the poker. But he tagged along when Sikes fled London after murdering Nancy. Fearing that he would be traced through the dog, Sikes tried to tie a weighted kerchief around his neck to drown him. But Bull's-eye "scoured away at his hardest speed." Separately, they straggled back to their old haunts in the city, where the police closed in on the murderer. Sikes, intending to swing by a rope from a roof to a ditch, slipped and hanged himself. Bull's-eye came out of hiding to run back and forth on the parapet "with a dismal howl," and, collecting himself for a spring, jumped for the dead man's shoulders. He missed, fell into the ditch, "and striking his head against a stone, dashed out his brains."

THE BULLS OF BASHAN, formidable because they grew strong on the fertile plain of Bashan, typified the enemies who distressed David in Psalms 22:12–13: "Many bulls encompass me, strong bulls of Bashan surround me; they open wide their mouths at me, like a ravening and roaring lion."

BULLWINKLE, the moose in Jay Ward Productions' *Rocky and His Friends*, a television cartoon series begun in 1959, was so popular that in 1960 a Bullwinkle balloon floated over Macy's Thanksgiving Day parade and in 1961 *The Bullwinkle Show* appeared during prime time. A native of Frostbite Falls, Minnesota, who had served as a radar antenna aboard a navy

BULL'S-EYE

destroyer, then as an officer's hatrack, Bullwinkle blundered along, foiling the villains Boris Badenov and Natasha Fataly with the help of his friend Rocky the squirrel. In a voice supplied by Ward's partner, Bill Scott, the amiable moose also recited poetry and, wearing a turban, consulted a crystal ball—"The spirits are about to speak."

BUMMER and LAZARUS, two mongrels, roamed San Francisco accompanying

Joshua Norton, a British trader who had lost his fortune speculating in rice and, in 1859, proclaimed himself Norton I, Emperor of the United States and Protector of Mexico. San Franciscans cherished the gentle eccentric, fed him, kept him in grand uniforms, and bought his Imperial Bonds for fifty cents apiece. In 1862, Lazarus was run over by a fire truck. His public funeral, attended by 10,000 citizens, was the greatest ever held for a dog. Bummer was later killed by a kick from a drunk, who was arrested and fined. Both dogs, preserved by taxidermy, were exhibited at the de Young Museum in San Francisco for many years.

BURIDAN'S ASS is dying of hunger between two equal and equidistant bundles of hay in a famous allegory attributed to the French philosopher Jean Buridan (1300–58), illustrating the dilemma of choosing between two equally valid alternatives. Actually, Buridan's Ass was a dog. In his commentary on Aristotle's *De caelo (On the Heavens)*, Buridan discussed the method by which a dog chooses between equal amounts of food placed before him, and concluded that the dog chooses at random—an idea that anticipated probability theory.

BUSHMAN, a lowland gorilla captured in Equatorial West Africa in 1928 when he was only a few months old, was sold to the Lincoln Park Zoo in Chicago for $30,500. When he arrived there in August 1930, he weighed 79 pounds. Bright and friendly, he played football with his keeper until he became so strong that when he squeezed the ball, it burst. Bushman grew very tall for a gorilla—over 6 feet—and reached 565 pounds. He escaped from his cage once when the lock was not secured, and was forced back in by a keeper, who thrust at him the one thing he feared—a small live snake. When Bushman died on January 1, 1951, at the age of 23, Chicago mourned its popular "citizen," and his skin was stuffed and mounted for display at the Field Museum.

BUSTER, James Herriot's feline retriever: see DEBBIE.

BUSTER BEAR, in the Thornton Burgess nature books, was usually good-tempered but in the spring, after his winter sleep, he was lean and mean. In *The Adventures of Bobby Coon* (1918), Buster knocked over a rotten tree stump, hoping to find ants and grubs. Instead, he found his cousin BOBBY COON. Buster accused him of poaching, threatened to eat him, and chased him up a tree. Bobby escaped, and later found a cave to settle in. To his horror, Buster came sniffing. Having found food by then, the bear was his old genial self, had forgotten his threat, and just chuckled at his cousin, telling him to be neighborly.

BUSTOPHER JONES, a cat, eschews pubs for clubs in "Bustopher Jones: The Cat About Town" from T. S. Eliot's *Old Possum's Book of Practical Cats* (1939). In impeccable black, with white spats, Bustopher visits a series of clubs for refreshments such as shrimp, venison, and a noon drink:

> It can be no surprise that under our
>   eyes
> He has grown unmistakably round.

THE BYERLY TURK was an Eastern-bred stallion that Capt. Robert Byerly captured at Buda in 1688 while he was fighting the Turks in Hungary. Two years later, as a colonel, he rode the horse at the Battle of the Boyne in Ireland. The Byerly Turk was then put at stud in England, where a new breed of racehorse, the Thoroughbred, was being developed by crossing Eastern-bred stallions with the larger native English mares. The male lines of three of the imported stallions have survived through a single Thoroughbred descendant of each one—the Byerly Turk's great-great-grandson HEROD, THE DARLEY ARABIAN's great-great-grandson ECLIPSE, and THE GODOLPHIN ARABIAN's grandson MATCHEM. Every Thoroughbred racing today is a male line descendant of one of these three and thus of one of the founders of the breed.

CACARECO, a female rhinoceros, won election by a landslide—with over 50,000 write-in votes—to the municipal council of São Paulo, Brazil, on October 4, 1959. The vote, according to a front-page story in the *New York Times*, was a protest against Brazilian politics, high living costs, and shortages of meat and beans. Some ballot envelopes were even stuffed with beans instead of votes. Cacareco's ballots, 15 percent of the vote, were nullified, of course, but her victory caused "deep political concern." The rhinoceros was the second non-human candidate to win in Brazil. In 1954, a goat named Smelly was elected to the city council of Jaboata, Pernambuco.

CADPIG, in *The Hundred and One Dalmatians* (1956) by Dodie Smith, was the smallest and prettiest of PONGO's fifteen puppies. While the puppies were being held captive, Cadpig adored watching television with their keepers. When the puppies escaped and headed for London, she and her brother Patch found themselves in an empty church on Christmas Eve. Cadpig

thought the lighted crêche was television until she saw that nothing moved. "But I like it much better than ordinary television," she said. "Only I don't know why."

CAESAR (1) and his brother LARIDON in "L'Education," one of the *Fables* of Jean de La Fontaine (1621–95), are dogs of fine pedigree who are raised by different masters. Laridon hangs around a kitchen. In the forest, Caesar lives up to his breed: he is a hunter, renowned for felling boars and bringing stags to bay. Caesar is kept from mating lesser bitches so that his issue will not have tainted blood.

CAESAR (2), in "Twa Dogs" (1786) by Robert Burns, is a rich man's pet, a dog "o' high degree," but not too proud to mount a gypsy's mongrel or to wander around with local dogs. He and LUATH (2), the plough-man's collie, compare their lives. Caesar describes his among the gentry and remarks, "But surely poor-folk maun [must] be wretches!" Then he observes that although the privileged "need na starve or sweat," even educated people are fools:

> That when nae real ills perplex them,
> They mak enow themsels to vex them.

As the friends parted at twilight, they "Rejoic'd that they were na *men* but *dogs.*"

CAESAR (3), a wirehaired fox terrier, sported a collar with the inscription, "I belong to the King." The king was Edward VII of England (1841–1910), who let the dog sleep on an easy chair by his bed and usually took him along on country weekends or trips abroad. When the king shook his stick at the dog and called him a "naughty, naughty boy," Caesar simply wagged his tail. On May 20, 1910, representatives of seventy nations, including nine kings, in the largest gathering of royalty ever seen in one place, were part of the spectacular funeral procession for King Edward. So was Caesar. Escorted by a Highland servant, the little dog trotted along directly behind the gun-carriage bearing his master's coffin.

CALLISTO, the daughter of LYCAON in Greek mythology, was seduced by Zeus and bore him a son, Arcas. Zeus's wife, Hera, was infuriated and turned Callisto into a bear. When Arcas grew up and became a hunter, Hera placed Callisto before him, intending that he kill his mother. But Zeus snatched up the bear, putting her among the stars as the constellation Ursa Major (Great Bear), then placing Arcas nearby as Ursa Minor (Lesser Bear). The honor given Callisto so enraged Hera that she persuaded the sea-gods to prohibit the bears' descent into the ocean. That is, supposedly, why they are the only constellations that never set below the horizon.

CALVIN, a large Maltese cat, was a stray that Harriet Beecher Stowe gave to Charles Dudley Warner, the editor of the *Hartford Courant.* The cat died eight years later, and Warner wrote a memorable essay about him in *My Summer in a Garden* (1882). The first time Calvin killed a bird, Warner had tried to convince him it was wrong, "for he is a reasonable cat, and understands pretty much everything except the binomial theorem." When Warner came home at night, Calvin was usually waiting near the gate, "as if his being there were purely accidental." The dignified cat liked companionship but disliked being petted. "If there was any petting to be done, however, he chose to do it. Often he would sit looking at me, and then, moved by a delicate affection, come and pull at my coat and sleeve until he could touch my face with his nose, and then go away contented."

THE CALYDONIAN BOAR, in Greek mythology, was sent by Artemis to ravage the country of Calydon because King Oeneus had failed to offer sacrifices to her

THE CALYDONIAN BOAR

at harvest time. The enormous wild boar, with tusks like an elephant's, trampled the crops, slaughtered the livestock, and killed the men who tried to kill him. Meleager, the king's son, summoned the bravest men of Greece to hunt the beast. Atalanta, the young huntress, joined them, and for Meleager it was love at first sight. The others objected to her but he insisted that she stay. Surrounded by hunters, the boar rushed them, killing two men before the first arrow, Atalanta's, hit him. The beast was only slightly wounded but Meleager was then able to drive a spear into his side, killing him. Although the honor of the kill belonged to Meleager, he handed the trophies, the boar's head and hide, to Atalanta, an act that led to his death: The Fates had told his mother, Althea, soon after he was born that Meleager would die when the log burning on the hearth turned to ash. Althea had then quenched the flame and hidden the log. But when Meleager killed her brothers for protesting the award to Atalanta, Althea was enraged. She brought out the log and threw it into the fire. Meleager fell to the ground, dying.

CAPILET, in Shakespeare's *Twelfth Night* (ca. 1601), is Sir Andrew Aguecheek's horse. In act 3, scene 4, Sir Toby Belch persuades Sir Andrew to challenge his young rival for the affections of Olivia, a rich countess, then tells the silly knight that the fellow is an expert fencer. Sir Andrew decides not to meddle with him: "Let him let the matter slip, and I'll give him my horse, grey Capilet."

CARLO (1), the vicious mastiff in Sir Arthur Conan Doyle's "The Adventure of the Copper Beeches" (1892), belonged to Mr. Rucastle, whose servant Toller was the only one who could handle the animal. "We feed him once a day, and not too much then, so he is always as keen as mustard," Rucastle told Viola Hunter, the governess he hired. When Miss Hunter told Sherlock Holmes about the strange goings on at Copper Beeches, Rucastle's home in Hampshire, she added that her heart was chilled by the sight of the giant dog, "as large as a calf, tawny-tinted, with hanging jowl, black muzzle, and huge projecting bones." Holmes and Dr. Watson went to Hampshire to confront the villainous Rucastle, who tried to escape. He let the dog loose but Carlo, unfed for two days because Toller was drunk, attacked Rucastle and mangled him horribly before Dr. Watson blew the dog's brains out.

CARLO (2), in "The Adventure of the Sussex Vampire" (1924) by Sir Arthur Conan Doyle, was Robert Ferguson's spaniel. When Sherlock Holmes and Dr. Watson accompanied Ferguson to his home in Sussex to investigate the circumstances that had led him to fear his wife was a vampire, they observed Carlo get out of his basket to walk with difficulty toward his master. "Its hind legs moved irregularly and its tail was on the ground." Holmes asked what was the matter with the dog. Ferguson said it was a sort of paralysis that the puzzled veterinarian thought was spinal meningitis. "The dog's mournful eyes passed from one of us to the other," said Dr. Watson. "He knew that we were discussing his case." From his observations of the contents of the house and its occupants, Holmes was soon able to deduce the cause of Ferguson's fear. As for Carlo, Holmes concluded, "I did not foresee the dog, but at least I understand him and he fitted into my reconstruction."

CATARINA, a cat, had been in the household of Edgar Allan Poe since she was a kitten. After Poe's consumptive young wife, Virginia, collapsed in 1842, the sight of Catarina curled up on the bed with her inspired Poe to write his horror story about PLUTO (1), "The Black Cat." In December 1846, a few weeks before Virginia died, the Poes were so destitute that Mrs. Gove Nichols, visiting their cottage in Fordham, found Virginia lying on a straw bed, "wrapped in her husband's great coat, with a large tortoiseshell cat in her bosom. The wonderful cat seemed conscious of her great usefulness. The coat and the cat were the sufferer's only means of warmth, except as her husband held her hands, and her mother her feet."

CAVALL, in Alfred Lord Tennyson's *Idylls of the King: Enid* (1859), was "King Arthur's hound of deepest mouth." His baying could be heard for great distances and would send hunted animals to their lairs. While he was chasing a wild boar in Breconshire, Wales, Cavall left a paw print on one of the rocks. A cairn built on the spot is thought to be Cavall's grave. According to legend, if anyone removes a boulder from it, the rock is mysteriously restored to the place where King Arthur put it when he buried his dog.

CCOA, the malevolent feline spirit that haunted the Quecha Indians of ancient Peru, was a striped cat, or wildcat, 2 feet long with a foot-long tail and a large head. Hail streamed from his eyes and ears, and he brought forth lightning at will. The Quechas constantly propitiated the dreadful cat with offerings, in the hope that he would stop using hail and lightning to kill people and ruin crops.

CECILY, in H. A. Rey's first book for children, *Cecily G. and the Nine Monkeys* (1942; earlier in France), was a lonely giraffe who had no one to play with until she met nine monkeys who needed a place to live. One of the monkeys went on to fame as CURIOUS GEORGE.

CECILY PARSLEY, in *Cecily Parsley's Nursery Rhymes* (1922) by Beatrix Potter, was a rabbit in a long white apron who "lived in a Pen and brewed good ale for Gentlemen."

CELESTE, a winsome elephant, marries BABAR in Jean de Brunhoff's *The Story of Babar* (1932). When Babar is crowned King of the Elephants, she is crowned Queen. In subsequent stories, they live interestingly ever after in Celesteville, the city of the elephants. Celeste wears pretty dresses and looks after their children, POM, FLORA, AND ALEXANDER.

CERBERUS, the monstrous watchdog of Hades in Greek mythology, guarded the gate of the nether world, through which all the spirits of the dead were permitted to enter, but none to leave. Those who tried, he ate. According to Hesiod (eighth century B.C.), Cerberus had fifty heads, but most writers said he had three, and a snake's tail. The twelfth and last labor that King Eurystheus demanded of Heracles was to bring the hound to him. Pluto, the ruler of the underworld, gave Heracles permission to try, provided he used no weapon other than his hands. Heracles overpowered Cerberus, carried him up to earth, and then carried him back. Orpheus, descending into Hades to retrieve his bride, Eurydice, lulled the dog to sleep with his music, and in Vergil's *Aeneid* (30–19 B.C.), Aeneas was escorted past Cerberus by the Sybil of Cumae, who mollified the beast with cake.

CHAMPION, Gene Autry's horse, was almost as famous as his owner. Starting with *Tumbling Tumbleweeds* (1935), Autry starred in ninety musical westerns in eighteen years, became a top box-office star, and made countless personal appearances with Champion in the United States and abroad. In the 1950s, the horse appeared on television in "The Gene Autry Show" and in "The Adventures of Champion," which was developed from a comic book series. Autry had several Champions, all with blaze faces and, except for the first one, four white stockings. The first touring Champion was originally named Lindy, because he was foaled on the day Charles A. Lindbergh flew the Atlantic. Billed as "the world's wonder horse," the chestnut stallion danced, knelt, and untied knots; at rodeos in New York City's Madison Square Garden, he made a spectacular leap through a paper poster. Doubles were used for dangerous stunts in the films, and since the intended audience was children, romance was kept to a minimum, with help from Champion. One leading lady recalled that as she and Autry went into their fade-out clinch, the horse stuck his nose between them to nudge them apart.

CH.* CHINOE'S ADAMANT JAMES, a liver-and-white English springer spaniel, born in 1968, was known as D. J.—for Diamond Jim—because of a white diamond on his back. In 1971, he took forty-seven

* "Ch.," for champion, is the title a dog earns by accumulating fifteen points in conformation (breed standard) competition at shows recognized by the American Kennel Club.

best-in-shows, including the prestigious Westminster Kennel Club Championship in New York City. His exuberant personality made him a popular champion. "Applause seems to be his song," said his owner, Dr. Milton E. Prickett, a Kentucky veterinarian. In 1972, D. J. won his second Westminster best-in-show and was retired with a career total of sixty.

CH. MY OWN BRUCIE, the black cocker spaniel who won best-in-show at the Westminster Kennel Club shows in 1940 and 1941, was sired by Red Brucie. Bred by Herman Mellenthin of Poughkeepsie, New York, the man most responsible for developing the American cocker, Red Brucie never became a champion but was the greatest stud dog the breed had known. My Own Brucie was his thirty-fourth champion and a valuable sire himself. When he took best-of-breed on the way to best-in-show at the 1940 Westminster, My Own Brucie's closest rival was his own son.

CH. NUNSOE DUC DE LA TERRACE OF BLAKEEN, the first poodle to win the Westminster Kennel Club best-in-show, was a huge, snow-white standard whose string of names reflected his international celebrity. Born in 1929 at La Terrace kennels in Switzerland, the Duc had won four continental championships when Jane Lane bought him for her Nunsoe kennels in England. After winning the English championship and siring six litters, he was brought to the United States in 1934 by Mrs. Sherman Hoyt for her Blakeen kennels. In eighteen American shows, he was undefeated best-of-breed, took sixteen group titles, and won nine best-in-shows, including the Westminster in 1935. The Duc had such awe-inspiring presence that he became known as the emperor of poodles, and his great popularity revived American interest in the breed, now the most popular in the United States.

CH. RANCHO DOBE'S STORM, a Doberman pinscher whelped in California in 1949, was never defeated for best-of-breed in his twenty-five-show career, took twenty-two group firsts, and won best-in-show seventeen times. In 1953, at the age of 38 months, he was retired from competition after winning his second best-in-show at the annual Westminster Kennel Club. Black with tan markings, Storm stood 28 inches high at the withers, weighed 90 pounds, and lived with his owners, Mr. and Mrs. Len Carey, in Greenwich, Connecticut. Children were safe around him; once when he was pestered by a small child, the dog walked up to him, lifted off the child's hat, and buried it in the garden. Storm was the second Doberman to receive the Westminster's top award. The first was his great-grandfather, Ferry v Rauhfelsen of Giralda, who won it in 1939.

CHAPERONE, a gray marmoset that Maud Gonne bought in Marseilles in 1887 to take along on a trip to Constantinople, was named for the fact that her owner was traveling alone, an unusual venture for a beautiful 20-year-old debutante in the Victorian era. The future "Irish Joan of Arc" already had a lover, Lucien Millevoye, a prominent Boulangiste, who gave her an ivory-handled revolver for more practical protection. In aid of his cause the following spring, Gonne made a journey from Paris to Russia with secret documents sewn into her dress. Again she was alone, with only Chaperone and the little gun to protect her. Her mission was successful but the cold St. Petersburg winter killed Chaperone.

CHARLEY (1), "a noble animal of the Camanchee wild breed," was the pony that George Catlin rode across 500 miles of prairie in the 1830s to study and paint American Indians. He described getting acquainted with his horse in *North American Indians* (1841). Stopping at dusk near the bank of a stream, Catlin tethered Charley to a picket but the pony slipped free. After chasing him for ½ mile, Catlin gave up, returned to his bivouac, and went to sleep. In the middle of the night, he woke up to a shock: a huge figure was looming over him. The "faithful" horse had filled his belly and "with his head hanging directly over me, . . . was standing fast asleep." Next morning, Charley was gone again. Catlin spent half an hour trying to catch him, then decided to test the pony's "attachment and dependence." Packing up his things and slinging the saddle over his back, he started walking. When he looked back, Charley merely looked at him and then at the campsite. Seeing nothing there, he neighed "very violently," raced to overtake Catlin, and wheeled about in front of him, "trembling like an aspen leaf. . . . I took good care after that night to keep him under my strict authority."

CHARLEY (2), a large, 10-year-old French poodle, was John Steinbeck's companion in 1960 on his 10,000-mile tour of the United States. The journey, described in *Travels with Charley* (1963), was made in a pickup truck fitted with a small cabin in the back. When they drove into Yellowstone National Park, the peaceful dog, who couldn't fight his way out of a paper bag, went berserk at his first sight of a bear. The writer drove on, with the windows rolled up. Two more bears appeared, and "Charley became a maniac," leaping and snarling at them. After locking him in the cabin, Steinbeck could hear him thrashing around, knocking things over as they passed more bears. "What could have caused it? Was it a pre-breed memory of the time the wolf was in him?" Hours after the exhausted dog collapsed into sleep at the auto court that night, Steinbeck was awakened by yapping and whining, to find Charley sleeping with his eyes open, twitching, and making running motions, "but it was only a night bear."

CHATTERER THE RED SQUIRREL, in the Thornton Burgess nature books, was impudent because he could easily get away from all the other animals except SHADOW THE WEASEL. Perched high on an isolated pine tree in *The Adventures of Buster Bear* (1916), the squirrel happily joined the birds in taunting BUSTER BEAR, not knowing that bears can climb trees. When Buster started up, Chatterer wished he had never opened his mouth. The frightened squirrel jumped, landed hard, and scurried off.

CHECKERS, a cocker spaniel, became famous on September 23, 1952, when Senator Richard Nixon appeared on television to save his candidacy for Vice President. A secret fund at Nixon's disposal, more than $18,000 donated mostly by oilmen, had been revealed, and Dwight D. Eisenhower, the presidential candidate, would not defend him. Nixon spoke of his humble background and denied any impropriety; the fund was for "necessary political expenses" and "to fight communism." Then he reported another gift from a political admirer, a little cocker spaniel sent in a crate from Texas. "Black and white spotted. And our little girl—Tricia, the 6-year-old—named it Checkers. And you know, the kids love the dog, and I just want to say this right now, that regardless of what they say about it, we're gonna keep it!" Many, including Nixon himself, were moved to tears by his plea for support. It succeeded and has been called the Checkers Speech ever since.

CHEE-CHEE, an organ-grinder's monkey, was given a good home with the other animals at Puddleby-on-the-Marsh in *The Story of Doctor Dolittle* (1920) by Hugh Lofting. The only one with hands, he took over the cooking and mending after the doctor ran out of money. When the monkeys in Africa took sick, Chee-Chee persuaded Doctor Dolittle to go help them, led his party through the jungle, and then decided to stay. Like the parrot and the crocodile, Chee-Chee had been born in Africa. As the doctor sailed away, the three of them stood on the rocks, "crying bitterly and waving till the ship was out of sight."

CHEETAH, Tarzan's chimpanzee pal, was a character created to add a comic touch to *Tarzan the Ape Man* (1932), the sixth of forty-two movies based on Edgar Rice Burroughs' Tarzan stories, and the first with Johnny Weissmuller in the title role. In his twelve films between 1932 and 1948, Weissmuller worked with at least eight different chimpanzees because, as they matured, they became potentially dangerous and had to be replaced. Cheetah was one of the most popular animals in the movies and continued to provide comedy with subsequent Tarzans until, for the first time, filming was done in Africa. Two chimpanzees shipped from England to Kenya for *Tarzan's Greatest Adventure* (1959) were so terrified by the jungle noises that one was used only in a brief scene, with Tarzan saying, "So long, Cheetah."

THE CHESHIRE CAT, in *Alice's Adventures in Wonderland* (1865) by Lewis Carroll, was first seen grinning on the kitchen hearth while the Duchess nursed her baby. When Alice went outside, she was startled to find the Cat sitting in a tree. She asked it which way she should go and the Cat replied that there were mad people in every direction, that it was mad, and that Alice was mad. Alice wondered how the Cat knew it was mad. "To begin with," said the Cat, "a dog's not mad. You grant that? . . . Well then, you see a dog growls when it's angry, and wags its tail when it's pleased. Now *I* growl when I'm pleased, and wag my tail when I'm angry. Therefore I'm mad." Alice said she called it purring, not growling. "Call it what you like," said the Cat. After it disappeared, then reappeared a couple of times, Alice complained that the sudden appearings and vanishings made her giddy. The Cat obliged with a slow fade-out, "beginning with the end of the tail, and ending with the grin, which remained some time after the rest of it had gone."

The expression "to grin like a Cheshire cat" came either from grinning cats painted on inn signboards in Cheshire, England, or from an old custom of forming Cheshire cheese into the shape of a cat and incising a grin. There is no Cheshire breed of cats.

THE
CHESHIRE
CAT

CHESSIE, the snoozing kitten, first appeared in the September 1933 issue of *Fortune* magazine in an advertisement for the Chesapeake and Ohio Railway's first fully air-conditioned train. A C&O executive had obtained commercial rights to the picture of the kitten after seeing a newspaper reproduction of the original etching by Guido Gruenwald, a Viennese artist whose favorite subjects were cats and

CHESSIE

kittens. Captioned "Sleep Like a Kitten," the picture was an immediate success as a corporate symbol, attracting hundreds of requests for copies. When the first Chessie calendar appeared in 1934, fan mail poured in from all over the world, with gifts ranging from catnip mice to crates of oranges. The kitten still receives birthday cards each September, the month of her debut in *Fortune.* Chessie later acquired a tom, Peake, and two kittens, and in 1948 the C&O began royalty-free licensing of all sorts of Chessie merchandise, using some

for their own promotions. In 1973, Chessie System, Inc., was formed as the parent company for the C&O, B&O, and Western Maryland railroads, and other subsidiaries. It has no more sleeping cars, just freight cars, but the sleepy kitten is still the symbol.

CHIA-CHIA, the London Zoo's male giant panda, was flown to the United States in March 1981, in the hope that he would impregnate Ling-Ling, the female panda at the National Zoological Park in Washington, D.C. Hsing-Hsing, the male panda who accompanied her from the People's Republic of China in 1972, had proved himself "inept." (See HSING-HSING AND LING-LING.) When Chia-Chia was let into Ling-Ling's pen on April 14, he followed her to the farthest end and hit her. After they exchanged blows for an hour and a half, a hose was turned on them to separate them. London Zoo officials "asked us to try to put them together again," said a Washington spokesman, "but Ling-Ling was too sore." Chia-Chia was returned to London, where his pen bore a sign:

WELCOME HOME
CHIA-CHIA
WELL-TRIED!

CHIMPANZEES A, B, C, D, E, and F, in Russell Maloney's short story "Inflexible Logic" (1940), were set to work by Mr. Bainbridge to test an assertion that, according to the science of probability, six chimpanzees pounding six typewriters would, in a million years, turn out all the books in the British Museum. In four weeks, each chimpanzee produced a foot-high pile of typescript. Chimpanzee A had finished *Oliver Twist*, word for word, and comma for comma. The others were typing works by John Donne, Anatole France, Sir Arthur Conan Doyle, et al. Bainbridge's friend James Mallard, a mathematics professor, was shocked by what he saw, but predicted the chimpanzees would soon produce gibberish. They did not. Eleven weeks later, Mallard visited again, saw they were still at it, and went berserk. He shot the chimpanzees and Bainbridge, who managed to shoot him. All died immediately except Chimpanzee F, who, with his left hand, pulled the final page of Florio's trans-

lation of Michel de Montaigne's essays out of his typewriter, inserted a fresh page, "and typed with one finger, 'UNCLE TOM'S CABIN by Harriet Beecher Stowe. Chapte . . .' Then he too, was dead."

CHINOOK, a white German shepherd billed as "The Wonder Dog," was Kirby Grant's co-star from 1949 to 1954 in a series of B-movies about a Canadian Mountie and his dog. The episodes were based on the stories of James Oliver Curwood. The dog had a reputation as a biter but Grant, quoted in David Rothel's *The Great Show Business Animals* (1980), said that he had been spared and, "surprisingly," got along fine with Chinook. "He was not vicious. He was just very temperamental." The dog was evidently manageable enough to work with children because he next played White Shadow in the Corky and the White Shadow serial on television's "Mickey Mouse Club" from 1955 to 1959.

CHIP and DALE, a peppy pair of chipmunks, were added to Walt Disney Productions' short animated cartoons in the 1940s to bother the already irascible Donald Duck.

CHIPPY HACKEE, a small striped chipmunk in *The Tale of Timmy Tiptoes* (1911) by Beatrix Potter, had a grand time inside a hollow tree, cracking nuts and singing songs with his squirrel friend, TIMMY TIPTOES. After a big wind knocked the tree over, Timmy went home, but Chippy Hackee camped out for another week, until a bear came sniffing around.

CHIPS, the first war dog sent overseas during World War II, was a shepherd-husky-collie mix owned by Edward J.

Wren of Pleasantville, New York. Wren offered Chips to Dogs for Defense, a civilian organization supplying recruits to the army's newly formed K-9 Corps. When Chips and his handler, Pvt. John R. Rowell, landed in Sicily with the 3rd Infantry Division in July 1943, the American forces were pinned by machine guns in a pillbox camouflaged as a peasant hut. Unleashed, the dog made his way to the emplacement, where he leaped at the throat of one of the Italian gunners. The man fled and Chips drove out the other two. The army awarded him the Purple Heart and the Silver Star, then took them away a short time later because commendations for animals were deemed "contrary to Army policy." Chips' company replaced the decorations with some of their own. Chips was discharged in 1945, "demilitarized," and sent home to his owner.

CHOLMONDELEY, a mature chimpanzee with the airs of a "fascinating, mischievous, courtly old man," was shipped from Africa to the London Zoo by Gerald M. Durrell, who described him in *The Overloaded Ark* (1953). Known as Chumley, the chimpanzee smoked cigarettes, uttered expressive "hoo hoos" when he was pleased, and had perfect table manners—until the end of a meal, when he would throw his empty plate and mug as far as possible. He was the only animal Durrell had ever known to share things, and would "grunt with satisfaction" when his offer of a banana was accepted. Chumley became a television star in London, but when his teeth went bad, he had to be moved to the sanatorium at Regent's Park. After escaping twice and biting a passenger on a bus, "the fine, intelligent animal" shown on television came to be regarded as a "fierce and untrust-

worthy monster." Lest he escape and bite again, Chumley was shot.

CHOUGNA, a very exasperating dog, prompted Victor Hugo (1802–85) to ask, in *"La Dernière Gerbe,"* why he behaved so badly in front of people when they went out:

Why . . .
Do you run, yapping, through the bushes
After young dogs and little boys?
Why can you not see a cock without chasing it?
So that I look as if I had a drunken dog?

CHRYSOMALLUS, in Greek mythology, was the marvelous ram with a fleece of pure gold that Hermes sent to save two children, in answer to their mother's prayer. A Greek king named Athamas had tired of his wife, Nephele, and sent her away so that he could marry the Princess Ino. After Ino bore him a son, Nephele's fears about the safety of her daughter, Helle, and, especially, her son, Phrixus, were confirmed. Ino arranged an elaborate plot that required Athamas to sacrifice his first son. As Phrixus was led to the altar, Nephele prayed to Hermes. Chrysomallus suddenly appeared, the boy and his sister climbed on his back, and the ram vaulted into the sky. Helle fell off as they crossed the strait between Europe and Asia. Because she drowned there, the strait was named for her—the Hellespont, or sea of Helle. The golden ram kept going until he reached the land of the Colchians on the eastern shore of the Black Sea. He landed there and, in an odd expression of gratitude for being saved, Phrixus sacrificed Chrysomallus to Zeus, then gave the ram's Golden Fleece to

King Aeetis. Aeetis placed it in a sacred grove where it was guarded by a dragon who never slept, until Medea put it to sleep with a magic potion so that Jason could recover the Fleece.

CHURCHY LA FEMME, a turtle, was a busybody in Walt Kelly's comic strip *Pogo*. In a 1959 episode, he turned up with cap and guns to guard the border between Pogo and Li'l' Orphan Abner, and seemed to speak for Kelly when he said, "A comic strip is like a dream—a tissue of paper reveries—it gloms an' glimmers its way thru unreality, fancy an' fantasy."

CINCINNATI (or CINCINNATUS), a gift from the people of Cincinnati, Ohio, was Gen. Ulysses S. Grant's favorite mount during the Civil War, and one of several horses that Grant took to Washington in 1869 when he became President.

CIPION, in Miguel Cervantes' "Colloquy of the Dogs" from the *Novelas exemplares* (1613), was courteous about listening to BERGANZA, a fellow watchdog, tell his life story but urged him not to digress or gossip. In Cipión's opinion, dogs were famous for their memory, gratitude, and fidelity and had become the symbol of friendship, but they, like other animals, were devoid of reason. The fact that he and Berganza had been given the power of speech was, to Cipión, all the more miraculous because their discourse was rational.

CITRON, a "filthy cur," is put on trial for devouring a capon in *Les Plaideurs* (1668), a farce by Jean Racine that is based on Aristophanes' *Wasps* (422 B.C.). In the Greek play, the dog LABES is tried for a similar offense. Citron's trial is staged by

Leander to keep his half-demented father, Dandin, a judge, quiet and at home. After an oration by the porter as prosecutor, the clerk defending the dog reminds the court that it was Citron who kept watch at the doors and never failed to bark at thieves. The speech puts the judge to sleep. Roused by Leander, he sentences the dog to the galleys. But when the clerk pulls Citron's puppies out of his pocket and pleads on their behalf, the judge admits to being sympathetic, even while they spray the room.

CLARENCE, a cross-eyed lion, was the reason for and star of the movie *Clarence the Cross-Eyed Lion* (1965), which begat the television series "Daktari" (1966–69). In 1964, Ralph Helfer and Ivan Tors had become partners in Africa, USA, a compound in Soledad Canyon near Los Angeles, where animals were given "affection training." When a cross-eyed lion cub arrived, Tors chose Clarence as a funny name for the animal and guessed correctly that the public would enjoy him. Filmed at Africa, USA, the movie and the series were set in a game preserve and research center supposedly in East Africa. Clarence was a gentle lion who did not seem to mind having JUDY the chimpanzee sit on his back or pull his tail. A novel touch was to let the audience see as Clarence saw, by showing his point of view in double vision.

CLAVILENO, in part 2 of Miguel Cervantes' *Don Quixote* (1616), was a magic horse. La Trifalda, the Distressed Duenna, persuaded Don Quixote and Sancho Panza to ride him by telling them that the horse had been created by Merlin and traveled

CLAVILENO

through the sky so smoothly that a rider could carry a full glass of water without losing a drop. The creature was made of wood with a peg in its neck for guiding it, she said—hence his name, which means "wooden peg." (The similarly wondrous "stede of bras" in Geoffrey Chaucer's unfinished "Squire's Tale" [1400] had a peg in its ear.) After dark, Don Quixote and Sancho mounted Clavileño, were blindfolded, and, as soon as the knight turned the peg, felt air rush by—because bellows were blown at them. The hoax ended when Clavileño's tail was set on fire, detonating rockets inside the horse. Don Quixote and Sancho were hurled to the ground, convinced they had sailed past the moon.

CLEO, the basset hound in the television series "The People's Choice" (1955–58), belonged to Socrates "Sock" Miller (played by Jackie Cooper), an idealistic young city councilman constantly at odds with Mayor Peoples and in love with his daughter, Amanda. The basset did not converse directly with the characters in the show, but with her glum face in close-up, and voiceover by Mary Jane Croft, Cleo did comment on the goings on.

CLEVER HANS (KLUGE HANS), a famous performing horse in Germany at the turn of the century, tapped out answers to mathematical problems written on a blackboard, using his right forefoot for digits, his left for tens. Scientists were baffled by his apparent ability to calculate until Oskar Pfungst, a young psychologist, analyzed his performance in 1907. Hans failed if he was blindfolded or if the questioner did not know the problem's solution. Further, after signaling Hans to start tapping, the questioner would relax with some slight movement when the horse reached the right number of taps, unwittingly giving him the cue to stop. Pfungst's conclusion that Hans had learned to react to this sensory clue has given psychologists a term for the result of inadvertent signals during tests—the "Clever Hans effect."

COLO, born on December 22, 1956, at the Columbus, Ohio, zoo, was the first gorilla born in captivity. Her father, Baron, was 11 years old and weighed 380 pounds; her mother, Christiana, was 9 and weighed 260 pounds. Found on the floor of the cage, the 3¼-pound newborn was brought to life by artificial respiration, then placed in an incubator. She matured into a healthy gorilla who mated and reproduced.

COLONEL, the English sheepdog who organized the puppies' escape in *The Hundred and One Dalmations* (1956) by Dodie Smith, was, according to TIB the cat, "a perfect master of strategy—you ask the sheep." After teaching the puppies to obey orders, and seeing them safely off to London, Colonel promoted himself to Brigadier-General.

COMANCHE, Capt. Myles Keogh's mount, was the sole survivor of Gen. George Armstrong Custer's force of 264 men of the 7th U.S. Cavalry at the battle of the Little Big Horn in Montana on June 25, 1876. The 13-year-old horse was seriously wounded in the neck, lung, and groin, but recovered to live seventeen more years. At Fort Lincoln (North Dakota), and subsequent posts, he was paraded at all ceremonies and allowed to wander free the rest of the time. By special order, no one was permitted to ride him. After his death in 1893 at Fort Riley, Kansas, his body was stuffed and put on display at the University of Kansas.

CONGO, a popular chimpanzee of "Zootime," a weekly show that was televised live from the London Zoo in the 1950s, became famous for his drawing and painting. Desmond Morris, who hosted the show, reported in *Animal Days* (1980) that as soon as he showed Congo how to hold a pencil, the chimpanzee began producing scribbles, mostly in radiating fan shapes, all in "a recognizable, personal style." A guest appearance by Baltimore Betsy, a finger-painting chimpanzee from the United States, prompted Morris to give brushes and paints to Congo, who became even more obsessed with making pictures. In 1957, an exhibit of his paintings at an avant-garde gallery in London caused an uproar in the press, pro and con, and attracted collectors. Salvador Dali ranked the chimpanzee above Jackson Pollock, Pablo Picasso was said to be delighted with the Congo painting he was given, and several years later, Joan Miró made a trip to the zoo to get one.

COPENHAGEN, the Duke of Wellington's famous charger and a grandson of ECLIPSE, was 4 years old when the duke bought him in 1812 for the Peninsular Campaign. At the battle of Waterloo against Napoleon's forces on June 18, 1815, Wellington rode out on the small chestnut stallion at 6 A.M. for an inspection tour and stayed on him all day, galloping in and out of the action, or observing it. When the Prussian allies finally arrived around 7:30 P.M., the duke waved his hat toward the French, spurred Copenhagen forward, and began the final charge. By nine o'clock, the battle was won. Two hours later, Wellington reached his inn at Waterloo. As he dismounted, he gave the horse a pat. Instantly, Copenhagen turned on him and the duke, unscathed through the day's fighting, narrowly escaped injury.

Retired to the duke's estate at Strathfield Saye, Copenhagen died in 1836 and was buried there with military honors. In tribute to him, Wellington declared: "There may have been many faster horses, no doubt many handsomer, but for bottom and endurance I never saw his fellow."

CORNELIUS (1), in Jean de Brunhoff's *The Story of Babar* (1932), is a bespectacled, wise, old elephant. When BABAR, dressed like a boulevardier, drives home to the forest in a red sports car, Cornelius is so impressed that he chooses Babar to be king. Babar likes the idea so much that, after he is crowned, he gives his derby hat to Cornelius and makes him a general. From then on, in subsequent stories, General Cornelius is often seen officiating in a splendid uniform.

CORNELIUS (2), a chimpanzee in *Planet of the Apes* (1964) by Pierre Boulle, is an archaeologist in a world ruled by civilized talking apes—not unlike Jonathan Swift's HOUYHNHNMS—who have subjugated the wild brutes that men have become. In *Escape from the Planet of the Apes* (1971), one of three sequels to the 1968 movie version of the book, Cornelius and his mate ZIRA travel 2,000 years back to the present world, where they are treated as celebrities. He is taken to a boxing match and calls it "beastly." When he explains how future apes will overthrow their human masters, sterilization is ordered for both chimpanzees. Cornelius accidentally kills a man for calling Zira a monkey, they hide with a circus until she gives birth, and both of them are shot when they flee—without their baby.

CORNELIUS (3), a rhinoceros born on December 10, 1979, at the Granby Zoo in Montreal, was made the titular leader of the fifth-largest federal political party in Canada, the Rhinoceros Party. It had been formed in 1963 by nationalist Quebecers who had been inspired by the election victory in São Paulo, Brazil of the rhinoceros CACARECO. Such an animal, declared the founders, was "the perfect symbol of the Quebec Member of Parliament—myopic, clumsy, and thick-skinned, indeed somebody who loves to wallow in mire but is quick to sense danger and run from trouble." In January 1980, the party declared war on Belgium after the Belgian cartoon character Tintin blew up a rhinoceros. It was, the party charged, Cornelius' mother, Elizabeth. A peace treaty was signed on January 30 with the Belgian ambassador, who served lunch for reparations. Cornelius ate the leftovers.

CORNPLANTER

CORNPLANTER, a performing horse, starred in the first real circus in the United States. Produced by John Bill Ricketts, an English equestrian who built an eight-hundred-seat amphitheater in Philadelphia, the circus opened on April 3, 1793, presenting a clown, a rope walker, and "the most surprising Equestrian Feats in America." While riding Cornplanter, Ricketts juggled, did headstands, and vaulted over a ribbon suspended 12 feet off the ground. He also jumped Cornplanter over a horse of the same size. The show was a sensation. President George Washington was an enthusiastic spectator, as was his successor, John Adams. Ricketts built another theater in New York and toured as far as Albany.

In 1799, both theaters burned down and he was ruined. No one knows what happened to Cornplanter.

COTTON-TAIL, like her sisters FLOPSY and MOPSY, is a good little bunny who obeys her mother and does not get into mischief like her brother PETER RABBIT (1), in *The Tale of Peter Rabbit* (1903) by Beatrix Potter.

COURTAUD, a bobtailed wolf, was a famous outlaw who led a pack of ten or twelve other wolves in chasing horses and attacking small flocks of domestic animals being driven to the walled city of Paris in the summer of 1447. In February 1450, it was said that the pack got into Paris through a breach in the walls and killed forty people. After hunters failed to kill the wolves in their lairs, a trail of fresh meat was laid to lure them into the city, to the square in front of Notre Dame. Trapped there, the wolves were stoned and stabbed to death.

THE COWARDLY LION, in L. Frank Baum's *The Wonderful Wizard of Oz* (1900), leaped into the story with a roar, sending the Scarecrow flying, knocking over the Tin Woodman, and getting a rap on the nose from Dorothy for threatening her little dog, TOTO. Admitting he was a coward, the Lion joined their expedition to the Emerald City in the hope that the Wizard would give him courage. Carrying his friends, the Lion vaulted a big ditch, despite his fear of falling, and towed their raft across a river. On the mission to destroy the Wicked Witch, his roars were intimidating. When the Lion claimed the courage the Wizard had promised him, the Wizard poured it from a green bottle into

THE COWARDLY LION

for more movie work and returned to Broadway, saying, "Well, after all, how many lion parts are there?"

COWPER'S HARES, three leverets given to William Cowper by neighbors as he emerged from his third siege of mental illness in 1774, were immortalized in his article in the June 1784 issue of *Gentleman's Magazine.* Puss, Tiney, and Bess, "notwithstanding the two feminine appellatives," were all males, and Cowper "commenced carpenter" to build them a little house with a separate compartment for each one. Puss "grew presently familiar" and would leap into his lap to nibble the hair at his temples. Tiney was ferocious while Bess, tame from the start, was "a hare of great humour and drollery." A sportsman, concluded Cowper, "little knows what amiable creatures he persecutes, . . . how cheerful they are, . . . what enjoyment they have of life."

Bess died young. Puss was almost twelve when he died "of mere old age." Cowper wrote "Epitaph on a Hare" for "Old Tiney, surliest of his kind," who lived nine years:

> Though duly from my hand he took
> His pittance every night,
> He did it with a jealous look,
> And, when he could, would bite.

a dish. Asked how he felt after drinking it, the Lion replied, "Full of courage." Dorothy went home to Kansas and the Lion retired to the jungle, where he had been invited to rule as King of the Forest.

In *The Wizard of Oz* (1939), the M-G-M movie that has become as much a classic as Baum's book, Bert Lahr was a memorable Cowardly Lion, lumbering around in a 100-pound lion suit, while a stagehand managed the tail with a fishing rod, and gurgling the song "If I Were King of the Forest." One reviewer could not resist writing, "The Lion is fion." Lahr was disappointed in his hope

THE COWS OF BASHAN, well-fattened on the fertile plain of Bashan, typified the self-indulgent women of Samaria in Amos 4:1–2:

> Hear this word, you cows of Bashan, who are in the mountains of Samaria, who oppress the poor, who crush the needy, who say to their husbands, "Bring, that we may drink!". . . the days

are coming upon you when they shall take you away with hooks.

COYOTE, the smartest and most powerful of the great animal people of American Indian mythology, was a trickster god who also appeared in the creation myths of many western tribes. The Crows said that back when there was only water and the only living things were four little ducks, Coyote told the bravest one to dive to the bottom and bring up some dirt. After it dried, Coyote cast it over the water to form land. In several tales he was swallowed by a monster (WISHPOOSH, for example), cut his way out, then sliced up the corpse to create different tribes. The Ashochimis of California said the tribes sprouted from bird feathers Coyote had planted. He caught the sun and arranged the seasons, according to the Nez Percés. The Shoshones said that Coyote stole fire from the Crane people by dancing so near it that his head-dress caught on fire. In a Flathead tale, he outwitted a huge ram by asking it to prove its power before attacking him by butting a tree. The ram got stuck, its horns embedded in the tree. Just before meeting the ram, Coyote broke Meadow Lark's leg by accident. He promptly used his powers to heal it but to this day, she still limps.

CRAB, the only dog who actually appears in a play by Shakespeare, belongs to Proteus' servant, Launce, in *The Two Gentlemen of Verona* (1595). In act 2, scene 3, Launce enters with Crab, calling him "the sourest-natured dog that lives." The news that he was going to the court of the Duke of Milan, says Launce, left his mother weeping, father wailing, sister crying, "our maid howling, our cat wringing her hands, . . . yet did not this cruel-hearted cur shed one tear." Throughout the tirade, the dog just sits there.

In act 4, scene 4, Crab is led onstage in disgrace. Delivered to Mistress Sylvia as a gift from Proteus, the dog had stolen her capon's leg and then misbehaved under the table. To spare Crab a whipping, Launce had taken the blame for the smell, just as he had previously sat in the stocks for pudding the dog stole, and stood on the pillory for geese that were killed. Launce then reminds the dog, "Did I not bid thee still mark me and do as I do? When didst thou see me heave up my leg and make water against a gentlewoman's farthingale, Didst thou ever see me do such a trick?" Again, Crab just sits there and, according to one critic, "invariably runs away with the play."

THE CRETAN BULL, in Greek mythology, was running wild on Crete, and the seventh labor of Heracles (or Hercules) was to bring it to King Eurystheus. Heracles went to Crete, caught the bull singlehanded, and took it back to Greece in a boat; in one tale, he swam it back. The king was so frightened by the bull that he dedicated it to Hera, the goddess of the city of Argos, and set it free. Unimpressed by the dedication, Hera drove the bull out of town. It wandered to Marathon, where it went on another rampage until Theseus caught it and killed it in sacrifice to Apollo.

In some stories, the bull had been given to Minos, the king of Crete, by Poseidon. When Minos failed to sacrifice it to him, the enraged god made the king's wife, Queen Pasiphae, fall madly in love with the bull, who sired her half-human, half-bull monster, the Minotaur.

CRYSTEL, a female capuchin monkey, was selected by Dr. Mary Joan Willard, a psychologist at Tufts-New England Medical Center in Boston, to assist William Powell, a quadriplegic, in his home. The idea of using a monkey, with its grasping ability, to help a paralyzed patient had occurred to Willard when she was a research assistant to B. F. Skinner, the pioneering behavioral theorist. She chose capuchins—organ grinders' monkeys—for their size, alertness, and longevity. After a year of training by both Willard and Powell, Crystel was turned over to Powell in the fall of 1978. Within six months, she was feeding him, however sloppily, responding to signals he made with a flashlight pointer, turning lights off and on, placing phonograph records on the turntable, fetching small articles, and putting them away. "Crystel has her own personality," said Powell, "and she won't take any guff."

CURIOUS GEORGE, a little African monkey, was so inquisitive about an explorer's hat that he was captured and taken to a big city in *Curious George* (1941), the first of seven books about him written and illustrated by H. A. Rey in collaboration with his wife, Margret. The confusions resulting from George's curiosity—after watching a man dial a telephone, for example, George does it and gets the fire department—have made the books internationally popular. They have been translated into a dozen languages. Curious George is known in Denmark as Peter Pedal, in France as Fifi, and in Great Britain as Zozo—the first book appeared during the reign of King George VI and the original name might have been disrespectful.

CURTAL, in Shakespeare's *All's Well That Ends Well* (ca. 1602), is a horse owned by the elderly Lord Lafeu. In act 2, scene 3, when the king of France lines up four or five young bachelor lords for Helena to choose from, old Lafeu declares:

> I'd give bay Curtal and his furniture,
> My mouth no more were broken than
>   these boys',
> And writ as little beard.

(He would give his horse and harness to have the good teeth and slight beard of the boys.)

THE CUSTER WOLF is reputed to have destroyed $25,000 worth of livestock in a six-year rampage through ten counties around Custer, South Dakota, starting in 1915. When the land was strewn with strychnine-filled bait during a rabies epidemic in 1916, thousands of wild animals perished but the outlaw wolf, whose tracks were found all around the bait, kept killing. Roger Caras reported in *The Custer Wolf* (1966) that the renegade would slaughter thirty sheep in one night, ten steers in another, and that his habit of killing a cow to get its unborn calf made him "one of the most hated animals this land has ever known." Scores of bounty hunters failed to get him; in one two-month period, his trail covered 600 miles. H. P. Williams, the professional hunter who succeeded, joined the search in March 1920. When Williams put the scent of a female wolf on his boots, the Custer Wolf began tracking the hunter, even tunneling 50 feet underground to prepare a den for his phantom mate. But the elusive predator was finally trapped in October, lured by the scent of another outlaw, THE SPLIT ROCK WOLF. As Williams approached, the Custer Wolf jerked the trap free and ran 3 miles with it clamped to his leg before he was shot. People were surprised at what a small wolf he was.

CUT, in Shakespeare's *Henry IV, Part One* (1597), is the horse that the first Carrier wants the ostler at the Rochester inn to take care of, in act 2, scene 1: "I prithee, Tom, beat Cut's saddle, put a few flocks in the point, poor jade is wrung in the withers, out of all cess."

CUWART, the hare in the twelfth-century beast epic *Reynard the Fox*, was flattered into accompanying REYNARD on his proposed pilgrimage to Rome. At the first stop, Reynard's house, the hare was invited in to help the fox say farewell to his wife and children. The family ate him.

CYLLAROS and HARPAGOS, in Greek mythology, were the magnificent horses of Castor and Polydeuces (better known by his Latin name, Pollux). These two sons of Leda were such devoted brothers that when Castor, the mortal son of the king of Sparta, was killed, Pollux, whose father was Zeus, was inconsolable. Zeus answered his prayers by reuniting the brothers to share their lives—one day in the underworld, the next in Olympus, always together. Finally, they were placed among the stars as the Gemini, or Twins. In some tales, they occasionally returned to earth on their snow-white steeds to join battles.

THE CYPRIAN CAT, a large gray and black tabby, plagued the ailurophobic narrator of Dorothy L. Sayers' short story "The Cyprian Cat" (1940). While visiting a friend and his wife at an inn, the narra-

CUWART
Cuwart and Bellin the ram prepare to accompany Reynard on his pilgrimage

tor observed as many as fifteen cats in the garden every night, sitting in a circle, while the Cyprian cat danced around them, "in and out like a weaver's shuttle." Afterward she would climb the wisteria to his closed window. One oppressively hot night, the narrator opened the window during a thunderstorm and, as fifty cats howled below, the great Cyprian suddenly appeared at his shoulder, glaring. He struck her. At the same time, his wife's friend became ill. When the cat invaded his room the next night, the narrator shot at her. She vanished and as he stood in his doorway with the gun, his friend's wife fell dead at her door.

DAISY (1), the Bumstead family dog in the comic strip *Blondie,* was created by Murat ("Chic") Young and first appeared on September 15, 1930. Blondie, a feather-brained flapper, married Dagwood Bumstead on February 17, 1933, and they lived frantically ever after, with a son, a daughter, and Daisy, who produced five puppies.

DAISY (2), the Scottish terrier whose obituary by E. B. White appeared in *The New Yorker* and in *Quo Vadimus?* (1932), was run over by a taxi in December 1931 while she was "smelling the front of a florists' shop. . . . The cab skidded up over the curb," White wrote, "just the sort of excitement that would have amused her, had she been at a safe distance." Born in 1928, Daisy was the smallest of a litter of seven, "and the oddest. . . . She was subject to moods, and her feeling about horses laid her sanity open to question." Her "curious habit of holding people by the ankle without actually biting them" was beyond explaining to the owner of the ankle but White decided that Daisy

"suffered from a chronic perplexity, and it relieved her to take hold of something."

DAISY (3), in *Raising Daisy Rothschild* (1977) by Betty and Jock Leslie-Melville, was a giraffe. Because there were only one hundred eighty Rothschild giraffes left in Kenya, with little chance of survival where they were, the authors adopted Daisy when she was 2 months old. Eight feet tall and weighing 450 pounds, the baby was lassoed cowboy style, then transported 225 miles to a corral on their property near Nairobi Game Park. An appealing creature with 2-inch eyelashes who gave big, slobbery kisses, Daisy thrived on milk and carrots. At the end of four months, she was 9 feet tall and weighed 700 pounds. Betty and Jock decided to turn her loose by knocking down a section of her corral. "When the opening was ready we stood back with our cameras and sang 'Born Free.' Daisy just stood there." Cheered on, she emerged to traipse around the garden, eating every flower in sight, then tried to follow Betty and Jock into the house for lunch. To move more of the endangered Rothschilds to safety, the Leslie-Melvilles started raising money, with some success, and acquired their own second giraffe, a young male named Marlon. Daisy greeted him with a swift kick.

DALI, a 12-year-old African elephant at the Edinburgh Zoo in Scotland, had refused to leave her indoor pen for almost four years and had become sickly for want of fresh air and exercise when the public was invited in January 1980 to suggest how to get her out. She had apparently been frightened by something—and "an elephant never forgets." Thousands of letters arrived, proposing such measures as hypnosis, building a fire under her, and combining the powers of drugs and a tractor. The problem solved itself, however, after Sally, an old Indian elephant in the next pen, died in late February. On March 3, Dali emerged, backwards. She continued going in and backing out for several weeks but began to put on weight and in September, a zoo official reported: "Dali now takes a bath, begs from the public, and behaves as though nothing had been wrong."

DAN, an English bulldog, belonged to George Robertson Sinclair, the organist of Hereford Cathedral and a friend of Sir Edward Elgar. In 1899, Elgar dedicated his *Variations on an Original Theme for Orchestra, Opus 36*—known as the "Enigma" Variations—to "friends pictured within," but later declared that Variation XI (G.R.S.) had "nothing to do with organs or cathedrals, or . . . G.R.S." Instead, it represents his friend's "great bulldog Dan (a well-known character) falling down the steep bank of the river Wye, . . . his paddling up stream to find a landing place, . . . and his rejoicing bark on landing. . . . G.R.S. said, 'Set that to music.' I did; here it is."

DANDY, a shaggy old dog, made W. H. Hudson believe the story of LUDLAM'S DOG, who was so lazy that he had to lean against a wall to bark. In *A Traveller in Little Things* (1921), Hudson declared that Dandy, an incessant barker, was lazier. The dog would sit at the garden gate, barking to be let out or in, but if no one came, "would deliberately open the gate himself, which he could do perfectly well."

DANNY MEADOW MOUSE, in the Thornton Burgess nature books, usually stayed out of sight, scampering along his private trails under the grass. In *The Adventures of Grandfather Frog* (1915), the mouse bravely accompanied GRANDFATHER FROG on an open path because the frog could not hop in the deep grass. The nonchalant frog thought Danny was timid, but Danny knew that "the only way to feel safe was to feel afraid." Suddenly, he dived into the grass and called to Grandfather Frog to do the same. The frog saw no reason to. A moment later, Farmer Brown's boy grabbed him.

DAN PATCH, a big, easygoing brown stallion, set a world record in 1905 that lasted for thirty-three years when he paced the mile in 1:55¼. Foaled in Indiana in 1896, he ran and won his first race when he was 4 years old. In 1901 and 1902, he toured the harness-racing Grand Circuit, lost only two of the fifty-six heats he ran, and won every race. M. W. Savage, a

Minneapolis feed merchant, bought the horse in 1902 for a record $60,000 and took him on an exhibition tour. In 1904 alone, Dan Patch traveled 10,000 miles and was seen by 600,000 people. He also became a household word. All kinds of products were named for him—cigars, chewing tobacco, toys, sleds, pillows, ladies' scarfs. People danced the Dan Patch Two Step and there was even a Dan Patch washing machine. When the horse was retired in 1909, he was undefeated, held nine world records, and had earned $3 million for his owner. Dan Patch died on July 11, 1916, and the nation mourned. Mr. Savage died the next day.

THE DARLEY ARABIAN, foaled in 1700, was a bay stallion that Thomas Darley, Queen Anne's consul in Aleppo, bought from Sheik Mizra III for 300 gold sovereigns in 1704, then had to smuggle out when the sheik decided that he wanted to keep the horse. Shipped to Darley's brother, a breeder in Yorkshire, the Darley Arabian became one of the three Eastern-bred stallions (see THE BYERLY TURK and THE GODOLPHIN ARABIAN) that founded a new breed of racehorse, the Thoroughbred. Through his great-great-grandson ECLIPSE, 90 percent of the Thoroughbreds racing today are male-line descendants of the Darley Arabian.

D'ARTAGNAN'S HORSE, a parting gift from M. d'Artagnan the elder, in *Les Trois Mousquetaires* (1844) by Alexandre Dumas, was a 13-year-old yellow Bearn pony with a hairless tail and a manner of traveling with his head lower than his knees. On his way to Paris to join the musketeers, young D'Artagnan stopped at an inn where a stranger burst out laughing at the horse, remarking, "This color is well known in botany, but up to the present very rare among horses." The incensed youth drew his sword, and was knocked unconscious. When he recovered, the innkeeper charged him two crowns because "the yellow nag . . . had eaten three times more than his size justified." But as soon as D'Artagnan reached Paris, he sold his steed for three crowns, "in consequence of the originality of his color."

DASH (1), a big, unruly dog, first belonged to the English poet Thomas Hood; Hood then handed him on to Charles Lamb. During Lamb's evening strolls, the dog's habit of tearing off in different directions or simply disappearing in the bush led Lamb and his sister Mary to ask P. D. Patmore, a friend in Fulham, to accept the dog—"if only out of charity," pleaded Mary, "for if we keep him much longer, he'll be the death of Charles." A few weeks later, in September 1827, Lamb wrote to Patmore:

> Excuse my anxiety, but how is Dash? . . . Goes he muzzled or *aperto ore*? . . . All the dogs here are going mad. . . . Does his tail wag horizontally or perpendicularly? . . . Has he bit any of the children yet? If he has, have them shot, and keep *him* for curiosity, to see if it was the hydrophobia. . . . If the slightest suspicion arises in your breast that all is not right with him, muzzle him and lead him in a string . . . to Mr. Hood's, his quondam master, and he'll take him in at any time.

DASH (2), a King Charles spaniel who was given to the Duchess of Kent in 1833, was soon adopted by her 13-year-old daughter,

Princess Victoria, who took to dressing him up in blue trousers and a scarlet jacket. On the death of King William IV in 1837, the princess became Queen Victoria and moved to Buckingham Palace where, she noted in her journal, "dear *Dashy*" loved the garden. After her coronation, a five-hour ceremony at Westminster Abbey on June 28, 1838, the young queen rode in state back to Buckingham Palace, and gathering up her skirts, ran upstairs to give Dash a bath. The dog died in 1840 and was buried at Windsor Park under a marble effigy with an inscription that concluded:

READER
If you would be beloved and regretted
Profit by the example of
DASH

DAVID GRAYBEARD, a chimpanzee in the Gombe Stream Chimpanzee Reserve in Tanzania, was the first to accept the presence of Jane van Lawick-Goodall when she began her ten-year study of wild chimpanzees in 1960. As she reported in her book *In the Shadow of Man* (1971), his lack of fear allowed her to observe him eating meat and using, even making, tools —two important discoveries. David would poke a grass stem into the hole of a termite mound, then withdraw the stem to eat the termites clinging to it. Or he would use a twig after stripping off its leaves. The "calm and gentle" chimpanzee was also the first to visit her camp, to take a banana from her hand, and to let her touch him. Van Lawick-Goodall acknowledged his contribution to her work in a personal way: when she married Hugo van Lawick, who had been sent to photograph her project in 1961, "a clay model of David Graybeard crowned the wedding cake."

DEACON MUSHRAT, the muskrat whose bombast was printed in Old English type in Walt Kelly's comic strip *Pogo*, was entrusted with 34 cents to pay off two kidnappers but decided to pocket the money because he could not abide dishonesty. At Christmastime in a 1952 strip, he lectured Pogo and Albert about peace: "If a man of good-will like me could get his hands on this new bomb—Ha! I'd show those who live by the sword—I'd drop that Bomb and I'd force Peace right down their blood-thirsty throats!"

DEBBIE, a timid little black cat in James Herriot's *All Things Wise and Wonderful* (1976), began making brief visits to Mrs. Ainsworth for a little food and, in the fall, would stop to gaze at the glowing coals in the fireplace before she ran off. After staying away for several weeks, Debbie staggered in on Christmas Day thinner than ever, caked with mud, and carrying a tiny black kitten in her mouth. She placed it on the hearth rug, then lay down beside it. She had been motionless for several hours when Herriot, a veterinarian, arrived. Even as he reported that Debbie was in a coma, she died. The kitten grew into a big boisterous cat named Buster, who forced Mrs. Ainsworth's three basset hounds to wrestle with him. On the following Christmas, Herriot watched Buster fetch a ball repeatedly for Mrs. Ainsworth and declared him "a feline retriever!"

THE DEMOCRATIC DONKEY, the creation of cartoonist Thomas Nast, first appeared as a jackass labeled "Copperhead Papers"—a symbol of the Democrats—in the January 15, 1870, issue of *Harper's Weekly*. In February 1872, a cartoon of

THE DEMOCRATIC DONKEY

Horace Greeley offering himself the combined Democratic and Republican presidential nominations showed a donkey in the background, kicking at being yoked with a Republican ox. In November, after Greeley lost, the bucking donkey threw him to the ground. Nast also used other animals to represent the Democrats—in 1874, a fox appeared with THE REPUBLICAN ELEPHANT and in 1875, THE TAMMANY TIGER was retitled "Democratic (Party) Tiger." But the donkey, shown with the elephant for the first time in 1879, remains the party symbol.

DEN-DEN, a 450-pound Yorkshire sow, was the model for *Pig*, a 5-by-7-foot oil by James Wyeth, who first exhibited the painting in 1971 at the newly opened Brandywine River Museum at Chadds Ford, Pennsylvania. Soon after she began posing, Den-Den ate seventeen tubes of paint and for the next week deposited colorful droppings around the Wyeth farm. At other times, she was so mean that she had to be soothed with music, but, said

Wyeth, "I became purely enamored of her. There were good vibrations." In the realistic, life-size portrait, the massive beige pig is shown in profile, standing in a pen and, in the opinion of some viewers, grinning.

DENMARK, the thoroughbred stallion sired by Imported Hedgeford, was foaled in Kentucky in 1839. In 1908, the American Saddle Horse Breeders' Association named Denmark sole foundation sire of the American Saddle Horse, a breed that existed before he did. Originally called the Kentucky Saddle Horse, it was developed from several strains, including Thoroughbred, Standardbred, and Morgan, for the riding needs of pioneer settlers. Denmark and his son Gaines Denmark 61, who passed on the easy saddle gaits of his dam, a Cockspur mare, were deemed the most important contributors to the breed.

DESIREE, a white Arabian mare, was sometimes Napoleon's mount instead of MARENGO, his white Arabian stallion. It has been said that Napoleon rode Desirée during at least part of the battle of Waterloo in 1815.

DIABLO, in "The Cisco Kid," a western series that began on radio in 1942 and appeared on television in the 1950s, was Cisco's horse. The original Cisco Kid in "The Caballero's Way" from *Heart of the West* (1907) by O. Henry (William Sydney Porter) was a Mexican bandit who rode around on his unnamed speckled roan, killing "for the love of it." But in a string of movies that preceded the radio show, the Kid became a romantic adventurer. At the end of each radio episode, Cisco's pal Pancho would make a terrible pun, then each man would call his horse and, whooping with laughter, gallop into the sunset.

DIAMOND, Sir Isaac Newton's dog, was as fictitious as the story about him that began to circulate more than fifty years after Newton died. The reason that Newton suffered a nervous breakdown at Trinity College in 1693, it was said, was that he returned from chapel one morning to find his irreplaceable scientific notes burned by a candle the dog had knocked over. In the story, Newton forbears striking the dog, saying only, "Oh, Diamond, Diamond, thou little knowest the mischief thou hast done!" There was no dog. There was a fire, ten years earlier, that did little damage. In 1693, Newton was not working on any important problem. His temporary illness was probably caused by exhaustion and the strain of seeking the post of Comptroller of the Mint.

DIANA OF WILDWOOD, a Shetland sheepdog, was sent from Michigan to President and Mrs. Calvin Coolidge after their white collie, ROB ROY, died in 1928. The dog was shipped by airplane and arrived so covered with grease that she was first described as black-and-white spotted. A good scrubbing revealed her to be mostly white with a few brown spots. Mrs. Coolidge renamed her Calamity Jane.

DICKIE, in Jean Giraudoux's play *La Folle de Chaillot* (1945), is the imaginary dog that Constance, the Madwoman of Passy, rebukes for barking while she and Gabrielle, the Madwoman of St. Sulpice, descend to the underground home of the Countess Aurelia, the Madwoman of Chaillot. When the ladies have settled down to their tea, Constance tells Dickie it is all right for him to jump up on "Aunt Aurelia's" lap. Though he is only the memory of a real dog, the Countess does not want him on her lap because she has a serious matter to discuss. Gabrielle offers her lap, the ladies bicker, Constance begins to weep. The penitent Countess summons her servant to walk the dog. "No. He doesn't want to go," says Constance. "Besides, I didn't bring him today. So there!"

DICK WHITTINGTON'S CAT was the only possession of poor, orphaned Dick, a scullery boy for Hugh Fitzwarren, a rich merchant in London. Before sending out his ship, the *Unicorn*, Fitzwarren invited his servants to invest in the cargo for a share of the profits because he believed it would bring them all luck. The boy offered the cat that he had bought for a penny to clear his room of rats and mice. Ship and cat landed on the Barbary coast, where the king's palace was also overrun with rats and mice. The cat got rid of them and the king paid a fortune for her, plus the cargo. Dick, meanwhile, tormented by the cook, ran away on All Hallow's Day. As he sat on a stone to rest at Halloway, the bells of Bow Church began to peal and seemed to say to him:

Turn again, Whittington,
Lord Mayor of London.

Back he went to his kitchen. When the *Unicorn* returned, Dick received his fortune, married Fitzwarren's daughter Alice, and became Lord Mayor of London.

There was, in fact, a Richard Whittington who was elected mayor three times. He was a textile merchant married to Alice, daughter of the wealthy Sir Ivo Fitzwaryn, but nothing is known of his boyhood or arrival in London. Whittington died in 1423 and is remembered chiefly for his charities. The earliest reference to the legend of Whittington's cat appeared in 1605 and the story survived in ballads and chap-books. Older and similar tales have been found in such disparate cultures as Buddhist, Scandinavian, Russian, and Persian. In the folklore of Brittany, there was a cat who made silver, and in Denmark, a dog who barked money.

DINAH, in *Alice's Adventures in Wonderland* (1865) by Lewis Carroll, was the cat that Alice began to miss as she fell down the rabbit-hole. "I hope they'll remember her saucer of milk at tea-time." Later, swimming in the Pool of Tears with the Mouse who had just cried, "Would *you* like cats, if you were me?" Alice couldn't stop talking about Dinah:

I think you'd take a fancy to cats if you could only see her . . . she is such a nice thing to nurse—and she's such a

DICK WHITTINGTON'S CAT

capital one for catching mice—oh, I beg your pardon!

Alice finally saw that the bristling Mouse was offended, and she promised not to say more. She did, though, again to the wrong audience. She told the Duck, the Dodo, the Lory, and the Eaglet what a great mouser Dinah was, "And oh, I wish you could see her after the birds! Why, she'll eat a little bird as soon as look at it!"

DINAH THE MULE, in Hal Roach's *Our Gang* comedies, often provided locomotion for the kids. In *Back Stage* (1922), she was strapped inside a bottomless bus and pulled it along as she tried to reach the open feed box in front of her. Instead of tooting a horn, the driver pulled a string attached to a feather duster that tickled Dinah, making her produce a loud "Hee-Haw." In *Free Wheeling* (1932), she had to push a contraption that the kids called a taxi, until one of them left a bottle of rubbing alcohol within her reach. Dinah downed it, went berserk, and broke loose.

DINNY, in *Alley Oop,* the comic strip created by Vincent T. Hamlin in 1933, was Alley Oop's pet dinosaur. Alley, a sturdy caveman in the Kingdom of Moo, would ride Dinny into battle against Moo's enemies and against Moo's incompetent king. When Professor Wonmug, the inventor of a time machine, entered the strip in 1939, Alley and Dinny turned up as startling anachronisms in several other centuries.

DIOGENES, in Charles Dickens' *Dombey and Son* (1848), was a gruff, disheveled dog, "continually acting on a wrong idea that there was an enemy in the neighborhood, whom it was meritorious to bark at." Mr. Toots took him to Florence Dombey after her brother Paul died, because the boy had asked that the dog be cared for. Diogenes was "far from good-tempered, and certainly not clever," but she loved him. Her father had never shown affection, and when Florence offered sympathy after his second wife left him, Dombey struck his daughter. She fled the house, to rush through the streets of London. Suddenly she saw a familiar shadow dart past, wheel around, and circle her with joyful barks. "Dear, true, faithful Di" had found her.

DIOMED, a grandson of HEROD, won the first English Derby at Epsom in 1780. Legend has it that a coin was flipped to decide if the race would be named for the twelfth Earl of Derby, or for Sir Charles Bunbury, who lost the toss—depriving America of a Kentucky Bunbury—but, as the owner of Diomed, won the race. The horse raced a few times more but never won again. At stud, he was a failure until an American bought him in 1798 and shipped him to Virginia where, at the age of 23, he became a prolific and prepotent sire, producing fifty-five sons, winners and influential stallions, in eight years. Diomed has been called the most important Thoroughbred ever sent to America, and his death in 1808 was regarded by Virginians as a national catastrophe.

DJALI, a little white goat with gilt horns, hoofs, and collar, belonged to Esmeralda, the gypsy street-dancer in *The Hunchback of Notre-Dame* (1831) by Victor Hugo. After the girl danced, the goat performed, tapping Esmeralda's tambourine to tell time and strutting on her hind legs to imitate the captain of the pistoleers. When Quasimodo, the hunchback, rescued Esmeralda, condemned to death for murder and witchcraft, "the nimble Djali" escaped with her to the sanctuary of the cathedral. The goat rubbed her shaggy head against the girl's knees until Esmeralda realized she was there and was comforted. Although the gypsy was recaptured and hanged, Gringoire, the poet, saved Djali.

DOBBIN, in Shakespeare's *The Merchant of Venice* (ca. 1596), is Old Gobbo's horse. In act 2, scene 2, Old Gobbo, who is nearly blind, arrives in Venice looking for his son Launcelot, a servant of Shylock, and asks directions, not knowing that he is talking to his son. After fooling a little, Launcelot kneels to ask his father's blessing, but with his back to the old man. "What a beard hast thou got!" exclaims Old Gobbo, peering at the back of Launcelot's head, "Thou hast got more hair on thy chin than Dobbin my fill-horse has on his tail."

THE DOG OF MONTARGIS: see HERCULES.

THE DORMOUSE, in *Alice's Adventures in Wonderland* (1865) by Lewis Carroll, dozed most of the time at the mad tea party, wedged between THE MARCH HARE and the Mad Hatter. When the latter sang "*Twinkle, twinkle, little bat!*" the Dormouse sang "*twinkle twinkles*" in his sleep until they pinched him to make him stop. They pinched him awake again when Alice could not think of a story to tell, but his tale became so confusing that the hare and the hatter tried to stuff him into the teapot.

At the trial of the Knave of Hearts,

Alice began to grow larger again, squeezing the Dormouse. "You've no right to grow *here*," he complained and crossed in a sulk to the other side of the court, where he met his doom for interrupting a witness. "Collar that Dormouse!" the Red Queen shrieked. "Behead that Dormouse! Turn that Dormouse out of court! Suppress him! Pinch him! Off with his whiskers!"

DOUGAL, "a huge tawny mastiff, with body and limbs almost as big as a lion's," belonged to the Earl of Dorincourt, Cedric Errol's grandfather, in *Little Lord Fauntleroy* (1886) by Frances Hodgson Burnett. The crusty old earl began to be disarmed by his 7-year-old American grandson when he saw "how quietly the brute sat under the touch of the childish hand . . . and deliberately laid its huge lion-like head on the boy's black velvet knee."

DUCHESS (1), the little black dog invited to tea by RIBBY, the cat, in *The Pie and the Patty Pan* (1905) by Beatrix Potter, tried and failed to avoid eating mouse pie.

DUCHESS (2), the elegant Parisian cat in Walt Disney Productions' animated feature, *The Aristocats* (1970), is abducted to the French countryside, where she meets a Dickensian assortment of animal characters and charms O'MALLEY, the alley cat, into helping her and her three kittens get home.

DUKE (1), the puppy given to Jean Jacques Rousseau in 1756, was "no beauty," said Rousseau in his *Confessions,* but "certainly deserved the name better than the majority of those who had assumed it." After the Duke of Montmorency befriended him and the "sensible and affectionate" dog became a favorite at the duke's château, Rousseau, "in a moment of foolish weakness," changed the dog's name to Turk. The Marquis de Villeroy then forced him to admit, in the presence of several dukes, that Turk was originally named Duke, and Rousseau complained that the Marquis "cruelly enjoyed the embarrassing position in which he had placed me." Rousseau, who had a gift for alienating people, mourned in a letter when the dog died, "My poor Turk was only a dog but he loved me. He was sensitive, disinterested. . . . How many so-called friends were not worth this one!"

DUKE (2), Penrod Schofield's "wistful, scraggly, little old dog," in *Penrod* (1914) by Booth Tarkington, had to be hoisted in a basket to Penrod's hideaway, a sawdust box in the stable. Ordered back in the basket to leave, Duke would just sit, facing a corner with his back to Penrod, until he was picked up. When Penrod, going on 12 and often in trouble, once tried to hide from his mother by locking himself in the stable's storage room, he was betrayed by his faithful dog, who had been trained to sit up and beg, then "speak" when he wanted something. Duke kept performing in front of the locked door, even after being hit by a paint can hurled over the door's transom.

DUMBO, a baby elephant delivered to the circus by a stork, was separated from his mother and rejected by the other elephants because he had such big ears, in *Dumbo*

(1941), the sixty-four-minute animated feature by Walt Disney Productions, based on the book by Helen Aberson and Harold Pearl. When the little elephant discovered he could fly by flapping those big ears, he became a star circus performer and a national celebrity.

THE DUN COW, in Walter Wangerin, Jr.'s *The Book of the Dun Cow* (1978), was God's messenger to the animals, entrusted with keeping Wyrm, the serpent who was evil incarnate, underground. When his creatures above ground murdered the sons of Chauntecleer the rooster, the animals' leader, the Dun Cow arrived to comfort Chauntecleer and to encourage him. The rooster led a successful battle against basilisks sent by the serpent and killed Cockatrice, Wyrm's surrogate, but the war was not over. After speaking softly to Mundo Cani Dog, the Dun Cow suddenly smashed her head against Chauntecleer's coop, breaking off one of her lethal-looking horns. The horn became the dog's weapon for the final fight when Wyrm burst through the earth's crust.

THE DUN COW OF DUNSMORE, "a monstrous wyld and cruell beast" in English legend, belonged to a giant who kept her on Mitchell Fold in Shropshire. The cow's supply of milk was inexhaustible but when an old woman filled her pail and then wanted to fill her sieve, the cow was so enraged that she broke loose. She wandered to Dunsmore heath and it was there that Guy of Warwick slew her.

ECLIPSE, a great-great-grandson of THE DARLEY ARABIAN, has been called the greatest thoroughbred racehorse of all time. Foaled in England on April 1, 1764, during a solar eclipse, the chestnut stallion with a white blaze and one white leg was 5 years old when he ran and won his first race, a 4-mile heat at Epsom Downs. Before the second heat, an Irish gambler named Dennis O'Kelly made a prediction that has become the most famous in racing history, "Eclipse first, the rest nowhere." That was literally true in nine of the horse's eighteen starts in his 17-month racing career, when no other horses were entered and Eclipse simply walked the course to collect the purse. He also won the other nine starts, eight by more than a furlong. At stud for nineteen years, Eclipse became one of the three principal thoroughbred progenitors (see HEROD and MATCHEM) through whom all of the Thoroughbreds now racing are descendants of the three Eastern-bred stallions who founded the breed. He is also the direct forebear of 90 percent of today's racehorses.

EDAL, the female otter described in Gavin Maxwell's *Ring of Bright Water* (1960), proved a "perfect successor" to MIJBIL, the first otter that Maxwell had kept as a pet at his cottage on the northwest coast of Scotland. Born in West Africa, Edal was 8 months old when she was given to Maxwell in 1959. Her skin was so much bigger than she was that it drooped in velvety folds. In the house, she would dribble a ball, batting it with her tail, or would play with a small object and then deposit it in a boot or shoe, whether occupied or not. Maxwell received several black beetles that way. At the beach, she would lie on her back to begin her water-splashing specialty, spinning "like a chicken on a spit that has gone mad." While willing to swim, Edal was at first reluctant to go in over her head, but within two months had lost her fear of depth and was staying underwater for as long as two minutes.

EEYORE, the Old Grey Donkey in A. A. Milne's *Winnie-the-Pooh* (1926), reacted with his usual gloom when he was told

EEYORE

that Christopher Robin was giving a party. "I suppose they will be sending me down the odd bits which got trodden on," said Eeyore. In *The House at Pooh Corner* (1928), Eeyore brightened up a little to remark that even though it was snowing and freezing, "We haven't had an earthquake lately."

EL-AHRAIRAH was the trickster rabbit hero of the lapine mythology in *Watership Down* (1972) by Richard Adams. During their perilous adventures, the rabbits led by HAZEL were comforted and inspired by the retelling of El-ahrairah's exploits.

ELMER was invented by The Borden Company in 1940 to be the "husband" of ELSIE the Cow, the star of its exhibit at the New York World's Fair. While Elsie was in California making a movie, a meek bull originally named Sybil's Dreaming Royalist was put on display at the Fair in Elsie's "Barn-Colonial" boudoir, which had been disarranged with such masculine props as copies of the *Police Gazette* and poker chips. The public loved him. The bull proved too stubborn for continued personal appearances but Elmer survived as a cartoon character in magazine advertisements showing Elsie and her family recommending Borden food products. In 1951, the company's Chemical Division produced a new white glue, and since Elsie was associated with food, Elmer was chosen to promote the glue, with a drawing of his head for its trademark. Ironically, when Borden resumed having a live Elsie, their great star, make public appearances in 1971 after a long absence, children asking who she was were simply told, "Elmer's wife."

ELSA, the lioness in *Born Free* (1960) and *Living Free* (1961) by Joy Adamson, was the smallest of three newborn cubs rescued in 1956 by the author's husband, George Adamson, a game warden in Kenya, after he had to shoot their mother in self-defense. Six months later, the larger cubs were sent to the Rotterdam-Blydorp Zoo, while Elsa was kept as a pet. "Neither force nor frustration was ever used" on the affectionate, fast-growing cat who liked to suck Joy's thumb, roll in elephant droppings—"an ideal bath powder"—and lie on top of the Land Rover.

When she was 27 months old, the Adamsons, determined to set her free, moved Elsa to a game reserve where they spent over a year training her to hunt and kill her own food. She mated, gave birth to three cubs in December 1959, and, after hiding them for six weeks, began bringing them along on her regular visits to the Adamsons' camp. "She always knew exactly how much . . . was fitting for her to give to each of her two worlds."

Born Free, its sequels, a motion picture, and a television series made Elsa worldfamous. Joy Adamson established the Elsa Wild Animal Appeal, an international conservation project, with the royalties. Elsa died of a parasitic infection in 1961.

ELSIE the Cow originated in 1936 as a cartoon character in The Borden Company's advertisements in medical journals. By 1939, radio commercials and general advertising had made her so well known that visitors to the Borden exhibit at the New York World's Fair (1939–40) kept asking which was Elsie among the hundred and fifty cows being used to demonstrate a new milking machine. A 7-year-old Jersey named You'll Do, Lobelia was chosen for the part and a star was born. The following summer, RKO borrowed the new Elsie to play Buttercup in their production of *Little Men*. Elsie was temporarily replaced at the Fair by her alleged husband, a bull renamed ELMER. She returned with her newborn calf, Beulah, and when the Fair ended, they went on tour.

The Borden cow became a national celebrity. Represented by a series of borrowed purebred Jerseys, Elsie was credited with raising $10 million at War Bond rallies during World War II, received keys to six hundred cities, became an honorary Indian chief, and was awarded such honorary degrees as Doctor of Bovinity. In 1947, she gave birth to a bull calf in Macy's department store in New York City. In 1950, her birthday was celebrated at New York's Roosevelt Hotel, where Guy Lombardo called her the sweetest cow this side of heaven. The tours tapered off in the 1960s, until a poll showed that Elsie was the most popular trademark in the country. Borden resurrected her in 1971, and by 1974, the fifteenth and sixteenth live Elsie had appeared at Disney World, the Kentucky Derby, the Indianapolis 500, and the Rose Bowl Parade.

The cartoon Elsie thrived in magazine advertisements through the 1950s. Her peak of popularity was reached in 1957, Borden's centennial year, when she gave birth to twins. The contest to name them drew a record three million entries. The graphic Elsie lives on in a 1951 trademark that is still used for Borden's dairy products. It shows her head in the center of a daisy.

EMILY, the chimpanzee in John Collier's *His Monkey Wife* (1931), could not speak but she learned to read and to understand spoken English at the school for Boboma bushmen. She also fell in love with the teacher, Mr. Fatigay, who took her back to England as a present for his fiancée, Amy. In London, Emily charmed the elderly habitués of the Reading Room at the British Museum and infuriated Amy, who treated her as a servant. Jealous and upset, the chimpanzee took Amy's bridal veil by force to stand at the altar and be married to Fatigay. Amy departed, Fatigay became a derelict, and the resourceful Emily not only earned a fortune as a dancer but also taught herself to type, which enabled her to verbalize her devotion when she rescued Fatigay. The pair retired to Boboma, where Fatigay gradually accepted the chimpanzee as his wife—"*my gracious silence* he sometimes laughingly called her."

EMPRESS OF BLANDINGS, Lord Emsworth's black Berkshire sow in P. G. Wodehouse's *Pig-hoo-o-o-o-ey!* (1927), stopped eating ten days before the Shropshire Agricultural Show in which she had been entered in the Fat Pigs class. Offered acorns, skim milk, and potato peels, she touched none of them. The problem was solved when Lord Emsworth told James

Belford that her fasting began after the pigman was sent to prison. She missed the pigman's call, explained Belford, who had become an expert on hog calls in America. One that he cited was made by a man in Nebraska tapping his wooden leg; unfortunately, his pigs broke their necks trying to climb a tree after hearing a woodpecker. But, Belford said, there was a universal call that "is to the pig world what the Masonic grip is to the human." Standing before the Empress of Blandings' pen, he bellowed, "Pig-hoo-o-o-o-ey!" and as the sound died down, a new "gulpy, gurgly" sound was heard. "The Empress was feeding." And she won the silver medal at the show.

ENOS, a male chimpanzee, was the first creature launched by the United States to orbit the earth. He went around twice, in fact, in 1961. He was trained to press a lever when a light flashed, to avoid mild electric shocks, and to be rewarded with banana pellets and water. A faulty circuit gave him some shocks along with the pellets, but he kept performing correctly. Photographs taken during the flight showed that he just bared his teeth and carried on. Back on earth, he even continued to relish banana pellets.

EPONA, a horse-goddess of the Celts of Gaul, may have originally been the deity of a spring or river, worshiped as a spirited steed. Later, as a goddess in human form, she was always shown with horses, usually riding sideways on a mare and often feeding a foal. Her popularity as the protectress of horses and mules spread to Rome, where the cavalry adopted the cult of Epona and displayed her portrait in their stables.

EPONINE, a well-mannered black cat named for a character in Victor Hugo's *Les Misérables,* belonged to Théophile Gautier (1811–72). She charmed his guests by greeting them, escorting them to the salon, and then purring around them until he came in. If Gautier dined alone, a place was set for her at the table. She was always in her chair when he entered the dining room, "her paws folded on the tablecloth, her smooth forehead held up to be kissed, like a well-bred little girl who is politely affectionate to relatives and older people." Occasionally, she tried to refuse the soup but Gautier had only to say, "Mademoiselle, a young lady who is not hungry for soup is not expected to have any appetite for fish," to make her lap it up.

ERIK, a gorilla, appeared in the movie *Murders in the Rue Morgue* (1932). In Edgar Allan Poe's story with the same title, an unnamed orangutan killed two women. In the film, which bore little resemblance to the story, Dr. Mirakle (played by Bela Lugosi) gave a belled bracelet to each lady who visited his salon to see Erik on display as a living example of Darwin's theory. At night the gorilla was turned loose to trace the tinkling bells and bring back victims to supply human blood for Mirakle's experiments.

ERSWIND, the gullible she-wolf in the twelfth-century beast epic *Reynard the Fox,* accompanied the fox to a lake one winter's day in the foolish belief that he would teach her to fish with her tail. She lowered it into the water, it froze fast, and REYNARD ravished her. He fled when her husband, ISEGRIM the wolf, arrived to break the ice so that Erswind could pull out her tail, or

ERSWIND
*Reynard flees while Isegrim rescues
Erswind, whose tail is stuck in the ice*

most of it. A chunk was left behind and her cries of pain brought the men of the village running with all sorts of weapons; the wolves ran for their lives. Another time, Erswind found Reynard in a well whose rope ran through a pulley and had a bucket at each end. The fox was at the bottom moaning because, he said, he had eaten so many fish. Erswind, liking fish, decided to join him and he told her to get into the bucket at the top. While she went down, Reynard went up, and away. Erswind sat there all day, cold and hungry.

THE ERYMANTHIAN BOAR, in Greek mythology, was ravaging the countryside around Mount Erymanthus and had to be captured alive, in one of the twelve labors required of Heracles (or Hercules) by King Eurystheus. Heracles chased the boar up the mountain into deep snow where he

could not run, then leaped on his back and chained his legs. He carried the boar down to show to Eurystheus, who was so frightened that he climbed into a large bronze vase and hid there until the beast was taken away.

ESME, the hyena in *The Chronicles of Clovis* (1911) by Saki (H. H. Munro), strayed from Lord Pabham's park, stared down a dozen baffled hounds, and cheerfully trotted off with two horsewomen who were heading for the Crowley Road. One of them, the Baroness, chose the animal's name. A gypsy child burst into tears at the sight of the trio and after the women rode past, they heard wailing. The lagging hyena caught up with them, then suddenly bounded ahead into some bushes where a wail "rose to a shriek and then stopped altogether." A few minutes later, Esmé turned up again looking pleased with himself, but just as they reached the road he was struck and killed by a car. The Baroness let the owner of the car believe that the "valuable animal" was hers by improvising, "He took second in the puppy class at Birmingham last year." She gave no details because, she told a friend later, the gypsies were "unobtrusive" about missing offspring. "I don't suppose they really know to a child or two how many they've got." For reparation from the car owner, the Baroness got "a charming little diamond brooch, with the name Esmé set in a sprig of rosemary."

ESMERALDA, a cat, was introduced in 1933 in *Cicero's Cat*, a new Sunday comic strip by Al Smith, ghost cartoonist for Bud Fisher's *Mutt and Jeff*. For about thirty years, the cat, who belonged to Mutt's son

Cicero, talked and often wore clothes in her slapstick adventures with local animals. In one episode, she persuaded a caged wildcat to hang his head in shame for eating a steak at a time when meat was rationed. When the poor boob finally dared to look around, the steak was gone and Esmeralda was lolling outside his cage, picking her teeth.

EXTERMINATOR, a scrawny chestnut gelding nicknamed "Old Bones," was an obscure 3-year-old when he was bought as a lead horse for Sun Briar, a favorite in the 1918 Kentucky Derby. When Sun Briar was scratched, Exterminator ran the race as the 30 to 1 long shot and won. He went on to become one of America's greatest Thoroughbreds and when the public cheered their beloved Old Bones, he bowed to them. The big gelding raced in Canada, Mexico, and the United States until 1924, when he went lame in his one hundredth race; he had won fifty of them. In retirement, Exterminator would not eat unless he had a Shetland pony for a stable mate, so a series of ponies named Peanuts kept him company until he died in 1945 at the age of 30.

FAGOTIN, the monkey in "The Lion's Court," one of the *Fables* of Jean de La Fontaine (1621–95), entertained the beasts who had been summoned to a banquet by their ruler, the lion. The year the fable was published, 1678, a celebrated performing monkey named Fagotin was drawing crowds to a marionette theater in Paris.

FALA, Franklin D. Roosevelt's Scottish terrier, was a puppy named Big Boy when a cousin gave him to the President in 1940. Roosevelt renamed him Murray the Outlaw of Fala Hill in honor, he said, of a remote Scottish ancestor. Fala slept in the President's bedroom and often traveled with him. When Roosevelt conferred with Winston Churchill aboard the U.S.S. *Augusta* near Newfoundland in 1941, Fala was there. When the President and his dog traveled from San Diego aboard the U.S.S. *Baltimore* in July 1944, Fala was almost bald by the third night out—sailors had been snipping locks of his hair for souvenirs. Some Republicans, critical of the voyage in an election year, later spread a rumor that Fala had been left behind while the ship was in the Aleutians and that a destroyer was sent from Seattle to pick him up. On September 23, the President responded in a speech to the Teamsters Union that was broadcast to the nation. He did not resent such attacks, said Roosevelt, but when Fala heard the story that a destroyer had been sent for him at a cost to the taxpayers of millions of dollars, "his Scotch soul was furious. He has not been the same dog since."

On April 5, 1945, Fala was at Warm Springs, Georgia, with the President when he collapsed. About two hours later, Roosevelt was pronounced dead. Fala jumped up, crashed through a screen door, and, barking loudly, ran up a nearby hill where he just stood, refusing to come down. He lived seven years more, cared for by Mrs. Roosevelt, who often said, "Fala was always my husband's dog. He merely accepted me."

FALINE, in *Bambi* (1928) by Felix Salten, was a pert and nimble fawn when she and her brother GOBO first romped with BAMBI. When they matured, Bambi found her beautiful and declared his love. Faline turned coy and skittish. As Bambi chased her happily, another buck challenged him. Bambi kept attacking until the buck fled. When a second one ran after Faline, Bambi fought him off. "That was wonderful," Faline said laughingly.

FANCHETTE, the cat in Colette's *Claudine à l'école* (1900) and *Claudine à Paris* (1901), stayed on the bed when Claudine was ill, playing with her feet under the blanket or sitting, "big as a donkey," on her chest. In Papa's library, "the most intelligent cat in the world" would nudge Claudine to pull out several fat volumes so that she could settle into the space they left. In heat, and preoccupied by a local Tom, the cat seemed, by her expression, to be telling Claudine, "Don't despise me too much, nature has her urgent demands. But I'll soon come home again and I'll lick myself for ages to purify myself of this dissolute life." After Claudine and her father moved to Paris, the maid arranged a mating for Fanchette because "the poor darling did want it so cruel." Three kittens were born, two were taken away immediately, and Fanchette, who could count to three, proved "a rather indifferent mother"—she rolled the remaining kitten over in case the other two were under him, then simply decided to "lick that one twice more. That was all."

FEATHERS was a kitten when Carl Van Vechten began writing *The Tiger in the House* (1920), a treatise on *Felis domestica* in folklore and the arts that is still regarded as a cat bible. Discussing feline behavior,

Van Vechten noted that Feathers had no respect for slumber, but woke him up at *her* breakfast time. She licked his cheek, nibbled his toes, then marched up and down his body. When he brought another kitten home, Feathers kept biting its tail and spitting at Van Vechten until the newcomer was evicted. She understood the words "dinner" and "meat," heading for the icebox when she heard either one. She was also a nocturnal pianist, waking Van Vechten at 2 A.M. to hear her "attempting prodigious scales." By the time he finished his book fourteen months later, Feathers was about to become a mother: "She is less active and she wishes more repose. . . . See, Feathers, I am nearly done. . . . You can come to me now and spend the hours of preparation in my lap."

FELIX THE CAT, one of the greatest characters in animated films, was introduced in *Feline Follies* (1919), produced for Paramount by Pat Sullivan, an Australian cartoonist who emigrated to the United States in 1914. His associate, Otto Messmer, designed and animated the cat whose name, "Felix" for felicity, was chosen for contrast to superstitions about black cats. Felix was a jaunty loner surviving in a hostile world. His distinctive walk, stooped over, paws clasped behind his back as he pondered his next move, inspired a popular song of the 1920s, "Felix Kept On Walking" (1923). His tail could serve as an oar, a telescope, a cane for his Charlie Chaplin imitation. When only his outline appeared, he used shoe polish to blacken in his body. Felix cartoons were even more popular in Europe than in the United States and several hundred were made before Sullivan died in 1933, including in 1930 the first animated film seen on television. *Felix the Cat*, a comic strip also drawn by Messmer, was launched in 1923. It, too, had ingenious graphics. In one strip, Felix played "hot tunes" on a saxophone, and the music notes poured into the cellar of an elderly couple to become their coal supply for the winter. In 1960, Felix was revived by Joe Orilo, who produced 260 episodes of "Felix the Cat" for television.

FENRIS (or FENRIR), the terrible wolf of Norse mythology, was one of the offspring of Loki and the giantess Angerboda. Raised at Asgard, the home of the gods, the wolf became so ferocious that only the war god Tyr dared feed him, and he grew so rapidly that the gods chained him, saying it was a game to test his strength. Fenris burst the chain. A second chain, twice as strong, was tried with the same result. A third one was sent for, from the land of the dwarfs. This chain, called Gleipnir, was as fine as silk. It was made from the sound of a cat's footsteps, the beard of a woman, the roots of a mountain, the sinews of a bear, the breath of fishes, and the spittle of birds; for this reason, cats now walk silently, women do not have beards, and so on. Fenris agreed to test the chain if one of the gods would put a hand in his mouth as a pledge of release if the chain could not be broken. Tyr inserted his hand. Fenris was bound. The more he strained, the tighter Gleipnir held. The enraged wolf bit off Tyr's hand. The gods anchored the chain to the earth, propped the wolf's jaws open with a sword, and left Fenris there to howl until the end of the world.

The twilight of the gods—Ragnarok, or Götterdämmerung—began with an eclipse when the wolves SKOLL and HATI (also known as MANIGARM) swallowed the sun and the moon. The stars fell out of the sky, the earth shook, and Fenris broke free to rush forth with jaws gaped wide. Odin advanced, leading the gods into their final battle. The wolf swallowed him whole. Odin's son Vidar avenged his father's death. With one foot on Fenris' lower jaw, he gripped the upper jaw, and with his boot, he tore out the wolf's throat. The earth was consumed with fire and all things perished. A new world, free of evil, rose out of the sea.

FENRIS ULF, the huge gray wolf who protected the wicked Snow Queen in *The Lion, the Witch and the Wardrobe* (1950), the first of the Chronicles of Narnia by C. S. Lewis, was sent to attack the children who had entered Narnia. When Peter, the oldest one, slashed at him with a sword, Fenris was so angry that he howled instead of going for the boy's throat. Peter's second lunge killed him.

FERDINAND, a Spanish bull, would rather sniff than fight, in Munro Leaf's *The Story of Ferdinand* (1936), illustrated by Robert Lawson. While the young bulls around him were butting their heads together, Ferdinand spent his days sitting in the shade of his favorite cork tree, smelling the flowers. When he was full-grown, men came to select the fiercest bull to fight in Madrid. The other bulls showed off. Ferdinand went to his cork tree and sat down, on a bee. His jumps and snorts and pawings of the ground made him the choice. Paraded into the bull-ring as Ferdinand the Fierce, "he saw the flowers in all the lovely ladies' hair and he just sat down quietly and smelled."

FIDDLEBACK, a decrepit pony, replaced the good horse that young Oliver Goldsmith (1728–74) with £30 in his pocket rode to Cork, intending to emigrate to America. After he sold the horse to pay for his passage, the voyage was delayed by unfavorable winds. The wind shifted while Goldsmith was on a jaunt in the country and the ship sailed without him. Forced to spend most of his last two guineas on a pony so swaybacked that he named him Fiddleback, the penniless young man made his way home to Ballymahon, 120 miles away. His desperately poor mother, a widow with younger sons to raise, refused to welcome him and Goldsmith brooded about it for the rest of his life.

FIDELE, in Nicolai Gogol's *Diary of a Madman* (1834), was a little dog that Poprishchin, the diarist, saw talking to MEDJI, the dog who belonged to a young lady he adored. Convinced that the dogs were corresponding, Poprishchin went to Fidèle's home, rummaged around her basket, and pulled out a bundle of papers while the dog barked and tried to bite his nose. She did bite him on the thigh but when she discovered he had the papers, she started whining and pawing him. Poprishchin fled, noting that the "stupid" child who had let him in "must have thought I was mad as she seemed scared out of her wits."

FIDO, a yellow mongrel, part hound, belonged to Abraham Lincoln's two younger sons, Willie and Tad, in Springfield, Illinois. When the President-elect and his family moved to Washington in February 1861, Fido was photographed, then left behind with John E. Roll's family, which included two boys old enough to take care of him. Two years later, Lincoln received a newsy letter from his barber in Springfield, a black man named William Florville, who requested, "Tell Taddy that his (and Willys) Dog is a live and Kicking doing well he stays mostly at John E. Roll with his Boys."

FIGARO, a kitten, was created for *Pinocchio* (1940), Walt Disney's animated film version of Carlo Collodi's book *Pinocchio* (1883). When the Blue Fairy finally transformed the puppet Pinocchio into a real boy, Figaro celebrated by diving into the fishbowl to kiss Cleo the goldfish.

FIGURE: see JUSTIN MORGAN.

FIRAPEEL, the leopard in the twelfth-century beast epic *Reynard the Fox*, held high rank in the court of his close relative, NOBLE the lion. When the king realized that REYNARD's duplicity had misled him into imprisoning his friends, BRUIN the bear and ISEGRIM the wolf, Firapeel found the way to make amends. He freed the bear and the wolf, and gave them the right to "hunt and do the worst you can to Reynard and all his lineage."

FIVER, in *Watership Down* (1972) by Richard Adams, was the clairvoyant little rabbit whose precognition that his warren would be destroyed frightened him so much that his brother HAZEL persuaded other yearling bucks to join them in flight. In their subsequent adventures, Fiver's premonitions saved his companions time and again.

FLETCHER RABBIT, who bustled about making himself understood with expressive and repeated use of his one-word vocabulary, "tui," was one of Burr Tilstrom's puppets on "Kukla, Fran, and Ollie," the long-lived television show that was first seen nationally in 1949.

FLICKA, a wild filly, was chosen by 10-year-old Ken McLaughlin from the yearlings on his father's Wyoming ranch despite the prospect of her being as loco—untamable—as her mother, in *My Friend Flicka* (1941) by Mary O'Hara. Resisting capture, Flicka (whose name in Swedish means "little girl") clawed her way out of a corral and crashed through a barn window but when she failed to clear a barbed wire fence, her injuries nearly killed her. With Ken's devoted care, she survived and learned to trust the boy enough to submit to a halter.

FLIPPER, the dolphin introduced in the movie *Flipper* (1963), produced by Ivan Tors, was played by Mitzi, a pet kept in the Florida Keys by Milton Santini, who captured dolphins for aquariums. Mitzi was the first dolphin to be trained to work in the water with people. Trainer Picou Browning easily taught her to fetch a ball, then threw his 9-year-old son in the water to be retrieved. The boy was soon riding on her back. Several more female dolphins performed in the second film, *Flipper's New Adventure* (1964) and in the television series "Flipper" (1964–67).

FLO, a female chimpanzee, was supreme in the hierarchy of female chimpanzees in the Gombe Stream Chimpanzee Reserve in Tanzania where, in 1960, Jane van Lawick-Goodall began her ten-year study of wild chimpanzees. In her book *In the Shadow of Man* (1971), van Lawick-Goodall reported that despite a bulbous nose and a ragged ear, scrawny old Flo had great sex appeal. When she came in heat, "one after the other, all the adult males" mated her, even while her 4-year-old daughter Fifi tried to push them off. Flo was a solicitous and sometimes playful mother not only to Fifi and to Flint, her new baby, but also to two older sons who often accompanied her, making the family "formidable indeed."

FLOPSY, one of PETER RABBIT(1)'s sisters in the Beatrix Potter books, married BENJAMIN BUNNY in *The Tale of the Flopsy Bunnies* (1909). "They had a large family and they were very improvident and cheerful." In *The Tale of Mr. Tod* (1912), the rabbit-babies were stolen after their grandfather, OLD MR. BOUNCER, invited TOMMY BROCK the badger into the rabbit hole. Flopsy was so angry that she wrung her ears, berated her father-in-law, took away his pipe, and did a complete spring cleaning "to relieve her feelings." As soon as Benjamin recovered the bunnies, all was forgiven.

FLORA TEMPLE, the first harness trotter to do the mile in less than 2:20, was a bobtail mare foaled in New York State in 1845. She was also a bay and some people thought that Stephen Foster referred to her in the last line of his song, "De Camptown Races" (1850): "I'll bet my money on the bob-tail nag. Somebody bet on the bay." Untrainable at first, Flora Temple was sold several times, once for a paltry $13, until she began showing speed when hitched to a wagon at the age of 4. Trained for harness trotting, the "little cricket," as she was called, started winning. The older she

FLORA TEMPLE

got the faster she went, and she lowered the world trotting record for one mile six times. At the age of 14, she made her final record, 2:19¾. When she was retired from racing in 1861, Flora Temple had appeared in 112 events and won 95 of them.

FLORIAN, the Lippizaner stallion in Felix Salten's novel *Florian* (1934), was foaled in 1901 and, at the age of four, was sent to the Spanish Court Riding School in Vienna for training in the *haute école*. He was an outstanding performer, but after a year at the Royal Stud he was transferred to the Imperial Palace, where he became Emperor Franz Joseph's favorite carriage horse, an "incomparable trotter, soft of mouth," who led a team of six on state occasions. The emperor died in 1916, his successor preferred automobiles, and Florian was sold to a cabman who mistreated him. The famous old Lippizaner was 20 years old and starving when the cabbie sold him, but his new owners, a kindly couple, let him live out his days in comfort.

FLOSSIE, a black and white Holstein cow, gave birth to a brown, 73-pound gaur, a wild ox native to India, on August 14, 1981, at the Bronx Zoo in the second known successful use of a domestic animal as a surrogate mother for a completely different wild species. (In 1977 at Utah State University, a mouflon, a wild Sardinian sheep, was born to a domestic sheep.) The procedure began in August 1980, when four Holstein cows and a female gaur were given injections to synchronize their reproductive cycles. Superovulation was then induced in the gaur (rhymes with power) and she was mated. Eight days later, on October 15, five embryos, invisible to the naked eye, were recovered by flushing and one was inserted into the uterus of each Holstein. Three of the cows became pregnant. Flossie alone, after a 308-day gestation, had a live birth. The male gaur baby was given an Indian name, Manhar, which means "one who wins everyone's heart." The procedure that produced him, interspecies embryo transplant, may eventually increase the chance for survival of a number of endangered species.

FLOSSY, the small black and white spaniel given to Anne Brontë in 1843, became as beloved a pet as Emily Brontë's mastiff, KEEPER. The dogs would sit quietly beside the sisters at their breakfast of Scotch oatmeal and milk, waiting for the share that was always handed down at the end of the meal. After five years, Anne reported, "Flossy is fatter than ever, but still active enough to relish a sheep-hunt." Anne died in May 1849, six months after Emily, and Charlotte Brontë was left with the dogs. "Keeper may visit Emily's little bed-room . . . and Flossy may look wistfully around for Anne, they will never see them again— nor shall I," she mourned. But when the fat little spaniel died at the age of 11, Charlotte concluded, "No dog ever had a happier life or an easier death."

FLOWER, a skunk, was created for *Bambi* (1942), Walt Disney's animated film version of the book by Felix Salten (1928). Although BAMBI the deer was presented fairly realistically, his friends and advisers about life in the forest, Flower and THUMPER the rabbit, were deliberately made cute and funny to brighten the story.

FLUSH, Elizabeth Barrett Browning's pet, was the cocker spaniel of belles-lettres. His owner wrote two poems about him and often mentioned him in her correspondence. Virginia Woolf's *Flush* (1933) is a biography of the dog from his point of view, and he was featured in Rudolf Besier's play *The Barretts of Wimpole Street*, first produced on Broadway in 1931 and subsequently made into a movie. The red cocker was given to Miss Browning around 1842 when she was a semi-invalid. He spent most of the next three years lying at her feet on the sofa in her bedroom, but during his occasional outings, he was stolen three times. Dognapping in London was profitable. It cost Miss Barrett a total of £20 to buy him back. When Robert Browning began to court her in 1845, Flush bit him twice. Nevertheless, the dog was taken along to Italy after their marriage. "He goes out every day and speaks Italian to the little dogs," wrote Mrs. Browning. Flush lived out his days in contentment, except when warm weather brought fleas. Mrs. Browning sympathized, "Savonarola's martyrdom here in Florence is scarcely worse than Flush's in the summer." The dog finally got so mangy that Browning "clipped him all over into the likeness of a lion."

FLYBALL, the enterprising cat introduced in Ruthven Todd's *Space Cat* (1952), wore an inflated suit with a tail like a "fat frankfurter" to accompany Captain Fred Stone on his pioneer flight to the moon. Finding a subterranean cave where weird plants exuded sticky stuff, Flyball used it to patch Fred's helmet and saved both their lives. In subsequent adventures, the two of them learned to communicate telepathically on Venus, and on Mars, the Space Cat realized that a metallic mouse was playing with him instead of the other way around. He also went swimming, reluctantly, in one of the canals with Moofa, the sole surviving Martian cat whose stripes went lengthwise. After their two kittens were born on the moon, the whole family donned space suits to fly off with Fred to explore a planet of Alpha Centauri.

FOP, a spaniel, belonged to a friend of William Cowper (1731–1800). Cowper's "Epitaph on Fop" concludes:

> Ye squirrels, rabbits, leverets, rejoice,
> Your haunts no longer echo to his
> voice. . . .
> He died worn out in vain pursuit of
> you.
> "Yes!" the indignant shade of Fop
> replies,
> "And worn with vain pursuit, man
> also dies."

FOSS, a fat, striped tomcat with a stub of a tail, was Edward Lear's beloved companion for seventeen years. Lear often included caricatures of Foss and himself in his letters, and in "The Heraldic Blazon of Foss the Cat," published in later editions of *Nonsense Songs, Stories, Botany and Alphabets,* he presented his owl-eyed cat gravely couchant, rampant, regardant, etc. When Foss died in 1887, he was buried in the garden of Villa Tennyson, Lear's home

FOSS

Fop, Passant

in San Remo, Italy; his tombstone inexplicably gives his age as 31.

FOZZIE BEAR has a pink nose, a little brown hat, and an earnest manner. In *The Muppet Movie* (1979), he drives to Hollywood with his friend, KERMIT the frog. In "The Muppet Show" on television, he tries self-improvement therapy, then announces proudly as he makes his entrance, "There! *I* opened the door; and *I* wanted to!"

FRANCIS, the talking mule, made his debut in *Francis* (1950), a movie based on Donald Stern's novel about an army private befriending a mule who talks. With actor Chill Wills supplying the mule's voice and Donald O'Connor as the private, the film was so popular that five sequels were made in as many years, showing Francis at the races, at West Point, covering "Big Town," joining the WACs, and in the navy. A sixth sequel, *Francis in the Haunted House* (1956), co-starred Mickey Rooney. The success of the films inspired a television series about a talking horse, MR. ED, and in 1951, Francis received the first Patsy (Picture Animal Top Star of the Year) Award, presented by the American Humane Association, which supervises the treatment of animals in movies and television.

FREDDY, an enterprising pig on Mr. Bean's farm, was the hero of a series of animal adventures—twenty-six books between 1927 and 1958—by Walter Brooks. In *Freddy Goes to the North Pole* (1930), originally titled *More To and Again,* the pig operated Barnyard Tours, Inc. for vacationing animals. But after JINX the cat taught him to read, he found his real vocation. Inspired by *The Adventures of Sher-*

lock Holmes, the pig began solving mysteries in *Freddy the Detective* (1932) with the help of a wardrobe of disguises and advice from Jinx.

FRIEND HARE, in Felix Salten's *Bambi* (1928), raised and flopped one spoonlike ear, then the other, and then both together while he inspected the fawn named BAMBI. The hare's nose twitched as though a sneeze was coming. Bambi laughed. So did the hare. Then he congratulated Bambi's mother and hopped away. "The good Hare," she said; "he is so suave and prudent. He doesn't have an easy time of it in this world." In the Disney animated film *Bambi* (1942), Friend Hare was replaced by THUMPER the rabbit.

FRITZ was William S. Hart's beloved pinto pony. Hart, a former Shakespearean actor, was the first big star of western movies, and the first to co-star with his horse. Two of his films, in fact—*Pinto Ben* and *The Narrow Trail*—were tributes to Fritz. Hart and Fritz performed together from 1915 to 1925 and did all their own stunts. In *Truthful Tolliver* (1916), Hart rode Fritz right through a plate glass window without a scratch on either of them. In *Tumbleweeds* (1925), they made a spectacular leap across an overturned wagon. Only once was Fritz replaced for part of a stunt. In a scene with Hart riding him along the edge of a cliff, Fritz was to be shot by the bad guy, fall, drop off the cliff, and then roll down a gorge. Fritz played the scene through the fall from the shot, then Hart mounted a dummy in Fritz's place for the rest of the tumble. The action was so convincing that Hart had to show the censors how it had been put together, to prove that Fritz had not been exposed to possible

FRITZ

injury or death. Fritz died at the age of 31 and was buried at Hart's Horseshoe Ranch in Newhall, California, which was opened to the public in 1958 as the William S. Hart Park.

FRITZ THE CAT, in comic strips that Robert Crumb drew for his own amusement as a teen-ager, was originally based on the family cat, Fred, but turned into an uninhibited tom who walked upright, often wore a shirt and tie, used four-letter words, and had a fantastic sex life. In 1965, several years after the strips were drawn, they began to appear in underground comic books and were a huge success with the underground "hippie" sub-culture of the 1960s. *Time* magazine called Crumb "a kind of American Hogarth, a moralist with a blown mind," who "gave back to cartooning the scatological vigor and erotic exuberance it had during the Regency, and then some." Ralph Bakshi made Fritz nationally famous with his animated film *Fritz the Cat* (1972), America's first X-rated cartoon. Crumb detested it so much that he drew a final strip, *Fritz the Cat "SUPERSTAR"* (1972), in which a rejected female ostrich killed "this silly and unambitious creation of my adolescence" with an icepick through the cat's skull.

FROU FROU, in *Anna Karenina* (1876) by Leo Tolstoy, was the thoroughbred English mare that Anna's lover, Count Vronsky, rode in his regiment's steeplechase. As the mare gained the lead on the approach to the next-to-last and most difficult barricade, Vronsky sensed uncertainty in her ears, raised his whip, then realized she knew what she was doing. Frou Frou accelerated, soared over the brush-covered mound, and, landing well beyond the ditch behind it, effortlessly resumed her pace. Aware that she was tiring, Vronsky began to work the reins as they neared the final water ditch. She cleared it like a bird but Vronsky, to his horror, knew that he had landed wrong in the saddle. Frou Frou fell. He tugged at the reins to get her up and then, in a rage, kicked her belly. She just looked at him with her speaking eyes. Her back was broken.

FROUDE'S CAT asked, "What is my duty?" in "The Cat's Pilgrimage" from James Anthony Froude's *Short Studies on Great Subjects* (1867–82). One animal replied, "Get your own dinner," but the Owl said, "Meditate, O Cat!" The Cat asked what to meditate about and the Owl suggested she consider which came first, the Owl or the egg.

FURY, the black stallion star of the television series "Fury," was an American Saddlebred foaled in Missouri and originally named Highland Dale. Trained by his owner, Ralph McCutcheon, he first appeared as BLACK BEAUTY in the 1946 movie version of Anna Sewell's book and went on to win acting awards from the American Humane Association for performances in *Gpysy Colt* (1955), *Giant* (1957), and *Wild is the Wind* (1958). His name would be changed to the name of the role he was playing, but he became permanently famous as Fury. The television series, about an orphan boy learning to be responsible for the horse, began in 1955, ran for over five years, and made Fury second only to LASSIE (2) as the highest money earner among Hollywood animals up to that time. Fury also changed owners during his career. In *The Gentle Jungle* (1980), Toni Ringo Helfer wrote that in the 1960s, she and her husband Ralph, owners of Africa USA, an animal park in southern California, were forced to buy a mistreated, starving black horse from a seedy cowboy to save its life. The horse recovered and a few months later was identified by an old Hollywood wrangler as Fury.

FUWCH GYFEILIORU, in Welsh lore, was a pure white, elfin cow who produced endless streams of milk and had the power to heal the sick, make fools wise, and make everyone in the world happy.

GABILAN, in John Steinbeck's "The Red Pony" (1933), was given to young Jody Tiflin by his father as a colt. Billy Buck, the ranch hand, taught the boy how to take care of his pony and, in the fall, to train it with the long halter. Jody's father set Thanksgiving as the day the boy could try to ride Gabilan but the pony took sick after being drenched in a downpour. Billy Buck's remedies were useless: Gabilan was dying. On the last night, a strong wind blew the barn door open. By morning, the pony was gone. Jody followed his trail on the dewy grass toward a ridge where he saw buzzards circling. From the top of the ridge, he found his pony lying in a clearing below, his legs barely moving. As the boy plunged down the hill, Gabilan died and the buzzards attacked. Jody rushed at them, grabbed the one who didn't fly off in time, and, in a terrible fight, killed it.

THE GADARENE SWINE, 2,000 of them, were feeding on a hillside above the Sea of Gallilee when a madman who called himself Legion because he was possessed by so many devils implored Jesus to cast them out. The evil spirits entered the swine, who then rushed down a steep bank into the sea and drowned. Since the story, in Mark 5:1–19 and Luke 8:26–39, begins with Jesus entering "the country of the Gadarenes" in the King James Bible but "the country of the Gerasenes" in subsequent translations, "the Gerasene swine" is another, less familiar name for the unfortunate herd.

GALATHE is Hector's horse in Shakespeare's *Troilus and Cressida* (1609):

> There is a thousand Hectors in the field;
> Now here he fights on Galathë his horse,
> And there lacks work.
>
> (act 5, scene 5)

GAMIN, a black poodle, was presented to Julia Atwater by a beau in Booth Tarkington's *Gentle Julia* (1922). Kitty Silver, the maid, was baffled by the way the "poogle dog" whom she called Gammire trotted on his hind legs or sat up with his forepaws over his nose as in prayer. "Is you a dog, or isn't you a dog?" she demanded. "Whut *is* you anyway?" When Julia's father came home, he threw a stone at the "idiot poodle" and missed. Gamin fetched it, then resumed his praying position as though to say, "There's your rock. Let's get on with the game." The dog was allowed to stay.

GARFIELD, the fat cat with drooping eyelids and a lust for lasagna, was created in 1977 by the cartoonist Jim Davis for the comic strip *Garfield.* In January 1982, the strip was appearing in more than 450 newspapers, and three paperbacks—*Garfield at Large* (1980), *Garfield Gains Weight* (1981), and *Garfield Bigger Than Life* (1981)—were all listed as national bestsellers. Although Garfield is lazy—a yawn is his idea of exercise—and refuses to diet, he is basically forceful, chasing dogs, biting the mailman, and getting his own way.

"Groveling is not one of my strong suits," he muses.

GARGANTUA, the gorilla star of Ringling Brothers and Barnum & Bailey Circus from 1938 until his death in 1949, was the most publicized animal since Barnum's JUMBO (1). Billed as "The World's Most Terrifying Creature!" Gargantua looked it. Acid thrown in his face when he was a baby had given him a permanent vicious scowl and a disposition to match. Copywriters were carried away: "With a smirk of cruel calculation and a sadistic scowl of challenge on his huge bestial face, Gargantua the Great now defies civilization from behind the heavy, chilled steel bars of the strongest cage ever built." Even his trainer was afraid of him. Gargantua often demonstrated his great strength. He would tear up a burlap bag as if it were tissue paper, or twist a truck tire into a figure eight. An estimated 40 million people went to see Gargantua, making him one of the greatest circus attractions of all time.

GARGANTUA

GARGANTUA'S MARE, in book 1:16 of *Gargantua and Pantagruel* (1535) by François Rabelais, was as big as six elephants. Her feet were cloven into toes, her coat was burnt sorrel with some dapple-gray spots, and she had a terrible tail, as tall as the tower of St. Mars near Langeais. Entering a great forest just past Orléans that was teeming with horseflies and hornets, the mare switched her tail so furiously that she not only demolished the stingers but also uprooted the trees. The spectacle delighted Gargantua, who gazed at the leveled wasteland and exclaimed, *"Je trouve beau ce."* The area has been called Beauce ever since.

GARMR (or GARM), in Norse mythology, was a dreadful, blood-spattered dog who was chained at the gate of hell to watch over the dead. He could be appeased with a special cake only by those who had given bread to the poor. One of the signs that Ragnarok, the twilight of the gods, had begun was his ferocious barking. As the world ended, Garmr burst free of his fetters to fight Tyr, the god of war. They killed each other.

GARRYOWEN, the citizen's "bloody mangy mongrel" in the *Cyclops* episode of James Joyce's *Ulysses* (1922), was known to have chewed the pants off a constable who came around about a license. While the men at Barney Kiernan's pub drank and talked, the dog nosed around for crumbs and growled occasionally. The "citizen" mauled him and talked to him in Irish. The "old towser" growled back, in Irish, "like a duet in the opera." Moreover, the "famous old Irish red wolfdog setter" cursed in verse. Barney got cursed for not providing water:

> The curse of my curses
> Seven days every day
> And seven dry Thursdays
> On you, Barney Kiernan.

Water was brought to the dog and "gob, you could hear him lapping it up a mile off." Joyce based the dog on a real one, a Garryowen who belonged to his Aunt Josephine Murray's father.

GEIST, a dachshund, was Matthew Arnold's pet for only four years. The poet recalled the dog's "winning ways" in "Geist's Grave" (1881):

> We see the flaps of thy large ears
> Quick raised to ask which way we go.

In "Poor Matthias" (1882), an elegy to his canary, Arnold mourned Geist again:

> All that gay courageous cheer,
> All that human pathos dear.

GELERT, a wolfhound, belonged to the Welsh Prince Llewelyn in a thirteenth-century legend retold in "Beth-Gelert," a ballad by William Robert Spencer (1769–1834). The prince returned from hunting one day because his "peerless hound" had not appeared. Bounding out of the castle to greet him came Gelert, covered with gore, blood dripping from his fangs. Llewelyn rushed inside to find his infant son's bed overturned and the room spattered with blood. There was no sign of the child nor answer to the father's call. Convinced that the dog had devoured the baby, the prince plunged his sword into Gelert's side. The hound's dying cry woke the child, lying unharmed under a heap of bedclothes. Beneath the bed was the torn body of an enormous wolf:

Ah, what was then Llewelyn's pain!
For now the truth was clear;
His gallant hound the wolf had slain.
To save Llewelyn's heir.

To this day, thousands of tourists each year visit a spot near Snowdon in North Wales where a stone marks Gelert's grave.

THE GENERAL, John Tyler's favorite horse, was buried at Sherwood, Charles City County, Virginia, with the inscription:

Here lies the body of my good horse, The General. For years he bore me around the circuit of my practice and all that time he never made a blunder. Would that his master could say the same—John Tyler.

Tyler was President of the United States from 1841 to 1845.

GENERAL WOUNDWORT, in *Watership Down* (1972) by Richard Adams, was the vicious, power-hungry rabbit, almost as big as a hare, who organized the Efrafa warren into a police state. When several does escaped to Watership Down, he refused HAZEL's offer of a peaceful settlement because he wanted to fight. He lost.

GENEVIEVE was a dog who "kept its head" and fished Madeline out of the Seine in *Madeline's Rescue* (1953) by Ludwig Bemelmans. Madeline and her eleven schoolmates kept the dog until she was evicted by the trustees. After the girls searched Paris in vain for Genevieve, she came back on her own to produce a litter, "enough hound to go all around."

GEORGE, a Masai bull from Kenya, was the tallest giraffe ever held in captivity. He arrived at Chester Zoological Gardens in England when he was about 18 months old. When he was 7 years old and fully grown, his head almost touched the 20-foot-high ceiling of the zoo's Giraffe House. George got a charge, literally, out of licking the telephone lines running past his enclosure. The wires were salty and he enjoyed the tingle he got from the 50 volts they carried. For six months, zoo personnel were puzzled by crossed calls and phones ringing for no reason. After they located the problem and solved it by raising the lines 3 feet, George appeared to be very much annoyed. He died in 1969 at the age of 12.

GEORGE and MARTHA, in a series of books by James Marshall, starting with *George and Martha* (1972), were an inseparable pair of hippopotamuses. George broke off his right front tooth when he was rollerskating and replaced it with a gold one. He boasted of his courage but came out of a scary movie "white as a sheet," asking Martha to hold his hand so that she would not be afraid walking home. Martha wore a flower behind her left ear, had a flair for tightrope walking, and liked to make split pea soup more than George liked to eat it. To spare her feelings, he poured it into his shoes. Martha was happy to switch to chocolate chip cookies; she did not like split pea soup either.

GEORGE TIREBITER, an irritable mongrel who resembled an unkempt Airedale, began scrounging food and chasing cars on the campus of the University of Southern California in 1940 and became the mascot of its football team, the Trojans. He received national publicity in 1947 when he was stolen before the UCLA–USC game and then recovered, shaved so that the remaining fur on his back formed the letters U-C-L-A. The Trojans' victory at that game sent USC to the Rose Bowl, where George wore a sweater to conceal his defacement. After his death in 1950, two more Tirebiter mascots served briefly, but since 1961, USC has been represented by a white horse named TRAVELER.

GERI and FREKI, two wolves, always attended Odin, the supreme deity of Norse mythology. When he gave banquets to the gods and heroes in Valhalla, Odin took only wine—it was both food and drink for him. He gave the meat that was served to him to the two wolves crouching at his feet. Their names mean "the ravenous one" and "the greedy one."

GERTIE, the first animal to star in an animated cartoon, was a dinosaur created by Winsor McCay for his Sunday comic strip, *Little Nemo in Slumberland*. Intrigued by flip-books that his son had acquired, McCay began animating a Little Nemo film in 1908, produced a second one four years later, and, in 1914, toured vaudeville with his third animated cartoon, *Gertie, the Trained Dinosaur*. McCay would stand on the stage, talking to Gertie on the silent screen, and she would react—laughing, eating, dancing the tango. She would turn mischievous, he would scold her, and she would start to cry. The effect was sensational. McCay had brought the creature to life.

GERTRUDE, a sturdy, bespectacled kangaroo reading a book, with another one in

GERTIE

her pouch, first appeared in June 1939 as the trademark for Pocket Books, the first mass market paperback publisher in the United States. During the next thirty-eight years, she appeared on over a billion books, was registered as a trademark in thirty-seven countries, and was redesigned five times. She lost weight and her reading glasses were eliminated lest the public think the small books had small print that required them. In her latest design, by Milton Glaser in 1977, she is hopping. The original Gertrude was designed and named by Frank J. Lieberman, who received $25 for the marsupial colophon. Why Gertrude? "For some unknown reason," Lieberman recalled, years later, "I named it after my mother-in-law."

GEUSH URVAN, in Persian mythology, was the soul of the primal bull, or cow in some legends, that was sacrificed for the re-creation of the world. In the Zoroastrian version, the bull was created before the first man in order to give him food (see Audhumla), then the god of evil killed them both for resisting him. Plants grew out of the blood of the bull, and its seed, carried to the moon, returned as animals. Others believed that the bull was slain by the god Mithra, who plunged his hunting knife into its side. Twelve different plants and 55 types of grain sprang from its limbs, 282 pairs of animals, led by a pair of oxen, emerged from its seed, and the soul of the bull rose to heaven to watch over them.

GINGER (1), a yellow tomcat, and Pickles the terrier had a little shop in Beatrix Potter's *Ginger & Pickles* (1909). When mice came in, Ginger asked Pickles to wait on them because they made the cat's mouth water. The partners gave unlimited credit and soon went out of business. Ginger was last seen living in the warren, where "he looks stout and comfortable."

GINGER (2), the silky-voiced "slyboots" of a cat in *The Last Battle* (1956) by C. S. Lewis, conspired with Calormene invaders to take over Narnia for their own profit by manipulating Shift the ape. Shift had convinced the Narnian beasts that he spoke for Aslan the Great Lion. The cat was punished, lost its power of speech, and disappeared.

GIP, a large tabby with opaline eyes, was an edgy kitten when W. H. Hudson got him. "I never really looked at this animal without finding these panther . . . eyes fixed with a fierce intensity on me," Hudson recalled in *A Shepherd's Life* (1910). "The native wildness and suspicion in him could never be wholly overcome." After he injured a foreleg while hunting, the cat purred occasionally when the leg was rubbed with warm, melted butter but at the slightest movement or sound, he would dart to the door. If it was closed, "he would sit down, recover his domesticity, and return to my feet." In the agricultural village where they lived, Gip killed more than three hundred rats a year. This made him, big and heavy as he was, "worth much more" than his weight in gold, declared Hudson, because "the value of the grain and other foodstuffs he saves from destruction in a single year" was even greater.

GIPSY, a "needlessly tall" cat who was "half broncho and half Malay pirate," had an uproarious fight with Penrod's dog, Duke (2), in *Penrod and Sam* (1916) by Booth Tarkington. Startled awake by the sight of the cat with a whole fishbone in his mouth, Duke shrieked. Gipsy laid back his ears, shrank into himself "like a concertina," arched his back, and gave Duke "three lightning little pats, . . . these were no love-taps," on the ear. Duke howled and Gipsy chimed in with "a vocabulary for cat-swearing certainly second to none out of Italy."

GISSING, the hero of *Where the Blue Begins* (1922) by Christopher Morley, was a dog who talked, walked on his hind legs, and had a dog named Fuji for a butler. To explore life, Gissing left his adopted puppies, managed a department store, served in the church, and went to sea. He pondered the task of raising a family, "No one who is not a parent realizes, for example, the extraordinary amount of buttoning and unbuttoning necessary in rearing children," and he met God, who is also a dog. Newly reverent, Gissing went home to his family responsibilities.

GLADLY, a TEDDY BEAR so worn from love that one shoe button eye hung by a thread, was named for a line in a hymn, his young owner said. "The one where we sing 'Gladly the cross I'd bear.' "

GOANNA, the lizard god of the Yungnara tribe in the Kimberley region of western Australia, dwells beneath Pea Hill—where the Amax Petroleum Australia Company started drilling for oil on August 29, 1980. On the day after the drilling began, three tribesmen and a spokesman for the Aboriginal Legal Service arrived in Geneva to ask the United Nations Human Rights Commission to condemn the activity at their sacred site. The aborigines believe that if Goanna is disturbed he will command the 6-foot monitor lizards—an important food source for the Yungnaras—not to mate.

GOBO, in *Bambi* (1928) by Felix Salten, was the sickly deer who collapsed in the snow and was taken away by a hunter. In the summer, Gobo returned to the forest, fat and sleek, insisting that he had been well-treated, that there was nothing to fear from people, that they were good and kind. One morning, oblivious to the warning cries of the birds and the instincts of the other deer, Gobo stood confidently in a meadow. He was shot.

THE GODOLPHIN ARABIAN, a brown bay stallion foaled in the Yemen in 1724, is often called the Godolphin Barb because he was exported to Tunis on the Barbary Coast. The Bey of Tunis gave him to the king of France, Louis XV; around 1731,

THE GODOLPHIN ARABIAN

Edward Coke of Derbyshire sent the horse to England, where he was finally acquired by the second Earl of Godolphin. Legend has it that Coke discovered the stallion pulling a water-cart in Paris. Used sparingly at stud, the Godolphin Arabian got only about ninety foals but he was one of the three Eastern-bred stallions (see THE BYERLY TURK and THE DARLEY ARABIAN) who founded a new breed of racehorse, the Thoroughbred. His grandson MATCHEM was one of the three principal thoroughbred progenitors through whom all of today's Thoroughbreds are male-line descendants of the three Eastern horses who founded the breed. Another grandson, JANUS, in Virginia, was an important progenitor of the American Quarter Horse.

The Godolphin Arabian was so devoted to a cat named Grimalkin that, when his little companion died, he took to detesting cats and whenever he saw one, tried to kill it.

THE GOLDEN ASS was what the second-century philosopher-satirist Lucius Apuleius turned into for a year, in *Metamorphoses*, a first-person tale that strongly influenced the development of the novel. Lucius' alleged adventures took place in Greece, where, fascinated by magic, he started an affair with Fotis, a slave girl, in order to observe her mistress, a witch named Pamphile. After seeing Pamphile apply an ointment that transformed her into an owl, Lucius begged Fotis to let him do the same, but she gave him the wrong ointment. Instead of growing feathers, he became an ass. Fotis assured him, however, that he could easily restore himself by chewing roses, which were in bloom at the time.

Before he could do that, bandits dragged him away, their loot on his back. Escaping from them, Lucius had many strange experiences with different masters. Finally, a Corinthian official, amused that the ass liked food meant for humans, put him on display. When a rich noblewoman paid to be serviced by the ass, Lucius, full of wine, obliged. His delighted owner hired a harlot to partner the ass in a public performance but Lucius, realizing it was time for the roses to bloom again, bolted from the amphitheater. He galloped 6 miles to the coast, to collapse on the beach, exhausted. The goddess Isis appeared, saying that the High Priest celebrating her festival the next day would be carrying a garland of roses. Lucius found the priest, ate the roses, and recovered his human form.

THE GOLDEN CALF was fashioned by Aaron because the Israelites, disturbed by the long absence of Moses on Mount Sinai, demanded a god to lead them. According to Exodus 32, Aaron took their jewelry, melted it, and with a graving tool shaped it into the form of a calf. Then he built an altar. On the next day, the people made offerings and feasted and danced. Up on the mountain, the Lord (Yahweh) told Moses that his "stiff-necked" people had corrupted themselves by worshiping the molten calf. Carrying the tablets of the Covenant, Moses went down to the camp, saw the calf and the dancing, and, in a rage, smashed the tablets. He melted down the calf, pulverized the gold, threw the powder into the stream, and made the Israelites drink it. He then called for volunteers to serve the Lord. The Levites responded and, commanded by Moses, slew 3,000 of the idolators. "And the Lord plagued the people, because they made the calf, which Aaron made" (Exodus 32:35).

GOLDSMITH MAID, "the trottin'st mare in history," did not start racing until she was 8. Foaled in New Jersey in 1857, she grew up on Alden Goldsmith's farm near Goshen, New York, where she first raced in 1865 as Lady Goldsmith. Two years later, she showed such speed in a close loss to the famous champion Dexter that Budd Doble, a trainer-driver, bought her for $20,000. In his expert hands she raced brilliantly for ten more years. Renamed Goldsmith Maid, the beautiful bay (a granddaughter of HAMBLETONIAN) broke the world record for trotting the mile seven times. When she was 17, she set it at 2:14, an incredible speed in those days. Sulkies were much heavier that they are now and she carried 16-ounce shoes on her forefeet. In thirteen seasons, "The Maid" won 350 heats and 97 of her 123 races. She stopped racing at the age of 20 and her winnings, estimated at $364,200, were not surpassed for almost seventy years. Goldsmith Maid was popular, too. She crossed the continent three times in her own railroad car and was seen in action by more people than any horse had been up to that time.

GOLIATH (1) was a prize ram at Marshfield, Daniel Webster's farm in Massachusetts, where an 1852 inventory listed seventy-five cattle, seventy-five sheep, twenty-five hogs, and a herd of llamas from Peru. Webster reveled in his livestock. Three favorite horses were honored by being buried upright (see STEAMBOAT) and whenever Webster came home from a long absence, he would go right to the barn to give each of his oxen an ear of corn. He was said to have been prouder of Goliath than of his historic Plymouth Oration. Embellishing the legend in *The Devil and Daniel Webster* (1937), Stephen Vincent Benét declared that Goliath "had horns with a curl like a morning-glory vine and could butt through an iron door." And when a visitor arrived early one morning, "Dan'l was up already, talking Latin to the farm hands and wrestling with the ram."

GOLIATH (2), billed by the Ringling Brothers and Barnum & Bailey Circus as "The Greatest Sea Monster Ever Exhibited Alive," was a sea elephant bought from the Hagenbeck Zoo in Hamburg for the 1928–29 circus season. The enormous creature weighed 3¼ tons, ate 150 pounds of fish every day, and was hauled around on a platform wagon drawn by six horses. The sea elephant is the largest member of the seal family. When the bull is aroused during the mating season, his proboscis swells to twice the usual size. This has no perceptible effect on attracting the females, but does give the bull a fierce appearance and makes his trumpeting more resonant.

GOMA, the second gorilla born in captivity (see COLO), was born at the Basel Zoo in Switzerland in September 1959 and raised at home by Dr. Ernest M. Lang, the zoo's director, because her mother did not know how to feed the infant. In *Goma, the Gorilla Baby* (1961), Dr. Lang reported that she was very much like a human baby, although she developed twice as fast since the life span of gorillas is half ours. She had a security blanket, "was more inclined to play than eat," reached up for hugs, and took sick when her surrogate parents were away. She sucked a forefinger because gorilla thumbs are tiny. At the age of 9 months, she would instinctively arrange twigs and branches into a sleeping nest, then climb into Dr. Lang's lap. Goma (Swahili for "dance of joy") was a year old when a young male gorilla, raised in a West African home, was acquired and became such a compatible playmate that Dr. Lang could plan to move them together to the zoo.

GOODY TIPTOES and her husband, Timmy Tiptoes, were prudent squirrels who prepared for the winter by gathering nuts in bags and storing them in hollow stumps near their nest, in *The Tale of Timmy Tiptoes* (1911) by Beatrix Potter. Timmy disappeared. Goody kept gathering nuts. Then she learned her husband was in the bottom of a tree, singing and cracking nuts with Chippy Hackee the chipmunk. Goody stuck her head in the woodpecker hole above them and said, "O fie, Timmy Tiptoes!"

GOOFY, first seen as Dippy Dawg in the Mickey Mouse animated cartoon *Mickey's Revue* (1932), was one of Walt Disney's most popular characters. The scrawny black hound was an amiable dimwit and, with voice provided by Pinto Colvig, was given stardom in his own series in 1939. One of Goofy's best bits was in *Clock Cleaners* (1937) when he performed perilous pirouettes on the ledge of a clock tower to the strains of Moses Mendelssohn's "Spring Song."

GORGON was young Barnaby Baxter's dog in Crockett Johnson's comic strip *Barnaby* (1942–52), which made its debut in the New York City newspaper *PM*. The

dog was a gift from Barnaby's fairy godmother, Mr. O'Malley, who smoked cigars and wore earmuffs as well as wings. Gorgon looked like a sawed-off Airedale, talked, and, in one strip, taught himself to respond to his own commands. When the dog said, "Heel!" Barnaby had to assure O'Malley that Gorgon did not mean him.

GRANDFATHER FROG usually had good sense in the Thornton Burgess nature books but he could be stubborn. When Old Mr. Toad shamed him into leaving his lily pad to go see the Great World, in *The Adventures of Grandfather Frog* (1915), the frog kept getting in trouble. Each friend who rescued him urged him to go home but Grandfather Frog was more afraid of being laughed at than of dangers ahead. Among his misfortunes, he was toyed with by Bowser the Hound, trapped in a spring barrel, and carried around by a cat before he wound up in Farmer Brown's boy's coat pocket. Then his luck changed. On the bank of the Smiling Pool, the boy took his coat off to go fishing. Out of the pocket and into the water the frog hopped home.

GRANE, the horse that Brünnhilde gives to Siegfried in the Prologue of Richard Wagner's opera *Götterdämmerung* (1876), had been the Valkyrie's trusted steed in battle. When Siegfried is murdered in act 3, Brünnhilde orders a funeral pyre for him, ignites it, and rides Grane into the flames to join her beloved in death (see Grani).

GRANI, in Norse mythology, was the wonderful horse that Odin gave to Sigurd the Volsung, the hero known as Siegfried in the German *Nibelungen* epic and

Richard Wagner's *Ring* cycle. When Odin punished Brynhild for her disobedience by putting her into an enchanted sleep and surrounding her with a wall of fire, the dauntless Sigurd rode Grani through the flames to bring her to life (see GRANE).

GRANNY FOX, in the Thornton Burgess nature books, tried to raise her grandson REDDY Fox to be as smart and sly as she was. In *The Adventures of Reddy Fox* (1913), she taught him how to steal chickens without waking up BOWSER THE HOUND. Granny had a temper. When PETER RABBIT (2) saw her sneaking up on him and got away, she was so mad that she hopped up and down, tore up the grass, and ground her teeth. When Reddy did not want to move out of their hole, she boxed his ears. The next day, Farmer Brown's boy arrived with a shovel and dug out the empty hole. Granny watched from a distance, grinning.

THE GRAY OF MACHA, the prescient chariot horse of the Celtic warrior-hero Cuchulainn, fled when his master ordered him yoked for their final battle, and when Cuchulainn's charioteer caught him, he shed tears of blood as he was forced into harness. In battle, the Gray was mortally wounded by a spear in his side. Cuchulainn drew the spear out and said farewell to his horse, who galloped off but returned to kick and bite the enemy closing in on his dying master.

GREYFRIARS BOBBY, a Skye terrier, worked with a shepherd named John Gray in the Scottish Pentlands. Auld Jock, as the shepherd was called, died in Edinburgh in 1858 and was buried in the Greyfriars

GREYFRIARS BOBBY

Churchyard there. The day after the burial, Bobby was discovered sleeping on his master's grave. James Brown, the Greyfriars sexton, evicted him from the churchyard, but night after night the little dog came back. In bad weather, he huddled under a toppled headstone near Jock's grave. A neighborhood innkeeper fed Bobby and each day when the one o'clock gun was fired, the dog trotted over to get his meal. He kept his nightly vigil at

Jock's grave for fourteen years and tourists came from as far away as America to see him. When Bobby died on January 14, 1872, church officials consented to his being buried next to Jock. American friends contributed a headstone, and the memorial donated by the English philanthropist Baroness Burdett-Coutts has become an Edinburgh landmark. Located on Candlemaker Row, it is a large drinking fountain for dogs with a bronze statue of Bobby seated on a pillar in the center.

GREYHOUND, regarded by many as America's greatest trotter, was foaled in 1932 and, as a gelded yearling, was bought for $900 by Col. E. J. Baker of St. Charles, Illinois, and turned over to trainer-driver Sep Palin. In 1934, Greyhound set a record for 2-year-old geldings of 2:04¾, and in his seven years of racing he won seventy-one of his eighty-two heats. At one time, "The Gray Ghost" with the 27-foot stride held fourteen world records. The final one he set was in 1940 when, ridden by Mrs. Frances Dodge Johnson, he lowered the trotting-under-saddle record from 2:05¼ to 2:01¾. Colonel Baker retired him that year and started exhibiting him around the country. Greyhound was a sight after he turned white with age. With a red halter, a red ribbon, and his hoofs painted red, he received standing ovations.

GRIMALKIN is another word for cat, but it may once have been the name of a particular one, Gray Malkin. Gray was its color, and Malkin, the diminutive form of the name Maud or Matilda. The word also means both an old female cat and a malicious, bad-tempered old woman.

The word first appeared in 1605, in Shakespeare's *Macbeth*. At the opening of the play, the three witches plan their next meeting, then part. The First Witch cries, "I come, Graymalkin!" In this usage, Graymalkin is her familiar, or demon spirit, in the form of a cat later described as "brinded" (brindled).

GRIMBERT, the dasse (badger) in the twelfth-century beast epic *Reynard the*

GRIMBERT

Grimbert rebukes Reynard for eyeing the poultry

Fox, offered a countercharge to every accusation the other animals made against his uncle, REYNARD, then rushed to warn the fox that his life was in danger if he did not go to the king and defend himself. On the way, Reynard promised to stop plundering and made a full confession to his nephew. Grimbert absolved him. As they passed a barnyard, however, Reynard leaped at a capon. Feathers flew but it got away. Grimbert rebuked his uncle. Reynard said he had forgotten himself. Further on, Grimbert had to scold him again, "Foul false deceiver! How go your eyes so after the poultry!" At the court, Reynard talked the king out of hanging him and went home. Grimbert soon had to take the fox back to answer new complaints. On the way, Reynard confessed more misdeeds and gave his cynical reasons for committing them. Acknowledging that he could not understand his worldly uncle, Grimbert simply tried to cheer him up. The fox thanked his nephew for the comfort and soon talked his way free again.

GRIZZLE is the old gray mare in *The Tour of Doctor Syntax in Search of the Picturesque* (1812), a series of hand-colored aquatints by Thomas Rowlandson with a narrative in Hudibrastic verse by William Combe. The first plate shows Dr. Syntax, a parson and schoolmaster, preparing to mount his bony nag to set forth on an eight-week sketching tour of England. He manages to lose Grizzle, then he finds her. When he paints, he eschews the natural beauty he sees and rearranges the landscape to make it more "picturesque." Where sportsmen bow to a fine steed like "the far-famed ECLIPSE," he prefers Grizzle. In one plate, Syntax is shown sketching an ugly bunch of braying farm animals while Grizzle appears to be sniggering in the

GRIZZLE

background. Later, Syntax sells her before going to London, then buys her back to ride home. In her final appearance, knobby-kneed but high-stepping old Grizzle is drawing the chaise bearing Dr. Syntax and his wife to his new parish, where:

> . . . the good parson, horse, and wife
> Led a most comfortable life.

GRIZZLY BEAR, one of the animal people, or spirits, in American Indian mythology, was worshiped for his curative powers by Fox and California tribes, whose ceremonial Grizzly Bear Dance included a tribesman in bearskins and mask impersonating him. Since the Kootenais believed that Grizzly Bear was in charge of all plants, roots, and berries, their dance, performed at the beginning of berry-picking season, was a prayer that he tell them where to find berries. The Flatheads were less respectful. COYOTE, the principal character in their myths, went to the camp where Grizzly Bear was head chief, made him walk around the circle of tipis, and ordered the dogs to bite him. Grizzly Bear could not finish the walk. Bleeding and tired, he lay down and died. The subchiefs were glad because he had been cruel.

GRYLL, in book II, canto XII of Edmund Spenser's *Faerie Queene* (1590), was a hog in the Bower of Acrasia, one of many men who had been transformed into "unruly beasts." When they were changed back to men, Gryll "repyned greatly" and Sir Guyon remarked:

> . . . See the mind of beastly man,
> That hath so soon forgot the excellence
> of his creation.

The palmer accompanying the knight added:

> . . . The donghill kinde
> Delightes in filth and fowle
>   incontinence:
> Let Gryll be Gryll, and have his
>   hoggish mind.

The incident was taken from a dialogue by Plutarch about GRYLLUS.

GRYLLUS was a man changed into a pig by Circe, a witch in Greek mythology, then given the power of speech for a conversation with her and Odysseus in a dialogue by Plutarch (ca. A.D. 46–120), Odysseus wanted Circe to restore the animals on her island to their original human form, but Gryllus ("grunter") preferred to remain a pig. Beasts are morally superior to men, he argued, because nature has endowed animals with such virtues as bravery, temperance, and general contentment, while the so-called virtues of men are prompted by self-interest. Further, it is men, not animals, who are guilty of bestiality.

GUB-GUB was the lachrymose baby pig in *The Story of Doctor Dolittle* (1920) by Hugh Lofting. In Africa with Doctor Dolittle and the other animals, Gub-Gub cried when they were captured. As they escaped through the jungle, he cried because he was tired and scared. On the voyage home, Gub-Gub was frightened by eagles flying overhead. He was sure their terrible eyes were looking right into him "to see what he had stolen for lunch." It was a great relief to Gub-Gub to get back to Puddleby-on-the-Marsh. He went right to the garden wall and dug up the horse-radish.

GUDANNA, in the Babylonian epic poem *Gilgamesh* (ca. 2000 B.C.), was the bull of heaven sent to punish the hero Gilgamesh. Gilgamesh had not only refused to marry Ishtar, the insatiable goddess of fertility, but had also reminded her of the terrible things she had done to previous lovers. Enraged, Ishtar appealed to her father, the god Anu, and he created Gudanna, the constellation Taurus. The celestial bull descended from heaven with breath so lethal that each snort destroyed two hundred men, but Gilgamesh and his friend Enkidu killed him. Ishtar climbed up on the wall of the city to shriek curses at Gilgamesh. Enkidu tore off Gudanna's right leg and threw it in her face.

GULLINBUSTI, in Norse mythology, was a marvelous boar that Brokk the dwarf fashioned from a pigskin and hundreds of little pieces of gold wire and gave to Freyr, the God of Plenty. Hitched to Freyr's chariot, Gullinbusti could speed across the earth, the sky, or the sea faster than any horse, and was always surrounded by a brilliant light from his golden bristles.

GUNPOWDER, in Washington Irving's *The Legend of Sleepy Hollow* (1820), was the broken-down old horse, blind in one eye, that Ichabod Crane had borrowed and was riding home when he encountered the headless horseman, allegedly the ghost of a Hessian soldier. The massive rider on the powerful black horse kept pace on Gunpowder's blind side until the old horse, "who seemed possessed with a demon . . . plunged headlong downhill." As they thundered over a bridge, Ichabod looked back to see his pursuer "in the very act of hurling his head at him." Crane fell to the ground. The next morning, his hat was found near a shattered pumpkin and Gun-

powder was "soberly cropping the grass at his master's gate." There was no body. Ichabod had simply left the neighborhood.

GUS, short for "Asparagus," had reached his anecdotage, in "Gus: The Theatre Cat" from T. S. Eliot's *Old Possum's Book of Practical Cats* (1939). The thin, palsied old cat loved to recall past triumphs when his friends gathered behind the neighborhood pub. He remarked that the Theatre had certainly changed:

> But there's nothing to equal, from
>   what I hear tell,
> That moment of mystery
> When I made history
> As Firefrorefiddle, the Fiend of the
>   Fell.

GWYLLGI is the huge Dog of Darkness in Wales. According to English folklore, Gwyllgi's terrifying howl can paralyze a man, and a glance from the creature can knock him down.

GYB was the "savage cat" in *The Boke of Phyllyp Sparowe*, a 1,400-line poem by John Skelton (ca. 1460–1529), in which a school-girl mourned her dead bird by cursing the cat who caught him by the head "and slew him there starke dead." She wished the cat were blind so that leopards and lions could catch him and chew him, that serpents could sting him, that dragons might poison his liver, and that manticores might feed on his brains. She would have the bears of Arcady pluck away his ears, and "the wylde wolfe" LYCAON bite the backbone of the "foule cat." Finally, she cried, let Mount Etna ignite his tail in a blaze that could be seen all the way to Salisbury plain.

HACHIKO, an Akita dog, accompanied his master, Dr. Eisaburo Ueno, to the Shibuya railroad station in Tokyo to see him off every morning, and was there every evening to meet his return train. In May 1925, Dr. Ueno died during the day at Tokyo University, where he was a professor. That night, Hachiko waited for him at the station until midnight. The next day and every day for almost nine years the dog arrived at the usual time, and waited. He became famous throughout Japan. After he died in March 1934, a statue of Hachiko was placed in the Shibuya station and an annual ceremony is held there to honor his memory.

HAM, known as the Space Chimp, was lobbed into suborbital flight by a Redstone 2 rocket on January 31, 1961. His Mercury capsule reached a maximum speed of 5,800 mph and an altitude of 156 miles before splashing down in the Atlantic 16½ minutes later, 414 miles from the Cape Canaveral launch site. The freckled, 40-pound chimpanzee had been known simply

as test subject Number 61 until the day of the flight, when he was given the name Ham, an acronym for Holloman Aerospace Medical Center. A faulty mechanism in the rocket added two minutes to the flight, the oxygen supply ran short, and during the ascent, Ham was pushed down into his cushioned couch with a force of seventeen g's (seventeen times his own weight and five g's more than expected). Nevertheless, having been trained to respond to flashing lights by working various switches to avoid mild electric shocks, he performed so well during the flight that he received only three shocks. Ham was recovered in good condition and two years later became a celebrity at the National Zoological Park in Washington, D.C.

HAMBLETONIAN, a great-grandson of MESSENGER, was foaled in 1849 in Orange County, New York, and sold, with his dam, for $125 to William Rysdyk, an illiterate but shrewd farmhand who saw the colt's breeding potential. Rysdyk began exhibiting Hambletonian (named for a well-

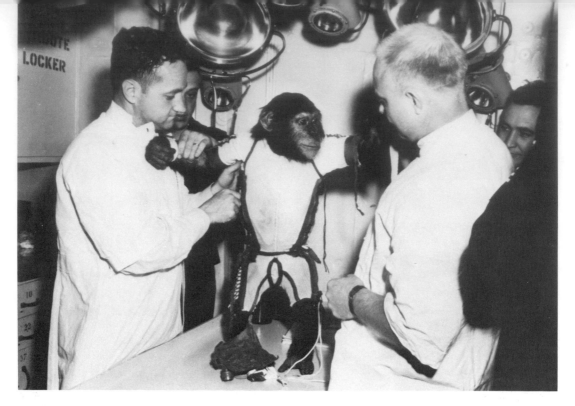

HAM

known English Thoroughbred) at county fairs, raced him only once to win a time trial against a rival stallion, and started him covering mares as a 2-year-old. By the 1860s, the success of such foals as Dexter and George Wilkes made Rysdyk's Hambletonian the most famous trotting stallion in America. The "old bull," as the little bay was called, sired 1,331 horses between 1851 and 1874. His Thoroughbred blood contributed to their excellence, which they passed on, and today, nearly all of America's harness racers trace back to Hambletonian, the father of the modern Standardbred.

HAMILCAR was Bonnard's Angora cat in *Le Crime de Sylvestre Bonnard* (1881), a novel in diary form by Anatole France. When Bonnard spoke softly, Hamilcar accompanied him "with a throat-like sound like the song of a kettle on the fire,"

but when he raised his voice, the cat notified him with lowered ears and wrinkled brow "that it was bad taste on my part so to declaim." Ten years later, after remarking that the aging cat's air of gravity intimidated him, Bonnard dropped a book while Hamilcar was washing himself. The cat stopped and "looked angrily at me with his paw over his ear. Was this the tumultuous existence he must expect under my roof?" Bonnard, a bibliophile, felt obliged to explain that he was a victim of a passion and that without passions, "there would be no arts or industries in the world. . . . and you would not be able, Hamilcar, to repose all day on a silken cushion."

HANDSOME DAN, the original Yale bulldog, was sitting in front of a New Haven blacksmith's shop in 1889 when Andrew B. Graves, class of 1892, saw him and bought him. Graves began taking him to sports events, leading him across the field at football games. Handsome Dan became Yale's mascot and served for ten years. The big white bulldog was also a prize-winning show dog in the 1890s, regarded as the best American-bred bulldog up to that time. His stuffed body is in a sealed glass case in the trophy room of Yale's Payne Whitney Gymnasium.

Handsome Dan II, another white bulldog, was presented to the university in 1933. On the eve of the 1934 Yale–Harvard football game, he was kidnapped. The next day, newspapers ran a photograph of Handsome Dan II licking the feet of the John Harvard statue. The feet had been smeared with hamburger. The dog was kept as mascot until his death in 1937. Ten more bulldogs have served, some of them briefly because they couldn't stand crowds. Yale had become coeducational when the latest one was designated in 1975. Handsome Dan XII is a bitch named Bingo.

HANUMAN, in Hindu mythology, was the monkey god whose loyal service to Rama was related in the epic poem *Ramayana*. When Sita, the wife of Rama, was abducted to Lanka (Ceylon) by Ravanna, Hanuman managed to get to the walled city where she was imprisoned. Palace guards caught him, oiled his tail, and set it on fire. He swished it around and set the city on fire. After he returned to Rama, he and an army of monkeys and bears helped build a bridge to Lanka for their invasion. Rama killed Ravanna, rescued Sita, and rewarded Hanuman with per-

HAMBLETONIAN

petual life and youth. In modern Hinduism, Hanuman became a village deity, worshiped especially by women who want children and by wrestlers. To this day, monkeys and apes are sacred in India. Some villages stage a ceremonial wedding of apes at great expense as a religious service.

HAPPY JACK SQUIRREL, usually a blithe spirit in the Thornton Burgess nature books, blew up when he found UNC' BILLY POSSUM sleeping in his nut supply in *The Adventures of Unc' Billy Possum* (1914). Being startled awake made Unc' Billy so mad that he showed his teeth, until he realized where he was and grinned. Both animals burst out laughing, and Happy Jack helped Unc' Billy get home safely.

HARRY, the hero of a series of children's books written by Gene Zion and illustrated by Margaret Bloy Graham, is a white dog with black spots who plays in such dirty places that he turns into a black dog with white spots in *HARRY the Dirty Dog* (1956). When his family fails to recognize him, he digs up the scrub brush he has buried in the garden and actually begs for a bath.

HARRY CAT, in three books by George Selden, lived in a drainpipe in the Times Square subway station with his pal TUCKER MOUSE. Harry's heavy-handed—heavy-pawed—affection for Tucker was useful for calming the excitable mouse and stopped just short of squashing him. In *The Cricket in Times Square* (1960), Harry's recognition of the musical talent of Chester Cricket, who had turned up in the station, led to cricket concerts that

brightened the lives of subway travelers. In *Tucker's Countryside* (1969), the cat and mouse went to Connecticut to help Chester save a meadow from real estate developers. Harry advanced Tucker's scheme of drawing public attention to the area by letting RUFF (2), the Saint Bernard, chase him. In *Harry Cat's Pet Puppy* (1974), the striped tomcat charmed a female Siamese into letting the overgrown pup he had rescued share her home.

HARVEY (1), a 6-foot, 1½-inch-tall white rabbit, was visible only to Elwood P. Dowd and occasionally to his sister Veta in Mary Coyle Chase's play, *Harvey*. Produced by Brock Pemberton against the advice of his wife, director, and best friends, it opened in New York on November 1, 1944, became the fifth-longest-running play in Broadway history, and won the Pulitzer Prize. In the play, the bibulous Elwood introduces Harvey to everyone, explaining that he is a pooka, a Celtic spirit in animal form, very large animal form. During the play's Boston tryout, Pemberton hedged his bet by spending $600 for a rabbit suit and hiring an actor to walk around in it as a visible Harvey. The idea was abandoned after one performance. From then on, the only sight the audience had of Harvey was in a portrait placed on the mantel during the play, showing Elwood seated with his furry companion standing at his side.

HARVEY (2), a cranky black and white rabbit, was taken in by the New York City chapter of the American Society for the Prevention of Cruelty to Animals in the spring of 1977 after he bit six people. He had turned mean, it was reported, after being mistreated by the family who got him as an Easter bunny. Duncan Wright, the ASPCA director, labeled Harvey an "attack" rabbit for his tendency to bite "when people get within hopping distance," and said the 4½-pound *Oryctolagus cuniculus* would not be available for adoption. Instead, a securely caged Harvey was sent on tour with some other animals to educate people about the proper care of pets. He also raised thousands of dollars for the Society, partly through the sale of Harvey T-shirts. Ornery to the end, Harvey died on March 18, 1978, two days before a scheduled appearance on a program about treatment of Easter pets. An ASPCA official remarked, "It's incredible that he picked Easter to kick off."

HATHI, a wild elephant in *The Second Jungle Book* (1895) by Rudyard Kipling, bore a scar from a pointed stake that had raked him from heel to shoulder when he fell into a trap. He broke free as the hunters pulled him out and, after his wound healed, he returned at night with his three sons to ruin the men's crops and smash their huts. "We let in the jungle," said Hathi, "and in those villages, . . . there is not one man today who gets his food from the ground." Knowing this, Mowgli asked the elephant to let in the jungle at the village where his parents were being persecuted. Hathi and his sons demolished the area and "by the end of the Rains there was the roaring Jungle in full blast on the spot that had been under plough not six months before."

HATHOR, a cow-goddess of ancient Egypt, was both consort and mother of the great god Ra. She was the goddess of love and beauty, patroness of music and art, and, as the Great Mother fertility figure, protector of women and infants. When a baby was born, seven goddesses in her image, called Hathors, would surround the cradle and predict the child's future. At Thebes, as the deity of the dead, Hathor stood in a sycamore grove at the edge of the desert to welcome the dead with bread and water, then held the ladder steady while they climbed to the skies. When Ra was threatened by rebellion in his old age, she transformed herself into Sekhmet, the lion-headed goddess of battle, and began to slaughter his enemies. Fearing she would exterminate the human race, Ra covered the battlefield with a frothy liquid that looked like blood but was beer and pomegranate juice. Bloodthirsty Hathor drank it and passed out. Mankind was saved.

HATI, in Snorri's *Edda* (ca. 1220), was the wolf who joined his brother SKOLL in chasing the sun across the sky. The notion of such pursuit was inspired by the variegated rays of light seen when the sun breaks through clouds which are still called "sun-wolves" in Scandinavia. In other tales of Norse mythology, Hati was called MANIGARM because he chased the moon.

HAZEL, in *Watership Down* (1972) by Richard Adams, was the yearling rabbit who led an exodus from his warren because his brother FIVER had a premonition that it would be destroyed. Guided by Fiver's prescience and his own good sense about the abilities of the other bucks, Hazel directed their perilous journey across the English countryside to a hilltop, Watership Down, where they settled. In a subsequent battle with GENERAL WOUNDWORT, Hazel loosed a dog on the attackers in a daring move that left him lacerated by a cat. The attackers fled and Hazel lived many more years, venerated as Chief Rabbit.

An animated film version of the story, *Watership Down*, written and directed by Martin Rosen, appeared in 1978.

HEATHCLIFF, the chubby cat who outwits dogs and ambushes the milkman, was created in 1973 by George Gately for his comic strip *Heathcliff*. Eight years later, the strip was appearing in more than 700 newspapers, Gately's paperbacks, *Heathcliff Banquet* (1980) and *Heathcliff Feast* (1981), were big sellers, and Heathcliff became a star of Saturday morning television cartoons. A tough cat, whose zest for birds can ruin an expedition of birdwatchers or a woman's spring hat, Heathcliff can be tender, too. To charm Sonja, the pretty Persian, he sets out a can's worth of sardines in the outline of a heart.

THE HEFFALUMP, in A. A. Milne's *Winnie-the-Pooh* (1926), gave WINNIE-THE-POOH nightmares after PIGLET dug a Heffalump Trap and he baited it with his honey jar. Neither of them had seen a Heffalump but Christopher Robin said that he had. Going back during the night to finish his honey, Pooh got his head stuck in the jar, fell into a hole, and landed on Piglet. Both were convinced that the Heffalump had made a trap for them until Christopher Robin pulled them out of the gravel pit.

HEIDRUN, in Norse mythology, was the goat who stood on the roof of Valhalla, munching the leaves of Yggdrasil, the wondrous ash-tree that supported the universe. Each day, the Heroes drank mead that flowed from her udder while they dined on boiled SAEHRMNIR.

HERCULES, Aubry of Montdidier's dog in a medieval French legend, witnessed the murder of his master and effectively accused Richard of Macaire of the deed by attacking him in the presence of the king. A duel between man and dog was decreed, Hercules felled Macaire by fastening on his throat, and the murderer confessed. After Charles V had a mural of the duel placed in his castle at Montargis in 1371, Hercules became known as the Dog of Montargis and a statue illustrating the story was placed in the town's public garden. In 1814, *The Dog of Montargis, or the Forest of Bondy*, a melodrama by R. C. G. de Pixéricourt, had its premiere in Paris and became so popular that three years later the Grand Duke Charles Augustus of Weimar insisted that the play, complete with live poodle in the title role, be presented at the Court Theater. Johann Wolfgang von Goethe, the long-time director of the theater, detested dogs and when the poodle arrived for rehearsal, resigned.

HEROD, a great-great-grandson of THE BYERLY TURK, was a Thoroughbred foaled in England in 1758. The bay horse won only six of his ten races, but at stud, from 1768 to 1780, he passed on his size and stamina to his foals, who won over £200,000. Although his line accounts for only about 4 percent of today's racehorses, Herod was one of the three principal thoroughbred progenitors (see ECLIPSE and MATCHEM) through whom all of the Thoroughbreds now racing are descendants of the three Eastern-bred stallions who founded the breed.

HIDDIGEIGEI, a tomcat with sable coat and majestic tail, is a principal character in *Der Trompeter von Säckingen* (1854), a narrative poem by Joseph Viktor von Scheffel. By 1911, the romantic and humorous tale had appeared in more than 250 editions. An English translation appeared in 1893, and a restaurant in Capri was named for the cat. In his thirteen songs, Hiddigeigei reflects on human behavior and finds it absurd. People struggle through their lives while the tomcat, conscious of his worth, sits calmly on the roof. When cats sing of love, men scornfully call it caterwauling:

> Yet, alas! 'Tis ours to suffer
> That these same contemptuous mortals
> Call such sounds into existence
> As I have been forced to hear. . . .
> And in view of yonder damsel,
> Grasping yon abhorrent trumpet,
> Can a man, with front unblushing,
> Jeer when cats are making music?

HIGGINS, the dog in television's "Petticoat Junction": see BENJI.

HIM and HER, a pair of beagles, were taken along when President Lyndon B. Johnson and his family moved into the White House in 1963. On April 27, 1964, while strolling on the White House lawn with a group of bankers and the press, Johnson spotted the dogs, called them over, and playfully lifted Her, then Him, upright by the ears. The dogs yelped in pain. The President claimed it was good for them but the public immediately disagreed, in indignant letters and phone calls to the White House and stern statements from experts on dogs. Johnson, who truly loved dogs, was upset. "I don't want to be inhumane," he said the next day, but a week later he repeated the ear-pulling for photographers, insisting that the dogs' yelps were yelps of joy. When Her died the following November after swallowing a stone, more than 300 beagles were offered to the President. All were declined. Him expired in June 1966, run over by a White House car while he was chasing a squirrel.

THE HIND OF CERYNEIA, in Greek mythology, had brazen hoofs and horns of gold (some said it was a stag), and was sacred to Artemis. One of the twelve labors King Eurystheus set for Heracles (Hercules) was to bring the deer to him, alive and unharmed. The chase took a year. With the animal slung over his shoulders, Heracles was on his way to the king when he met Artemis. The goddess was furious but after Heracles explained that Eurystheus had ordered the capture, she let him go, provided he freed the deer as soon as he proved that he had caught it.

HINSE OF HINSFIELD, the family cat, kept Sir Walter Scott's enormous hound MAIDA in a state of terror. Soon after Scott received the dog, he reported that the cat "insists upon all rights of precedence, and scratches with impunity the nose of an animal who would make no bones of a wolf." At dinner, Hinse joined the dogs crouched around the table and, if one was disrespectful, swatted it on the ear. In 1826, the old tomcat was killed in a fight with Nimrod the bloodhound. Even though Scott was sorry to lose the cat, he pointed out that Hinse always had been the aggressor.

HODAIN, in Arthurian legend, was a little "brachet" (female hound) that a daughter of the king of France gave to Sir Tristram to remember her by. Banished from Cornwall when his uncle, King Mark, discovered that he and Queen Isoude were lovers, Tristram hid in the forest, living off game that his faithful dog chased without barking lest she reveal his presence. Then, leaving Hodain with Isoude to remember him by, Tristram went on to other adventures. He died in Brittany, moments after the ship bringing his beloved Isoude was sighted. The news of his death killed her and after their bodies were returned to Cornwall, Hodain dashed through the forest to the chapel where Tristram lay. She kept vigil there until he was buried.

HODGE was Samuel Johnson's cat. In *The Life of Samuel Johnson* (1791), James Boswell reported that Johnson would go out himself to buy oysters for Hodge "lest the servants having that trouble should take a dislike to the poor creature." Boswell, who detested cats, "frequently suffered a great deal from the presence of the same Hodge," but faithfully recorded: "I recollect him one day scrambling up Dr. Johnson's breast, apparently with much satisfaction, while my friend, smiling and half-whistling, rubbed down his back, and pulled him by the tail; and when I observed he was a fine cat, saying, 'Why, yes, Sir, but I have had cats whom I liked better than this'; and then, as if perceiving Hodge to be out of countenance, adding, 'but he is a very fine cat, a very fine cat indeed.'"

HOFVARPNIR, in Norse mythology, was the horse that the goddess Gna rode through the air and over the waters when her errands for Odin's wife, Frigg, required speed. His name means "one who tosses his hoofs."

HORTON, the goodhearted elephant created by Dr. Seuss, agreed to do a favor for a bird in *Horton Hatches the Egg* (1940). He sat on her egg in a nest in a tree, after propping up the tree to support his weight, for fifty-one weeks, even while hunters transported him with the tree, nest, and egg to the United States to exhibit them around the country. When the tour reached Palm Beach, the egg hatched —a flying baby elephant. In *Horton Hears a Who* (1954), the elephant heard a small sound coming from a speck of dust. The other animals mocked him for insisting that a whole community of tiny creatures was there. Horton pleaded with the "Who's" to make themselves audible and they did.

THE HOUND OF THE BASKERVILLES, a ghostly black beast on the moors of Dartmoor, had killed wicked Sir Hugo Baskerville in 1648 and brought doom on his descendants, according to family legend in Sir Arthur Conan Doyle's *The Hound of the Baskervilles* (1902). When Sir Charles Baskerville suddenly died, apparently of fright since there was no mark on him, Sherlock Holmes was told that several reliable people had seen a "huge creature, luminous, ghastly and spectral" on the moor and that "the footprints of a gigantic hound" were discovered not far from the body. Soon after Sir Charles' heir, Sir Henry, moved into Baskerville Hall, Holmes and Dr. Watson heard terrible screams on the moor, mingled with a deep, menacing rumble, and they found the mangled body of an escaped convict dressed in Sir Henry's clothes. The next night, as they watched Sir Henry start across the moor, a hound such as mortal eyes had never seen sprang out of the fog to attack him. "Fire burst from its open mouth, its eyes glowed with a smouldering glare, its muzzle and dewlap were outlined in flickering flame." Knowing what had happened and why, Sherlock Holmes saved Sir Henry's life and said of the outcome, "We've laid the family ghost once and forever."

THE HOUYHNHNMS, an intelligent race of horses, ruled the South Sea island where Lemuel Gulliver was stranded during his fourth voyage in *Gulliver's Travels* (1727) by Jonathan Swift. An inferior race of hairy, savage humans, called *Yahoos*, worked as servants or beasts of burden for the horses, or ran wild. The Houyhnhnms had remarkable dexterity. Using the hollow part between the pastern and the hoof of their forefeet, they could thread a needle, milk cows, make simple tools, form earthenware vessels, and harvest their crops. They knew how to concoct medicine from herbs. They could not write, but they observed the solar year, understood eclipses, and held quadrennial General Assemblies on the vernal equinox.

Gulliver soon learned enough of their spoken language to answer the Master Horse's questions about the behavior of the *Yahoos* in his own land. He grew to venerate the Houyhnhnms, whose society was ordered by their grand maxim, "To cultivate *Reason,* and to be wholly governed by it." He admired their virtues of friendship and benevolence, their "*Decency* and *Civility* in the highest Degrees." He tried so hard to become like a Houyhn-

hnm that when he returned home, "My Friends often tell me in a blunt way, that I trot like a horse; which, however, I take for a great Compliment." Five years after his return, Gulliver was still not reconciled to *Yahoos* in general, but did permit his wife to sit at dinner with him, "at the farthest End of a long Table." Meanwhile, he bought two young horses who understood him tolerably well. "I converse with them at least four Hours every Day."

HRIMFAXI, in Norse mythology, was the horse with the mane of rime that the swarthy goddess Nott (Night) drove across the sky. Each morning, the earth was bedewed with the froth that fell from his bit.

HSING-HSING and LING-LING, a pair of giant pandas, were presented to the American people by the People's Republic of China following President Richard M. Nixon's historic visit in February 1972, and in response to a donation from the United States to the Peking Zoo of two musk-oxen, Matilda and Milton. At the time of the exchange, there were only two other live giant pandas outside the Orient but more have been sent to Western zoos since. The first of several seen in the U.S. had been Su-Lin, a male cub imported in 1936; the last one died in 1953. When Hsing-Hsing and Ling-Ling went on display at the National Zoological Park in Washington, D.C., on April 20, 1972, 1,000 people an hour filed by to see them.

Ling-Ling, the 135-pound female, was 18 months old and playful. The male Hsing-Hsing (pronounced shing-shing) was smaller, six months younger, and shy. They were compatible youngsters but, on the

HSING-HSING AND LING-LING

advice of Chinese zoo keepers, were raised in separate enclosures. When they matured, Hsing was officially deemed "inept" at breeding, nor did artifical insemination work. In April 1981, when Ling went into her annual heat, Hsing had at her again so clumsily that she sent him sprawling. CHIA-CHIA, a male panda borrowed from the London Zoo, was then admitted to her pen. They fought so hard that a hose had

to be turned on them. The possibility remains that Ling might breed with another male, perhaps PE-PE from Mexico. Meanwhile she and Hsing-Hsing are as popular as ever at the zoo.

HUCKLEBERRY HOUND was created by Hanna-Barbera Productions in 1958 for the first all-animated television series, "Huckleberry Hound," which won an Emmy Award in 1960 "for outstanding achievement in the field of children's programming." The intrepid little blue dog with the heavy-lidded eyes handled all sorts of adventures —with robbers, dragons, an amorous cocker spaniel—with a cheerful calm that approached lethargy. Even when he fell head first from a skyscraper, he simply picked himself up and drawled, "That was a purty big building."

HUNCA MUNCA, a mouse, and her husband, Tom Thumb, in *The Tale of Two Bad Mice* (1904) by Beatrix Potter, vandalized a doll's house. The mice smashed the imitation food made of plaster, pulled feathers out of a bolster, and removed a number of odds and ends to their hole. The two of them were not all bad, however. They left a coin to pay for breakage, and early each morning, Hunca Munca swept the doll's house.

In *Tom Thumb the Great* (1731), a burlesque of contemporary playwrights by Henry Fielding, Tom Thumb's wife was a daughter of King Arthur named Huncamunca.

HUNGARI, a dog, was involved in the history and naming of Hungary, according to Aventinus' *Annals of Bavaria* (1554). When the Magyars ravaged Bavaria and defeated the Germans in A.D. 910, the German king, Henry I, sent Hungari, a mangy dog with no tail and both ears missing, as a royal delegate to arrange the payment of tribute. In *Origins* (1958), however, Eric Partridge traced "Hungary" not from a dog but from a root of the word "ogre," the Byzantine Greek *Ogor*, which meant an inhabitant of the area. The word was "nasalized" in the medieval Latin of Germany to *Ungarus* and the place name became *Ungaria*, which led to "Hungary" in English.

HWIN, the talking mare carrying the girl Aravis in *The Horse and His Boy* (1954) by C. S. Lewis, joined Bree, the talking war horse, and the boy Shasta in flight from captivity to Narnia, where the horses had been born and then stolen when they were foals. Although Hwin was diffident with the proud Bree, she was practical about having their tails shorn in order to pass through their captors' city unrecognized and after crossing a great desert it was she, "the weaker and more tired of the two, who set the pace."

I

IGLOO, the fox terrier who accompanied Adm. Richard E. Byrd on his first Antarctic expedition (1928–30), was a handful from the time they boarded a train to California to begin the voyage. At one stop, the dog held up the train for ten minutes while he chased a gopher. "I fancied neither man nor beast could discompose him," said Byrd, but when the Eskimo dogs brought aboard at New Zealand strained at their chains to get at Igloo, the dog was discomposed enough to spend the rest of the voyage below deck. At Little America, he was fitted out in lined boots and a camel's hair coat that covered his legs. His wool-lined crate was at the foot of Byrd's bed and whenever an ailing sled dog or one about to produce a litter was brought in to share the quarters, Igloo raised hell. He also got loose occasionally. Bedlam would break out where the other dogs were kept and the men would rush to extricate him. "Igloo was as cocky and fierce as ever . . . no doubt he believed he was a great fighter because we saved his life so often." Byrd found it a miracle that the dog survived but he did, "unchastened."

IGNATZ MOUSE, in George Herriman's comic strip *Krazy Kat* (1913–44), devoted his time to hurling a brick at the head of KRAZY KAT, who loved him and wanted him to hurl it. OFFISA BULL PUPP, who loved Krazy, incarcerated Ignatz when he could, but the mouse was tricky, at one point even drawing a picture of a tree to hide behind.

IMOGENE, a large spotted calf, replaced TOTO as Dorthy's pet in the musical comedy *The Wizard of Oz*, adapted by L. Frank Baum from his book *The Wonderful Wizard of Oz* (1900). The show opened in Chicago in 1902, was a smash hit, and moved to New York the following year. Toto was too small to be played by an actor in a dog suit (see LUATH [3]), hence the substitution of Imogene.

INCITATUS was Caligula's favorite horse. Caligula (Gaius Caesar), the third emperor of Rome, A.D 37–41, was a fanatic about horse racing. On the days before the races at his Circus Maximus, he would send soldiers around the neighborhood to order silence so that his horse's sleep would not be disturbed. Incitatus was given a marble stable and a furnished house with a retinue of slaves to wait on the human guests invited to dine with him. It was even said that Caligula intended to make the horse a consul.

IO, in Greek mythology, was a maiden loved by Zeus, who tried to conceal the romance by covering the earth with a cloud. Hera, his wife, suspected the cloud and ordered it removed. There stood Zeus, with a beautiful white heifer that he swore had just sprung from the earth. Not believing a word, Hera asked for the heifer— Io, of course—as a gift. Zeus could not refuse. Hera put Argus, a monster with a hundred eyes, in charge of her. Even when he slept, some of the eyes stayed open, watching. One day, Io saw her father and sisters. She ran to them and tried to speak but could only produce a bellow that frightened even her. Then she traced her name in the sand with her hoof. As her father embraced her in sorrow, Argus drove her away. Zeus finally sent Hermes to free her, which he did by telling such a long story to Argus that all hundred eyes closed. Io fled but she was not free. Hera sent a gadfly to plague her. The tormented heifer roamed the world. The Ionian Sea and the Bosphorus, which means "cow ford," were both named for her. At last, Io reached the Nile, where Zeus restored her to human form. She bore him a son and lived happily ever after.

IOSKEHA and TAWISCARA, in the mythology of the Iroquois and other eastern tribes of American Indians, were twin rabbits whose grandmother was the moon. When they grew up, the twins quarreled so violently that they came to blows. Ioskeha, the White One, took the horns of a stag for a weapon. Tawiscara, the Dark One, grabbed a wild rose to defend himself and was soon badly wounded. The drops of blood that fell as he fled turned into flint stones. Ioskeha settled in the east, where he became the father of mankind, slaying monsters, stocking the woods with game, and teaching the Indians such useful arts as cultivating crops and making fire.

IROQUOIS, the first American-bred horse to win the English Derby, was foaled in Pennsylvania. He was one of several yearlings taken to England in 1879 by Pierre Lorillard and his trainer, Jacob Pincus. Iroquois ran so well as a 2-year-old that the great Fred Archer asked to ride him in the 1881 Derby. When the news of the victory reached the New York Stock Exchange, there was such bedlam that trading was suspended. The stallion was returned to the United States to stand at stud, and was champion sire in 1892.

ISEGRIM, the wolf in the twelfth-century beast epic *Reynard the Fox*, suffered continual humiliations from REYNARD. When the fox tied him to a monastery bell rope, the resulting racket earned Isegrim a beating. While the wolf was stuck in a hole leading to a priest's pantry, the fox dropped a stolen capon beside him. Isegrim was caught and beaten senseless. Entering a barn that Reynard said was full of fat hens, the wolf fell through a trapdoor. When he complained about the fox to the king, Reynard talked himself back into the king's favor and Isegrim out of it. The exasperated wolf cast his glove in challenge to the fox. They fought viciously. Isegrim lost an eye but finally pinned Reynard to the ground and told him to yield or die. Reynard talked and talked. Then, as Isegrim replied that he would be a fool to spare the fox, Reynard reached between the wolf's legs and squeezed his testicles. The fight was over. Isegrim barely survived.

ISLERO, an unusually vicious bull of the Miura strain, killed and was killed by Manolete, the world's greatest bullfighter, in 1947 at Linares, Spain. At the age of 30, Manolete was at the peak of his thirteen-year career and had announced that he would retire at the end of the season. On August 28, he faced a large Miura bull, Islero, for the first time in years. Spaniards said of the ferocious breed: "A matador who turns his back on a Miura is a dead matador." Manolete did not turn his back, but as he drove his sword down into Islero's heart, he was gored by the bull's right horn. Islero fell dead. Ten hours later, Manolete died and the entire Spanish-speaking world went into mourning.

JACK (1), a chacma baboon, became a railroad signalman near Uitenhage, South Africa, earning twenty cents a day and half a bottle of beer on Saturdays. His owner, James Edwin Wide, had been given the job after losing both legs in a railroad accident. Getting around on wooden legs, Wide trained the baboon to pull signal levers or fetch the key to the coal bin according to the number of whistles from an approaching train. "This he does with an imitation of humanity which is as wonderful as it is ludicrous," reported the *Cape Argus Weekly* on February 6, 1884. "He puts down the lever, looks around to see that the correct signal is up, then turns round to the train and gravely watches its approach." Some passengers were uneasy about signals being handled by a baboon, but the railroad company found Jack quite competent and put him on the payroll. At home, he pumped water from the well, did garden chores, and, each morning, pushed his master to work in a trolley that Wide had devised. After nine accident-free years on the job, Jack died in 1890 and was buried next to the signal box.

JACK (2) was Tom's little pony in "Tom and his Pony, Jack" from Hilaire Belloc's *New Cautionary Tales for Children* (1931). Tom galloped for miles on Jack, leaping hedges for several days:

> Until the pony, feeling tired,
> Collapsed, looked heavenward and
> expired.

JACK HARE, in Kit Williams' *Masquerade* (1979), was a swift hare sent by the lady Moon to deliver a "splendrous jewel" to her beloved, the elusive Sun. After traveling through earth, air, fire, and water, Jack leaped beyond earth's gravity to reach the Sun, only to discover he had lost the jewel. The story and the painting illustrating it were filled with riddles that yield the exact location in Great Britain of a pendant in the shape of Jack Hare, fashioned of 18-carat gold and studded with rubies and turquoise. Williams claimed that a bright

JACK (1)

child of 10 could solve the riddles but it was not until March 1982, after 1.5 million copies of *Masquerade* had been sold in eight languages in eleven countries, that a 48-year-old design engineer unearthed the treasure. He recognized the final clue while walking his dog in a park in Ampthill, a village 35 miles from London.

JACKIE (1), a chacma baboon that Albert Marr took along to his South African regiment in World War I, was so friendly and intelligent that he became the regimental mascot, entitled to his own rations, paybook, and uniform. His acute hearing made Private Jackie a valuable guard at the front, where he warned his comrades with little barks or by tugging Marr's tunic before they could hear the enemy approach. When Marr was felled by a bullet in 1916, Jackie licked his wound until help came. In April 1918, they were both wounded during a barrage in Flanders and Jackie's right leg, shattered by shrapnel, had to be amputated. The surgeon later recalled thinking it might be best if the baboon died under anesthetic but "he lapped up the chloroform as if it had been whisky" and recovered fully. Promoted to corporal and given a medal, Jackie appeared in the Lord Mayor's victory parade through London in 1919, perched on a captured German howitzer. Then, with discharge papers that stated he was "bilingual," Corporal Jackie retired to Marr's farm. He died there in 1921.

JACKIE (2), a lion born at the California Zoological Gardens in Los Angeles, was a third-generation movie actor whose career began when he was 4 months old. His mother and grandmother had both appeared in Col. William Selig's early animal thrillers. He had no name until his tenth feature, *Burning Sands* (1922), when the leading lady, Jacqueline Logan, suggested he be named for her. Handled by William Koontz, Jackie was so tractable that he was used in more than 250 movies, silent and sound, and appeared as Leo, the M-G-M lion, for nearly eighteen years.

JACK RABBIT (JEAN LAPIN), in "The Eagle and the Beetle," one of the *Fables* of Jean de La Fontaine (1621–95), darted for cover when the eagle chased him. All the rabbit could find was a beetle's hole. The eagle pounced and dug her talons into his fur. The beetle pleaded with the eagle to spare Jack Rabbit, his friend and neighbor. The eagle struck the beetle with her wing and carried off the rabbit. To avenge Jack Rabbit's murder, the beetle destroyed the eagle's eggs for three years in a row until Jupiter changed the bird's mating season to winter, when beetles hibernate.

JACKSON is my dog.

JACQUES and GUS, two mice in the Walt Disney Productions animated feature *Cinderella* (1950), added a comic touch with their chittery voices, provided by Jim MacDonald, while they looked after Cinderella and looked out for the dreadful cat, Lucifer.

JAMBAVAT, king of the bears in Hindu mythology, was related to Rama, who gave Prince Satrajit a magic jewel that protected or destroyed its owner, depending on his behavior. The prince, fearing that Krishna would take it from him, gave the gem to his brother. The brother misbehaved and was killed by a lion, who put the jewel in his mouth. Jambavat killed the lion, retrieved the stone, and retired to his cave. Krishna followed him in. After twenty-one days of fierce single combat, the bear surrendered the jewel and gave Krishna the hand of his daughter.

JANUS, a grandson of The Darley Arabian, was foaled in England in 1746 and, after a respectable racing career and two years at stud, was sent to Virginia in 1757. There and in North Carolina, where the quarter-mile sprint was the preferred race, he was bred to mares of a breed developed from Spanish horses by the Chicasaw and Cherokee Indians. During the next twenty-two years, he produced an immense number of sprinters, and when his daughters and granddaughters were bred back to him, his get was even more successful. His ability to pass on his early speed and muscular, compact build established Janus as the first great thoroughbred progenitor of the American Quarter Horse, a breed that now has more registered horses than any other in the world.

JEAN, the first dog to star in American films, was discovered in 1911 by Florence

Turner, Vitagraph's leading lady, when she saw actor-writer Larry Trimble playing with his collie outside the Vitagraph studios in Brooklyn. Miss Turner had found working with a Pomeranian difficult but Jeannie took direction like a pro and was put on the payroll at $25 a week. The dog also appeared with John Bunny, the first famous film comedian, in such pictures as *Bachelor Buttons* (1911). Trimble became a director, and nine years later, launched the career of STRONGHEART.

JENNIE, the Sealyham terrior in Maurice Sendak's *Higglety Pigglety Pop! or There Must Be More to Life* (1967), was discontented because she had everything. Packing her belongings in her black leather bag with gold buckles, she went off in search of something she did not have. She found that The World Mother Goose Theatre needed a leading lady with experience. Having no idea of what that was, she set out to get some. During her adventures, she ate a lot of food and pulled her head out of a lion's mouth just as it snapped shut. It caught only the tip of her beard. Jennie became the star of The World Mother Goose Theatre.

JENNIE BALDRIN, a scrawny tabby loose in London, taught PETER BROWN, a boy who had been transformed into a cat, how to act like one, in Paul Gallico's *The Abandoned* (1950). "When in doubt—wash," was Rule No. 1, "because it feels so good to be clean." While they were stowaways aboard a ship headed for her native Glasgow, Jennie continued the training, showing Peter how to change direction in midair, catch a mouse, kill a rat, and defend him-

self in practice bouts with her. " 'Soon,' she said with satisfaction, 'you'll be cat through and through.' "

JEOFFRY, the cat who belonged to Christopher Smart (1722–71), was the subject of a long tribute that may have been written while the poet was in an insane asylum:

For when he takes his prey he plays with it to give it a chance.
For one mouse in seven escapes by his dallying. . . .
For he keeps the Lord's watch in the night against the adversary.
For he counteracts the powers of darkness by his electrical skin and glaring eyes.
For he counteracts the Devil, who is death, by brisking about the life. . . .
For he is the quickest to his mark of any creature.
For he is tenacious of his point.
For he is a mixture of gravity and waggery. . . .
For he is good to think on, if a man would express himself neatly. . . .

JERRY MUSKRAT helped and was helped by GRANDFATHER FROG in the Thornton Burgess nature books. In *The Adventures of Jerry Muskrat* (1914), Jerry took the frog's advice after nearly losing his tail in one of Farmer Brown's boy's traps and learned to spring the traps. In *The Adventures of Grandfather Frog* (1915), Jerry slapped his tail in the water as a signal to Grandfather Frog that Whitetail the Marsh Hawk was approaching. The frog dived into the water just in time. The furious hawk whirled and swooped at the muskrat. "But Jerry just laughed in the most provoking way and ducked under water."

J. FRED MUGGS, a chimpanzee, helped save the "Today" show and made millions of dollars for NBC. He was 10 months old and in diapers when he joined the one-year-old show on February 2, 1953. The ratings immediately soared, attracting the additional sponsors that "Today" needed to survive. For four and a half years, the likable chimp cavorted around in a variety of costumes, bedeviled the star, Dave Garroway, and generally raised Cain.

During Queen Elizabeth's coronation in 1953, "Today" supplemented radio coverage of the ceremony with photographs, but interposed occasional live shots of Fred's antics. The British took such offense that it was discussed in the House of Commons, and the London stop on Fred's 1954 world tour was canceled. In the 1970s, Muggs entertained visitors to a Florida amusement park, and in 1975, he was taken back to New York, this time to ABC's morning show, to celebrate his twenty-third birthday. Not long after that, he was finally retired.

JIMMY SKUNK, in the Thornton Burgess nature books, just ambled along, poking under things to find beetles for his breakfast. In *The Adventures of Peter Cottontail* (1914), when he was tricked into jumping on top of REDDY FOX, who was dozing in the sun, Reddy accepted his apologies. He had very great respect for Jimmy Skunk. GRANNY FOX did not. In *The Adventures of Reddy Fox* (1913), she accused the skunk of eating the chicken she had stolen. The more he chuckled and denied it, the angrier she got but as he moved toward her, she backed away, into a bramble bush. "Jimmy Skunk just rolled over and over on the ground and shouted, he was so tickled."

JIMMY THE GROUNDHOG emerges from his burrow in Sun Prairie, Wisconsin, "Groundhog Capital of the World," at 7:00 A.M. on February 2 while adults toast his health with a concoction called Moose Milk and reporters hover. If he sees his shadow and goes back into his hole, there will be six more weeks of winter—probably. In the twenty-three years that the prognostications of five successive Jimmies have been recorded, the groundhog has been right eighteen times, which means he is batting .783 (see PUNXSUTAWNEY PHIL).

JINX, a "reckless swashbuckler" of a cat on Mr. Bean's farm, was the outspoken pal of FREDDY the pig in a series of animal adventures by Walter Brooks. Sitting on Mrs. Bean's lap while she read the newspaper to Mr. Bean, Jinx learned to read. By then teaching Freddy to read, the cat launched the pig's career. Inspired by Sherlock Holmes, Freddy took on his first case in *Freddy the Detective* (1932). When he admitted he was worried about solving it, Jinx said, "Sure you will, old pig, . . . Because *I'm* going to help you."

JIP (1), in Charles Dickens' *David Copperfield* (1850), was Dora Spenlow's little black spaniel. Wherever Dora was, there was Jip (for Gipsy), gnashing his teeth with jealousy and "barking madly." The first time David approached the dog, "he showed his whole set of teeth, got under a chair expressly to snarl, and wouldn't hear of the least familiarity." The sight of David's aunt gave Jip fits, once "to such a furious extent that he couldn't keep straight, but barked himself sideways." And when their friend Traddles came to dinner after Dora and David were married, the dog, as usual, walked on the table.

JIP (1)

David "began to think there was something disorderly in his being there at all, even if he had not been in the habit of putting his foot in the salt or the melted butter." But Jip stayed, barking at Traddles and making "short runs at his plate."

JIP (2), the dog in *The Story of Doctor Dolittle* (1920) by Hugh Lofting, had a fantastic nose that made him a hero on the voyage back from Africa with the Doctor. As they sailed along the Barbary Coast, Jip scented and described in his sleep six pirates, their dinner, and the brave man they were attacking 10 miles away. After

a whiff of the man's kerchief, redolent of snuff, Jip identified the brand—Black Rappee—and navigated by nose to a far-away island where the victim had been stranded.

JO-FI, a chow whom Sigmund Freud got to replace his short-lived first one, was his constant companion for seven years. Freud had not had much contact with animals until he was 70, when his daughter Anna acquired an Alsatian. He took an interest in the dog and, in 1928, was given his first chow. In December 1936, in a letter to Marie Bonaparte, who had written a book about her chow Topsy, Freud noted "the remarkable fact that one can love an animal like Topsy (or my Jo-fi) so deeply: affection without any ambivalence. . . . There is . . . a feeling of close relationship, of undeniably belonging together." Ten days later, after enduring more oral surgery, he wrote to her again: "Constant pain above all. . . . I wish you could have seen what sympathy Jo-fi shows me in my suffering, just as if she understood everything." The dog died suddenly in January and Freud immediately got another chow.

JOHN JOINER, the terrier in Beatrix Potter's *The Roly-Poly Pudding* (1908), was a busy carpenter. TABITHA TWITCHIT summoned him when her son TOM KITTEN was captured under the attic floor by the two rats SAMUEL WHISKERS and ANNA MARIA. They fled at the sound of the yelping dog sawing from above and the grateful cats invited John Joiner to stay for dinner. He declined because he had to finish a couple of hen coops.

JOHNNY CHUCK, in the Thornton Burgess nature books, pulled a fast one on REDDY FOX by telling him where PETER RABBIT (2) was sleeping. Reddy dashed off and slammed right into a hornets' nest. In *The Adventures of Johnny Chuck* (1913), the woodchuck decided to see the world. After winning a fight with the first Chuck he met, he was all set to fight the second, until she introduced herself as Miss Polly Chuck. They played peekaboo and fell in love. The naturally lazy Johnny was soon busy teaching danger signals to his three baby Chucks.

JOHNNY TOWN-MOUSE, in *The Tale of Johnny Town-Mouse* (1918) by Beatrix Potter, was giving an elegant dinner party when TIMMY WILLIE, a frightened country mouse, crashed into it, breaking three glasses, but the urbane host made the newcomer welcome. After Timmy Willie went home, Johnny Town-mouse paid a visit, carrying his tail over his arm to keep it out of the mud and jumping at the sound of a cow or a lawn mower. He went back to town as soon as possible. Country life was too quiet.

JOHN WESLEY WEASEL, in *The Book of the Dun Cow* (1978) by Walter Wangerin, Jr., raged when the invading basilisks killed his beloved Wee Widow Mouse and kept on fighting until he was so badly wounded that MUNDO CANI DOG carried him away. The battle ended when the dog and the monstrous serpent who had sent the basilisks were buried by an earthquake. John Wesley recovered but burrowed into his hole to mourn the Widow Mouse until someone remarked that only the bravest would try to rescue Mundo Cani. Shamed into surfacing, the weasel shouted at Chauntecleer the rooster, "Is more love in a Weasel than in a Rooster—proud, silly bird! . . . Is Double-u's what dig; but Roosters only flutter-gut about!"

JONI, a male chimpanzee, was raised by Nadia Kohts in her home in Moscow from 1913 to 1916 so that she could observe and test him from the age of 18 months to 4 years. When her son Roody was born in 1925, she made the same exhaustive study of his behavior until he was 4. Her report, *Infant Ape and Human Child* (1935), has been called a classic. Kohts found that Roody and the chimpanzee had traits in common, such as curiosity, the way they played, and some gestures—a hand extended forward to ask for something, face and head averted to reject food, and a tug at her dress to get attention. But even though he lived with humans, Joni made no attempt at vocal communication beyond making sounds to express emotions. Kohts concluded that this showed a qualitative difference between the intelligence of an ape and of a man.

JOSEPHINE (1) was a tame wild boar that Albert Schweitzer bought while he was in Africa and described in *The Animal World of Albert Schweitzer* (1950; translated and edited by Charles R. Joy). Neither pen nor harness could hold Josephine and when church services were held, she attended. "Fresh from the marsh, covered with black mire," she strolled through the open door and wandered around the benches, rubbing herself against the ladies' white skirts. Dr. Schweitzer praised her wisdom in avoiding gnats at night by sleeping under some boy's mosquito net in the dormitory, and in coming to the hospital to have sand fleas excised from her feet, but when she began killing hens, she was "expeditiously and artistically slaughtered." A short time later, a visiting official admired the smoked bacon he was served at lunch. Told it was wild boar, he recalled the one he brought up with a nursing bottle. It had been stolen, he said. It was Josephine.

JOSEPHINE (2), a black miniature poodle who belonged to Jacqueline Susann and her husband, Irving Mansfield, inspired Susann, an actress who had always intended to write, to produce her first book,

Every Night, Josephine! (1963). She always said it was her favorite.

JUDGE, the bear mascot of Baylor University in Waco, Texas, is usually a North American black bear and is replaced every two years because he gets too big and is hard to control. In 1969, Judge strangled on his chain while trying to climb a tree but cynics called it suicide because Baylor had just lost to LSU, 63–8. The mascot tradition began in the late 1920s when a bear was abandoned in town by a traveling circus. An enterprising student persuaded the president of Baylor to make the bear the school's official mascot and, in exchange for its care and feeding, to give him—the student—free tuition.

JUDY, the chimpanzee in the movie *Clarence the Cross-eyed Lion* (1965) and the subsequent television series "Daktari" (1966–69), was trained by Frank Lamping. Judy knew seventy-five signals, including the one for lunch. The chimpanzee was such a pro that, after lunch, she would return to her position on the set, ready to resume her scene.

JUMBO (1), the world's most famous elephant, was probably the largest one ever held in captivity. The London Zoological Gardens acquired him in 1865, and for seventeen years he was the delight of English children who took rides in a howdah on his back. When P. T. Barnum bought him in 1882 for $10,000, even Queen Victoria joined in the uproar over the loss of the popular pachyderm. Crated and shipped on the steamship *Assyrian Monarch*, Jumbo was soothed with beer during his fifteen-day crossing. In New

JUMBO (1)

York, he received a hero's welcome, hauled through the streets in a crate pulled by sixteen horses and pushed by two elephants.

Jumbo was about 11 feet tall at the shoulder and weighed 6½ tons. His daily diet was 200 pounds of hay, 3 bushels of oats and biscuits, 5 buckets of water, plus bread, onions, fruit, nuts, candy, and an occasional bottle of whisky. He could knock back a quart of it in one gulp. For three and a half years, until he was struck and killed by an unscheduled freight train in Canada, Jumbo was Barnum's greatest star. A million children rode on his back, and Jumbo products—hats, cigars, fans, etc.—flourished. His name came to mean anything of great size, including olives and shrimps. The word probably came from an eighteenth-century expression for a West African spirit, Mumbo Jumbo.

JUMBO (2), played by a female elephant named Rosie, was the title character of Billy Rose's *Jumbo* (1935), a musical comedy–circus extravaganza that was the last show staged at the Hippodrome in New York City. Leading the elephant on stage, co-star Jimmy Durante pointed to Jumbo's trunk and his own nose, saying, "Me and him's related." Durante's finest moment came when, trying to kidnap Jumbo, he was accosted by a tax collector who demanded, "Where are you going with that elephant?" Durante's bland reply: "What elephant?"

JUSTIN MORGAN, the only horse for whom a distinct new breed was named, was a prepotent little work horse of unknown lineage, whose unique combination of traits was inherited by his offspring and by their descendants. Originally named Figure, he was foaled in Massachusetts in 1793 and taken to Randolph Center, Vermont, two years later by Justin Morgan, a music teacher and innkeeper. The chunky bay stallion, only 14 hands high and weighing less than 1,000 pounds, soon showed exceptional intelligence, strength, and speed. Tireless at hauling logs, he was also said to have won every weight-pulling match, quarter-mile dash, and trotting race that he entered. At stud, he covered as many as twelve mares a day. After Morgan's death in 1798, a series of owners continued to work Figure hard and to breed him until, around 1821, he died of neglect after being kicked in the flank.

Twenty years later, a lot of fine little horses, nearly identical in appearance and stamina, began attracting attention in New England and New York. Their progenitors were all traced back to Vermont and, in 1842, the founding sire was identified as Figure. In 1857, D. C. Linsley, a Vermont farmer, published *The Morgan Horses*, in which he declared the Morgan horse a new breed and renamed its founder for his first known owner. Morgans became the most popular breed in the United States, serving as family horses, farm horses, runners, trotters, pacers, and military mounts. The American Saddle Horse, Standardbred, and Tennessee Walking Horse were developed in part from Morgans. In 1961, the Morgan horse was named the state animal of Vermont.

JUSTIN MORGAN

KAISER and MAX were Matthew Arnold's dogs in 1882, when he wrote "Poor Matthias," an elegy to his canary. In the poem, Arnold recalled other pets—ATOSSA the cat, GEIST the dachshund, and another dog—then mentioned his present ones:

> Max a dachshound without blot—
> Kaiser should be, but is not. . . .
> Kaiser with his collie face,
> Penitent for want of race.

Arnold, who was 60, added that he would probably not write a dirge for either of them because, with advancing age, "poet's fire gets faint and low." But in 1887, he wrote "Kaiser Dead," his last poem:

> Yes, Max and we grow slow and sad;
> But Kai, a tireless shepherd-lad,
> Teeming with plans, alert, and glad
>   In work or play,
> Like sunshine went and came, and bade
>   Live out the day!

KALA, in *Tarzan of the Apes* (1912) by Edgar Rice Burroughs, was the female ape in West Africa who, after losing her newborn, adopted the year-old orphan son of Lord and Lady Greystoke. She raised the infant and gave him the name Tarzan because, in the ape language that Burroughs invented, *tar* meant white, and *zan* meant skin.

KALA NAG, in Rudyard Kipling's "Toomai of the Elephants" from *The Jungle Book* (1894), was an old fighting elephant whose job was to subdue wild elephants rounded up by the Indian government. One night, after a faraway hoot from a wild elephant, Kala Nag broke free of his light rope. As he moved away, Little Toomai, the great-grandson of his first mahout, pleaded to be taken along. Swinging the boy up on his neck, Kala Nag slipped into the forest. He trudged over a hill, across a riverbed, and up the next hill. At the top, Kala Nag joined scores of elephants entering a moonlit clearing of several acres that had been "trampled down as hard as a brick floor." One elephant trumpeted, then they all did. The elephants began stamping their forefeet, "one-two, one-two, as steadily as trip hammers." The dull booming shook the ground until daybreak, when it stopped "as though the light had been an order." After Kala Nag shambled back to camp, men traced his tracks to find the clearing, freshly enlarged by the elephants' dance, 15 miles away.

KAMADHENU, "the cow of plenty" in Hindu mythology, emerged from the Churning of the Ocean and became the property of the sage Vasishta. Her power to grant his every wish enabled him to lavish hospitality on a visiting sage, Visvamitra, who promptly offered to buy the cow. Refused, he tried to drag her away but Kamadhenu broke free and conjured up an army of warriors to defend her and her master. Kamadhenu was also known as SURABHI, "the fragrant one," and was revered as the symbol of nature's abundance. The many cows she bore were regarded as the mothers of the world.

KANGA and ROO, the marsupial mother and son in A. A. Milne's *Winnie-the-Pooh* (1926), were not welcome when they first appeared but Christopher Robin intervened and the other animals made friends with them. Roo liked adventures and one day, when his mother kept him home in *The House at Pooh Corner* (1928), he asked about tomorrow. "We'll see," she said. "You're always seeing, and nothing ever happens," Roo said sadly.

KANTHAKA was the magnificent stallion that Gautama Buddha (ca. 563–483 B.C.), the founder of Buddhism, sent for when he decided at the age of 29 to renounce his luxurious life as Prince Siddhartha to seek enlightenment as an ascetic. The prince's father, King Suddhodana, ruled the Sakya people at Kapilavastu on the Nepalese border. Recalling how often his father rode the noble beast into battle, the prince spoke to Kanthaka as to a friend: "Lend me your strength and your speed; the world's salvation and your own is at stake." The king had surrounded the palace with guards to prevent his son's departure but Kanthaka moved so silently that no one was roused and the barred gates of the city opened soundlessly of their own accord. The prince rode a long distance through the moonlit night. At dawn, he dismounted and gave his jewels to his groom, Chandaka, to take back with Kanthaka to his father. The weeping groom implored Siddhartha to return to his family, and Kanthaka licked his feet. The prince stroked the horse, saying, "You have shown that you are a noble animal." Then Siddhartha cut off his hair and exchanged robes with a hunter whose coarse red garment was more suitable for a hermit. With a heavy heart, Chandaka took Kanthaka home.

KASHTANKA, the scrawny little red mongrel in Anton Chekhov's "Kashtanka" (1887), had been following her master, Luka Alexandritch, on his drinking rounds when the music of a military band "unhinged her nerves" and she got lost. The kind man who rescued her was a clown with an animal act involving a pig, a gander, and a cat. Although Kashtanka was troubled by dreams of old Luka and his mischievous son, she thrived with her new master, who fed her well and began teaching her tricks. Her bark of delight each time she accomplished one clearly showed talent, he said. When the gander died unexpectedly, Kashtanka was bundled off to the circus, where she performed well until the clown started to play a tune on his pipe. The dog "who could not endure music" howled, and a "cracked drunken tenor" called out, "It's Kashtanka!" She leaped off the stage to scramble up to Luka and his son—"the delicious dinners, the lessons, the circus, . . . now like a long-tangled, oppressive dream."

KASMIR (or KATMIR or KITMIR), the dog of the Seven Sleepers in Muslim lore, was one of the animals Mohammed admitted to Paradise. In a story similar to the Christian tale of the Seven Sleepers of Ephesus, but said to have come from a Hebrew legend, seven youths who believed in God fled persecution to hide in a cave. While they slept, the dog lay at the threshold, his paws outstretched. When the young men woke, one went into the city to buy food. After he returned, they all went back to sleep—for 309 years, according to the Koran (XVIII:10–26). During that time, the faithful dog kept his watch, neither eating nor drinking nor sleeping.

KASWA, Mohammed's favorite camel in Muslim legend, was awarded a place in heaven for carrying the Prophet from Jerusalem to Mecca in four bounds. In A.D. 622, Mohammed fled from Mecca. When he reached Kuba, on the outskirts of Medina, his camel knelt. The Prophet regarded the kneeling as a sign from God and stayed at Kuba for four days. A mosque was later built to cover the spot where Kaswa knelt.

KEEPER, the bull mastiff that 19-year-old Emily Brontë drew "from life" in 1838, had

been given to her father, but she was the only one who could control the dog. To break his early habit of sneaking upstairs in the daytime to sprawl on the beds, Emily dragged him down the stairs one day, pushed him into a corner, and before he could spring at her, punched him in the eyes with her bare fists. Then, with swollen hands, she bathed his swollen head. Keeper adored her. A few years later, Emily was told that he had gotten into a fight with another large dog. Rushing to the scene with a box of pepper, she found they had each other by the throat. Several men stood watching, but the frail Miss Brontë waded in, grabbing Keeper with one hand while she peppered the noses of both dogs. That separated them.

Emily Brontë died in 1848. Her father and Keeper followed the coffin to the church for the funeral and, at Mr. Brontë's wish, the dog proceeded inside to the family pew for the service. For weeks afterward, Keeper stationed himself at the door of Emily's room and howled.

KELLY, the hound with the pince-nez and the pipe in George Herriman's comic strip *Krazy Kat,* baked the bricks that IGNATZ MOUSE heaved at KRAZY KAT. He taught Ignatz how to throw a curve, even with a brick: "Y'can put a coive in anything y'can toss—it's the 'ARM.' "

KELSO, America's greatest gelding, raced for seven years, won thirty-nine of his sixty-three starts, and was named Horse of the Year five times, from 1960 through 1964. The big brown-bay Thoroughbred, an inch over 16 hands high, won at distances from 6 furlongs to 2 miles on turf or dirt at twelve different tracks. When he

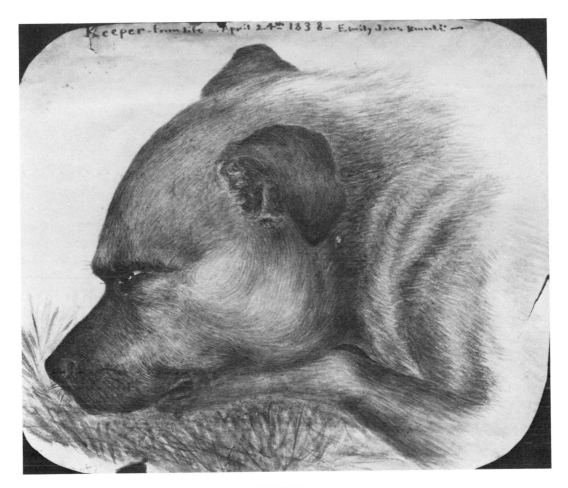

Keeper from life — April 24th 1838 — Emily Jane Brontë —

KEEPER

began his great stretch runs, the crowd would chant, "Kelly! Kelly!" but at Aqueduct on October 31, 1964, there was a sudden silence as he caught the leader at the quarter pole. Then 51,000 people started clapping in time to his stride as Kelso came on to win his fifth Jockey Club Gold Cup in the record time of 3 minutes, 19 1/5 seconds for the 2-mile race. And on November 11, he finally won the Washington, D.C., International, after

coming in second three years in a row. Kelso was retired in 1966 at the age of 9, with record earnings of $1,977,896.

KERMIT, the frog created by Jim Henson in 1956, became a star when "The Muppet Show" made its debut twenty years later. By 1979, the show was the most popular television entertainment in the world, seen by 235 million viewers in 102 countries.

Worked by Henson, the puppet Kermit is the enthusiastic M.C. who introduces the show and keeps it moving through a minefield of zany creatures. The spindly-legged green frog is also a love object. MISS PIGGY wants him, in marriage, to be the daddy of a little "pog," but he winces at the prospect of a parade of "bouncing baby figs." In *The Muppet Movie* (1979), Kermit leaves his Georgia swamp to head for Hollywood, hotly pursued by the owner of a fast-food chain featuring fried frogs' legs, and by Miss Piggy, aflame with other consuming desires. Whatever happens, Kermit is philosophical: "There are two openings in life for a frog. He can go into show business— or wind up on a plate. It isn't easy being green."

KICHE, the she-wolf who lured sled dogs to her ravenous wolf pack in *White Fang* (1906) by Jack London, was half dog herself, whelped by an Indian's dog. A year after running away to join the wolves during a famine, Kiche whelped WHITE FANG, who was still a puppy when they were separated. The next time he saw her, "she met him with shrewd fangs that laid his cheek open to the bone." Kiche had a new litter and no memory of White Fang.

KICKUMS, in R. D. Blackmore's *Lorna Doone* (1869), was a mean horse who lost the use of an eye in the beating John Ridd gave him for biting Ruth Hackabuck. But Ridd used "good Kickums" to search for his brother-in-law, Tom Faggus, among the Duke of Monmouth's rebels. The horse was "worth ten sweet-tempered horses, to a man who knew how to manage him." Kickums also snored and had to be wakened on the second morning of the journey.

After Faggus was found wounded and sent home tied to his mare WINNIE, Ridd was detained by the Royalists. And since "man might go his way and be hanged, rather than horse would meet hardship," Kickums headed back to his barn.

KIKI-LA-DOUCETTE, a male Angora cat, and TOBY-CHIEN, a French bulldog, are the interlocutors in *Dialogues de bêtes* (1904), the first book by "Colette Willy." In real life, the two animals were companions for Colette during her marriage to Henri Gauthier-Villars, who collaborated with her on the *Claudine* novels and signed them with his pen name, Willy. In the dialogues, the cat and dog reveal not only themselves but also "He" and "She," with whom they live. "The Cat is a guest and not a plaything," says Kiki, comparing Toby's exuberant devotion to Her with his own "secret and shy and deep" understanding with Him. "Try to imitate my serenity," the cat tells Toby, but when they are shut in a room, Kiki talks of a bone and a bitch to torment the dog into howling until they are freed. When Kiki is let out of his basket in a train compartment, He and She cannot talk him back into the basket, but before either He or She can touch him, Kiki arches his back, yawns, and saunters over to lie in it "with a calm deliberation so insolent as to compel admiration."

KILKENNY CATS, according to legend, kept fighting until only their tails were left. The legend may have been an allegory for the 300 years of squabbling that began late in the fourteenth century between the town of Kilkenny and the adjacent Irishtown. Another source for the legend was a story about some Hessian soldiers in

Kilkenny during the rebellions of 1798 or 1803. They were said to have tied two cats together by the tail for the fun of it, then hung them over a line to fight. Another soldier freed the cats by cutting off their tails. The cats fled as an officer arrived and the soldier, still holding the tails, coolly explained that the cats had devoured each other, except for the tails. Or the legend may have been invented by J. P. Curran, an Irish politician who died in 1817. In a sarcastic protest against cockfighting in England, Curran claimed that he had seen trained cats in Ireland fight so fiercely that all that was left were their tails. Whatever its origin, the legend lives on in the expression, "fight like Kilkenny cats."

KING KONG, a 50-foot gorilla, was perched on the top of the Empire State Building, swatting at navy biplanes, in the climactic scene of *King Kong* (1933), a movie conceived by Merion C. Cooper, an explorer and documentary filmmaker, with help from the mystery writer Edgar Wallace. At the start of the film, King Kong was terrorizing the natives of an island in the Indian Ocean when a group of American movie people arrived. Fascinated by the group's lone woman, Ann (Fay Wray), the gorilla carried her away, cradled in one hand while he fought off prehistoric monsters. Ann escaped and Kong was captured. Taken to New York City to be exhibited in a theater, he broke free in a rage, convinced that Ann was being attacked. When he found her, he headed for the city's highest point, the tower of the Empire State Building. Gently placing Ann on a ledge, King Kong tried to bat away the oncoming planes but the pilots opened fire and he toppled to the ground. The film-maker who had brought him to the city gazed at the dead gorilla and said, "It wasn't the airplanes. It was Beauty killed the Beast."

The movie's special effects were created by Willis O'Brien, who manipulated an 18-inch model of Kong on miniature sets for frame-by-frame shots of his movements. Superimposed images established the relative sizes of man and beast. For close-ups, a huge head with eyes as big as soccer balls was used, as well as a massive foot to show stomping, and a giant paw in which Fay Wray screamed. *King Kong* inspired several sequels and imitations and, in 1976, was remade in color by Italian producer Dino De Laurentiis. But even with jet fighters buzzing Kong astride the twin towers of the World Trade Center, the new version could not surpass the original.

KING LOUIE OF THE APES was created by Walt Disney Productions for *The Jungle Book* (1967), an animated feature based on Rudyard Kipling's stories. His ambition is to act like a human being, and with his voice provided by bandleader Louis Prima, he walks and talks in Dixieland style.

KING TIMAHOE, an Irish setter puppy, was presented to President Richard Nixon by his New York campaign staff in January 1969. The President named him for "the little village in Ireland where my mother's Quaker ancestors came from," and added the title because "even a President's dog gets the royal treatment." While he was still a puppy, Tim chased deer at Camp David with such zest that he once ran headfirst into a tree. At the White House,

Nixon liked to have his dog with him. Tim would sit in the Oval Office with his muzzle propped on the President's top right desk drawer, which held a supply of dog biscuits. One time, the dog started chewing the rug while the President was conferring with national security adviser Henry Kissinger. Instead of rebuking Tim, Nixon gave him some biscuits, which inspired Kissinger to remark, "Ah, Mr. President, I see you are *teaching* your dog to chew the rug."

KING TUT, a police dog, was acquired by Herbert Hoover in 1917, when he was organizing war relief in Belgium. In 1928, a widely circulated photograph of Hoover holding the dog and smiling was credited with helping his presidential campaign by revealing a warmth that his public manner belied. At the White House, King Tut became a self-appointed sentry, patrolling the grounds nightly in all weather to check fences, gates, and guards. He fetched the President's newspaper during the day and, if Hoover was outdoors, King Tut sat on the sections that had been read to keep them from blowing away. The dog rarely slept. When the President tried to keep him indoors at night, King Tut barked until he was let out to resume his rounds. In his old age, the dog turned mean and since muzzling made him worse, he was removed to the Hoovers' house on S Street, where he soon died.

KITTIWYNK, in Rudyard Kipling's "The Maltese Cat" from *The Day's Work* (1898), was the lone mare among the twelve polo ponies for the Skidars' team. She felt "undersized and unhappy" about playing against the opponents' larger and fresher ponies but performed smartly in the first chukker, following the ball "as a cat follows a mouse." The Skidars had a two-goal lead when she went in for the second time, for the fourth chukker (of six). At the end of the period, "Kittiwynk and the others came back with the sweat dripping over their hoofs and their tails telling sad stories." The opposing team had scored.

KOKO, the first gorilla to learn sign language, was a year old in July 1972, when Dr. Francine ("Penny") Patterson, then a graduate student in psychology at Stanford University, began teaching her the hand signs of the American Sign Language for the deaf. Although chimpanzees, starting with WASHOE in 1966, were the first apes trained to use a visual language, Koko confirmed the belief of some primatologists that gorillas match if not surpass chimpanzees in intelligence. By 1979, Koko had acquired over 400 signs and, according to Dr. Patterson, was using them—with more sense than syntax—to refer to the past or future, to argue, to joke, even to lie. Caught chewing a red crayon, for example, Koko quickly signed *lip* and moved the crayon across the outside of her mouth like a lipstick. She also began learning the sounds of words by punching symbols on the keyboard of a speech synthesizer—and by eavesdropping. The word c-a-n-d-y had to be spelled out in her presence. In 1976, a young male gorilla, Michael, moved in to share her trailer and Koko began teaching him signs, notably *Koko* and *tickle*. When a reporter once asked what sort of person Koko was, Dr. Patterson signed to her, "Are you an animal or a person?" Koko immediately replied, "Fine animal gorilla."

KOSHIN

KOSHIN is the collective name for the Three Wise Monkeys of Japan: Mizaru, "see no evil"; Kikazaru, "hear no evil"; and Iwazaru, "speak no evil." It is said that the legendary monkeys striking their poses, to convey the command of the Buddhist god Vadjra, originated in China and that the Tendai sect introduced them into Japan around the eighth century A.D. Little statues of the trio holding their hands over their eyes, ears, and mouths have been widely reproduced ever since.

KRAZY KAT sashayed around Coconino County with a tiny parasol, longing to be beaned by a brick hurled by IGNATZ MOUSE, in George Herriman's comic strip *Krazy Kat* (1913–44). Sketchily drawn with a scratchy pen, the strip was a surrealistic vaudeville with flying bricks and mangled words. A cat-mouse-dog triangle informs what plot there is. Krazy, sometimes referred to as "he," was in love with Ignatz. OFFISA BULL PUPP loved Krazy and incarcerated Ignatz when he could. Ignatz loved to "Krease that Kat's bean with a brick," but conspired with Krazy to thwart Offisa Pupp. When Krazy chased Ignatz into his hole during a "relapse" of atavism, she apologized, "I can't help it, dollin'—rilly, I can't." When she carried a picket sign calling Ignatz unfair, did it mean that he had thrown his last brick? No, she bawled, "His foist miss."

Krazy Kat was not widely syndicated but is still admired; some call it the greatest comic strip of all. It inspired several animated cartoons, a full-length ballet by John Alden Carpenter in 1922, and remarkable praise from critic Gilbert Seldes in *The Seven Lively Arts* (1924). A collection of strips, with an affectionate introduction by e. e. cummings, was republished in 1964.

KUHAYLAH, in Arab legend, was a wild mare that Ishmael saw while hunting. Thinking it was an antelope, he prepared to shoot it with an arrow. The angel Jabrail (Gabriel) stopped him, saying the beautiful animal was a gift from Allah that would become a great treasure to the Arab people, whom Ishmael would father. In time, the mare foaled. The newborn colt was placed in a saddlebag while Ishmael and his tribe crossed the desert. When he lifted out the foal, it appeared to be deformed. The camel's jogging had twisted its spine. This is the legendary reason why many Arabian horses have, in fact, fewer vertebrae than other horses. Ishmael wanted to destroy the colt. Again, the angel stopped him. When the colt matured, he was bred back to his mother and, according to legend, all Arabian horses are descended from them.

KUNTZE, a little spaniel, advanced the cause of Dutch independence by saving the life of Prince William of Orange, who led the fight for it. When the Spaniards attacked on the night of September 11,

1572, the dog, who had been sleeping at his master's feet, had to bark at the prince and scratch his face to wake him up. William escaped and from then on, he always kept a little spaniel in his bedroom. Several statues of the prince, including the one on his tomb, have a small dog at his feet.

KURMA, Vishnu's second avatar in Hindu mythology, was the tortoise that Vishnu turned into when he ordered the Churning of the Ocean for the purpose of restoring the strength of the gods. Telling them that Mount Mandara would be the churning stick with Vasuki the serpent coiled around it as the spinning rope, Vishnu then took the form of Kurma and descended to the bottom of the Milky Ocean. There, the tortoise's back both supported the mountain and served as the pivot on which it spun.

KYRAT, a chestnut horse of "wondrous speed" in Henry Wadsworth Longfellow's "The Leap of Roushan Beg" (1877), saved Roushan Beg, the bandit known as Kurruglou, when he was alone and lost north of Koordistan. Pursued by Reyhan the Arab and a hundred men, the bandit raced Kyrat up a mountain path that ended suddenly at a precipice overlooking a torrential river. The ravine was 30 feet wide. Hugging and kissing the horse, Roushan Beg implored him to jump across. Kyrat drew his feet together, eyed the space, then leaped:

> And the shadow that he cast
> Leaped the cataract underneath.

LABES is a family dog in Aristophanes' *Wasps*, first produced in 422 B.C. In the play, the elderly Philokleon has become a fanatic about jury service after having retired and turned over the management of his property to his son Bdelykleon. To keep his father from spending all his time on juries, Bdelykleon persuades him to conduct a court at home. As the appropriate setting is prepared, a servant announces that Labes has just rushed into the kitchen, snatched a whole Sicilian cheese, and devoured it. Philokleon is ready to convict at once but his son, insisting on a trial, defends the dog as the best they have, capable of guarding a whole flock, etc.: "Forgive his larceny! He is wretchedly ignorant, he cannot play the lyre. . . . Take pity on the unfortunate!" He even summons Labes' puppies to whine and beg. Philokleon admits his anger is cooling and Bdelykleon tricks him into acquitting the dog.

LAD, the thoroughbred collie in Albert Payson Terhune's *LAD: A Dog* (1919), had the "gay courage of a d'Artagnan,"

an "uncanny wisdom," and a soul. At home in New Jersey, he slept in his "cave" under the piano, treed a prowler, caught a burglar, and saved two children, one from a snake, the other from a fire. He stopped the charge of a crazed bull by leaping over its horns onto its back. Trained to "absolute obedience," Lad silently tracked a sheep-killer through two miles of woods, but he was a "furry martyr" when he was groomed for the Westminster Kennel Club show. Accidentally lost in New York City, where he had been muzzled in accordance with the law, the "superdog" made his way to the Hudson River, swam across, and was attacked by a mongrel. When the mongrel chewed through the straps of Lad's muzzle, he faced "not a helpless dog but a maniac wolf" and fled, howling. Most of Lad's adventures, said Terhune, actually happened to his collie, Sunnybank Lad, who lived sixteen years, "gallant of spirit, mighty of heart."

LADDIE BOY, formally named Caswell Laddie Boy, was the first gift Warren G.

Harding received after he became President in 1921. The Airedale puppy grew into a handsome dog and Harding adored him. Laddie Boy delivered the morning paper to the President, fetched lost balls on the golf course, and was trained to sit in his own chair at Cabinet meetings.

After the death of President Harding in San Francisco, his widow returned to Washington and on August 18, 1923, the *New York Times* ran the headline: "Mrs. Harding Quietly Leaves White House; Laddie Boy Greets Coolidge Warmly." In tribute to Harding, who had been a newspaper publisher, newsboys all over the country donated pennies for a statuette of Laddie Boy to be presented to Mrs. Harding. She died before the statue was made; it is now at the Smithsonian Institution.

LADDIE BUCK, a half-brother of President Harding's LADDIE BOY, was presented to President Calvin Coolidge shortly after he succeeded to office in 1923. Mrs. Coolidge renamed the dog Paul Pry because he was always sniffing around. Unfortunately, the Airedale turned mean, he bit Mrs. Coolidge's maid, and was banished to a Marine Corps detachment.

LADY (1) is a "brach" or bitch hound mentioned by Hotspur in Shakespeare's *Henry IV, Part One* (1598). In act 3, scene 1, Hotspur and his wife, Kate, are at a castle in Wales where Kate's sister-in-law is about to sing. Kate tells her husband, "Lie still, ye thief, and hear the lady sing in Welsh." Hotspur replies, "I had rather hear Lady my brach howl in Irish."

LADY (2), in Walt Disney Productions' *Lady and the Tramp* (1955), the first animated feature in CinemaScope, was a pretty cocker spaniel whose placid life with Jim Dear and his wife was disrupted when Aunt Sarah arrived to take care of their baby. Aunt Sarah's Siamese cats got Lady blamed for their vandalism and she was muzzled. TRAMP, the raffish mutt who loved Lady, persuaded a beaver to chew off the muzzle, then took her along on a chicken raid. She alone got caught. After other inmates of the pound told her what a rogue Tramp was, Lady would have nothing to do with him, until she had to implore him to save the baby from a rat. Tramp became a hero and she, the mother of his puppies.

LADY JANE, a large gray cat in Charles Dickens' *Bleak House* (1853), belonged to Mr. Krook, the strange proprietor of the Rag and Bottle Shop. She sat on his shoulder, "her tail sticking up on one side of his hairy cap like a tall feather." At his command, Lady Jane ripped at a bundle of rags with her claws, making a sound to set teeth on edge. Miss Flite, an upstairs lodger who kept at least twenty caged birds in her room, said that she could not air the place because the cat crouched on the parapet outside for hours, "greedy for their lives." A visitor to the other lodger, an old man, found him dead in his room. Krook appeared and sent for a doctor. "Don't leave the cat there!" said the surgeon; "that won't do!" Krook drove Lady Jane out and she went "furtively down-stairs, winding her lithe tail and licking her lips."

LADY MAUD, a pedigreed Jersey cow, was exhibited at the Philadelphia Centennial Exposition in 1876. Having obtained exclusive rights to reproduce her likeness,

John Dwight & Company began selling their baking soda (sodium bicarbonate) with Lady Maud's picture on the label. Customers started asking for "the soda with the cow on the package," the product was soon called "Cow Brand," and it still is. Church & Dwight Company, Inc.—the result of a merger in 1896—continues to sell it, chiefly in Canada.

LAIKA, also known as Kudryavka (Curly) and Limonchik (Little Lemon), was the first living creature to orbit the earth. The 11-pound Samoyed husky bitch was launched in Sputnik II on November 3, 1957, a month after the beginning of the Space Age, when the Soviet Union's Sputnik I became the first man-made object in orbit.

Conditioned to confinement, the little dog was strapped into an air-conditioned chamber with a food supply suspended in gelatin. Her body was wired with sensors connected to radio transmitters so that scientists 1,050 miles away could monitor her pulse, respiration, and movements to learn about life in space. Laika adapted to weightlessness with no apparent ill effect. Reentry and recovery were not feasible for this pioneer flight, however, so when the oxygen supply gave out after ten days, she died.

LANA was the first of several chimpanzees trained at the Yerkes Primate Research Center in Atlanta to write and read Yerkish, a language of words represented by abstract symbols that appear on a computer keyboard and are projected on a screen when the keys are pressed. Psychologist Duane Rumbaugh of Georgia State University first taught her nouns by rewarding her. When she pressed the symbol

for candy, she got candy. She learned to put *please* before the noun and a period after it, to use verbs like *give* and *open*, and to read unfinished sentences like *"Please machine open . . ."* that she then completed, in this case, with *window*. In 1975, after three years of training, Lana had a vocabulary of 120 words that she could arrange in declarative and interrogatory sentences. The latter were mostly about refreshments, including twenty-three different ways of asking for a cup of coffee. Without claiming that Lana and her successors have mastered syntax, Rumbaugh has said that their accomplishments may provide a useful approach to the learning problems of mentally retarded children.

LANGBOURNE was the favorite cat of Jeremy Bentham (1748–1832), the English philosopher who shunned general society as a waste of time but honored his pet, advancing him in rank to "Sir John Langbourne," then to "The Reverend Sir John Langbourne, D.D."

LAN LAN, a female giant panda, and a male, Kan Kan, were presented to the Japanese people in 1972 by the Chinese government to celebrate the normalization of relations between their two countries. The pandas became an adored national treasure. In seven years, 32 million people lined up to see and photograph them at Tokyo's Ueno Zoo. Lan Lan was 10 years old when she was stricken with a kidney disorder in August 1979. As she neared death, hourly reports of her condition were broadcast to the nation. The zoo was swamped with inquiries, and thousands of visitors filed past her empty cage. When Prime Minister Masayoshi Ohira spoke of her, his voice broke. Lan Lan died on September 4. The autopsy revealed that she was pregnant. Had she lived one more month, she might have given birth to the first giant panda born in captivity outside of China. (See YUANJING.)

LARIDON, in *"L'Education"* from the *Fables* of Jean de La Fontaine (1621–95), is a descendant of famous hounds. His brother CAESAR (1), raised by a different master, becomes a great hunter and is carefully bred to preserve his strain. But Laridon grows up in a kitchen, mating with any bitch who passes by. France is populated with his turnspits, cowering dogs that have no resemblance to Caesar. A good breed degenerates with neglect and time, La Fontaine writes. When nature's gifts are not cultivated, how many Caesars become Laridons?

LASSIE (1), the faithful Yorkshire collie in Eric Knight's short story "Lassie Come Home" (1938), met young Joe at the school gate every day for four years until the boy's father had to sell the dog when the family went on the dole. Taken to the north of Scotland, 400 miles away, Lassie escaped in late summer and resolutely headed south. She was injured and mistreated during her trek, but after covering 1,000 miles, she finally plowed through a snowstorm to return to her station at the school gate.

The story appeared in *The Saturday Evening Post* and was so popular that Knight expanded it into a book. Published in 1940, it was soon available in twenty-five languages. With *Lassie Come Home* (1943), the movie based on the book, and seven film sequels as well as both a radio and television series, the fictitious female collie inspired a male dynasty of real ones (see LASSIE [2]).

LASSIE (2), the collie in *Lassie Come Home* (1943), the movie based on Eric Knight's book (see LASSIE [1]), was a male named Pal who replaced the female intended for the part when she began losing her coat during summer filming. Trained by Rudd Weatherwax, Lassie-Pal inspired one reviewer to call him "a Greer Garson in furs." He starred in six more Lassie pictures, and barked, whined, and growled on "The Lassie Radio Show." From 1954 to 1973, males from four generations of his descendants appeared in the Lassie television series, and in 1978, a sixth-generation male starred in the film *The Magic of Lassie.*

LASSIE (2)
From Lassie Come Home *(1943)*
© *Loew's Inc. Ren. 1970 MGM*

LELAPS

LAUGHING GRAVY, in the two-reeler *Laughing Gravy* (1931), was a little mutt that Stan Laurel and Oliver Hardy had to hide from their landlord, who did not allow dogs. When Laurel got the hiccups, the dog started barking and the boys put him out on the roof in a snowstorm. One catastrophe after another occurred as Laurel and Hardy tried to fool their landlord and rescue Gravy. Out in the cold, the dog had a high old time, wagging his tail at every mishap.

LELAPS, an infallible hound in Greek mythology, was destined by Zeus to catch whatever he chased. The dog came into the possession of Procris, a beautiful nymph who gave him to her husband, Cephalus, a hunter. After a series of misunderstandings, Cephalus unwittingly killed Procris. (In a painting inspired by the tale, *The Death of Procris* by Piero di Cosimo [1462–1521], Cephalus is shown kneeling at the nymph's head while Lelaps, a big red dog,

sits forlornly at her feet.) Cephalus later set the hound after a Teumessian vixen, which had been destined by Hera never to be caught. The chase could have lasted forever, but Zeus resolved the impasse by turning both animals to stone.

LEO, the trademark lion for Metro-Goldwyn-Mayer, was inherited from Goldwyn Pictures, one of the three companies that formed the corporation in 1924. A few years earlier, when Sam Goldwyn asked the advertising agency promoting his company to create a trademark, young Howard Dietz, fresh from Columbia College, proposed the lion; he got the idea from the laughing lion decoration of the college magazine *The Jester.* Dietz also suggested the motto *Ars Gratia Artis* ("Art for Art's Sake") for the loop of film around the lion's head. Of the many lions who have played Leo, Slats was the first, JACKIE (2) starred for M-G-M, and Tanner was the first seen in Technicolor. Leo's roar was heard for the first time in *White Shadows in the South Seas* (1928), M-G-M's first movie with sound effects and one dubbed word of dialogue—"Hello."

LEONCICO, Vasco Nuñez de Balboa's yellow hound, accompanied his master across the Isthmus of Panama to the Pacific in September 1513. He was such a great fighter, it was said, that he drew the pay of a crossbowman.

LEXINGTON, a direct male-line descendant of DIOMED, was the greatest Thoroughbred foaled in the United States in the nineteenth century. The Kentucky-bred horse was called Darley for his first two races in 1853, which he won, then was renamed for the town where the track was, by his new owner, Richard Ten Broeck. Lexington ran only seven races, in 4-mile heats, and won six of them. In 1855, racing the clock, he set a new record for 4 miles, 7:19¾. Twelve days later, in a rematch with the only horse who ever beat him, his half-brother Lecomte, Lexington won easily. It was his last race. He was going blind. Ten Broeck sold him to Woodburn Farm in Kentucky, then the world's biggest stud farm. Lexington became one of the greatest sires of winners in racing history —236 of his 600 foals. "The Blind Hero of Woodburn" died in 1875.

LILLIAN, in Damon Runyon's "Lillian" from *Guys and Dolls* (1931), was a scrawny black kitten that Wilbur Willard found in the snow one morning and took home to his hotel on Eighth Avenue. She grew up to follow him "like a pooch" on his drinking rounds and even to hunt pooches, once carrying a Peke home by the scruff of the neck. She also took to playing with a little boy in the hotel. When the hotel caught fire one morning, Wilbur brought Lillian out but she raced back in. He went after her, the two of them appeared on the roof with the boy, and they all jumped into the safety net. After Wilbur gave up drinking, he decided to "expose Lillian." She was no hero. She was a "rum-pot." He had been lacing her milk with Scotch from the time she was a kitten. The first time he went in for her, he forgot to "Scotch her up," and she ran back in because she was "looking for her shot." The two of them stumbled on the kid by chance.

LINCOLN'S DOCTOR'S DOG would be a sure-fire subject for a best-selling book, according to George Stevens in *Lincoln's Doctor's Dog* (1939), a survey of best-sellers of the 1930s. Stevens, editor of the *Saturday Review of Literature*, cited a story going around the trade that since all books on Lincoln sell, all books by doctors sell, and all books about dogs sell, "the man who writes a book about Lincoln's doctor's dog is going to clean up." In *80 Years of Best Sellers: 1895–1975* (1977), Alice Payne Hackett suggested that the old formula for the best-seller be revised to suit more recent developments in publishing: "*Lincoln's Doctor's Dog's Favorite Recipes for Beginners* might just do the trick."

THE LION OF LUCERNE (LOWENDEN-KMAL) is carved in deep relief, high on the wall of a natural grotto that was discovered when geologists excavated a moraine at the site now called the Glacier Gardens. The dying lion, his head on a shield and with a broken spear sticking out

THE LION OF LUCERNE

of his ribs, is a memorial to the Swiss Guards who fought and died to a man defending King Louis XVI during the French Revolution, when a mob stormed the Tuileries on August 10, 1792. The heroic figure, over 42 feet long, was designed by Danish sculptor Bertel Thorvaldsen and, in 1821, was carved out of the sandstone surface by Lucas Ahorn. Mark Twain called it "the saddest, most poignant piece of rock in the world."

LITTLE BROWNIE, in *The Wonderful Adventures of Paul Bunyan*, "retold" by Louis Untermeyer (1945), was such a small heifer when Paul Bunyan got her to keep company with BABE the Blue Ox that one lick from Babe's tongue could knock her down. Paul built a barn to shelter her but she remained puny until the camp cook fed her a mixture of buffalo milk and whale milk, with a little rattlesnake oil thrown in for strength. That made her grow overnight. Next morning, the loggers found her miles away with what was left of the barn on her huge shoulders like a tattered coat. Little Brownie grew into the greatest milk cow in the world. It took twenty men to milk her and another ten to skim the cream. And she was always hungry. After she gorged herself on pine needles and balsam boughs, her next day's milk was undrink-able, so Paul bottled it as "Little Brownie's Pine and Balsam Cough Syrup," and used the cream for axle grease.

LITTLE DIAMOND, born on March 2, 1978, at the Knoxville Zoological Park in Tennessee, was the first African elephant foaled in captivity in the Western Hemis-phere. She was less than 3 feet tall, weighed 200 pounds, and her oversized ears looked like cabbage leaves. As a precaution against stress for mother and baby, the zoo was closed for the weekend.

Her mother, Toto, 16, was on breeding loan from the Bronx Zoo. Her father Diamond, 28, the largest African elephant in captivity, had been donated to the zoo in 1960 by the Ringling Brothers and Barnum & Bailey Circus. Old Diamond was productive. On May 16, 1978, his second mate, Sapphire, gave birth to Hilary.

THE LITTLE GENTLEMAN IN VELVET was what the Jacobites called the mole that raised the molehill that tripped the horse of William III of England, successor to James II. The king fell, broke his collar-bone, and on May 8, 1702, he died from the combined effects of his injury and a chill. During the reign of Queen Anne, who succeeded William, the Jacobites, who sought to restore the Stuart line to the throne, often raised a glass to "the little gentleman in velvet."

LITTLE JOE OTTER, in *The Adventures of Buster Bear* (1916) by Thornton Burgess, tried to keep BUSTER BEAR from catching trout in the Laughing Brook and was in-censed when the bear outwitted him. Little Joe thought the fish belonged to him.

GRANDFATHER FROG advised the otter to make friends with those who are bigger, smarter, and stronger. When Little Joe calmed down, he accepted the idea and set out a trout as a peace offering to the bear.

LITTLE SORREL, a small gelding, was chosen by Gen. Thomas J. ("Stonewall") Jackson as his mount in the spring of 1861 at Harpers Ferry, when his troops seized a train that included a carload of horses intended for the federal cavalry. For the next two years, Jackson rode the sturdy little horse almost exclusively. On the afternoon of May 2, 1863, the general moved his men to within earshot of the Union troops at Chancellorsville, Virginia. As darkness fell, he rode Little Sorrel into the woods to reconnoiter. By mistake, his own troops fired at him, hitting his right hand and shattering his left arm. The terri-fied horse bolted toward the enemy. Jack-son managed to turn Little Sorrel around, but could not stop him. Two staff officers galloped after them to catch the runaway. Eight days later, Jackson died. Little Sorrel was sent to the general's family and died in 1886. His stuffed hide is on display at the Virginia Military Institute in Lexington.

LOBO, the "King of Currumpaw," led a small pack of wolves that ravaged live-stock in northeastern New Mexico for five years, reportedly slaughtering over 2,000 animals by 1893. Ernest Thompson Seton was invited to try to catch him after several hunters, attracted by the $1,000 bounty, had failed. In *Wild Animals I Have Known* (1898), Seton reported that his first move was to cover his own scent with the blood of a freshly killed heifer and then to bait a trail with bags of meat containing odorless poison capsules. The wolf dragged three of the bags over to a fourth one and defecated on them. Seton then buried traps. Lobo exposed over a dozen by scratching away the earth.

The wolf was finally undone when his mate, Blanca, was killed. Reasoning that Lobo would keep on looking for her, Seton dragged Blanca's body around his camp, buried 100 steel traps in sets of four, and made prints near them with one of her paws. Two days later, the Currumpaw Wolf was found, securely trapped. "Poor old hero, he had never ceased to search for his darling." Carried back to camp and chained in the pasture with meat and water nearby, Lobo just lay there, staring across the prairie. Next morning, he was found in the same position, dead.

LOCO was Pancho's horse in the radio and television series "The Cisco Kid" (see DIABLO).

LOLA, Henny Jutzler-Kindermann's "talking dog," was sired by Rolf, the famous Airedale terrier of Mannheim, who, having allegedly mastered arithmetic and the alphabet (using numbers for letters), would tap out sums and words with his paw (see CLEVER HANS). Rolf was said to have given warning of the Mannheim earthquake in 1912 and to have replied to a woman asking what she could do for him, "Wag your tail." In similar fashion, Lola forecast weather and, after dallying in the woods, correctly predicted the number of puppies she would have. She declined to explain how she knew so much, saying only that, like magicians, dogs had sworn not to reveal their secrets. Reports of such talking by Lola, Rolf, and an "unbearable"

dachshund named Kurwenal prompted Graham Greene to comment in his essay "Great Dog of Weimar" (1940) that dogs, "solid, well-meaning, reliable, . . . seem to possess all the least attractive human virtues. What bores, I have sometimes thought, if they could speak, and now my most appalling conjectures have been confirmed."

LOOTIE, a fawn and white Pekingese, was the first of her breed to be taken to the West, according to *The Butterfly Lions* (1977), Rumer Godden's history of the "lion dogs," as they were called in China. For centuries, they had been bred exclusively as pets for the imperial family and when the Summer Palace in Peking was ransacked in 1860, Lootie was one of the little dogs discovered there. In 1861, John Hart Dunne, a young captain, offered her, "a most affectionate and intelligent little creature," to Queen Victoria. Although Dunne hoped the dog would become a pet of the royal family, she was placed in the Royal Kennels at Windsor, where she lived eleven more years. Queen Victoria commissioned a portrait of Lootie and the public read about her in the *Illustrated London News*, but as far as is known, the queen never saw her.

LORD RUSSEL, the Fox of Good Sense in Walter Wangerin, Jr.'s *The Book of the Dun Cow* (1978), grieved that one of his clever tricks indirectly caused the death of the sons of Chauntecleer the rooster. Russel had another trick, however, that helped protect his fellow animals from the basilisks sent to destroy them. Since the bitter scent of rue was as repugnant to other creatures as it was to him, the fox had his comrades rub themselves in the plant. When the serpents advanced, Russel darted out of his hiding place, the last to withdraw. Not one serpent attacked him but he killed three of them as he raced to safety.

LOVELL THE DOG appeared in a satirical couplet composed by William Collingbourne after the coronation of Richard III in 1483:

The catte, the ratte, and Lovell our
   dogge
Rulyth all Englande under a hogge.

William Catesby was the "cat," Sir William Ratcliffe was the "rat," and Francis, Viscount Lovell, was known as "the king's spaniel." The three were close friends of the king, whose emblem was a white boar. Collingbourne paid for his impudence with his life.

LUATH (1) was Cuthullin's dog in *Fingal* (1762) by James Macpherson, who claimed to have translated the Gaelic poems of Ossian, the legendary third-century bard and son of Fingal. (In fact, Macpherson had written his own version of Ossianic legend.) The dog is noteworthy for his name, which was subsequently given to other dogs by at least three other writers, starting with Robert Burns.

LUATH (2), in "Twa Dogs" (1786) by Robert Burns, is a ploughman's collie, wise and faithful, with a shaggy black coat and a white breast. He ambles around with his friend CAESAR (2), the dog who lives with the gentry. When they tire of rooting out mice, they sit down to talk. Caesar wonders how poor folks live. "They're nae sae wretched's ane wad think," says Luath. They're used to being poor, he explains. Their wives and children are "the dearest comfort of their lives," and they forget their private cares to discuss church and state affairs. On New Year's Day, they have such a grand time, "That I for joy hae barkit wi' them."

LUATH (3), a shaggy, black and white male Newfoundland who belonged to J. M. Barrie and his wife, Mary, was the model for NANA (2), the Darling children's nurse in the play *Peter Pan* (1904). Arthur Lupino, the actor who played Nana, was invited to Barrie's home to see the dog run through his tricks, which included beating his paws on the floor. Luath was then taken to the customers, who sketched his head and took a sample of his coat to make Lupino look as much like him as possible. They succeeded. Barrie later wrote that Luath's own brief appearance onstage during one performance was hardly noticed.

LUATH (4), the young Labrador retriever in *The Incredible Journey* (1961) by Sheila Burnford, suffered more than the other two pets, BODGER and TAO, as they made their way home through the Canadian wilderness. When the Labrador raided a chicken house, the farmer's collie nearly tore off an ear. After Luath attacked a porcupine, his face became swollen and infected from embedded quills. But as soon as a hunter extracted them and fed the three animals, the Labrador resumed leading his companions home.

LUCIFER, the spoiled house cat, was the nemesis of the mice in Walt Disney Productions' *Cinderella* (1950). Disney had been dissatisfied with preliminary renderings of the villainous character; then he happened to visit one of the animators, Walt Kimball, at his home and found the model for Lucifer—Kimball's big calico cat.

LUCKY, so-named because the dots on his back formed a horseshoe, was the most resourceful of PONGO's fifteen puppies in *The Hundred and One Dalmatians* (1956) by Dodie Smith. When the dogs were abducted, he scratched SOS (Save Our Skins) on an old bone.

LUCY, THE MARGATE ELEPHANT, 66 feet tall, 55 feet long, and weighing 90 tons, was built in 1881 by James V. Lafferty, a New Jersey real estate promoter, to attract buyers to what was then called South Atlantic City. He used her interior, with windows on her sides, for offices that were reached by stairs in her hind legs. She later served as a restaurant and a summer home. When Lucy started going to pieces in the 1960s and her owners wanted to sell the land she was on, the citizens of Margate rallied to their elephant, moving what was left of her to a park. Old Lucy was restored and, in 1976, became a National Historic Landmark.

LUDLAM'S DOG, in English lore, belonged to a sorceress named Ludlam, who

LUCY, THE MARGATE ELEPHANT

lived in a cave near Farnham, in Surrey. Her dog was so lazy that when people came to consult the witch, he hardly stirred, thus inspiring the old saying: "Lazy as Ludlam's dog, which leaned his head against the wall to bark."

LUFRA in Sir Walter Scott's *The Lady of the Lake* (1810), was Douglas' dog, "the fleetest hound in all the North." In Canto Fifth: The Combat, King James ordered a stag let loose for his two favorite grey-hounds to bring down, but Lufra raced past them:

> And dashing on the antlered prey,
> Sunk her sharp muzzle in his flank,
> And deep the flowing life-blood drank.

The king's groom struck the hound; Douglas knocked the man senseless.

LULU, a young gazelle of the bushbuck tribe, was raised by Isak Dinesen (Baroness Karen Blixen) in her house in Kenya and was described in *Out of Africa* (1937). The fawn so impressed the Scottish deerhounds that they would haul themselves away from their warm spot on the hearth to let her settle there "in the manner of a perfect lady who demurely gathers her skirts about her." Lulu grew up to be "unbelievably beautiful," moody, and no longer gentle. She disappeared for a week, then returned each dawn to eat maize set out for her, while a male bushbuck stood motionless at the edge of the forest. Later, she brought along a very small fawn, in the afternoon as well as at daybreak. Lulu would accept a piece of sugar cane that was handed to her but never came close enough to be touched. A year later, she brought a new fawn. Those years, wrote Dinesen, "were

the happiest of my life in Africa. . . . I came to look upon my acquaintance with the forest antelopes as . . . a token of friend-ship from Africa."

LYCAON, a king of Attica and the father of CALLISTO in Greek mythology, served human flesh to Zeus, who turned him into a wolf as punishment. His name is used to designate the now-endangered eastern timber wolf of North America, *Canis lupus lycaon*, and the Cape Hunting Dog, *Lycaon pictus*, an African wild dog that has only four toes on each foot, looks like a hyena, and hunts like a wolf.

LYCAS was a hound whose epitaph has been attributed to Simonides (ca. 556–ca. 468 B.C.), the first great lyric poet of Greece:

> Although beneath this grave-mound
> thy white bones are now lying,
> Surely, my huntress Lycas, the wild
> things dread thee still.

LYLE is the debonair crocodile in a series of books by Bernard Waber, starting with *The House on East 88th Street* (1962). The Primm family moves into the house to find Lyle in the bathtub, left behind by his im-poverished partner, Hector P. Valenti, a sometime star of stage and screen. Lyle has been trained for show business but he also does household chores, cheerfully. He has a sinking spell in *Lyle and the Birthday Party* (1966). Lyle is already green, so he turns sick with envy and has to be hospital-ized. He cures himself by doing acrobatics to amuse the patients.

MACARONI, the piebald pony who belonged to President John F. Kennedy's daughter, Caroline, inspired a New York composer to write a song titled "My Pony, Macaroni." From time to time during the Kennedy years at the White House (1961–63), the U.S. Navy Band played an arrangement of the tune, complete with whinnies and hoofbeats.

MACAVITY appears, or disappears, in "Macavity: the Mystery Cat" from *Old Possum's Book of Practical Cats* (1939) by T. S. Eliot. The tall, thin ginger cat is "outwardly respectable," but when glass is broken, or jewelry taken, or a treaty mislaid in the Foreign Office, he cannot be found:

He's the bafflement of Scotland Yard,
  the Flying Squad's despair:
For when they reach the scene of crime
  —*Macavity's not there!*

McINTOSH, "an Aberdeen terrier of weak intellect" in P. G. Wodehouse's *Jeeves and the Dog McIntosh* (1929), woke Bertie Wooster every morning by leaping onto his bed and licking his right eye, then curled up and went to sleep. The "loony hound" belonged to Aunt Agatha, and on the day of her return, he had to be retrieved from the hotel suite of a man who thought McIntosh had been given to him. Bertie feared the dim dog might not remember him but Jeeves, the resourceful butler, advised him to sprinkle his trousers with aniseed. "It is extensively used in the dog-stealing business," he explained. It worked. McIntosh shot out the door to Bertie. "If I had been a bird that had been dead about five days, he could not have nuzzled me more heartily."

THE MACK BULLDOG became a corporate symbol because English Tommies and American doughboys gave the nickname "Bulldog Mack" to the chain-driven, AC model Mack truck used in France during World War I. The blunt, snub-nosed hood gave it the look of a bulldog, and the legendary durability of the nearly 5,000 trucks shipped to France suggested the tenacity of the breed. In 1917, the Bulldog

THE MACK BULLDOG

was registered as Mack's corporate symbol. Alfred F. Masury, who designed the AC model, became the chief engineer of the company and in 1932 carved out of wood the original figure for the bulldog hood ornament subsequently used on all Mack trucks. "Mr. Mack," as the mascot is sometimes called, has also been reproduced in other forms, including a stuffed toy bulldog.

MADAME THEOPHILE, one of many cats who belonged to Théophile Gautier (1811–72), liked to listen to singers but piercing sounds made her nervous. "At the high A she never failed to close the mouth of the singer with her soft paw." Those who tested her by hitting the note learned that "the dilettante in fur was not to be deceived." She deceived herself, however, into a disastrous encounter with a talking parrot, apparently thinking it was a green chicken. Madame Théophile sprang to its perch, the parrot cried, *"As-tu déjeuné, Jacquot?"* ("Have you eaten, Pretty Poll?"), and "this utterance so terrified the cat that she fell backwards."

MADAME VANITY was the cat that Michel de Montaigne contemplated in his *Essays*, II:12 (1580):

When I play with my cat, who knows whether she diverts herself with me, or I with her! We entertain one another with mutual follies, struggling for a garter; and if I have my time to begin or refuse, she also has hers. It is because I

[152]

cannot understand her language that we agree no better; and perhaps she laughs at my simplicity in making sport to amuse her.

MAERA, a faithful dog in Greek mythology, belonged to Icarius, an Athenian whom Dionysus taught to make wine. When some drunken shepherds killed Icarius and flung his body into a well, Maera's howls led his daughter, Erigone, to the grave. Grief-stricken, she hanged herself from a tree that grew there, and the dog committed suicide by jumping into the well. Dionysus honored the three by placing them in the heavens—Icarius as the constellation Boötes, Erigone as Virgo, and Maera as Procyon, the brightest star in Canis Minor (Lesser Dog).

MAESTOSO BORINA, a long-lived favorite at the Spanish Riding School in Vienna, was one of the last stallions born at the Royal Stud at Lipizza before the city was ceded to Italy in 1918. As Maria Jeritza's mount in *The Girl of the Golden West* at the Vienna State Opera, he was so eager when he heard his cue that he once leaped over a rolled-up carpet to make his entrance. Col. Alois Podhajsky, a former director of the Spanish Riding School, recalled in *My Dancing White Horses* (1964) that when students rode Maestoso Borina to learn the *passage*, a high-stepping trot, the "especially cunning" horse would trick them by doing it with his forelegs only and simply shuffling along on his hind legs. In *White Stallion of Lipizza* (1964), Marguerite Henry noted that he could perform ten successive *courbettes*—rising on his hind legs then leaping forward. Maestoso Borino was still courbetting two or three times when he was retired at the age of 30, the

oldest performer in the history of the Spanish Riding School.

MAGGIE, in "The Auld Farmer's New Year Morning Salutation to his Auld Mare, Maggie" (1786) by Robert Burns, is droopy, "stiff, an' crazy," and her once gray hide is "as white's a daisie." The old farmer fondly recalls how hard she worked for him and that she produced colts that brought good prices. He and the old mare had been together for twenty-nine years:

> Yet here to crazy age we're brought,
> Wi' something yet.

MAIDA, a cross between "the deer greyhound and the mastiff with a shaggy mane like a lion," was Sir Walter Scott's favorite dog. He sat beside his master at the dinner table, his head as high as the back of Scott's chair. Although Maida was as big as a Shetland pony and, said Scott, "kills foxes most amiably," he was completely intimidated by HINSE OF HINSFIELD, the family cat. When the hound "set up most pitiful howls," the cause turned out to be "his fear of passing puss who had stationed himself on the stairs." Portraits of Scott often included Maida, but in 1820, Scott sat with another dog because, he explained, Maida was sick of posing, having "sate to so many artists that whenever he sees brushes & a pallet he gets up and leaves the room."

MAJOR, a prize Middle White boar in George Orwell's *Animal Farm* (1946), addressed the assembled animals at Mr. Jones's farm just before he died. He convinced them that Man was their enemy, taught them the rousing old anthem "Beasts of England," and urged them to rebel. Soon after his death, they did.

[153]

MALSUM, in the cosmogony of the Algonquin Indians, was the evil wolf-brother of the hero Gluskap. The brothers were created by mother earth and when she died, Gluskap used her body to form plains, edible plants, animals, and the human race. Malsum fashioned rocks, thickets, and venomous animals. Then, after saying that he could only be killed by a fern root, he jokingly asked his brother what could cause his death. Only an owl feather, said Gluskap. Malsum put an owl feather on the tip of an arrow and shot him. Gluskap recovered, so great was his magic, and when he found out about his brother's treachery, he struck Malsum with a fern root. Malsum did not recover. His evil magic sank into the ground and he was transformed into a cruel, vindictive wolf.

THE MALTESE CAT, the "old expert" of the Skidars' twelve polo ponies, was ridden by Luytens, the team captain, in Rudyard Kipling's "The Maltese Cat" from *The Day's Work* (1898). At the start of the final chukker of the Upper India Cup match, the score was tied. Luytens, with a broken collarbone, could not use his reins but he knew that his experienced horse could be played without a bridle. The Cat broke clear in the final rush, Luytens got his goal, and their momentum carried them straight at a pile-up of ponies. To save his rider, the Cat veered, straining a back tendon beyond repair. His polo career was ended but when Luytens, at his bride's insistence, gave up playing to become an umpire, everyone knew that his lame, flea-bitten gray pony was the "Past Pluperfect Prestissimo Player of the Game."

MAMELOUK, the big, black half-Persian cat in Margery Sharp's *The Rescuers* (1959), lived with the Head Jailer in the Black Castle and tormented the prisoners. When three mice arrived to release one of them, MISS BIANCA, the white mouse, baffled the cat by appearing to enjoy his toying with her. By distracting him while her friends explored the castle, she also induced him to brag that the jailers would collapse after the New Year's Eve Feast, but not he: "I am Mamelouk, the Irontummed."

MAMMY-BAMMY BIG-MONEY, in the Uncle Remus stories by Joel Chandler Harris (1848–1908), was the old Witch Rabbit who lived in a deep dark swamp. BRER RABBIT went to her for help when, because he could not fool the other animals anymore, he thought he was losing his mind. She pointed to a squirrel in a tree and ordered Brer Rabbit to bring it to her. He did. Then she said there was a snake in the grass that he must fetch. He figured out how to do that, too. But just as he dragged it toward her, old Mammy-Bammy disappeared. From way off yonder, Brer Rabbit heard, "Ef you git any mo' sense, son, you'll be de ruination ev de whole settlement."

MANABOZHO, the Great Hare, was the giver of life in the mythology of the Algonquin Indians in eastern North America. In one legend the Hare flooded the world to extinguish a fire set by his enemies. He and a few other animals survived, perched on a mountain. When the water receded, he ordered the muskrat to dive down and bring up some mud. With it, Manabozho formed a new earth and men to live on it. In another legend, Manabozho permitted a great fish, who was the symbol of evil, to swallow him. Then he

MANEKI NEKO

cut his way out, killing the fish and the evil.

MANEKI NEKO (BECKONING CAT) is a popular Japanese good-luck symbol. Little statues of the tricolor cat, sitting with one front paw raised to her ear, are placed in the windows of many shops and restaurants to invite business. The other front paw often holds a gold coin, in keeping with an old saying that a beckoning cat brings prosperity. There is also a general belief in the Orient that if a cat wipes its paw over its ear, distinguished visitors will arrive. The stylized figurine is said to have originated with a wooden statue of a cat who was killed while warning its owner of a dangerous snake.

MANHAR, a male gaur born to a Holstein cow: see FLOSSIE.

MANIGARM (MOON-HOUND), also called HATI, was the gigantic wolf in Norse mythology who chased the moon across the sky while his brother wolf, SKOLL, pursued the sun. At the end of the world, Ragnarok or Götterdämmerung, Manigarm swallowed the moon, spraying the heavens with blood and quenching the stars.

MAN O' WAR was the most famous thoroughbred racehorse in America, and the greatest. He won twenty of his twenty-one races, earned $249,465, and drew thousands of fans to the racetracks. Samuel Riddle paid $5,000 for him in 1918, when

"Man O' War"

MAN O' WAR

Maj. August Belmont, preoccupied with military service, auctioned off his yearlings. Mrs. Belmont had named the colt "My Man O' War" but he was nicknamed "Big Red" for his golden chestnut color. An unusually heavy eater, he matured into a big horse with a powerful, 28-foot stride, and he loved to run so much that he was almost unmanageable around starting barriers. (Starting gates came later.)

His only loss, to Upset on August 13, 1919, at Saratoga, was his best race. He was facing the wrong way when the race started, it took him half a mile to catch up, and after getting blocked on the rail, his jockey had to pull him out and around the other horses. Despite the bad start and inept ride, Big Red thundered down the stretch to finish second by only half a length.

Of his eleven wins in 1920, three were by twenty lengths or more. He did not run in the Kentucky Derby because, in his day, it was not considered that important. In his next to last race, he carried 138 pounds, the highest weight ever assigned a 3-year-old. With a higher impost likely the following year, Riddle chose to retire the horse at the end of the season. During his two years of racing, Man O' War had beaten the fifty best horses his age as well as the 4-year-old champion, Sir Barton. He also set five record times.

At stud at Riddle's Faraway Farms in Kentucky for twenty-three years, Man O' War sired 386 foals, who won nearly 1,300 races. War Admiral won the Triple Crown, and another son, Battleship, won the Grand National in England. Before Big Red died in 1947, half a million people had seen him at Faraway. Will Harbutt, his devoted old groom, would lead him out and say, "Ladies and gemmun, this is Man O' War. He's the mostest hoss there ever was."

THE MARCH HARE, in *Alice's Adventures in Wonderland* (1865) by Lewis Carroll, lived up to the old expression, "mad as a March hare," which is based on the wild behavior of hares during their mating season. This hare was not involved in mating but in a mad tea party with the Mad Hatter and THE DORMOUSE. The March Hare offered Alice wine that he didn't have, quibbled about words, knocked over the milk jug, and dipped his watch into his cup of tea. The Mad Hatter said the March Hare had tried to repair both their watches with butter on a bread-knife, which probably had crumbs on it. "It was the *best* butter," said the March Hare, meekly.

MARCHEVALLEE, in Carolingian legend, was termed "the best steed that ever fed in the vales of Mount Atlas" by Bruhier, the Sultan of Arabia, as he rode to meet Charlemagne's champion, Ogier the Dane, in single combat. During the contest, Bruhier kept healing his wounds with a magic balm from a vial attached to his saddle until, in one exchange, Ogier lopped off the Sultan's arm just as his own mount, BEIFFROR, fell dead from a blow by Bruhier. The Sultan leaped to the ground to retrieve his arm, but before he could get back to his horse and the vial, Ogier beheaded him. The Dane then jumped on Marchevallée, applied the balm to heal his own wounds, and rode off, refreshed, to help defeat Bruhier's army.

MARENGO, the white Arabian stallion who was Napoleon's favorite charger, was credited with saving the First Consul from capture by sprinting away from a surprise encounter with enemy cavalry the night before the battle of Austerlitz in 1805. (Although Napoleon is shown on a white charger in Jacques Louis David's painting of his crossing the Alps in 1800, he actually rode a sure-footed mule, not Marengo, across the St. Bernard Pass.) At the age of 22, Marengo carried Napoleon through the early part of the battle of Waterloo on June 18, 1815, then suffered a slight wound, his eighth in action. Taken to England as a prize of war, he died there in 1829 and his skeleton is still exhibited in London, now at the National Army Museum. One hoof was made into a snuffbox with a silver lid inscribed: "Hoof of Marengo, barb charger of Napoleon, ridden by him at Marengo, Austerlitz, Jena, Wagram, in the Russian campaign, and at Waterloo."

THE MARES OF DIOMEDES, four horses who belonged to the king of the Bistones in Thrace, fed on human flesh. The eighth labor of Heracles (Hercules) was to bring the animals to King Eurystheus. Heracles went to Thrace, overpowered the grooms, and hauled the four horses out on a single halter. Alerted by the commotion, the king and his guards attacked. While Heracles fought off the guards, the vicious mares ate Diomedes, which immediately made them tame. Heracles took them back to show to Eurystheus, then set them free.

MARGATE, a black kitten, turned up on the doorstep of 10 Downing Street and was taken in on October 10, 1953, the day of Prime Minister Winston Churchill's speech to the Conservative Party at Margate. That evening, as Churchill savored the success of his speech, an important demonstration of his recovery from a second stroke, the kitten jumped on his knee. "It has brought me luck," he said, fondling the purring cat. "It shall be called Margate." Lord Moran, his physician, noted the remark (in *Churchill: Taken from the Diaries of Lord Moran*, 1966) and added that, on a visit ten days later, he found the P.M. in bed reading the *Times* while Margate, "lying on its back, pawed the fluttering edges of the paper."

MARIAN was Bear Number 40 in the long-range study of grizzly bears in Yellowstone National Park that Frank C. Craighead, Jr. described in *Track of the Grizzly* (1979). She was 30 months old in 1960, when she was captured, sedated, and tagged on the ear. In September 1961, she became the first grizzly to be tracked by radio collar. Craighead and his associates were trailing her when an unexpectedly loud signal from their receiver made Marian pop up just 40 feet ahead. She sprinted away but paused to glare at them, "or was that merely a glance of curiosity?" During the next eight years, they observed her mating, preparing winter dens, and raising several families, while she evidently decided that "though we were pests we were harmless." In the spring of 1964, Marian emerged from hibernation with her first two cubs, "tiny ten-pound balls of fur." The one who survived weighed over 100 pounds by September; she weaned him the following June by chasing him away. In 1966, Marian was seen nursing a second pair of cubs, romping with them, then stopping their play with a sharp cuff to remind them that obedience was "demanded by all mother bears." In October 1969, a ranger trying to tranquilize one of her yearlings in order to move it away from a campground had to shoot Marian in self-defense.

MARIGOLD, a cat, was neatly described by Richard Garnett (1835–1906):

> She moved through the garden in
>   glory, because
> She had very long claws at the end of
>   her paws.
> Her back was arched, her tail was
>   high,
> A green fire glared in her vivid eye;
> And all the Toms, though never so
>   bold,
> Quailed at the martial Marigold.

MARJORIE, a black and white mongrel, was the first diabetic creature to be kept alive by insulin. In May 1921, using laboratory dogs at the University of Toronto, Dr. Frederick Grant Banting and Charles Herbert Best, a graduate student, set out to isolate the hormone in the pancreas, knowing that removal of the dog's pancreas caused a form of diabetes, the invariably fatal "sugar disease." On July 27, an active extract from the pancreas of a dog was injected into Marjorie, who had been made diabetic by the removal of her pancreas, and her blood sugar was immediately reduced. Banting and Best quickly discovered that a more potent and less impure insulin, as they named the hormone, could be extracted from unborn calves. They used it to prolong Marjorie's life for more than seventy days. On January 11, 1922, Leonard Thompson, a 13-year-old diabetic who weighed only 65 pounds, became the first human patient to receive the lifesaving therapy.

MARMADUKE, the enormous Great Dane in Brad Anderson's Sunday comic strip and daily panel *Marmaduke*, patiently submits to such indignities as being dressed up in Mom's old clothes or having hand lotion slathered on his paws because they are "very rough" when he shakes hands. Anderson, who created the strip in 1954, was inspired by his stepbrother's boxer, Bruno.

MAROCCO, Mr. Banks's educated horse, was so famous in Elizabethan England that many writers, including Shakespeare, Ben Jonson, and Sir Walter Raleigh, mentioned his accomplishments. The horse with the silver shoes could dance, count, recognize colors, and read dice. When Marocco performed in France, monks and friars in Orléans accused Banks of being a witch or a conjurer. The trainer asked one of them to hold up a crucifix, the horse knelt before it, and the charge was dismissed. In 1600, Marocco performed his greatest exploit, climbing to the top of the old cathedral of St. Paul's.

MAROCCO

MARRAMAQUIZ, a cat in Lope de Vega's *La Gatomaquia* (*The Battle of the Cats,* 1634): see ZAPAQUILDA.

MARYLAND, a big bay gelding, was the mount used by Brig. Gen. J. E. B. Stuart for his spectacular ride around Gen. George McClellan's army, June 12–15, 1862. Federal troops were massed on the outskirts of Richmond when Gen. Robert E. Lee, preparing to defend the city, sent his cavalry commander to probe McClellan's right flank. Stuart and his men started raiding enemy outposts and just kept going, making a complete circuit of McClellan's position. Rattled by the harassment, McClellan did not attack, and in the ensuing Seven Days' Battle he was forced to retreat.

MASTER MAGRATH, Lord Lurgan's celebrated greyhound courser, raced from 1867 to 1873, was beaten only once, and, after winning the Waterloo Cup three years in a row, was presented at court at the express desire of Queen Victoria. According to legend, Lurgan rescued the dog when he was a puppy about to be drowned by a drunken tenant farmer, and named it for the orphan boy who raised him.

THE MASTER'S CAT was the one kitten that Charles Dickens (1812–70) kept from the litter born to Williamina, a cat he had previously called WILLIAM (2). The kitten had a habit of using her paw to snuff the candle Dickens was reading by in order to get his attention.

MATCHEM, a brown bay grandson of THE GODOLPHIN ARABIAN, was foaled in England in 1748, when a new breed of racehorse was being developed by crossing Eastern-bred stallions with the larger native mares. Over two hands taller than the Godolphin Arabian, Matchem has been called the first Thoroughbred. In five years of racing, he won eleven of his thirteen races. At stud, he became one of the three principal thoroughbred progenitors (see ECLIPSE and HEROD) through whom all of the Thoroughbreds racing today are descendants of the three Eastern-bred stallions who founded the breed. In the United States, Matchem's most famous descendant was MAN O' WAR.

MATHE was Richard II's favorite greyhound, according to the *Chronicle* of Froissart (ca. 1338–1410). Whenever the king went riding, the dog would run straight to him to fawn and leap up to put his forefeet on the king's shoulders. Richard surrendered to Henry of Lancaster in 1399 at Flint Castle, and as they talked in the courtyard, Mathe left the king and went to Henry, offering him "the same frendly countinaunce and chere." It was a great good token for Henry, the next king of England, said Richard, and an evil sign for him, about to be deposed. "The grayhounde hath this knowledge naturally . . . he wyll folowe you and forsake me." (In Shakespeare's *Richard II*, the king lamented the defection of his horse, ROAN BARBARY.)

MATILDA and MILTON were a pair of shaggy North American musk-oxen who were donated to the Peking Zoo by the United States in April 1972, following President Richard Nixon's February visit to the People's Republic of China. The gift prompted one in return, the giant panda couple HSING-HSING AND LING-LING, who were presented to the people of the United States.

MAUD, the mule with the rolling eyes, wicked grin, and flying heels, began to appear in Sunday comic pages on July 24, 1904. The strip *And Her Name Was Maud!* alternated with *Happy Hooligan* and *Alphonse and Gaston*, all created by Fred Opper, one of the first great comic strip cartoonists. Three Maud books were published before 1910, and, with a few years' absence in the 1920s, the weekly strip ran until 1932. Maud belonged to the tubby, bewhiskered farmer Si, who bought her for $10 and then kept trying to sell her. As often as possible, Maud would plant her front legs, let fly, and kick somebody, usually Si. One time, he landed on top of the grandfather clock. Si's wife, Mirandy, said, "Lands sakes alive!" a lot.

THE MAUTHE DOG (or MODDEY DHOO) is a spectral hound that has been haunting Peel Castle on the Isle of Man for centuries. The ghostly black spaniel stayed in the guardroom from the time the candles were lit until dawn, and soldiers dared not curse in his presence because a drunken trooper who had reeled in alone, swearing, had lost his speech and died three days later.

MAVERICK originally referred to an unbranded or stray calf, then to other unattached animals, such as steers or horses, eligible for "finders-keepers." The name came from a Texas pioneer, Samuel Augustus Maverick, who bought and branded 400 head of cattle in 1845, then left them to graze—and breed—on an open range below San Antonio. Two years later, he sold the herd. Cowboys rounding up the cattle assumed that any unmarked yearlings were Maverick's, and the name stuck. It now extends to people as well.

MEDJI, a little dog in Nicolai Gogol's *Diary of a Madman* (1834), belonged to Sophie, a young lady whom Poprishchin, the diarist, adored. After seeing Medji chat with another dog, FIDELE, about their correspondence, Poprishchin stole Medji's letters. The first one, "impeccably written, . . . lapses into dogginess" as Medji boasts of her fine fare—woodcock in sauce or roast chicken wings—and her suitors—a coarse mongrel, a terrifying great Dane, and a muzzled gallant named Trésor. Medji went on to describe Sophie's admirers, those in St. Petersburg society and the "ugly" civil servant, Poprishchin himself, "just like a tortoise in a sack. . . . Sophie can't stop laughing when she looks at him."

"Damn it!" cursed Poprishchin. "It's enough to make you weep. I tore that stupid little dog's letter into little bits."

mehitabel, the alley cat, was a pal of archy the cockroach, who allegedly began writing columns for Don Marquis in the New York *Sun* in 1916 by hurling himself down head first onto the keys of Marquis' typewriter. Capitals and punctuation marks were impossible but he could, with difficulty, work the shift to start a new line. Archy explained,

> expression is the need of my soul
> i was once a vers libre bard

For eighteen years he produced a torrent of poetry, philosophy, and Boswellian reports of mehitabel, who considered herself an artist, a modern dancer. She claimed to have been Cleopatra in an earlier incarnation, he said, and reveled in the freedom of her present life, "so romantic capricious and corybantic." Mehitabel tried a "plutonic attachment" with a theater cat, took

mehitabel

what have i done to deserve all these kittens

up with various toms, went to Hollywood to get into the movies, and left with seven platinum blond kittens. When she got home to Shinbone Alley, a new set of kittens arrived, strange ones who acted like pups. Mehitabel seemed to remember a coyote who chased her across Arizona and New Mexico. Archy admired her spirit. With all the ups and downs, and a limp in her left hind leg, mehitabel sang:

> my youth i shall never forget
> but there s nothing i really regret
> wotthehell wotthehell
> there s a dance in the old dame yet
> toujours gai toujours gai

MEPHISTOPHELES, in Johann von Goethe's *Faust*, Part One (1808), first appears to Faust as a large black poodle circling him and Wagner, Faust's assistant, as they return from a stroll outside the city. Faust believes he saw fire whirling around the dog's tail, and wonders if it is some sort of magic snare. Wagner says it is just a poodle wagging his tail and wanting to play. Faust takes the dog home. In his study, he tells him to go lie down behind the stove. As Faust begins to work, the dog growls and howls and spirits are heard in the hall. The dog is transformed into a monster. Faust tries to exorcise it with spells. A cloud of vapor looms and Mephistopheles emerges, dressed as a traveling student. "So you were in the poodle's heart!" cries Faust. "A wandering scholar? It's the best joke yet!"

MERRYLEGS, the "highly trained performing dog" in Charles Dickens' *Hard Times* (1854), belonged to Sissy Jupe's father, a juggler in Sleary's circus. Several years after Jupe and the dog disappeared, Merrylegs turned up at the circus. Lame and nearly blind, he walked around the children in the company, as though seeking Sissy, the child he had known, then went to Sleary. The old dog threw himself up to stand on his forelegs, weak as he was, wagged his tail, and died. Sleary was convinced that Jupe was dead since Merrylegs would never have deserted him.

MESSENGER, a big, gray Thoroughbred foaled in England in 1780, won ten of his sixteen races, two by forfeit. At the age of 8, he was imported to America to sire runners, which he did. MAN O' WAR was his most famous Thoroughbred descendant, but the outstanding result of Messenger's twenty years at stud in Pennsylvania, New Jersey, and New York was that many of his foals inherited and passed on a strong instinct for the trotting gait. From them and from descendants of JUSTIN MORGAN, a new breed of American trotter, now called Standardbred, was developed for the new American sport of harness racing. Over 90 percent of today's standardbred trotters and pacers are descendants of Messenger through his great-grandson HAMBLETONIAN.

MEUZZA was Mohammed's beloved cat. One day, when he was sleeping on his robe the Prophet was summoned to prayers. Mohammed cut off his sleeve rather than disturb the cat. When the cat woke up, he arched his back in appreciation, and Mohammed stroked him three times, assuring Meuzza a permanent place in Islamic Paradise, and granting all cats perpetual freedom from the danger of falling by giving them the ability always to land on their feet.

MICETTO, a large, grayish-red cat with black stripes, was born in the Vatican and raised by Pope Leo XII. The vicomte de Chateaubriand, the French ambassador to Rome, often admired the cat as it nestled in the folds of the pope's white robe, and in 1829 he inherited the "bereaved animal." In his memoirs, Chateaubriand declared, "I am trying to ease his exile and help him forget the Sistine Chapel and the sun on Michelangelo's cupola, where he used to walk, far above the earth." The comtesse de Chateaubriand was more prosaic, noting in a letter that although the pope loved the cat, it was not well-fed "because all they knew in the Vatican in the way of sought-after dishes was cod and beans."

MICIFUF, a cat in Lope de Vega's *La Gatomaquia* (*The Battle of the Cats*, 1634): see ZAPAQUILDA.

MICKEY MOUSE made his debut on November 18, 1928, in *Steamboat Willie*, the first animated cartoon with sound. Walt Disney created him and provided his squeaky voice for the next twenty years, but it was Ub Iwerks, Disney's principal collaborator, who designed and animated the mouse. More mischievous boy than mouse, Mickey made music by playing a cow's teeth like a xylophone, and her udder like a bagpipe. The public adored him. In his second cartoon, *Plane Crazy* (1928), he wound up a dachshund like a rubber band to power his airplane, and in the cartoons that quickly followed, he romped through such roles as a gaucho, fireman, violinist, auto mechanic, moose hunter, and ringmaster.

He became an international star, known as Topolino in Italy, as Musse Pigg in Sweden, Miki Kuchi in Japan, etc. His films were shown in thirty-eight countries and his fans included Franklin D. Roosevelt, Benito Mussolini, and the Nizam of Hyderabad. The *Mickey Mouse* comic strip and the first licensed Mickey Mouse product, a school writing tablet, appeared in 1930. Mickey's image soon adorned all sorts of merchandise and, in mid-decade, saved two corporations from bankruptcy —the Lionel Corporation, with its Mickey and MINNIE MOUSE wind-up handcar, and the Ingersoll-Waterbury Company, which sold 2,500,000 Mickey Mouse watches in the first two years.

In the cartoons, Mickey was made less rambunctious because his public objected when their idol did not behave like one. He gradually became a lovable little fellow, and feisty Donald Duck, introduced in 1934, soon eclipsed him. To restore Mickey's popularity, Disney decided to star the mouse as the young magician who could make a broom fetch water but could not make it stop, in an animation of Paul Dukas's scherzo, *The Sorcerer's Apprentice* (1897). The conductor Leopold Stokowski was so enthusiastic about the project that more compositions were animated and Mickey's comeback became a segment of the feature film *Fantasia* (1940).

Mickey acquired a huge new audience in 1955 with the advent of "The Mickey Mouse Club" on television. His name has become a slang expression for trite or trivial, as in "Mickey Mouse music" or "Mickey Mouse regulations," but thousands of products, including a real telephone, still bear his image. At Disneyland and Walt Disney World, lifelike "audio-animatronic" figures of Mickey and his friends perform in *The Mickey Mouse Revue*, and he makes "live" appearances. Represented by a small actor in a Mickey Mouse costume, he danced in the White House on November 17, 1978, at a party honoring Mickey's fiftieth birthday.

MIGHTY JOE YOUNG, the likable 10-foot gorilla in the movie *The Mighty Joe Young* (1949), had been raised in Africa by Jill Young (Terry Moore) and was devoted to her. When cowboys from America tried to capture him, Joe seized one and would have thrown him over a cliff had Jill not ordered him to put the man down. She in turn was persuaded by the rescued cowboy to appear with the gorilla in the United States, at a nightclub decorated with caged animals. The act opened with Mighty Joe striding onstage, holding a platform aloft on which Jill sat at a grand piano, playing "Beautiful Dreamer." Then, tormented by rowdies in the audience who forced liquor on him, the gorilla ran amok. Cages were smashed and lions got loose. Joe fought them into submission but the authorities said that he must be killed. Jill and the cowboy smuggled him into a truck and as they headed for a ship that would take the gorilla back to Africa, they saw an orphanage in flames. Joe risked his life to save a child on the roof and was redeemed.

Willis O'Brien, who had animated KING KONG, used several models of Joe Young, each with 150 moving parts, for frame-by-frame shots of the gorilla's movements, and won an Oscar for special effects. The movie got mixed reviews, ranging from "lunatic drivel" to "Kong was a mere beast, but Joe is the kind of fellow you can get to love."

MIGHTY MOUSE was created by Paul Terry's animated cartoon studio for a take-off of Superman in *The Mouse of Tomorrow* (1942). As one of the mice being terrorized by the cats in his city, he took refuge in a supermarket, plunged into a piece of Super Cheese, and emerged as Super Mouse, with a flowing red cape and a massive chest that deflected bullets. Zooming through the sky, he saved his fellow mice by banishing the cats to the moon. Renamed Mighty Mouse a year later, he became one of the most popular Terrytoon characters. He appeared in comic books from 1955 to 1968 and on television in 150 episodes of "The Mighty Mouse Playhouse" (1955–67), which has been rerun many times. As always, Mighty Mouse used his "superhuman strength" to rescue mice, usually from cats, "with a speed that annihilates time and space."

MIJBIL, an otter, was obtained by Gavin Maxwell in Iraq in 1956 to keep as a pet at his cottage on the northwest coast of Scotland. In *Ring of Bright Water* (1960), Maxwell reported that before they flew home, Mij had learned to respond to his name, to accept a harness for walks, and to fiddle with bathtub faucets for more water for splashing. On the flight, the intensely inquisitive otter managed to unzip a travel bag belonging to the woman in the next seat and flung out the contents while she, fortunately, was asleep.

In Scotland, Mij invented solitary games, like pushing a Ping-Pong ball underwater, then pouncing on it when it popped up. When he came out of the sea, he dried himself on the nearest person. He slept with Maxwell and woke up at 8:20 every morning. If nuzzling and tickling failed to rouse Maxwell, Mijbil simply unmade the bed by rooting around under the covers. Unlike any otter Maxwell had seen, Mij was covered with velvety brown fur and the underside of his tail was flat. He represented a new subspecies, according to zoologists in London, who named it *Lutrogale perspicillata maxwelli.* Two years after Mijbil was killed, senselessly, by a stranger, Maxwell found a "perfect successor," a female otter he named EDAL.

MIKE IV, the 500-pound Bengal tiger mascot of the Louisiana State University football team since 1976, appears at home games at Tiger Stadium in Baton Rouge and is looked after by the LSU School of Veterinary Medicine. The Bengal mascot tradition began in 1936, when students chipped in to buy the original Mike, named for Mike Chambers, then the team's trainer. Mike I served for twenty-one years, Mike II died after one season, and Mike III was so popular that news of his being injured in a highway accident prompted a number of people to offer to donate blood.

MILOU is Tintin's little white terrier in *Tintin,* the Belgian comic strip created in 1929 by Hergé (Georges Rémi). Occasionally muttering disapproval, the spunky dog goes everywhere, even to the moon, with Tintin, a resourceful teenager who foils villains and solves mysteries. Since 1930, twenty-two books of their fantastic adventures have been published in thirty languages. In South America in *The Broken Ear* (1947), Milou (Snowy in the English version) saves Tintin twice, by chewing ropes binding the boy and by biting a man aiming a gun at him. When Tintin completes his mission and tells the dog they'll take a rest, Milou gives him a big grin and a snappy bark.

MINNALOUSHE, a black cat, is the subject of three verses by William Butler Yeats, who wrote them to be sung, one at a time, at the beginning, middle, and end of his play *The Cat and the Moon* (1926). The play has nothing to do with cats but is about two beggars, one lame, one blind, and the choice each has of losing his affliction or of being blessed. The poem dwells on the mysterious way the pupils of the cat's eyes change shape with each phase of the moon:

Minnaloushe creeps through the grass
Alone, important and wise,
And lifts to the changing moon
His changing eyes.

MINNA MINNA MOWBRAY was the "outstanding personality" of the countless cats owned by Michael Joseph, the British literary agent and publisher who described her in *Cat's Company* (1931). Because she was voiceless, Minna wore a collar with two bells that she signaled with by shaking her head, but she could keep them silent to stalk a bird. As for toms, she favored a one-eyed "old roué with . . . a pronounced limp. . . . The uglier they were, the more eligible." Kittens arrived in regular batches and Minna was an "exemplary mother"— except to the family favorite of each litter. They disappeared. Joseph wondered about Minna's lack of anxiety for her missing kittens until he saw one, several weeks after birth, in fine condition in a neighbor's garden. He concluded that, as with the others, Minna had deliberately "lost" him.

MINNIE MOUSE and Mickey Mouse made their debut in Walt Disney's *Steamboat Willie* (1928) and have appeared together ever since, in cartoons, comics, merchandise, and the Disney parks. In the early cartoons, when Mickey played the piano, she tap danced on top of it. When she was a captive in a harem, he smuggled her out, disguised as a potted plant. In *Plane Crazy* (1928), Mickey gave Minnie a big kiss while they were aloft. She would have none of it and bailed out, her patched bloomers serving as a parachute. Mickey landed and laughed at her droopy drawers. Minnie decked him with a horseshoe.

MINON was the enchanted cat in *Prince Dorus* (1811), a poem for children by Charles Lamb. The King had to step on her tail to break a spell that kept the Princess from marrying him but when he approached the cat, "her back bristled, and her great eyes glared." When he sneaked up behind her, "Whisk—off she skips—three yards upon a bounce." He chased her for weeks, until he finally caught her asleep and stamped on her tail. "Loud squalls were heard, like howlings of a storm," as Minon instantly changed into a giant man who promised revenge after the Princess married the King. Their son, Prince Dorus, was born with a "foul deformity" of a nose, and the Queen was "fast widowed."

MINORU, carrying the purple, scarlet, and gold colors of Edward VII, won the English Derby at Epsom Downs on May 26, 1909, at odds of 4–1. As Prince of Wales, Edward had had two other Derby winners, Persimmon and Diamond Jubilee, but this was his first as king. Thousands of spectators began to sing "God Save the King" and when he left the Royal Box to lead Minoru in, they shouted, "Good old Teddy!" and "Teddy boy! Hurrah! Hurrah!" The aging king was in his glory. That night, he gave his annual dinner for the Jockey Club, went on to a ball, and then played bridge until dawn. When he returned to the track the next day, a bystander yelled, "Now, king. You've won the Derby. Go back home and dissolve this bloody Parliament!" The king roared.

MISHA, the official mascot of the 1980 Summer Olympics in Moscow, was a bright-eyed, grinning brown bear cub sporting a belt, striped in the five Olympic colors and buckled with the five-ring Olympic symbol. He was ubiquitous in

Moscow, appearing in every possible form —stadium flash card displays, posters, souvenir doodads, dozens of dancing children in bear suits, and, at the closing ceremonies of the games, an immense balloon that was lofted out of Lenin Stadium. In the United States, most Misha licensees were stuck with their merchandise as a result of the American boycott of the games; but R. Dakin & Company of San Francisco, licensed to produce a Misha teddy bear, may recoup part of their loss. After selling about 75,000 stuffed Mishas through the 1979 Christmas season, they Americanized their remaining 100,000 bears by replacing the Olympic belt with a T-shirt saying "I'm just a bear" or showing a hockey player under the initials USA. Rumors that Misha will join a U.S. ballet company have been denied.

MISS BIANCA, the elegant white mouse in a series of books by Margery Sharp, illustrated by Garth Williams, belonged to an ambassador's son and lived at the embassy in a Porcelain Pagoda. In the first book, *The Rescuers* (1959), Miss Bianca agreed to help free a Norwegian poet imprisoned in the Black Castle, then flew to Norway in a diplomatic pouch to recruit a mouse who could speak the prisoner's language. She returned with NILS the sailor, BERNARD the pantry mouse joined them, and the Prisoner's Aid Society arranged the trio's journey to the Castle. With so little time to shop, Miss Bianca took only a small valise and a fan. At the Castle, she saved her companions when they were pinned under the paw of the terrible cat, MAMELOUK, by confusing him with such dazzling arguments that he loosened his grip. The mice fled, freed the prisoner, and made their way home.

MISS BIANCA
Miss Bianca confounds Mamelouk

MISSIS, in *The Hundred and One Dalmatians* (1956) by Dodie Smith, was a Dalmatian bitch whose litter of fifteen puppies was stolen. On the way to find them, PONGO, their sire, was injured and had to be hidden in a haystack while Missis went on to look for food. She found some at a house where a spaniel tried to give her directions back to the haystack. Since Missis didn't know right from left, he looked at her feet and told her to remember, "Right paw, spot. Left paw, no spot." That was too hard, so he showed her the haystack in the distance and advised her to keep her eyes on it while she ran. As she led Pongo back to the spaniel's house, she asked him if dogs had spots on their right or left paws. He said it depended on the dog. Missis thought that was hopeless. "How can I depend on a thing that depends?"

MISS MA'M'SELLE HEPZIBAH, the dainty skunk in Walt Kelly's comic strip *Pogo*, was the sweetheart of the Okefenokee Swamp, although POGO had never proposed to her. "But who is need such?" she said. When she invited a dozen or so nieces and nephews for Thanksgiving, she told their mother, "I am get a nice big elephant." English seemed to be her second language.

MISS PIGGY, the zaftig leading lady of "The Muppet Show," created for television by Jim Henson in 1976, has blue eyes, a swirling blond wig, and a generous pink snout that twitches eloquently. "My beauty is my curse," she sighs. She also has a will of iron. What batting her eyelashes does not accomplish, a fast karate chop does. Miss Piggy loves being glamorous and adores KERMIT the frog. He does not reciprocate but her career thrives. On television, she dances the pas de deux from *Swine Lake* with Rudolf Nureyev—who flees in a towel when she follows him to the steam room. *The Muppet Movie* (1979) makes her a star, scores of Miss Piggy products are merchandised, and *Miss Piggy's Guide to Life* (1981) is published. Asked if all this celebrity has changed her, she replies, "I am still just little *moi*, the same gorgeous and supremely talented pig."

MR. ALDERMAN PTOLEMY TORTOISE, in Beatrix Potter's *The Tale of Mr. Jeremy Fisher* (1906), brought his own meal, a salad in a string bag, when MR. JEREMY FISHER the frog invited him to dinner.

MR. ED, "The Talking Horse," was the star of "Mr. Ed," a popular television series launched in 1961. Trained by Les Hilton, the golden palomino performed a variety of tricks with his mouth—untying knots, waving a flag, writing notes with a large pencil, etc. In one scene, when Ed saw a box of carrots on a table, he pulled a light plug out of the wall, then went back to the carrots to chomp away in the dark. When he appeared to talk, Ed was wearing a halter with a nylon line running from it through his mouth to Hilton, out of camera range. A slight tug on the line would make Ed move his lips as if he were saying the words dubbed in by the actor supplying his voice. A four-time winner of the American Humane Association's Patsy Award, Mr. Ed died in 1979 at the age of 13.

MR. JACKSON, a fat, amiable toad in *The Tale of Mrs. Tittlemouse* (1910) by Beatrix Potter, made himself at home at Mrs. Tittlemouse's, although he declined her dinner, calling it inedible. He was there, he explained, because he smelled honey. Finding the bees in her storeroom, he made such a mess getting rid of them that Mrs. Tittlemouse made her door smaller to keep him from coming back in. When she gave a party a fortnight later, Mr. Jackson stood at her window, "not at all offended," drinking her health with acorn cups of honeydew passed through to him.

MR. JEREMY FISHER

weather. Miss Dormouse refused to take them back and her father simply stayed in bed, murmuring, "How snug."

MR. THOMAS, a baby civet cat, was raised by Wyant Davis Hubbard and his wife, Isabella, at Ibamba, their home in Northern Rhodesia, from 1929 to 1934. In *Ibamba* (1962), Hubbard noted that civet cats were considered untamable but this one, "like all infant creatures, . . . adjusted to the environment in which it found itself." Tommy slept in the Hubbards' bed, took morning tea, relished baked custard, and adored Isabella. He accepted PADDY (1) the lioness cub as a member of the family but expressed jealousy of the Hubbards' baby daughter by defecating on her empty bassinet. After he was full-grown, Mr. Thomas disappeared for two days; he was found in a distant trap, badly mauled by a leopard. Repeatedly calling his name, Isabella got no response from Tommy until she held a spoonful of custard under his nose. The nose twitched and one eye slowly opened. "Beyond any question he recognized his foster mother. Which made it so much more heartbreaking." He died three days later.

MR. JEREMY FISHER, a frog, lived by a pond in *The Tale of Mr. Jeremy Fisher* (1906) by Beatrix Potter. One rainy day, intending to give his friends a minnow dinner, Mr. Jeremy packed fishing gear, put on his macintosh, and hopped over to his boat, a lily pad in the middle of the pond. An enormous trout snapped him off the pad but then spat him out because the raincoat tasted so awful. The frog hopped home and changed his menu to roast grasshopper with lady-bird sauce.

MR. JOHN DORMOUSE and his daughter began selling candles after GINGER (1) and PICKLES closed their shop in Beatrix Potter's *Ginger & Pickles* (1909). The candles drooped in warm

MR. TOD the fox detested TOMMY BROCK the badger and his smell, in *The Tale of Mr. Tod* (1912) by Beatrix Potter. Finding his bed occupied by the snoring badger provoked the fox into rigging a pail of water over it, with a rope to tip the pail leading outside. Mr. Tod chewed the rope through and when it gave way, nearly lost his teeth. Worse, Tommy Brock was not in the bed. He was in the kitchen, dry and grinning. The two of them got into a fight and demolished the kitchen before they rolled out the door and down the hill.

MISTIGRIS, the cat in Honoré de Balzac's *Le Père Goriot* (1835), belonged to Mme. Vauquer, the proprietress of the boarding-house where Goriot lived. Caught knocking over a plate that covered a bowl of milk, the cat fled, then promptly returned to rub against the landlady's ankles. "Oh! yes, you can wheedle, you old hypocrite!" said Mme. Vauquer. When most of her lodgers left at about the same time, she was convinced there would be a death in the house within ten days. Then the cook told her that Mistigris had not been seen for three days. " 'Ah! well, if my cat is dead, if *he* has gone and left us, I—' The poor woman could not finish her sentence . . . quite overcome by this dreadful portent." Goriot died a short time later.

MRS. CHIPPY HACKEE, a chipmunk in *The Tale of Timmy Tiptoes* (1911) by Beatrix Potter, declined to squeeze through a woodpecker hole into the hollow tree where TIMMY TIPTOES and her husband were because, she explained, CHIPPY HACKEE bites.

MRS. O'LEARY'S COW, according to legend, kicked over a lantern, which started a fire that spread to become the Great Chicago Fire on the night of Sunday, October 8, 1871. What is *known* is that a neighbor across the street from Patrick and Catherine O'Leary's house at 137 De Koven Street saw flames in their barn around 8:30 that evening, ran to it, yelling "Fire!" and managed to get the tethered cows loose. Whichever cow or whatever else caused the fire, it spread unchecked

through the entire city of mostly wooden buildings as the wind picked up. By Tuesday morning, October 10, an estimated 250 people had perished, 100,000 were homeless, and 17,500 buildings had been destroyed with a property damage of $196 million.

MRS. TIGGY-WINKLE

MRS. TIGGY-WINKLE, the hedgehog in Beatrix Potter's *The Tale of Mrs. Tiggy-Winkle* (1905), was a conscientious laundress: "Oh, yes if you please'm, I'm an excellent clear-starcher." She washed old Mrs. Rabbit's handkerchief separately because it smelled so of onions.

MISTY, one of the wild ponies foaled on Assateague Island and forced to swim over to nearby Chincoteague Island to be sold on the annual Pony Penning Day, was made famous in Marguerite Henry's story about her, *Misty of Chincoteague* (1947), and the movie based on it, *Misty* (1961). Henry's sequel, *Stormy, Misty's Foal* (1963), was also based on real events. When a six-day tidal storm hit the islands, most of the Assateague ponies perished, the people on Chincoteague were evacuated, and Misty, about to foal, was taken to an animal hospital in Pocomoke, Maryland. Soon after her foal was born, Misty began making public appearances with Stormy to raise money to restore the Assateague herd. Children all over the United States sent hundreds of dollars to the Misty Disaster Fund.

MITTENS, her sister MOPPET, and their brother TOM KITTEN, in Beatrix Potter's *The Tale of Tom Kitten* (1907), were put in the garden by their mother, Mrs. TABITHA TWITCHIT, with orders to keep their clothes clean. The sisters got grass stains on their pinafores, Tom Kitten's buttons burst, and as his clothes fell off, the Puddle-Ducks put them on. Mittens laughed so hard that she fell off the garden wall, followed by Moppet. Their pinafores dropped off and the ducks made off with them, too.

MITZ, a pet marmoset, facilitated Leonard and Virginia Woolf's holiday drive through Germany in May 1935. Since the British Foreign Office was officially advising Jews not to go there, and Leonard was Jewish, he carried a letter from Prince Bismarck of the German Embassy in London requesting that the Woolfs be well treated. But Mitz was all they needed. Arriving in Bonn in their open car with the marmoset perched

on Leonard's shoulder, they found the main road lined with enthusiastic Nazis awaiting the arrival of, probably, Hermann Göring. At the sight of Mitz, "the crowd shrieked with delight" and as Leonard slowly drove "between the two lines of corybantic Germans," they kept shouting "Heil Hitler!" and giving her the Nazi salute. Throughout Germany, right to the Austrian border where the customs officer summoned his wife and children, people "went into ecstasies over *das liebe, kleine Ding*," Leonard recalled in his autobiography, *Downhill All the Way* (1967). "It was obvious to the most anti-Semitic stormtrooper that no one who had on his shoulder such a 'dear little thing' could be a Jew."

MNEVIS, the sacred bull of Heliopolis in ancient Egypt, was the manifestation of Re, the chief god of the city. The black and white bull, shown with the disk of the sun and a cobra between his horns, was also a symbol of fertility.

MOBY DICK, the albino sperm whale in Herman Melville's *Moby Dick* (1851), had taken the leg of Captain Ahab, who sailed the *Pequod* out of Nantucket, passionately determined to catch him. Rounding Good Hope, crossing the Indian Ocean, entering the Pacific, the *Pequod* swept the sperm whale cruising grounds of the world. Soon after Ahab encountered two ships that had lost men and boats to the White Whale near the equator, Moby Dick blew. Whaleboats were lowered and Ahab sighted him under water. The whale bit Ahab's boat in half and thrashed around the wreckage until the *Pequod* drove him off. The next day, "the White Whale churning himself into furious speed, . . . rushing among the boats with open jaws, and a lashing tail, offered appalling battle." Two boats were smashed, a third upended. Again the *Pequod* bore down to the rescue. On the third day, Ahab "darted his fierce iron, and his far fiercer curse into the hated whale." The line snapped. Moby Dick charged the *Pequod* and breached its starboard bow. The fouled line of a second harpoon caught Ahab around the neck, flinging him out of his boat as the stricken whale flew forward. The vortex of the sinking *Pequod* pulled down the rest of the men, except for Ishmael, the narrator, buoyed by a coffin.

Countless writers have discussed Moby Dick as a symbol—of evil, of indifferent nature, of fate. In *The Golden Day* (1926), Lewis Mumford wrote, "The White Whale is the sheer brute energy of the universe, which challenges and checks the spirit of Man." There was also literal truth in Melville's story. During the first half of the nineteenth century, a notorious real whale known as "Mocha Dick" was encountered in every ocean. In the course of being harpooned nineteen times, he caused the death of more than thirty men, smashed fourteen boats, badly damaged three whaling ships, and sank two other vessels.

MODESTINE, "a diminutive she-ass, not much bigger than a dog, the colour of a mouse, with a kindly eye and a determined under-jaw," was bought by Robert Louis Stevenson for 65 francs and a glass of brandy. He acquired Modestine in the French town of Le Monastier to carry his gear on the casual journey south that he described in *Travels with a Donkey in the Cévennes* (1879). The journey was not easy. "The instinct of an ass is what might be expected from the name," he wrote, and after three days he noted, "my heart was still as cold as a potato." Modestine was stupid but she was patient and liked to eat black bread out of his hand. For twelve days, they struggled up and down mountains, meeting people, and getting lost. When they reached St. Jean du Gard, 120 miles from their starting point, Modestine was worn out and Stevenson, anxious to go on to Alais for his mail, sold her. As he rattled along on the stagecoach, he realized his bereavement: "Up to that moment I thought I had hated her; but now she was gone . . . we had been fast companions. . . . Her faults were those of her race and sex; her virtues were her own."

On September 22, 1977, *National Geographic* editor Carolyn Bennett Patterson and her donkey, Modestine, set out from Le Monastier to make the same trip, ninety-nine years after Stevenson started his. Avoiding paved highways, she traveled Stevenson's route as closely as possible in the same amount of time. "My Modestine," she reported, "is sweet, with warm brown eyes and a talent for listening."

MOLE, in *The Wind in the Willows* (1908) by Kenneth Grahame, moved in with RAT at River Bank one spring. When winter came, Rat was either sleeping or writing poetry, so Mole went looking for BADGER (2) and got lost in the Wild Wood. By tracking Mole's golosh prints, Rat found his friend and they stumbled on to Badger's place. Mole felt completely at home there because "Once well underground, you know exactly where you are. Nothing can happen to you, and nothing can get at you."

MOLLIE, the white mare in George Orwell's *Animal Farm* (1946), preferred sugar cubes and ribbons for her mane to chores, after the animals seized Mr. Jones's farm. She soon defected and was last seen hitched to a dogcart outside a public house.

MONSIEUR GRAT was a little dog that René Descartes took along on his walks after he resumed living in a small town in Holland in 1644. Descartes was 48, lived alone, and rose late after spending the morning in bed meditating, a lifelong habit. The fact that he had a dog for company was remarkable in view of his conclusions about animals. "The greatest of all the prejudices we have retained from our infancy is that of believing that the beasts think," he asserted. They could not reason, therefore they had no souls. Their cries were not emotional but the working of an intricate machine: "The animals act naturally and by springs, like a watch." Madame de Sévigné (1626–96), who adored her dog, later scoffed, "Machines which love, which prefer one person to another, machines which are jealous . . . come now! Descartes never thought he could make us believe that!"

MONSIEUR TIBAULT, in *The King of the Cats* (1929) by Stephen Vincent Benét, was a French conductor who dazzled New York society by facing the audience, his hands clasped in front of him, while he led the New Symphony—with his tail. At dinner parties, M. Tibault monopolized an exotic princess from Siam, to the dismay of young Tommy Brooks, who became suspicious when he saw black fur under the conductor's torn sock. A friend advised him to retell an old legend, involving cats at a burial, at the next social gathering. Brooks did and M. Tibault vanished instantly, "tail and all."

MOPPET, the kitten in Beatrix Potter's *The Story of Miss Moppet* (1906), tied a duster with a hole in it around her head and feigned illness to lure a curious mouse. Peeking through the hole, she caught the mouse, tied it up in the duster, and tossed the bundle around like a ball. When she untied it, the mouse was gone. Moppet had forgotten the hole. In *The Tale of Tom Kitten* (1907), she and her sister and brother, MITTENS and TOM KITTEN, not only failed to keep their clothes clean, they lost them.

MOPSA, in Francis Coventry's *The History of Pompey the Little* (1751), was "deservedly reckoned the most philosophic Cat in *England*," after twelve years of living with an "aged Virgin" devoted to reading sermons. When POMPEY, the Bologna lapdog, joined the household, Mopsa—still mourning her sister SELIMA (eulogized by Thomas Gray)—resolved to divert him from his interest in "trivial Gratification of his Senses" to the "sober Comforts of Philosophy." The pair became great friends until Pompey, engrossed in a debate on the *"Summum Bonum,"* disgraced himself and was evicted by their mistress. Later, in his misery at being a guide for a blind beggar, the memory of Mopsa inspired him to "call in the Aids of Philosophy."

MOPSY and her sisters, Flopsy and Cotton-Tail, were good little bunnies who got bread and milk and blackberries for supper because they obeyed their mother in *The Tale of Peter Rabbit* (1903) by Beatrix Potter.

MORRIS, the big, orange-striped tomcat who became the finicky spokesman for 9-Lives Cat Food in 1969, was discovered at the Hinsdale Humane Society shelter near Chicago by Bob Martwick, a manager of animal talent. Leo Burnett Company, the agency producing the commercials, named the cat Morris and, in a lucky inspiration, had him say in a haughty voice provided by John Irwin: "The cat who doesn't act finicky soon loses control of his owner." The 15-pound tiger stalked through forty commercials in ten years, drew an enormous amount of fan mail, and confounded the competition. Cats promoting other brands on television were seen wagging their tails in unison or doing the cha-cha but they could not match his popularity. He appeared in the movie *Shamus* (1972), received the first Patsy Award, in 1973, for an animal performing in commercials, and was the subject of a biography by Mary Daniels in 1974. Morris—the original Morris—was about 17 when he died of old age in 1978.

MORZILLO, one of sixteen horses taken from Cuba to Mexico in 1519 by Hernando Cortez, became his mount and saved his life. In a battle near the Aztec capital, Tenochtitlán, Cortez took a blow on the head when Indian warriors pulled him off his horse. They almost captured him but Morzillo, despite a painful wound in the mouth from an arrow, fought them off until help came. When Cortez led an expedition to Honduras in 1524, he had to leave his black stallion with friendly Mayan Indians at Lake Petén Itzá in Guatemala because a deep splinter in one hoof had crippled him. The Mayas, who had never seen a horse before, wreathed him with flowers, perfumed him with incense, and fed him delicacies including chicken, not the usual fare for a herbivore. They also worshiped him as Tziunchan, the god of thunder and lightning. After Morzillo died, the Indians worshiped a statue of him. The next Spaniards to arrive at Petén Itzá in 1618 saw the statue, a life-sized figure seated on its haunches like a dog. A zealous Franciscan friar destroyed the idol but a legend persists among the Indians that the horse can still be seen in the deep clear water of the lake.

MOUFLAR, the mastiff in "The Dog Whose Ears Were Cropped," from the *Fables* of Jean de La Fontaine (1621–95), wept as a pup, wondering what he had done to deserve being mutilated by his

MOUFLAR

master. When the dog grew up, he realized there was less of him to bite; he was a fighter who would not come home with torn ears. With his spiked collar and cropped ears, Mouflar had nothing to fear, not even a wolf.

MOUMOUTTE BLANCHE and MOU-MOUTTE CHINOISE were the subjects of *Lives of Two Cats* by Pierre Loti (Louis-Marie-Julien Viaud; 1850–1923), a French naval officer and novelist renowned for the story of *Madame Butterfly* and his sensitive observations of cats. Moumoutte Blanche, a magnificent black and white Angora, had lived with Loti and his mother and aunt for five years when Loti returned from China with Moumoutte Chinoise, a wan, stowaway kitten who had refused to leave his cabin during the seven-month voyage. The first meeting of the cats took place, inevitably, in the kitchen, where, "uttering unearthly yells, a shapeless package of fur and claws . . . rolled and bounded,—shattering glasses, plates, and dishes" until Loti emptied a carafe of water on them. Watching him comfort the newcomer, the Angora apparently deduced "in her jealous little brain" that Moumoutte Chinoise must be tolerated. "They never quarreled again."

MUGGS, the Airedale in James Thurber's "The Dog That Bit People" from *My Life and Hard Times* (1933), spared no one but Thurber's mother, who sent about forty boxes of candy each Christmas to the people Muggs bit. But she was inclined to think it was their fault. One victim was a congressman. Mother had never liked him or his horoscope and said, "Muggs could read him like a book." In his old age, the "big, burly,

choleric dog" stayed outdoors most of the time and the garbage man, the iceman, and the laundryman would not come near the place. Then it was found that Muggs would rush into the house when Mother rattled a strip of sheet iron. It sounded like thunder, the only thing that ever cowed him. When Muggs died at the age of 11, Mother had to be dissuaded from placing him in the family plot. He was buried along a lonely road and Thurber printed *Cave Canem* on a board marking the grave. "Mother was quite pleased with the simple, classic dignity of the old Latin epitaph."

MUNDO CANI DOG, the noisy hound in Walter Wangerin, Jr.'s *The Book of the Dun Cow* (1978), was often a nuisance to the animals' leader, Chauntecleer the rooster, who called him a "running pump" because he wept so often. But the good-hearted dog readily chauffeured animals on his back or in his mouth, herded dithering turkeys, and rescued JOHN WESLEY WEASEL from basilisks sent by Wyrm, the evil serpent imprisoned underground. When Chauntecleer gave up hope that Wyrm could be contained, Mundo Cani was inspired by God's messenger, THE DUN COW, to keep fighting. Armed with her broken-off horn, the dog leaped at Wyrm's monstrous, looming eye and blinded the serpent before the earth convulsed and buried them both.

MUSIC, the dog in two poems by William Wordsworth, was a greyhound bitch who belonged to his brother-in-law, Thomas Hutchinson. In "Incident Characteristic of a Favourite Dog" (1805), she and Dart, a male greyhound, were chasing a hare across a newly frozen river when the ice broke and Dart fell in. Music tried and failed to save him:

> From the brink her paws she stretches,
> Very hands as you would say!
> And afflicting moans she fetches,
> As he breaks the ice away.

Blind in her old age, Music fell into a well and died. In "Tribute to the Memory of the Same Dog" (1805), Wordsworth recalled how feeble she was:

> I saw thee stagger in the summer breeze,
> Too weak to stand against its sportive breath,
> And ready for the gentlest stroke of death.
> It came, and we were glad; yet tears were shed.

MUSTARD and PEPPER were the names of Dandie Dinmont's six terriers in *Guy Mannering* (1815) by Sir Walter Scott. "There's auld Pepper and auld Mustard," said Dandie, "and young Pepper and young Mustard, and little Pepper and little Mustard . . . and now they fear naething that ever cam wi' a hairy skin on't." The limited variety of names, he added, was "a faincy o' my ain to mark the breed." Scott later explained that although Dandie, a Liddlesdale farmer, was a fictitious character, there was, in fact, a Mr. James Davidson living in the area who bred little terriers that he called Mustard or Pepper, according to their color. After *Guy Mannering* was published, "an English lady of high rank and fashion" addressed a letter to Dandie Dinmont that was delivered to Davidson, who happily sent her, as she requested, a pair of the dogs. The breed, first recorded in 1700, is now called the Dandie Dinmont terrier.

MUTT, in *The Dog Who Wouldn't Be* (1957) by Farley Mowat, was a black and white mongrel with a lopsided gait and original ways. He was bought as a puppy in 1929 when Mowat, then 10 years old, and his parents lived in Saskatoon, Saskatchewan. Although Mutt tried to retrieve forty-three heifers on his first hunting trip, he soon learned to go after birds, by diving, running them down, or climbing a tree. He climbed trees in town, too, as well as ladders to chase cats. The dog's finest hour came when a visiting New Yorker bet $100 that Mutt could not outretrieve any dog in the United States. Mowat patted his dog, aimed his empty gun down the alley, and said quietly, "Bang—bang—go get 'em boy!" Mutt streaked down the alley, turned the corner, and two minutes later, rushed back with a superb ruffed grouse, already stuffed and mounted. It had beeen on display in the hardware store window.

MYOBU NO OMOTO, a cat, was so dear to Ichijo, the emperor of Japan (986–1011), that when she had to be rescued from a dog who was chasing her, he exiled the dog and imprisoned her female attendant. A cat who arrived from China and gave birth to five kittens at the Imperial Palace in Kyoto in 999 may have been the first one in Japan and Myobu no Omoto was undoubtedly her descendant. The name means "Omoto, the lady-in-waiting."

MYSOUFF I, the cat who lived with Alexandre Dumas and his mother, "ought to have been a dog," according to the writer in *Histoire de mes bêtes* (1867). When Dumas went to work in the morning, the cat accompanied him to a certain corner and was there to greet him in the evening.

Mysouff would lash the pavement with his tail, "dance about my legs like any dog," start home, then turn back to Dumas before rushing to the house. On days when Dumas happened to decide to dine out, the apparently clairvoyant cat refused to go out the door that had been opened for him at the usual time and "lay motionless on his cushion, in the posture of a serpent biting its own tail."

MYSOUFF II was the cat who succeeded MYSOUFF I many years later when Alexandre Dumas's household included PRITCHARD the Scottish pointer, three monkeys, and an assortment of birds. In *Histoire de mes bêtes* (1867), Dumas reported that after the monkeys squeezed out of their cage and opened the aviary door, Mysouff gorged himself on the whole collection of doves, quails, coral beaks, etc. Placed on trial before Dumas's Sunday guests, the cat was defended by an eloquent gentleman who managed to save his life. But the verdict was guilty with "extenuating circumstances" (the monkeys). Mysouff was sentenced to five years with them in their repaired cage. Then Dumas went broke and had to give the monkeys away, and the cat, like a political prisoner, "regained his liberty by reason of present events."

NALAGIRI, in Buddhist mythology, was the elephant whom Devadetta used in an attempt to kill Buddha. Devadatta, Buddha's cousin, was a former convert who had grown bitterly jealous and found an ally in King Ajatasattu. After making the royal elephant Nalagiri royally drunk, they sent him crashing through the town where Buddha was seeking alms. His disciples begged him to withdraw but the sight of him instantly sobered the elephant, who prostrated himself at Buddha's feet.

NANA (1), the protagonist's namesakes in Emile Zola's *Nana* (1880), was a chestnut filly who had been beaten on every racecourse in France before Count Vandeuvres entered her in the Grand Prix. Her odds, 50–1, inspired the human Nana to quip, "Hell, I'm not worth much, am I?" But when the race started, the filly had been bet down to 10–1. From far back, she gained slowly until, in the stretch, she took a slim lead over Spirit, the English horse. Spirit came on to challenge and Nana's jockey started whipping; "he poured his heart into the filly, picked her up and carried her forward, drenched in foam, her eyes all bloodshot." Nana won by a head. Having held her back in earlier races to lengthen her Grand Prix odds, Vandeuvres had bet everything on her and was swindled in turn by his bookmaker. Ruined, the count burned himself and his horses to death in his stable.

NANA (2), the Darling children's nurse in *Peter Pan* (1904) by J. M. Barrie, is a Newfoundland dog quite capable of turning down beds, turning on bathtub faucets, laying out nightclothes, and fetching young Michael's medicine. Chained in the yard when Peter Pan drops into the house, Nana barks at the goings on, breaks free, and summons the Darlings from a dinner party, but the children have meanwhile flown off to Never Land. When they return with six lost boys who want to be, and are, adopted, the happiest creature in the house is Nana, who promptly assumes "the importance of a nurse who will never have another day off." Barrie's own male Newfoundland, Luath (3), was the model for Nana.

NANDI

NANDI (or NANDIN), "The Happy One," is the milk-white bull of the Hindu god Siva and the chief of his personal attendants. At temples to Siva in the south of India, there is always a recumbent figure of Nandi gazing at the shrine.

NANDINI, "the cow of abundance" in Hindu mythology, was a symbol of the fertility of northern India and it was said that her milk rejuvenated mankind for a thousand years. Her mother was SURABHI, who was also known as KAMADHENU.

NANKO and NANNY were a pair of goats that President Abraham Lincoln bought for $5 apiece as pets for his youngest son, Tad, an obstreperous 10-year-old who once hitched them to a kitchen chair and drove them through the East Room of the White House. On August 8, 1863, the President wrote to Mrs. Lincoln: "Tell dear Tad poor 'Nanny Goat' is lost. . . . The day you left, Nanny was found resting herself and chewing her little cud on the middle of Tad's bed." Lincoln explained that the goat had been moved to the White House because the gardener had complained about her destroying the flowers. Two days later she had disappeared. "This is the last we know of poor 'Nanny.' "

NAPOLEON (1), one of the great dogs of newspaper comic strips, was created by Clifford McBride in 1929 for a Sunday panel titled "Uncle Elby Befriends a Lonesome Dog." Amiable Uncle Elby, a portly middle-aged bachelor, was based on McBride's own uncle, Henry Elba Eastman, who owned a 210-pound St. Bernard. Napoleon was a scraggly 250-pound black and white mongrel who spread confusion in Uncle Elby's life. The pair became so popular that a daily strip, *Napoleon and Uncle Elby*, was launched in 1932 and lasted until 1960, nine years after McBride's death. In a typical episode, Uncle Elby rummages in a cabinet for bread and onions to go with the Camembert a friend had given him. Napoleon sniffs at the cheese on the kitchen table and looks horrified by the odor. Uncle Elby, returning to the table, is stunned to see the cheese has vanished. Through the window, at a great distance, Napoleon can be seen burying the smelly thing.

NAPOLEON (2), the large Berkshire boar in *Animal Farm* (1946), a political fable by George Orwell, became dictator after the animals seized Mr. Jones's farm for their proposed egalitarian society. With sheep bleating to disrupt general meetings and a bodyguard of dogs trained to attack, Napoleon ousted a rival pig, SNOWBALL. Another pig, SQUEALER, persuaded the gullible animals that "our Leader, Comrade Napoleon" knew what was best for them. They slaved while the pigs luxuriated in Jones's house, dissenters were executed, Napoleon began doing business with men, and the basic principle of the rebellion was amended to:

ALL ANIMALS ARE EQUAL
BUT SOME ANIMALS
ARE MORE EQUAL THAN OTHERS

THE NAVY GOAT: see BILL XXII.

NEIL, the Saint Bernard dog in the television series "Topper" (1955), had perished in the same avalanche in Switzerland that killed George and Marian Kirby. The three of them returned as ghosts to bedevil Cosmo Topper, a staid banker. He alone could see and hear their shenanigans. The series was based on the movie *Topper* (1937), which was based on Thorne Smith's novel *The Jovial Ghosts*. Neil drank martinis.

NELSON, a light chestnut gelding, was 3 years old when Thomas Nelson, the governor of Virginia, gave him to George Washington in 1765. For the next ten years Nelson, so-named by Washington, was his favorite mount for cross-country hunting. When the Second Continental Congress appointed Washington commander in chief of the Continental Army in June 1775, he rode Nelson to Philadelphia and accepted command. He proceeded to Boston, traveling part of the way by coach, but Nelson went along. Nelson was with Washington at Valley Forge in 1777–78 and remained the only one of the general's several mounts used throughout the Revolutionary War. On October 19, 1781, Washington rode Nelson to the British surrender at Yorktown. After retiring to Mount Vernon,

Washington never rode the horse again, nor was anyone else permitted to. Nelson lived out his days as an "honorable pensioner."

THE NEMEAN LION, in Greek mythology, was a terrible beast who ravaged the valley of Nemea. The first of the twelve labors of Heracles (Hercules) ordered by King Eurystheus was to kill him and bring back his hide. Since no weapon could wound the lion, Heracles, the strongest man on earth, choked it to death. The sight of Heracles approaching with the carcass flung over his shoulder so terrified Eurystheus that he hid in a large bronze jar and ordered that future trophies be displayed outside the city's gates.

NEPTUNE, a pointer, belonged to Sir John Throckmorton, whose friend William Cowper (1731–1800) eulogized the dog in "An Epitaph":

> Here lies one, who never drew
> Blood himself, yet many slew. . . .
> Stout he was, and large of limb,
> Scores have fled at sight of him;
> And to all this fame he rose
> Only following his nose.

NERO, a little white terrier, part Maltese and part mongrel, brightened the life of Jane Welsh Carlyle, who was 48 and childless when a friend gave him to her in 1849. She adored the dog. Her husband, Thomas Carlyle, had mixed feelings. On walks, the dog's "happy gambollings" amused him but when Nero refused to follow him home and had to be fetched, the "miserable quadruped" became a "real nuisance and absurdity." One morning in 1850, Nero leaped from the library window at 5

THE NEMEAN LION

Cheyne Row in London and was carried in senseless. "Imagine his taking it into his head that he could *fly*—like the birds—if he tried!" wrote Jane. Virginia Woolf, in her biography of Elizabeth Barrett Browning's dog, *Flush* (1933), suggested that it might have been a suicide attempt: Perhaps "Nero was driven to desperate melancholy by associating with Mr. Carlyle. . . . For

[181]

the present, Nero's motives must remain obscure." In any case, the dog recovered and lived ten more years.

NEWCOMER, the mascot of the Baltimore Colts since 1975, is a brown and white pinto mare who dashes around the field when Baltimore scores. Her owner-rider Colleen Sarro wears a western outfit in blue and white that matches Newcomer's blanket. During her first years as mascot, Newcomer delighted fans by producing a filly. The foal's name, Gimme-a-C, was chosen in a big contest and the winner received season tickets.

NIATROSS, the greatest Standardbred in the history of American harness racing, won all thirteen of his starts as a 2-year-old and set five world records even before he completed his sweep of pacing's Triple Crown: the Cane Pace, the Little Brown Jug, and, on October 11, 1980, the Messenger Stakes. Earlier that month in Lexington, Kentucky, grown men wept when the big bay colt paced a time-trial mile in 1:49 1/5, shattering the world record by 2 4/5 seconds. Twice named harness horse of the year, he was sired by Albatross, who was similarly honored in 1971 and 1972. Niatross had such potential value at stud, with 150 advance bookings at $35,000 a service, that his racing career ended on December 27 at Pompano Park in Florida, where, in the style expected of "the perfect horse" and "living legend," he won by seventeen lengths and set a track record. In his two-year career, Niatross won thirty-seven of thirty-nine starts, earning $2,019,212, and, in the 1980 season, earned $1,414,313, more than any racehorse of any breed.

NILS, in Margery Sharp's *The Rescuers* (1959), was one of the three mice who freed a Norwegian poet imprisoned in the Black Castle. A hearty sailor, Nils was recruited in Norway because a mouse who spoke the prisoner's language was needed. He was also resourceful. When the trio arrived at the Castle, Nils advised his companions, MISS BIANCA and BERNARD, to follow the best boots. Since they belonged to the Chief Jailer and he had the best food, his quarters had the only mouse hole in the place. After two tedious months in hiding there, Nils found an escape route through the dungeon. He darted to each cell, calling out Norwegian words until he located the poet and the rescue was accomplished.

NIM CHIMPSKY, was a chimpanzee, taught to use sign language in an experiment designed by Herbert S. Terrace, professor of psychology at Columbia University, to determine if a chimpanzee could learn to use language the way people do, by creating sentences. (Nim was named for linguist Noam Chomsky of M.I.T., who considers this ability biologically unique to humans.) The experiment began in December 1973, when Nim was 2 weeks old, with caretaker-teachers treating him like a human child while training him to make hand signs. Nim started to put two signs together in 1975 and, a year later, was linking three, as in *me more eat* or *you tickle me*. At the end of forty-four months, when he was returned to the Institute for Primate Studies in Norman, Oklahoma, Nim understood 200 signs and could produce 125 of them. He had also signed combinations of two or more words 20,000 times.

These phrases appeared to indicate that a chimpanzee could form sentences, but

Terrace reported in his book *Nim* (1979) that after reviewing videotapes, photographs and transcripts, he found that he had overrated Nim's linguistic ability. The combinations had not increased in length as a growing child's do, and most of them were prompted by what the teacher had just signed. However, in view of what Nim had accomplished with sixty different teachers in less than four years, Terrace concluded that a longer experiment with fewer teachers might advance even further a chimpanzee's ability to communicate in sign language.

NIPPER (1), a black and white fox terrier born near Bristol, England, in 1884, was adopted by artist Francis Barraud after his brother, the dog's first owner, died. In the early 1890s, Barraud was inspired by the way the little dog cocked his head at the sounds coming out of the horn of the "talking machine" or "gramophone," as record players were then called. He painted the scene and titled it "His Master's Voice." No one bought the work so he brightened it up with a brass horn in place of the original black one. An executive of the Gramophone Company then asked that the cylinder machine in the picture be replaced with the more recent turntable. That done, Barraud sold the painting for £50 and the copyright for an additional £50. Nipper died in 1895. Barraud was kept busy for the rest of his life making copies of the original painting for record company executives.

In 1901, the Victor Talking Machine Company of Camden, New Jersey (later merged with RCA), acquired the American rights to "His Master's Voice" and adopted the picture as its trademark. Four stained glass windows of dog and phonograph were installed in the Victor tower in Camden in 1915 and served as landmarks for fifty-four years; one is now at the Smithsonian Institution. Millions of Nipper doodads—salt and pepper shakers, watch fobs, etc.—were distributed, and in the mid-1930s, Nipper statues appeared, à la cigar store Indians. Some were wired for sound to entice pedestrians with the latest hits. In 1954, the world's largest Nipper, 25½ feet high, was constructed on top of a four-story building in Albany, with a flashing beacon on his right ear to alert low-flying, very low-flying, planes. Nipper was relegated to limited use in the 1960s, mostly on records and album covers, but in 1978, RCA began promoting wider use of the trademark by the entire corporation.

NIPPER (2) the ferret was ready, if needed, to hook up the television cameras at the Queen Victoria Memorial in front of Buckingham Palace for the day of the Royal Wedding of the Prince of Wales and Lady Diana Spencer on July 29, 1981. Cables from those cameras had to be led by a draw wire through a 6-inch underground duct to equipment in St. James's Park. When rigging commenced for the Queen's Silver Jubilee in 1977, the draw wire was missing and a ferret was used to replace it. Inserted at one end of the duct, he scurried to his reward of bacon at the other end 75 yards away, easily negotiating a 120° bend in the center, and the nylon thread attached to his harness was used to pull through the first of increasingly larger lines. Four years later, Nipper was harnessed to demonstrate the procedure at Thames Television's studios in South London but the contingency he was prepared for did not arise.

THE NITTANY LION

THE NITTANY LION became the athletic symbol of Pennsylvania State University in 1904, when the baseball team, at Princeton for a game, refused to be impressed by a statue of THE PRINCETON TIGER and declared their imaginary lion "the fiercest beast of all." Penn State won. The lion cited was the North American *Felis concolor*—the mountain lion, cougar, puma, or panther who had roamed the Nittany Valley until about twenty-five years before the university was founded there in 1855. To end confusion with the African maned lion, the symbol was made tangible in 1942, when a 13-ton limestone statue of a crouching Nittany lion, carved by Heinz Warneke, was presented to Penn State. After vandals knocked off the lion's right ear in 1979, Warneke came out of retirement at the age of 84 to replace it.

NOBLE, the lion in the twelfth-century beast epic *Reynard the Fox,* was the king. He depended on advice from his council or his wife and believed whatever he was told. When REYNARD, sentenced to death, spoke of great treasure, Noble was persuaded by his wife and his own greed to pardon the fox. The king was soon enraged by more of Reynard's misdeeds. "I am not the first that has been deceived by a woman's counsel," he complained. Again the fox ingratiated himself. This time, Noble made Reynard his highest official, "For here is none that is like to you in sharp and high counsel nor subtler in finding remedy for a mischief."

NOBS, the horse who carried Dr. Daniel Dove of Doncaster on his rounds in Robert Southey's *The Doctor* (1834–47), was a big 17-year-old chestnut. Nobs compared favorably with famous horses in history and legend, and possessed "two properties of a man, to wit, a proud heart and a hearty stomach." In many cases, "the patient could not have been saved unless the Doctor by means of his horse Nobs arrived on time." When the Doctor left Nobs outside a farmhouse one day, the farmer's little boy began tugging his tail and hitting his legs with a switch. Before the mother could pull the child away, "Nobs lifted up one foot, placed it against the boy's stomach, and gently pushed him down. . . . This was what the Doctor called kindness of disposition in a horse."

NOX, in G. K. Chesterton's "The Oracle of the Dog" from *The Incredulity of Father Brown* (1926), was a big black retriever whose behavior on the afternoon of Colonel Druce's murder enabled Father Brown to solve it. While his friend Fiennes and the Colonel's nephews Herbert and Harry were strolling on the beach that afternoon, Herbert tossed his walking stick into the sea and Nox plunged in to fetch it. Then Harry threw his. The dog swam out again but stopped, returned to shore, and started to howl, just as a scream from the garden marked the discovery of Druce's body. At the garden, the three men met Traill the lawyer. Nox immediately blocked his path and barked at him. Fiennes thought the dog was an oracle, coming out of the sea to howl just as the body was found, then denouncing Traill. Nonsense, said Father Brown, "Dogs hate nervous people," and Traill was nervous. What mattered was the business on the beach. "Once a dog is actually chasing a thing, . . . he won't stop," and turning around because his mood changed was "unthinkable." Nox came back without the stick because he could not find it. It had sunk, the reason being that it was really a steel rod with a sharp point, a "sword stick"— the murder weapon.

NUTKIN, in *The Tale of Squirrel Nutkin* (1903) by Beatrix Potter, was the impertinent red squirrel who chanted silly riddles to Old Brown the owl. After singing out a riddle on the sixth day, the squirrel hopped onto Old Brown's head and the owl caught him. It cost Nutkin half his tail to escape.

OFFISA BULL PUPP, in George Herriman's comic strip *Krazy Kat* (1913–44), walked upright, sported a policeman's hat, badge, and night stick, and tried to keep Ignatz Mouse from heaving a brick at Krazy Kat. By putting the mouse in jail or, at one point, covering his brick with glue, Offisa Pupp occasionally interrupted the flow of bricks but just as often became the target of one as well.

OH BOY, a white English bulldog, was given to President Warren G. Harding after he had received and grown very fond of his famous Airedale, Laddie Boy, in 1921. Harding liked his new dog but, concerned that the two males might fight, had the bulldog quartered in the White House stables. As it turned out, there were no problems. Oh Boy and Laddie Boy became great friends.

OLD DRUM, a black and tan hound, belonged to a Missouri farmer named Charles Burden. Lon Hornsby, a neighbor who had lost a number of sheep to raiding dogs, had his nephew shoot Old Drum on October 28, 1869. Burden sued Hornsby for damages and won. Hornsby appealed and won a reversal. Burden then obtained a new trial on the ground of new evidence. This time, his lawyer was George Graham Vest, who later became a U.S. senator. In his summation on September 27, 1870, in the Warrensburg Courthouse, Vest spoke for an hour on the bond between men and their dogs in history, literature, and legend. His peroration has become a classic among dog lovers:

> The one absolutely unselfish friend that a man can have in this selfish world . . . is his dog. . . . If fortune drives the master forth an outcast in the world, . . . the faithful dog asks no higher privilege than that of accompanying him . . . and when the last scene of all comes, and death takes his master in its embrace, . . . there by his graveside will the noble dog be found, his head between his paws, his eyes sad but open in alert watchfulness, faithful and true even to death.

Burden won. Or, as one of Hornsby's lawyers observed, "The dog, though dead, had won." A memorial monument stands near the spot where Old Drum's body was found, a bronze tablet marks the site of the trial, and, in 1953, a bronze statue of Old Drum, with the text of Vest's "Eulogy on a Dog" on its base, was dedicated at Warrensburg's Courthouse Square.

OLD IKE, the tobacco-chewing ram, and thirteen ewes were pastured on the White House grounds during World War I to trim the lawn and thus save manpower. They trimmed it all right, and a lot of shrubbery, and several beds of perennials. The sheep were sheared regularly and the wool was auctioned off. The proceeds, a reported $100,000, were donated to the Red Cross. In 1920, the "Wilson flock" was given to Mr. Probert, who had a farm in Maryland, where, thanks to Old Ike, the flock expanded from fourteen to seventy.

Giving an animal chewing tobacco was something farm hands in the South did for the fun of it. Old Ike had become hooked on nicotine and the dribbling ram had been an amusing curiosity at the White House. On the farm, he would nudge Mr. Probert to get at his cigar when there was no plug forthcoming. By 1927, Old Ike had grown too feeble to rise. He was given his last chaw and, a few hours later, was put down.

OLD JOE, an Arabian dromedary featured in the Barnum & Bailey Circus, was the model for the picture on the Camel cigarette package. In 1913, the R. J. Reynolds Tobacco Company of Winston-Salem, North Carolina, was preparing to launch the world's first blended cigarette. Names that evoked exotic places were then popular in the tobacco business and Richard Joshua Reynolds, the company's founder, had just picked Camel for the brand name of his new cigarettes when the circus came to town. Reynolds sent his stenographer, R. C. Haberken, to take pictures of Old Joe. The camel, however, would not cooperate. He kept turning his head to look at the camera. The circus manager kept straightening the camel's head until finally, in disgust, Old Joe lifted his tail and raised his head. The art for the cigarette package was based on the photograph of that pose.

OLD MAN COYOTE, in *The Adventures of Old Man Coyote* (1916) by Thornton Burgess, had never seen a porcupine before the night he arrived from the Great West and was confronted by PRICKLY PORKY. Keeping his distance, the coyote kicked dirt on Prickly until the two of them realized that GRANNY FOX had arranged the fight. The next time she tried to get rid of him, Old Man Coyote figured out her plan and not only escaped but also stole the hen that she had stolen.

OLD MR. BENJAMIN BUNNY, in *The Tale of Benjamin Bunny* (1904) by Beatrix Potter, smoked a pipe, carried a switch, and since he had "no opinion whatever of cats," simply jumped off a wall onto one that was sitting on an overturned basket. After kicking the cat into the greenhouse and locking the door, he found his missing son BENJAMIN BUNNY and nephew PETER RABBIT (1) under the basket. Old Mr. Bunny pulled Benjamin out by the ears and gave him a switching. Then he pulled out Peter and marched them home.

OLD JOE

Camels

Tomorrow

there'll be more
CAMELS in
this town than
in all Asia and
Africa com-
bined!

OLD MR. BENJAMIN BUNNY

OLD MR. BOUNCER, the father of BENJAMIN BUNNY in *The Tale of Mr. Tod* (1912) by Beatrix Potter, was supposed to mind the rabbit babies while his son and daughter-in-law FLOPSY were away, but he fell asleep while entertaining TOMMY BROCK the badger. The bunnies were gone when Mr. Bouncer woke up. After a scolding from Flopsy, who took away his pipe, he sulked in a corner, barricaded behind a chair, until Benjamin returned with the babies. Old Mr. Bouncer was forgiven and a new pipe and fresh tobacco were presented to him. "He was rather upon his dignity; but he accepted."

OLD MR. TOAD, having seen the Great World, patronized his cousin GRANDFATHER FROG for being gullible, in *The Adventures of Grandfather Frog* (1915) by Thornton Burgess. The cousins exchanged sharp words until Farmer Brown's boy approached. Grandfather Frog dived into the Smiling Pool. Old Mr. Toad, who had boasted that he helped the boy in the garden and that they were friends, stayed put. The frog was so astonished to see the boy tickle Old Mr. Toad under the chin that he decided to have a look at the Great World himself.

THE OLD PRINCE, in *Bambi* (1928) by Felix Salten, was a majestic, dark red stag, the biggest in the forest. Few had seen him even once. Nobody knew his age, his family, or where he lived. BAMBI was a fawn, calling for his mother, when he first saw the Prince. The next time they met, Bambi was curious about the hunters. "Listen, smell and see for yourself," said the old stag. When Bambi was a young buck convinced he had heard his mate and straining to go to her, the Prince blocked his path, then led him soundlessly through the woods to show him a hunter imitating her call. The wise old stag taught Bambi how to survive in the forest. Then the time came to tell Bambi not to follow him any farther. "My time is up," the old Prince said calmly. "Now I have to look for a resting place. Good-bye, my son. I loved you dearly."

OLD RIP, a horned toad, had been inexplicably placed by Justice of the Peace Ernest Wood in the cornerstone of the Eastland, Texas, courthouse when it was dedicated in 1897. The building was demolished in 1928 to make way for a new one, and on February 28, 3,000 people gathered to watch County Judge Ed Pritchard open the cornerstone. Under a Bible and other assorted items lay the dusty toad. He was handed to the judge, who held him up by one leg for all to see. Suddenly, the other leg started to twitch; the toad had come back to life after thirty-one years. He was christened Old Rip and displayed around the country. President Coolidge allegedly canceled several appointments to see him. In 1929, Old Rip succumbed and was laid to rest in a fancy coffin that can still be seen in the Eastland County Courthouse. Was his story fact or legend? A local spokesman said, "Arguing the point is not recommended in these parts."

OLD ROWLEY was a favorite horse of Charles II of England (1630–85), who frequented the course at Newmarket, often riding in races. The king, seated on Old Rowley to watch the horses work out, was such a familiar sight that he was given the nickname "Old Rowley." A section of the Newmarket course is still called the Rowley Mile.

OLD WHITEY, a knock-kneed horse with a shaggy mane, was the favorite mount of Gen. Zachary Taylor, who was called "Old Rough and Ready" because the higher he rose in rank, the sloppier his dress became. His legs were so short that he had to be helped up on his horse; once mounted, he often sat sideways with one leg slung over the pommel. The general, in his farmer's straw hat, and his horse were a scruffy pair and a familiar sight in the Mexican War. Old Whitey was lethargic most of the time, even in the thick of battle, but always perked up at the sound of a band. When Taylor became President in 1849, his old war horse grazed freely on the White House lawn. Visitors gave him sugar and carrots, or pulled hairs out of his tail for souvenirs. One day, he tried to nudge his way into a parade of visiting firemen. After that, whenever there was band music, Old Whitey was tethered.

OLD YELLER, a big, ugly dog with one ear missing, adopted a Texas frontier family in the 1860s in Fred Gipson's *Old Yeller* (1956). While the father was away selling cattle, the half-starved stray turned up to steal a side of meat, but soon proved his worth. Named for his howl as well as his color, Old Yeller tracked game and fearlessly protected the family. He was nearly torn apart fighting killer hogs so that Travis, the older boy, could jump free. Old Yeller was still crippled when he had his last fight. He saved the boys' mother from a rabid wolf, was bitten, and had to be shot.

O'MALLEY, the alley cat in Walt Disney Productions' animated feature *The Aristocats* (1970), is smitten with DUCHESS (2), the elegant cat stranded in the French countryside with her three kittens. They have a high old time getting back to Paris, where they live happily ever after.

OSWALD THE LUCKY RABBIT, created in 1927, was Walt Disney's first successful animated cartoon character. The black rabbit was a forecast of MICKEY MOUSE, who appeared a year later, with his white face, wide grin, and big feet. Oswald's animation was innovative: in *Oh, What a*

OLD WHITEY

Knight (1928), the drenched rabbit wrung himself out to dry, and in *Bright Lights* (1928), he lifted the shadow of a large man, then slid under it to sneak into a show without paying. Disney did not own the rights to the character, however, and in 1929, Oswald became the star of cartoons produced by Walter Lantz for Universal Pictures. Aftr being changed into an undistinguished white rabbit in 1936, Oswald was gradually replaced by Lantz's new stars, ANDY PANDA and Woody Woodpecker.

OWD BOB, the gray collie in Alfred Ollivant's *Bob, Son of Battle* (1898), was the last of the Gray Dogs of Kenmuir to herd sheep for the Moores in the Daleland of Scotland, and the first in fifty years to win the Shepherds' Trophy. He had "that famous trick of coaxing the sheep to do his wishes, blending . . . the brains of a man with the way of a woman." In Bob's final competition for permanent possession of the trophy, one of three sheep being driven toward a plank bridge ran away. "Racing like the nor'easter over the sea," the Gray Dog retrieved it and when the sheep balked in the middle of the bridge, he leaped on the back of the hind one to force them across. A few nights later, Bob was discovered standing beside a dead sheep. For a terrible moment it appeared that he was the killer who had been raiding the flocks; then it became evident that he had run the killer to ground.

THE PACING WHITE MUSTANG, or White Steed of the Prairies, was a legendary wild stallion that frontiersmen from the Rio Grande to the Rocky Mountains claimed to have seen, sometimes with a large band of mares, most often alone. Thousands of dollars were offered for his capture and he was chased for hundreds of miles but he could pace faster than the swiftest horse could run. He had never been known to gallop or trot. Indians believed that he was a ghost horse, that neither fire nor bullets could stop him. J. Frank Dobie, who traced the lore in *The Mustangs* (1952), found the earliest mention of the pacing stallion in Washington Irving's *A Tour on the Prairies* (1835). Starting with George W. Kendall in *A Narrative of the Texan Santa Fe Expedition* (1844), other writers recalled "marvelous tales" they had heard of the White Steed; and Herman Melville, who had never seen a mustang, described him in "The Whiteness of the Whale" in *Moby Dick* (1851).

PADDINGTON, introduced in *A Bear Called Paddington* (1958), the first of a series of books by Michael Bond, is a small bear in a large hat who was wearing a tag saying, "PLEASE LOOK AFTER THIS BEAR. THANK YOU," when Mr. and Mrs. Brown discovered him in London's Paddington Station. He had emigrated from darkest Peru, he explained, after his Aunt Lucy moved to the home for retired bears in Lima. The Browns took him home, where he nearly flooded the house, not knowing that stoppered bathtubs overflow. But Paddington endeared himself with well-meaning projects that were somehow always diverted from disasters to triumphs. The Paddington books, television series, and toy bears have made him nearly as popular as WINNIE-THE-POOH and THE TEDDY BEAR.

PADDY (1), a lioness, was raised from infancy by Wyant Davis Hubbard and his wife, Isabella, at Ibamba, their home in Northern Rhodesia from 1929 to 1934. In *Ibamba* (1962), Hubbard reported that since Paddy was too young to know how lions behave, she made friends with everybody in the household, including small antelope, dogs, a crested crane, and MR. THOMAS, the civet cat. The playful cub wrestled with Hubbard, romped with Isabella, and let their baby daughter, Buncher, climb all over her. If anyone made Buncher cry, Paddy snarled a warning to be gentle. When the lioness outgrew the house, she was moved to an outdoor paddock, where an amorous wild lion made repeated visits. She kicked dirt at him but, at 350 pounds, she was "almost obnoxiously loving" to the Hubbards, "bouncing about like a tremendous rubber ball." In 1934, the Hubbards had to move back to the United States. Since they could not take Paddy and she was too tame to survive in the wild, Hubbard made his "awful decision." He shot her "between her great luminous, trusting eyes."

PADDY (2), an infant beaver whose mother had been killed by a wolf, was raised in the Ontario wilderness for four months by R. D. Lawrence, who related the experience in *Paddy* (1977). Rescued in May, the half-starved kit weighed only 1 pound and had to be fed milk through an eyedropper for the first two weeeks. By July, Paddy weighed 8 pounds and bounced along after Lawrence "like a well-trained puppy." He would announce his hunger in "long-suffering mumbles." Other beavers, including a buck who was probably his father, began visiting his chicken wire enclosure, and when Lawrence dismantled it in mid-September, Paddy—by then, weighing about 30 pounds—swam off to join them, "a natural reunion that just had to be."

PADDY THE BEAVER, in the Thornton Burgess nature books, dismantled his dam

in *The Adventures of Jerry Muskrat* (1914) as soon as he was told that it cut off the water to the animals who lived below it. He went down to see their homes and admired the Smiling Pool but declined to stay. The distant barking of BOWSER THE HOUND unsettled Paddy and, as he explained, he had to live up in the forest where he could eat the bark of trees.

PANGUR BAN, a cat, belonged to an Irish scholar in the ninth century, whose poem about him is the earliest known reference to a domesticated cat in European literature. The poet compared their lives: while Pangur hunted mice, he hunted words. Together they enjoyed their separate tasks. Pangur was glad when a mouse darted out of the wall, and the scholar was happy with his studies:

> Practice every day has made
> Pangur perfect in his trade;
> I get wisdom day and night
> Turning darkness into light.

PAN HU, a five-colored dog in Chinese folklore, belonged to Kaoshin, an emperor in the twenty-fourth century B.C., who was so distressed by an invasion of barbarians that he offered an enormous reward—including the hand of his youngest daughter—for the head of the invaders' chieftain. When Pan Hu brought it in and placed it at the foot of the throne, Kaoshin kept his promise. His daughter and the dog were married. They had twelve children, who intermarried; their descendants founded several barbarous tribes who venerated Pan Hu as their ancestor god.

PAPILLON, the fire-breathing horse in Carolingian legend, suddenly appeared just as Ogier the Dane, shipwrecked on the Isle of Avalon, headed inland. The horse (whose name in French means "butterfly") knelt for Ogier to mount, then dashed away to the garden of a magnificent palace where the fairy Morgana placed a crown of flowers on Ogier's head. The Dane lived there in an enchanted state for a hundred years until Morgana inadvertently removed the crown and broke the spell. With his memory restored, Ogier longed to return to the French court. He rode Papillon to the shore, sea-goblins bore them across the sea to France, and the horse sped to Paris. Hugh Capet, the king, welcomed the paladin from the past as well as his offer of help in lifting the Saracen siege of Chartres. As the Dane rode into battle, Papillon breathed fire from his nostrils, throwing the Saracens into confusion. Ogier finished them off with his magic sword, Cortana.

PATIENCE and FORTITUDE, the marble lions in front of the New York Public Library at Fifth Avenue and 42nd Street,

were named by Mayor Fiorello La Guardia, who always ended his Sunday radio broadcasts on WNYC in the 1940s with the exhortation, "Patience and Fortitude." Originally dubbed Leo Astor and Leo Lenox, in honor of two foundations that help support the library, the lions had also been known as Lord Lenox and Lady Astor, or Leo and Leonora, in spite of their manes—which clearly indicate they are both male. Set in place a few days before the building was dedicated by President William Howard Taft in May 1911, the statues, executed in pink Tennessee marble by Edward C. Potter, were not well-received. One critic thought the intelligent, industrious beaver would have been more appropriate. Theodore Roosevelt, who had wanted elk or moose, was overruled. The public called the recumbent lions "absurd," "squash-faced," and "mealy-mouthed," but they have since become a popular landmark, especially at Christmas, when each lion sports a great wreath with a big red bow. Patience and Fortitude have also in-

PATIENCE AND FORTITUDE

spired stories and poems and the inevitable pun about going to the library to read between the lions.

PATRIPATAN, a legendary white cat in India, was sent by his master, a prince of Salangham, to pluck a flower from a tree in the heaven of the gods and goddesses. The cat found life there so pleasant that 300 years passed before he remembered his errand, but during that time, the prince and his people waiting below did not age a minute. And Patripatan had been so charming that the king of the gods sent him back not with a single blossom but a whole flowering branch of his beloved tree. From that day on, Salangham was a land of gentleness and beauty.

PATTY CAKE, the first gorilla born in New York City's Central Park Zoo, was a complete surprise when she arrived on September 3, 1972. Her mother and father, Lulu and Kongo, had been imported from Africa in 1966 and it was unusually early for them to breed. Surprising also was the excellent care given by Lulu since over 98 percent of gorilla mothers in captivity reject their babies. For six months, Patty Cake lived with her parents and thrived, a zoo celebrity with press coverage and thousands of visitors. But in March 1973, a freak accident occurred when Kongo, in an adjoining cage, reached through the bars for her. Lulu grabbed her, knocking the baby's arm against the bars and breaking it. The arm was set in a plaster cast and Patty Cake was taken to the Bronx Zoo to be cosseted with other primate babies.

As she gained weight and recovered from the fracture, a dispute arose over where she should be kept—at the Bronx Zoo, which had better facilities, or at the Central Park Zoo, where her parents were. Dr. Ronald R. Nadler of the Yerkes Regional Primate Center in Atlanta then inspected both zoos. Noting that gorillas had become an endangered species, he concluded that Patty Cake should be returned to her parents, "to develop the normal social repertoire of a gorilla and thereby improve the chance that she can participate in the perpetuation of her species."

The reunion took place in June. Lulu recognized Patty Cake with a scream but, apparently sensing the baby's initial terror, hesitated before picking her up. Kongo was admitted to the cage about twenty minutes later and went right over to nuzzle her. In a few months, however, the parents were moved to a separate cage lest their strenuous sexual foreplay cause another accidental injury. Patty Cake stayed next door with Pansy, a chimpanzee, to keep her company.

PAULINE, a Holstein, belonged to President William Howard Taft (1909–13). She was the last of many cows pastured on the White House lawn to provide milk for the families of the Presidents.

PAUL PRY, a black and white Newfoundland dog, was carrying a basket of flowers in his mouth when Sir Edwin Landseer saw him for the first time. Impressed by the dog's beauty, Landseer posed him on a studio table for the painting *A Distinguished Member of the Humane Society* (1838), which depicted Paul Pry resting on a stone pier at high tide. It was said at the time that Landseer breathed "Promethean fire" into the portrait. The engraving of the picture, dedicated to the Royal Humane

PAUL PRY

Society, became so popular that, in honor of the artist, black and white Newfoundlands have been called Landseers ever since.

PAUL REVERE'S HORSE on the historic night ride of April 18, 1775, was a small chestnut mare that Revere borrowed in Charlestown from his friend Deacon John Larkin. She was a Narragansett Pacer, a breed now extinct, and her name is not known. When Revere was captured halfway between Lexington and Concord,

Massachusetts, at about two o'clock on the morning of the 19th, a British soldier rode off on Larkin's mare.

PEGASUS, the famous winged horse of Greek mythology, was born from the neck of Medusa when Perseus cut off her head. The horse created the spring Hippocrene on Mount Helicon, the home of the Muses, with a stamp of his hoof. The young warrior Bellerophon coveted Pegasus, so he tamed him with a golden bridle presented by the goddess Athena, rode him into the sky, and killed the monstrous Chimera by raining arrows down from above. After several more adventures, Bellerophon presumed to ascend to Olympus to join the immortals but the horse, stung by a gadfly sent by Zeus, threw him off. Pegasus flew on to Olympus and there he stayed, fetching thunderbolts for Zeus.

PEGLEG PETE, a raffish bulldog with a wooden leg, made his debut in Walt Disney's *Steamboat Willie* (1928), chasing his co-star, MICKEY MOUSE, off the ship's bridge. In *Gallopin' Gaucho* (1929), Pegleg tried to abduct MINNIE MOUSE, but Mickey rescued her from his clutches. Ever the villain, Pegleg appeared in many Mickey Mouse cartoons, chomping his cigar and being nasty, but always thwarted in the end.

PELLEAS, a small, black French bulldog with a "powerful head like Socrates and Verlaine," was a favorite of Maurice Maeterlinck (1862–1949), who adored dogs. The Belgian writer eulogized Pelléas in his essay "On the Death of a Little Dog": "He knows to what to devote the best in him. He knows to whom above him to give himself. . . . He possesses truth in its fullness."

PENNY, a female leopard cub, was acquired by Joy Adamson in 1976. Having raised ELSA the lioness and PIPPA the cheetah, Adamson wanted to compare the three great cats of Africa. In *Queen of Shaba* (1980), completed shortly before her death, Adamson described Penny's development from a "confident pet" to an alert,

wild leopardess roaming Kenya's Shaba Reserve. Fitted with a radio collar so that she could be tracked, and helped if necessary, Penny learned to catch and guard her prey, found a mate, and, in May 1979, gave birth to two cubs. Unlike Elsa and Pippa, Penny wanted to lead Adamson to them immediately; on the third day, Adamson went to see them. After seven weeks of keeping one cub out of sight, Penny again displayed them both. She was affectionate with Adamson, the only "mother" she had ever known, but unpredictable, "playfully" slashing or biting her several times. Adamson concluded that of the three big cats, leopards are "certainly the most difficult to understand, more intelligent . . . and less reliable. Although Penny was very good-natured . . . I could never relax with her."

PE-PE, a male giant panda at the Chapultepec Zoo in Mexico City, sired XENG-LI, who was born there in 1980. When a second successful mating with his consort, Ying-Ying, was reported in the spring of 1981, Pe-Pe was nicknamed *El Macho* and there was talk of borrowing him to service Ling-Ling (see HSING-HSING AND LING-LING) in Washington, D.C.

PEPE LE PEW, the amorous French skunk created by Chuck Jones and Michael Matlese for Warner Brothers' animated films, made his debut in *The Odor-able Kitty* (1945). In the Academy Award–winning *For Scent-imental Reasons* (1949), Pepé, who considered himself a great lover, relentlessly pursued what he thought was his ideal lady skunk. It was a romantic delusion. She was a cat who had accidentally acquired a white stripe down her back.

PERDITA, in *The Hundred and One Dalmatians* (1956) by Dodie Smith, was a liver-spotted Dalmatian who helped nurse the fifteen puppies whelped by Mrs. Dearly's MISSIS. When her milk supply ended, Perdita, a rescued stray, feared that she would be turned out, but Mrs. Dearly assured her that she was indispensable because she washed the puppies so well. Perdita was so relieved that she washed them all over again.

PERITAS was a favorite dog of Alexander the Great (356–323 B.C.). On his march of conquest eastward to India, Alexander founded cities along the way. Most of them were called Alexandria but one was named Peritas and had a monument to the dog in its public square.

PERSIMMON, carrying the purple, scarlet, and gold colors of Albert Edward, Prince of Wales, won the English Derby at Epsom Downs in 1896, at odds of 5–1, and made his owner the most popular man in the kingdom. The famous painting by S. Begg of the prince leading Persimmon in after the victory, as cheering spectators toss their top hats in the air, was said to understate the enthusiasm of the crowd. Persimmon, sired by the great, undefeated St. Simon, went on to win the St. Leger, the Astor Gold Cup, and the Eclipse Stakes in 1897. He also became an important sire, and a huge bronze statue of him was placed at the Royal Sandringham Stud.

PETER BROWN, in *The Abandoned* (1950) by Paul Gallico, was an 8-year-old boy who was transformed into a cat and taught to behave like one by JENNIE BALDRIN, a stray tabby. Amazed at how delicious mice were, he was trained by Jennie to catch them. Lacking her distrust of people, he had to learn—by the painful and humiliating experience of having his tail pulled—to be wary of children. Peter had courage. He killed a rat after seeing how Jennie did it, and won a fight to the death with an old tom who wanted her.

PETER CHAPIN, a black cocker spaniel, was the favorite of all the dogs owned by the Howard M. Chapins of Providence, Rhode Island. After Peter died, they decided to assemble a collection of books about dogs as a memorial to him, having learned that even the largest libraries in the United States had no more than ninety titles on the subject. By 1920, the Chapins had gathered more than 800 titles from bookshops in North America and Europe. When they presented their library to the College of William and Mary in Williamsburg, Virginia, in 1937, it contained 1,993 titles in ten languages, including the first book published in England about dogs, *De Canibus Britannicis* (1570). The Peter Chapin Collection of Books on Dogs now has more than 3,000 volumes as well as other items, each bearing a bookplate with a picture of the little cocker who inspired the collection.

PETER RABBIT (1), in Beatrix Potter's *The Tale of Peter Rabbit*, disobeyed his mother, sneaked into Mr. McGregor's garden to eat various vegetables, then lost his shoes and new jacket when Mr. McGregor chased him. When Peter got home, his mother put him to bed with a dose of camomile tea. The tale, originally written and illustrated in a letter to a sick child in 1893, was published in 1902 by

Frederick Warne & Company in London and launched a series of animal stories that have become classics collectively known as the Peter Rabbit books. Peter reappeared in three of them with cousin BENJAMIN BUNNY, who married Peter's sister FLOPSY. When their babies were stolen in *The Tale of Mr. Tod* (1912), Peter said to his distraught brother-in-law, "Cousin Benjamin, compose yourself," and the two of them rescued the bunnies.

PETER RABBIT (2), in the Thornton Burgess nature books, laughed a lot at the expense of REDDY FOX. Three times, in *The Adventures of Peter Cottontail* (1914), Reddy suggested they meet to enjoy a delicacy—carrots the first time, sweet clover the second, then cabbages—and three times, Peter got there early to eat them in safety. When Reddy arrived at the moonlit cabbage patch, Peter ducked under an old straw hat lying there and hopped the hat toward the fox. Reddy raced home, his tail between his legs. When autumn came, the joke was on Peter. Wanting to hibernate like the other animals, he settled into a hole, until he heard what sounded like Reddy Fox digging and barking. The rabbit shot out of the hole to find UNC' BILLY POSSUM, BOBBY COON, and JIMMY SKUNK laughing fit to kill. Peter learned his lesson—"he had no business to try to do what Old Mother Nature had never intended that he should do."

PETER RABBIT (3), in *Peter Rabbit*, the comic strip by Harrison Cady, was adapted from the PETER RABBIT (2) in Thornton Burgess' books, which Cady illustrated, and had nothing to do with the PETER RABBIT (1) created in England by Beatrix Potter. The strip first appeared in 1920 in the New York *Tribune*; it lasted about thirty years. Unlike Burgess' rural rabbit, this one had a wife and twin boys, lived in a house, and went to a job. The comic situations were those of a human husband and father. Pleading a high fever, for example, Peter Rabbit begged off babysitting for his wife and skipped happily down the road, enjoying his freedom—until she caught him.

PETE THE PUP, played by at least three different mongrels in Hal Roach's *Our Gang* comedies, had a black circle drawn around whichever eye did not have a colored patch. He appeared in more than eighty episodes. In *Lazy Days* (1929), he ran back and forth on a seesaw rigged to rock a cradle and a chair; in *Fly My Kite* (1931), he flew the kite to keep it away from robbers; and in *For Pete's Sake* (1934,) he mowed not only a lawn but also, unfortunately, a shaggy rug that was lying on it. When Stymie, his owner in *The Pooch* (1932), asked a woman for leftovers for Pete, she found an artichoke in the refrigerator and wondered aloud if the dog was a vegetarian. "No," said Stymie, "he's just like me. He's a Methodist."

PETRUCHIO'S HORSE managed to carry his master to the wedding in Shakespeare's *The Taming of the Shrew* (1623) despite being, according to a servant boy in act 3, scene 2:

> possessed with the glanders and like to mose in the chine, troubled with the lampass, infected with the fashions, full of windgalls, sped with spavins, rayed with the yellows, past cure of the fives, stark spoiled with the staggers, begnawn

with the bots, swayed in the back, and shoulder-shotten.

PHAEA, the Crommyonian sow in Greek mythology, was one of the nasty creatures that attacked and robbed travelers on the road to Athens. (The most famous one was Procrustes, who stretched his victims or amputated parts of them to make them fit his iron bed.) Theseus went along the road, killing each monster in the way it had claimed its victims, but instead of biting the sow, he ran her through with his lance.

PHANTOM (1), MISTY's dam in Marguerite Henry's *Misty of Chincoteague* (1947), had twice eluded the annual round-up of wild ponies on Assateague Island but, as a 3-year-old protecting her foal, she crossed the channel to Chincoteague Island. A year later, she won the Pony Penning Day race there, then returned to Assateague when PIED PIPER, the stallion who sired Misty, swam over to claim her.

PHANTOM (2) was Zorro's white stallion in "Zorro" (1957–59), the television series based on Johnston McCulley's novel *The Curse of Capistrano*, which also inspired two films titled *The Mark of Zorro*, starring Douglas Fairbanks in 1920 and Tyrone Power in 1940. The story is set in 1820 in the Spanish colony of Monterey, California, where Diego Vega, a Mexican aristocrat and apparent idler, led a second life as Zorro, the masked man in black who galloped around on Phantom to avenge the victims of the tyrannical Spanish governor.

PHINEAS T. BRIDGEPORT, in Walt Kelly's comic strip *Pogo* (1948–75) was the bear dressed like an alderman. His orotund phrases were printed in circus poster type, and sounded like utterances from W. C. Fields—"Ah there, friends of my youth! Yonder lies the swamp!! Sweet in succulent somnambulance!"

PICKLES the terrier and GINGER (1) the tomcat gave unlimited credit in their shop in Beatrix Potter's *Ginger & Pickles* (1909). When the customers failed to pay their bills, Pickles had no money for his dog license. The partners ate what was left of their merchandise, closed the shop, and Pickles became a gamekeeper.

THE PIEBALD, in *National Velvet* (1935) by Enid Bagnold, was a piebald gelding, part cart horse, part Arab, with one wall-eye and a habit of running wild in the village. He was a natural jumper. Velvet Brown, who was 14 and a fine rider, had seen him, running free, sail over a wall that was 5 feet, 2 inches high. When she won the horse in a raffle, Velvet resolved to ride him in the Grand National, England's greatest steeplechase. The first time she mounted Pie, she headed him toward a flint wall and, with no urging from her, "they cleared the wall together, wildly, ludicrously high, with savage effort and glory." After a little practice at a local gymkhana, Velvet entered her horse as The Piebald in the Grand National and, despite a rule against female jockeys, rode him—and won.

In the movie *National Velvet* (1944), Pie was a frisky sorrel gelding named King Charles. The film became a classic and made a star of 12-year-old Elizabeth Taylor, who played Velvet.

PIED PIPER, in Marguerite Henry's *Misty of Chincoteague* (1947), was the wild pinto pony on Assateague Island who sired MISTY. As a foal, Misty was taken across the channel to Chincoteague Island with her dam, PHANTOM (1). A year later, Pied Piper swam across to claim the mare and the two of them plunged into the surf to head home.

PIGLET, in A. A. Milne's *Winnie-the-Pooh* (1926), was doubtful about stealing baby Roo from Kanga, "One of the Fiercer Animals," and was accused of lacking pluck (see KANGA AND ROO). "It is hard to be brave," said Piglet, "when you're only a Very Small Animal." His size gave him an advantage over WINNIE-THE-POOH, however. When Christopher Robin went to school, Piglet was small enough to go in his pocket.

PIGLING BLAND, the "sedate little pig" in Beatrix Potter's *The Tale of Pigling Bland* (1913), was captured on the way to market. After he escaped with another prisoner, a little female Berkshire named PIG-WIG, they saw a tradesman's cart approach. Pigling began to limp. The grocer, assuming that such a lame pig could not run, asked them both to wait while he drove on to do an errand. As Pigling predicted, the grocer looked back. He saw the pigs standing in the middle of the road, but a moment later they scampered away.

PIG-WIG, "a perfectly lovely little black Berkshire pig" in *The Tale of Pigling Bland* (1913) by Beatrix Potter, escaped from Mr. Piperson's locked cupboard and ran away with PIGLING BLAND.

THE PINK PANTHER was created by David DePatie and Fritz Freleng for the animated title sequence of *The Pink Panther* (1963), Blake Edwards' movie starring Peter Sellers as Inspector Clouseau. The film was so successful that four sequels were made with Sellers. All had the Panther cavorting to Henry Mancini's bouncy theme music through the credits. DePatie-Freleng meanwhile launched a series of Pink Panther cartoons with *The Pink Phink* (1964), which won an Academy Award. The skinny Panther, who walks upright but never speaks, moved to television in 1969 and has also appeared in commercials.

PIPPA, the female cheetah whose return to wild life was described by Joy Adamson in *The Spotted Sphinx* (1969), had been raised as a pet until, in 1964, at the age of 8 months, she was given to Adamson. Like ELSA the lioness, Pippa was later moved to Kenya's Meru National Park, where she developed her stalking and killing instincts and mated. She was an aloof creature who lived in the bush several miles from camp but came in regularly for food during her pregnancies. As early as five days after her cubs were born, she would reappear to guide Adamson to them. "Her trust in showing me her new family while their eyes were still closed moved me deeply," Adamson wrote. Pippa had four litters before she was injured in a fight and died. Two litters were killed by predators but seven cubs survived in the wild. Adamson reported in her autobiography, *The Searching Spirit* (1978), that on a visit to Meru Park in 1976, she saw one of them, Whitey, who was 9 years old, playing with her sixth set of cubs.

PLATERO was the amiable little gray donkey of *Platero y yo* by the Spanish poet Juan Ramón Jiménez, winner of the 1956

Nobel Prize for Literature. Published in Madrid in 1917 when Jiménez was 36, the work presents a series of gently humorous observations on life in the Andalusian village of Moguer, the author's boyhood home. The book has become a classic in Spanish-speaking countries, required reading in schools, and as familiar to children as *The Tale of Peter Rabbit* is to the English-speaking world. Besides telling stories about the people they met as they meandered around the town and countryside, Jiménez mused aloud to his donkey about everything from eclipses to wildflowers. Platero (Spanish for "silversmith") liked mandarin oranges, preened after a bath, and leaned over the author's shoulder when he read poetry.

PLUTO (1), in "The Black Cat" from Edgar Allan Poe's *Tales* (1845), was a one-eyed cat whose mutilation and murder were avenged by the demoniacal cat who took his place in the home of the story's narrator, a drunken madman.

PLUTO (2), a gangling hound with rolling eyes and a silly grin, was one of Walt Disney's most popular characters. First seen as an anonymous bloodhound in the MICKEY MOUSE cartoon *The Chain Gang* (1930), he was given an identity in *Mickey's Pal Pluto* (1933) and eventually starred in his own series. Unlike most cartoon animals, Pluto did not speak. He acted and sounded like a dog, a simple-minded, inquisitive dog who was always getting into trouble—like being stuck to a strip of flypaper in *Playful Pluto* (1934)—and somehow finding a way to get out of it.

POGO, the possum in Walt Kelly's comic strip *Pogo*, was the amiable innocent among the denizens of the Okefenokee Swamp. Syndicated in 1949, the strip had become so popular by 1952 that Pogo for President clubs sprouted on college campuses and at least 50,000 "I Go Pogo" buttons were distributed. In the strip, Pogo was asked to contribute a plank to the platform being built for him; he offered a piece of his porch. Then he slept through the uproarious departure of the Pogo delegation to the convention. His most memorable remark appeared in 1970 on an anti-pollution poster. In a forest, surrounded by garbage and litter, Pogo declared, "We have met the enemy and he is us."

Walt Kelly died in 1973, and the strip ended two years later. The possum's wit and wisdom survive in fourteen Pogo books, in Kelly's recording of *Songs of the Pogo*, and in the minds of such men as Vice President Walter Mondale, who told a gathering of governors in July 1979, "It's like Pogo said. We face insuperable opportunities."

POGO

POM, FLORA, and ALEXANDER are the sons and daughter of BABAR, the King of the Elephants, in the books by Jean and Laurent de Brunhoff. When a boy named Colin jumped on Pom's head and pulled his ear in *Babar and the Professor* (1956), Pom gripped Colin's foot with his trunk and twirled the boy around until Babar made him stop. When Babar and his family visited San Francisco in *Babar Comes to America* (1965), Alexander had the bright idea of going down Telegraph Hill on roller skates. A policeman told him not to do it again. Flora was sweet.

POMPEY, a Bologna lapdog, was taken to London, where he traveled from owner to owner in *The History of Pompey the Little* (1751), Francis Coventry's satirical portrait of eighteenth-century English society. Pampered by the wealthy Lady Tempest, Pompey became a "Dog of the Town," servicing "*Bitches of the Highest Fashion*" until he was snatched out of the park, then handed on to social climbers, a rake, a poet, and a blind beggar, among others. The dog met a philosophic cat named MOPSA, whose counsel comforted him during later misfortunes. Some owners got rid of him because he barked too much or "wantonly did his occasions" on valuable objects. Others sold him. At Cambridge University, he escaped from a doctor preparing to dissect him and, by luck, was reunited with Lady Tempest in London, eight years after she lost him. From then on, "his chief Amusement was to sleep before the Fire" until, at the age of 14, Pompey "departed this Life . . . and was gathered to the Lapdogs of Antiquity."

PONGO, in Dodie Smith's *The Hundred and One Dalmatians* (1956), was the father of fifteen puppies, who were abducted by Cruella de Vil from London to her estate in Suffolk. She intended to make coats of their skins. Calling for help on the English dogs' jungle telegraph, a chain of informative barkings, Pongo learned where the pups were and headed there with their mother, MISSIS. He freed his pups and eighty-two more, shepherded them back to London, and let them into Cruella's town house, where they tore her furs to shreds.

PONTO, in Charles Dickens' *The Pickwick Papers* (1836–37), was the remarkable dog described by Mr. Jingles:

> Ah! you should keep dogs—fine animals—sagacious creatures—dog of my own once—Pointer—surprising instinct —out shooting one day—entering inclosure—whistled—dog stopped—

PONTO

whistled again—Ponto—no go: stock still—called him—Ponto, Ponto—wouldn't move—dog transfixed—staring at a board—looked up, saw an inscription—"Gamekeeper has orders to shoot all dogs found in this inclosure"—wouldn't pass it—wonderful dog—valuable dog that—very.

POOR MAILIE was a pet ewe that Robert Burns kept tethered in a field. One morning, a funny-looking boy told Burns anxiously that Poor Mailie was lying in a ditch, all tangled up. Burns easily set her right and was so amused by the boy that he composed "The Death and Dying Words of Poor Mailie" during his afternoon ploughing. The poem, one of the few he wrote before 1784, describes the dumbstruck boy standing like a statue while the dying ewe gives him a long message to her master, which concludes: "An' bid him burn this cursed tether." A year or so later, Burns wrote "Poor Mailie's Elegy," which begins:

Lament in rhyme, lament in prose,
Wi' saut tears tricklin down your nose.

THE POPE'S MULE, in Alphonse Daudet's *Lettres de mon moulin* (1866), had a happy life in Avignon until a new groom, Tistet Védène, and his friends began tormenting her and drinking the wine that Pope Boniface gave her every day. Worse, Védène forced her to climb the bell tower from which the humiliated mule had to be lowered by ropes. Védène went away for seven years; when he returned, he charmed the Pope into appointing him chief mustard-bearer at a grand ceremony. Arriving gorgeously dressed, with a tall ibis

feather in his hood, and making sure that the Pope was watching, the rogue stopped to pat the mule. She gave him so terrible a kick that "a whirlwind of blond dust, in which flew the feather of an ibis," was all that remained of Tistet Védène. "Mule kicks are not usually so destructive; but this was a papal mule; . . . she had kept it for him for seven years. There is no finer example of ecclesiastical rancor."

PORKY PIG, a durable star of Warner Brothers cartoons, made his debut in *I Haven't Got a Hat* (1935). His frequent co-star, Daffy Duck, was introduced in *Porky's Duck Hunt* (1936), and the character that became BUGS BUNNY was first seen in *Porky's Hare Hunt* (1938). The amiable pig in the big bow tie turned up in comic books in 1941 and in the *Bugs Bunny* comic strip a year later. In the films, with voice provided by the versatile Mel Blanc, Porky had an engaging stutter and was so popular that he was chosen to give the studio's famous sign-off, "That's all, folks!"

POT-8-Os, sired by ECLIPSE, was foaled in England in 1773 and called Potato as a colt. When Lord Abingdon, his owner, ordered the name painted over the horse's stall, the stable boy printed Potoooooooo, a spelling that was soon abbreviated to Pot-8-Os. His name aside, Pot-8-Os is memorable as the greatest of Eclipse's sons, on the track and at stud. His son Waxy and Waxy's son Whalebone, both Derby winners, founded the world's most important male line of Thoroughbreds, which includes KELSO.

PRICKLY PORKY, the porcupine in the Thornton Burgess nature books, had little to fear from the other animals, who kept their distance for obvious reasons. In *The*

Adventures of Unc' Billy Possum (1914), Porky prevented REDDY FOX and SHADOW THE WEASEL from ruining a party. He knew they were hiding in a hollow log, so he simply sat in the open end with his back to them, telling long stories and occasionally rattling his spears to remind the famished fox and weasel of their plight.

THE PRINCETON TIGER became the mascot for athletic teams at Princeton University for four reasons: in 1756, the original college building, Nassau Hall, was named for William of Orange of the House of Nassau; in the 1860s, students adopted a cheer based on the British Navy's "three cheers and a tiger," in which "a tiger" meant a roar; orange and black became the college colors in 1874, when the Princeton crew wore them at Saratoga; and in 1880, the football team began wearing orange and black striped jerseys. The colors, the roar, and the stripes inevitably produced the tiger symbol, currently represented at football and basketball games by two undergraduates, one male and one female, capering in tiger suits.

PRITCHARD was "the only dog in whom I found true originality," wrote Alexandre Dumas in *Histoire de mes bêtes* (1867). The irrepressible Scottish pointer was an escape artist and thief who snatched meat from the table, eggs from laying hens, and the hens themselves. When an older dog retrieved two partridges in the field, Pritchard stole both of them. Even the loss of a hind paw in a trap did not slow him down. After misbehaving on a hunting trip, Pritchard was incarcerated in an empty hen house, but 15 minutes later climbed out the roof. He then liberated the host's dog,

chained in the yard, by chewing through its collar. They reappeared at 10:00 that night, drenched with blood, Pritchard proudly carrying a hare. Surmising that they had devoured one, then brought along the second to avoid punishment, Dumas was pleased with his dog: "He used to carry off the day's dinner. Now he supplied it."

PUDLENKA, in "The Immortal Cat" from *I Had a Dog and a Cat* (1940) by Karel Capek, was so prolific that by the time the Czech writer tried to place her twenty-sixth kitten, he began to feel that people were avoiding him. She had appeared on his doorstep just as his little Angora tomcat expired from poison, and Capek suspected that she was a supernatural cat whose mission was to "revenge and replace a hundredfold the life of that tomcat." Her daughter Pudlenka II inherited her formidable fecundity, producing twenty-one kittens of all colors and breeds except Manx before a dog bit her to death. Pudlenka III, the equally fertile twenty-first kitten, is probably dreaming, Capek concluded, of "hosts of cats . . . seizing power to rule over the universe" as she continues the "Great Task" imposed by the Angora tom.

PUDMINI was Petersen Sahib's "clever she-elephant" in Rudyard Kipling's "Toomai of the Elephants" from *The Jungle Book* (1894). On the night that KALA NAG, the old fighting elephant, broke free to trek to the place where the elephants danced, Pudmini snapped the chain attached to her leg iron and followed him. The next morning, the double-chained elephants at the camp trumpeted when she shambled in, "mired to the shoulders."

PUNXSUTAWNEY PHIL, "Seer of Seers," is the resident groundhog at Gobbler's Knob in Punxsutawney, Pennsylvania, where the Punxsutawney Groundhog Club, founded in 1887, convenes every year on Candlemas Day, February 2, to observe his weather prediction. If he comes out of his hole, sees his shadow, and burrows back in, there will be six more weeks of winter, according to a tradition imported by German immigrants. They had been accustomed to watching badgers but, finding none in Pennsylvania, switched to groundhogs with apparent success. The Punxsutawney Groundhog Club claims that since 1887 Phil has never been wrong (see JIMMY THE GROUNDHOG).

THE PURPLE COW was introduced in May 1895, in the first issue of the *Lark*, a "little magazine" published by Les Jeunes, a lighthearted literary group in San Francisco. Frank Gelett Burgess, one of its founders, wrote:

> Reflections on a Mythic Beast
> Who's Quite Remarkable, at Least.
> I never saw a Purple Cow,
> I never Hope to See One.
> But I can Tell you Anyhow,
> I'd rather See than Be One.

The poem became so popular that Burgess was marked as "the purple cow man," not to be taken seriously, which drove him to add, a few years later:

> Ah, Yes! I Wrote the Purple Cow—
> I'm Sorry, now, I Wrote It!
> But I can Tell You Anyhow,
> I'll Kill You if You Quote It!

PUSHINKA, a 6-month-old puppy, was sent to Mrs. John F. Kennedy in 1961 by Soviet Premier Nikita Khrushchev. The pup's mother was Strelka, one of the two Samoyed husky bitches who were the first animals to survive orbital flight (see BELKA AND STRELKA). The little dog delighted President Kennedy by learing to climb the ladder of the children's slide on the White House grounds, and then skid down. Pushinka (Russian for "fluffy") also delighted young Caroline Kennedy's Welsh terrier, Charlie, and four puppies were born. When it was announced that two of them would be given to children chosen in a letter-writing contest, over 10,000 entries were received. One letter that might have won did not have a return address. It said: "I will raise the dog to be a Democrat and bite all Republicans."

PUSS IN BOOTS, in the story "Puss in Boots" from Charles Perrault's *Contes du temps passé* (1697), made his humble master's fortune. Demanding boots for walking in the woods, the cat began catching game and presenting it to the king in the name of the marquis of Carabas, a title Puss invented for his master. One day, knowing the king and his daughter would be riding along the river, the cat told his master to jump in, then hid his clothes and ran to the king's carriage, crying for help to rescue the marquis from drowning. He added, "Stop, thief!" to justify borrowing royal garments when his master was fished out. While the princess and the marquis fell in love as the carriage rolled on, the cat raced ahead to force peasants along the route to declare that all the land belonged to the marquis. Arriving at a castle owned by an ogre, Puss tricked him into changing into a mouse and ate him, just in time to welcome the king to the marquis's castle.

PUSS IN BOOTS

The princess married the marquis, and Puss in Boots became a very important personage who hunted mice only for amusement.

PUSS, TINEY, and BESS: see COWPER'S HARES.

PUSSYCAT PRINCESS was the kitten who ruled Tabbyland and tried to make the Earl of Sourface laugh, in *Pussycat Princess*, a Sunday comic strip launched in 1935 by Grace G. Drayton, the first successful woman cartoonist in the United States. Drayton had also created the Campbell Soup Kids, and, like them, the costumed kittens in the strip had moony faces. Soon after the *Pussycat Princess* began, Ruth Carroll took over the drawing and continued until the strip ended in 1947.

PUZZLE, an obliging donkey in *The Last Battle* (1956) by C. S. Lewis, let SHIFT the ape cover him with a lion's hide and exhibit him as ASLAN the Great Lion of Narnia. When Narnia's defenders captured the imposter, "his silly, gentle, donkey face peering out" of the lionskin, he explained apologetically, "The ape said Aslan *wanted* me to dress up like that. And I thought he'd know. I'm not clever like him. I only did what I was told." Everyone forgave him.

PYEWACKET, in *Bell, Book and Candle* by John van Druten, is Gillian Holroyd's cat. The play, which opened in New York in 1950, is a comic fantasy about love vs. witchcraft. Gillian is a witch and Pyewacket, a Siamese, is her familiar. By stroking the cat and mumbling a few words, Gillian makes her neighbor, Shepherd Henderson, fall in love with her. Later, when she loses her powers, Pyewacket disappears.

QUEENIE, a trick horse in silent movies: see SCRAPS.

RA, the sun-god in Egyptian mythology, was a cat in an ancient myth recounted in *The Book of the Dead*, a guide to the nether world that was buried with the dead as long ago as the sixth millennium B.C. At the British Museum, a papyrus copy from the XVIII Dynasty, ca. 1580 B.C., shows a striped cat with his left forepaw planted on the head of a snake while he slices its body with a cleaver held in his other forepaw. "Who is this cat?" says the text. "This male Cat is Ra himself, and he was called Mau." In the background is the Egyptian tree of life and knowledge, the Persea Tree in Heliopolis, where Ra was worshiped for his victory over the forces of evil, symbolized by the snake. (See BAST.)

RAB, the huge old mastiff in Dr. John Brown's *Rab and His Friends* (1859), had only one or two teeth, one eye, and a "tattered rag of an ear," but he could still make "expressive twinklings and winkings" with his stub of a tail. As a boy, Brown had made friends with the dog by cutting him free of his muzzle when a bull terrier had gotten him by the throat. Six years later, Rab's master, a cart driver named James, brought his wife, Ailie, to the hospital in Edinburgh where Brown was a medical student. The dog, permitted to stay in her room, "behaved well, never moving, showing us how meek and gentle he could be." When Ailie died, Rab stationed himself on the foot of her bed until James returned with his cart and mare to take her home. After James died a few days later, Rab stayed in the mare's stall, refusing to eat, and when the new driver tried to feed the mare, he growled and grabbed his legs. The driver had to kill the dog. "Fit end," wrote Brown. "His teeth and his friends gone, why should he keep the peace and be civil?"

RABBIT bustled about leaving notes and organizing plots that did not work in A. A. Milne's *Winnie-the-Pooh* (1926) and *The*

RA

House at Pooh Corner (1928). When he schemed to lose TIGGER, it was Rabbit who got lost and Tigger who found him. WINNIE-THE-POOH and PIGLET agreed that Rabbit was clever and "has Brain," but Pooh supposed, "that's why he never understands anything."

RABICAN, a coal-black charger with a white star on his forehead, was the fleetest of steeds in Carolingian legend. His sire was Wind, his dam was Fire, and the enchanted horse fed only on air. After his first master was killed, he lived in a cavern until Rinaldo fought the giant and the griffin guarding the entrance and rode him out. When Rogero borrowed Rabican, they were chased by a huntsman on foot, his falcon, his horse, and his dog, who was as swift as Rabican. Rogero stopped to fight. The dog bit, the other horse kicked, and the falcon overhead attacked with claws and wings. Rabican was so frightened that he became unmanageable. Fortunately, Rogero remembered he carried a magic charm and unveiled it. The attackers fell down in a trance.

RACAN and PERRUQUE were two of the fourteen cats that Cardinal Richelieu allegedly owned at the time of his death in 1642. It is said that the cardinal doted on cats and left a trust fund for the care of the ones who survived him. These two were named for the fact that they were born in the wig of the marquis de Racan, a poet and one of the original members of the French Academy, which Richelieu had founded in 1635.

RAGGYLUG, a cottontail rabbit in Ernest Thompson Seton's *Wild Animals I Have Known* (1898), paid attention to his mother, Molly, after he got his ear chewed by a snake for being so curious. She taught him to freeze in place to avoid being seen, to signal with hind foot thumps, and other "tricks of the trail." His favorite was to lead a pursuing dog or fox at a long slant toward barbed wire to be crippled or killed. Rag and Molly had a nice life until a bigger rabbit turned up to beat him and abuse her. Arranging to be chased by a hound, Rag lured the buck into position between them —and that was the end of him. Molly perished one night, while trying to get away from a fox. Rag killed the fox by using the old barbed wire trick. The rabbit grew up to be a big strong buck with a pretty wife and a large family.

RAKHSH, a horse, belonged to the legendary Persian hero Rustam, whose exploits were recounted in *Shah-nameh* (Book of Kings), the eleventh-century epic poem by Firdausi. (Matthew Arnold called the horse RUKSH in his 1853 poem "Sohrab and Rustum.") In one bout, when the Turanian warrior Chingish fled after Rustam deflected his arrows, lightning-swift Rakhsh overtook his horse. When Rustam grabbed hold of the tail, Chingish jumped off, and Rustam beheaded him. In another episode, Rustam had gone to sleep on the first night of an arduous journey when a lion attacked his camp. The brave horse killed the lion. Persian miniatures illustrating *Shah-nameh* traditionally show Rakhsh biting the neck of the hapless lion as he emerges from the reeds.

RAKKAE, in a legend similar to that of SAUR I, was a little dog whom King Athils of Sweden imposed on the Danes as their king in the early Middle Ages. Rakkae's reign ended abruptly. One day when he was seated at the table in the banqueting hall, the hounds on the floor began fighting over his scraps. King Rakkae barked at them, then jumped to the floor and started biting them. The hounds tore him to pieces.

RAKSHA, the Mother Wolf in *The Jungle Book* (1894) by Rudyard Kipling, suckled the infant Mowgli and defied SHERE KHAN the tiger, who wanted to carry him off. "He shall live to run with the Pack and to hunt with the Pack; and in the end, . . . he shall hunt *thee!*" she declared. When the boy left her to rejoin the world of men, she implored him to return, admitting, "I loved thee more than I ever loved my cubs." Mowgli later killed the tiger, fulfilling Raksha's prophecy. "It is well done," she said.

RALPHIE, a 1,000-pound American bison, was retired in 1978 after thirteen years as the mascot for the University of Colorado football team. Ralphie, whose name was chosen before it was discovered that the buffalo was a female, became so popular that she was once elected homecoming queen. In rousing appearances at Folsom Field in Boulder, she thundered the length of the field, wheeled around, then pounded back to her trailer at the other end. At one game, when she missed the trailer and kept going, the scoreboard flashed: RALPHIE COME HOME. Ralphie did. Her 3-year-old successor, Ralphie II, is also a cow buffalo. She weighs 1,400 pounds.

RAMBLING WILLIE, a pacer foaled in 1970, raced longer, won more purses, and broke more records than any horse in his-tory despite being disabled several times, twice by a bowed tendon. Still racing as an 11-year-old, the bay gelding had won over a hundred races, earned $1,838,982, and contributed more than $90,000 to the Church of Christ in West Mansfield, Ohio, by the time his biography, *Rambling Willie: The Horse That God Loved* by Donald P. Evans and Philip Pikelny, was published in April 1981. The church bene-fited because the pastor's daughter, Vivian Farrington, owned half of Willie and tithed her share of his earnings. In May, Willie began a farewell tour reminiscent of DAN PATCH's but unique in that it included a stop at the annual convention of the American Booksellers Association.

RAMINAGROBIS was a cat in several *Fables* of Jean de La Fontaine (1621–95). In "The Cat, the Weasel, and the Rabbit," the fat, sanctimonious feline recluse (whose name is also that of a poet in François Rabelais' *Pantagruel*, 1553) was asked to settle a dispute between the weasel and the rabbit. Claiming deafness in his old age, Raminagrobis asked them to come closer. They did. He pinned both of them with his claws and devoured them.

In "The Old Cat and the Young Mouse," the mouse pleaded to be spared because he was small and would grow into a fine meal for the cat's children. "Go to hell," said Raminagrobis. "My children will find their own food."

In "The League of Rats," a mouse asked the rats to protect him from Raminagrobis. Since they would be next when all the mice were consumed, the League marched to the rescue of their little friend. But they were too late. With the mouse's head in his

RAMINAGROBIS
*The Weasel and the Rabbit ask Raminagrobis
to settle their dispute*

mouth, Raminagrobis advanced on the troops, growling. The rats dispersed, each to his own hole.

RASCAL, a baby raccoon, was found by 11-year-old Sterling North in the Wisconsin woods in May 1918 and kept as a pet for a year. In *Rascal* (1963), North recalled how quickly the adaptable raccoon learned to take the cover off the sugar bowl and to undo the screen door latch to come sleep with him. Rascal loved a fast bicycle ride. Standing in the handlebar basket, the "cycling maniac" with his natural black goggles looked like Barney Oldfield, the famous racing driver. In August, Rascal became "drunk and disorderly" on sweet corn, and neighbors threatened to shoot him for raiding their gardens. He had to be caged but young North could still take him everywhere, even to school, on a leash. With the approach of the mating season in March, it was time to return the full-grown raccoon to his natural life in the woods. North took him a great distance in a canoe. Then, as they entered Koshkonong Creek by the light of a full moon, Rascal heard the "crooning tremolo" of a female raccoon, jumped overboard, and swam to shore.

RAT, in *The Wind in the Willows* (1908) by Kenneth Grahame, was a good-natured fellow, inclined to compose little songs or poems when he was in a dreamy mood. He lived at River Bank because he was a Water Rat. As he said to MOLE, "Believe me, my young friend, there is *nothing*—absolutely nothing—half so much worth doing as simply messing about in boats." Toward the end of summer, Rat found himself restless, wondering what lay beyond the horizon. A passing Sea Rat so entranced him with tales of faraway places that he went home to pack. With glazed eyes, Rat told Mole he was going south. "Seawards first, and then on shipboard, and so to the shores that are calling me!" Mole threw him to the ground, Rat sobbed hysterically, and Mole tactfully left him alone with paper and pencil. Before long, Rat began to scribble a little. "The cure had at least begun."

RATATOSK, in Norse mythology, was the squirrel who never stopped scurrying up and down the trunk of the wondrous ash tree Yggdrasil. Nidhogg, the serpent who gnawed at the tree's deepest root, would send the squirrel up the tree with an insult for the eagle in the top branches, and the eagle would have an insult for Ratatosk to take right back down to the serpent.

RATAXES is a tough old rhinoceros in the books about BABAR the elephant by Jean and Laurent de Brunhoff. In *The Travels of Babar* (1934), Rataxes declared war after Babar's cousin ARTHUR tied a firecracker to his tail. The rhinoceros army laid waste to the land of the elephants until Babar returned and tricked them into flight. Rataxes invaded again, in *Babar and the Wully Wully* (1975), but Babar's daughter Flora managed to tame him.

RATON (1)
Raton pulls out the chestnuts.
Bertrand eats them

RATON (1), the cat in "The Monkey and the Cat," one of the *Fables* of Jean de La Fontaine (1621–95), was flattered by BERTRAND the monkey into pulling chestnuts out of the fire. As the cat delicately pushed the ashes around, drawing out one chestnut, a second one, and then three more, Bertrand ate them. The maid came in and the animals fled. Raton was not very happy, they say. So much for flattery.

RATON (2), the dog that Mme. de Maintenon gave to her friend Ninon de Lenclos (1615–1705), was too tiny to frighten anybody, but Ninon had him wear a medal engraved: "Faithful to my mistress, I follow where she goes. Because I know she loves me, I will bite anyone who does not love her. So far I have not had to bite anyone." Ninon, a famous courtesan whose career lasted an extraordinarily long time, had to work hard to keep her figure and whenever she reached for something fattening, Raton barked at her until she put it down.

REBECCA, a raccoon, was sent to President Calvin Coolidge (1923–29) by some constituents in Mississippi, supposedly to be served for Thanksgiving dinner. Coolidge, one of the great pet lovers among American Presidents, named her and had a pen built for her near his office. In the evenings, he would take Rebecca for a walk on a leash. Sometimes he draped her over his shoulder for a stroll from his office to Mrs. Coolidge's sitting room. When the President decided Rebecca needed a companion, Horace, a male raccoon, was imported and an enlarged pen was built for the couple. But they didn't get along, and Horace escaped.

RECKLESS, a small Korean racing mare, was 4 years old in October 1952, when Lt. Eric Pedersen, commander of a U.S. Marine Recoilless ("Reckless") Rifle Platoon, paid $250 for her at the Seoul, South Korea, race track. He had her trained to carry ammunition. Reckless performed so well in combat that she was promoted to the rank of corporal. In 1953, during two days under heavy fire in the battle for the outpost Vegas, Reckless made fifty-one trips up a steep hill to haul more than 9,000 pounds of ammunition to the front, while men in the rear yanked out clumps of grass to keep her fed. Cited for "her absolute dependability," which "contributed materially to the success of many battles," the little red mare was promoted to sergeant in April 1954. Her story appeared in *The Saturday Evening Post,* and Andrew Geer retold it in *Reckless, Pride of the Marines* (1955). In November 1954, Sergeant Reckless was retired to Camp Pendleton in California.

REDDY FOX, in the Thornton Burgess nature books, could steal chickens and escape from BOWSER THE HOUND but PETER RABBIT (2) kept outwitting him. And Reddy hated to be laughed at. In *The Adventures of Peter Cottontail* (1914), the fox limped along with one eye closed, pretending he had not yet recovered from a collision with a hornets' nest. When Peter, who had been sympathetic, saw that eye open slowly, with a hungry look in it, he hopped into the briar patch, fast. Reddy shook his fist at him. The fox had jumped in after Peter once before and had come out torn and bleeding.

RED RUM, who won the Grand National steeplechase at Aintree, England, three times, might never have been entered in the race if Donald (Ginger) McCain, a taxi driver who also trained horses, had not had a wealthy passenger, Noel Le Mare, who shared his dream of having a Grand National winner. They bought Red Rum in 1972, unaware that the 7-year-old bay gelding had been treated for a form of equine arthritis. After he was trotted in the sea along Southport Beach, his limp disappeared and he won six of his first nine races for McCain, placing in the other three. In 1973, on his first try in the Grand National—a 4½-mile course with thirty jumps—Red Rum made up fifteen lengths to set a track record of 9:01.9. He won again in 1974, came in second the next two years, and in 1977, carrying the top weight of 162 pounds at the age of 12, won by twenty-five lengths. "He's like a cat," said his jockey, Tommy Stack. "He just measures all the jumps." Less than twenty-four hours before the 1978 Grand National, "Rummy" was withdrawn for an injury. He was paraded on the track before 60,000 fans in an emotional farewell to racing and went on to make a fortune in personal appearances.

REEPICHEEP, in the Chronicles of Narnia by C. S. Lewis, was the intrepid, chess-playing, 2-foot-tall Chief Mouse, who was always ready to fight, even an invisible enemy, with his very long sword. "I'd sooner meet them face to face than be caught by the tail," he declared. While piercing the feet of visible soldiers in a battle in *Prince Caspian* (1951), he lost his tail—"the honor and glory of a Mouse"—but ASLAN the Great Lion was persuaded to replace it. In *The Voyage of the Dawn Treader* (1952), Reepicheep disappeared in a great wave. After Narnia was destroyed in *The Last Battle* (1956), the mouse reappeared to welcome the survivors into the next world.

THE REPUBLICAN ELEPHANT was created by Thomas Nast for a cartoon that appeared in the November 7, 1874, issue of *Harper's Weekly*, just before Election Day. In the drawing, titled "The Third Term Picnic," an assortment of animals symbolizing various subjects mill about while the elephant, "The Republican Vote," stands near a pitfall. The Republicans lost control of the House of Representatives in the election, and a week later the elephant was seen tumbling into the hole. In 1875, Nast showed the elephant emerging, falling back in, and, after the November elections, finally standing aboveground, trumpeting Republican victories. Nast, who also created THE DEMOCRATIC DONKEY, occasionally used other animals to represent the Republicans, but the elephant remains the party symbol.

REX, "King of the Wild Horses," was the first horse to be starred on his own in

THE REPUBLICAN ELEPHANT

western movies. When the black Morgan stallion was chosen to play a wild horse in the Hal Roach film *Black Cyclone* (1927), it was type casting. Because he had been mistreated as a colt, Rex was mean and almost unmanageable, so for scenes with human actors, a double was used. But he was magnificent in action. His greatest sequence, accomplished by special effects, was a fight with a mountain lion. Rex, who had cost $150, continued to star in features and serials for almost fifteen years. *Black Cyclone* alone grossed $350,000

REYNARD the fox was the popular hero of the beast epic *Reynard the Fox* that evolved during the twelfth-century in France and the Low Countries from a series of animal folktales, some of which can be traced back to Aesop's sixth-century B.C. fables. By 1250, German, French, and Flemish versions of the epic had appeared and in 1481, William Caxton translated the Flemish version into English. Reynard was an impudent rascal who outwitted the other animals with cunning tricks that played on their weaknesses: BRUIN the bear, mad for honey, got wedged in a tree; TIBERT the cat, greedy for mice, was lured into a trap; BELLIN the ram was persuaded to take credit for something he did not do, and it cost him his life.

The king, NOBLE the lion, was forever infuriated by complaints about the fox and, to escape hanging, Reynard promised treasure that did not exist or a penitent pilgrimage to Rome that he did not make. He explained to his loyal nephew, GRIMBERT the badger, that he was corrupt because the world was corrupt. Loose prelates and rich priests did not practice what they preached; Lords, ladies, and clerks were full of deceit; therefore, said the fox, "I must flatter and lie also, or else I should be shut without the door." After winning yet another pardon by pleading in that fashion, Reynard was challenged by ISEGRIM the wolf, his favorite victim. The wolf missed his chance to win and barely survived. Noble made the fox his highest official.

The world is full of Reynard's heirs, the epic concludes, and they do not all have red

REYNARD
The fox's arrival at court

beards. They can be found in the pope's court, the emperor's, the king's, or any other lord's—wherever there is money. The final sentence of Caxton's translation—"And if anything be said or written herein that may grieve or displease any man, blame me not, but the fox"—is followed by the translator's disclaimer, "For they be his words and not mine."

RHUBARB, a cat, inherited a baseball team called the New York Loons in H. Allen Smith's satirical novel *Rhubarb* (1946). Orangey, a striped cat trained by Frank Inn, played the title role in the 1951 movie version of the book. Renamed Rhubarb, the cat took a dislike to Ray Milland, his co-star, but appeared to be affectionate after Inn smeared liver paste on the actor's hands. When the cat tired of liver paste, Milland was anointed with catnip. With the help of doubles and stand-ins, Rhubarb won a Patsy Award—for animals, the equivalent of an Oscar—and went on to play Minerva in the television series "Our Miss Brooks," from 1952 to 1955. In 1962, old Orangey-Rhubarb-Minerva won another Patsy as Cat in the film *Breakfast at Tiffany's.*

RIBBY, a hospitable cat, served mouse pie to her friend DUCHESS (1) the dog in *The Pie and the Patty-pan* (1905) and to an outspoken relative in *The Roly-Poly Pudding* (1908), both by Beatrix Potter. When Ribby dropped in on TABITHA TWITCHIT right after TOM KITTEN disappeared, she said, "He's a bad kitten, Cousin Tabitha; he made a cat's cradle of my bonnet last time I came to tea." But then she joined the search for Tom.

RIENZI was the big black Morgan gelding that Maj. Gen. Philip ("Little Phil") Sheridan rode out of Winchester, Virginia, on the morning of October 19, 1864, to rejoin his troops at Cedar Creek, about 14 miles away. Instead, he met thousands of them retreating from a surprise attack by Confederate Gen. Jubal Early. Exhorting the men to "Turn back, face the other way!" Sheridan galloped Rienzi across fields and over fences to reach his troops that still held their line. His counterattack, reinforced by the returning men, turned the apparent rout into a great victory.

The horse shared credit with the general in "Sheridan's Ride" (1865), the famous poem by Thomas Buchanan Read that had the wrong mileage but the right spirit:

> Be it said in letters both bold and
>   bright:
> "Here is the steed that saved the day
> By carrying Sheridan into the fight,
> From Winchester,—twenty miles
>   away!"

Rienzi, named for the town of Rienzi, Mississippi, the objective of a raid, had been given to Sheridan in 1862, when he was a captain commanding the 2nd Michigan Cavalry. The horse died in 1878 at the age of 20. His body, preserved by taxidermy, is on display at the Smithsonian Institution in Washington, D.C.

RIKKI-TIKKI-TAVI, the young mongoose in *The Jungle Book* (1894) by Rudyard Kipling, saved the English family he lived with from two cobras, Nag and his wife, Nagaina. Nag was asleep in the bathroom when Rikki-tikki pounced and held onto the snake's head even though he was sure the thrashing cobra would bang him to death. "For the honor of the family, he preferred to be found with his teeth locked." The Englishman shot Nag, but next morning Nagaina was discovered on the veranda, coiled and ready to strike at the Englishman's son. The mongoose, who had just destroyed all but one of Nagaina's eggs, rushed to distract her while the child was pulled to safety. Nagaina recovered her last egg and plunged into a rathole, followed by Rikki-tikki, his teeth clenched to her tail. From then on, after he dragged himself out, Rikki-tikki kept the garden the way a mongoose should, "with tooth and jump and spring and bite, till never a cobra dared show its head inside the walls."

RINKA, Norman Scott's Great Dane bitch, was shot dead on October 24, 1975, in England in what a local newspaper called the "Mystery of the Dog in the Fog." After shooting the dog, the assailant had then aimed the gun at him, said Scott, but it apparently jammed. Scott was a former stable lad and male model who claimed to have had a homosexual relationship in the early 1960s with Jeremy Thorpe, a Member of Parliament and, in 1975, the leader of Britain's Liberal Party. In August 1978, Thorpe was charged with conspiring to murder Norman Scott and with "inciting" a co-conspirator to murder him. A few days before the trial began in May 1979, Auberon Waugh, who reported it in *The Last Word* (1980), was one of Thorpe's opponents in a parliamentary election, declaring on behalf of dog lovers in North Devon: "Rinka is NOT forgotten. Rinka

lives. Woof, woof. Vote Waugh to give *all* dogs the right to life, liberty and the pursuit of happiness." Waugh lost. So did Thorpe, but at the so-called "Trial of the Century," he was acquitted.

RIN TIN TIN, the German shepherd who became a movie star, was one of a litter that American airmen rescued from an abandoned German dugout in France in September 1918. Corp. Lee Duncan named the pup for a tiny doll that French soldiers carried for luck, and took him home to California. Originally trained for dog shows, Rinty was so successful in his first film, *Where the North Begins* (1923), that in nine years, he made more than forty movies, earned over a million dollars, and kept Warner Brothers solvent. Among his great stunts, Rinty scaled walls—which had camouflaged cleats on them for leverage—and, coated with fireproofing chemicals, ran through flames. Translucent panes of sugar, the now-familiar replacement for glass, were devised for his safety when crashing through windows. He even projected emotions. In one closeup in *The Night Cry* (1925), Rinty, suspected of killing sheep, peered at his owners with an expression that changed from forlorn to hopeful to sad, then finally to joyful when the owners' baby was friendly to him.

The public loved Rin Tin Tin, sending him 10,000 fan letters a week. After he died in 1932, his son, Rin Tin Tin, Jr., starred in westerns until 1938, and another descendant appeared in *The Return of Rin Tin Tin* (1947). A popular television series, begun in 1954, "The Adventures of Rin Tin Tin," was rerun in the 1970s.

RIN TIN TIN

RIQUET, a tan puppy "of doubtful breed," became the companion of Lucien Bergeret, the philosophical professor in Anatole France's four-volume, satirical *Histoire contemporaine* (1896–1901). On the day his housekeeper gave him the dog, M. Bergeret stood on an old chair to reach a book on a high shelf and landed on the floor, his right leg through the cane seat. Riquet ran anxiously around him, approaching and retreating, then licked his nose. By the time M. Bergeret got to his feet and limped to his own chair, the pup was already curled up in it. "The sympathy you bestow on me is a charming mystery, and I accept it," said M. Bergeret, and he told the housekeeper he would keep the dog. Over the years, the professor often addressed his thoughts to Riquet, and the dog's own "Meditations" included:

> My master keeps me warm when I lie behind him in his chair. It is because he is a god. . . . It is impossible to know whether one has acted well towards men. One must worship them without seeking to understand them. Their wisdom is mysterious.

ROAN BARBARY, in William Shakespeare's *Richard II* (1595), is the favorite horse of King Richard II. After forcing Richard to abdicate and sending him to Pomfret Castle as a prisoner, Bolingbroke is crowned Henry IV. In act 5, scene 5, a loyal groom tells Richard that Bolingbroke rode Roan Barbary to the coronation. Richard asks how the horse behaved:

> GROOM: So proudly as if he disdained the ground.
> RICHARD: So proud that Bolingbroke was on his back!
> That jade hath eat bread from my royal hand;

> This hand hath made him proud with clapping him.
> Would he not stumble? would he not fall down,
> Since pride must have a fall, and break the neck
> Of that proud man that did usurp his back?
> Forgiveness, horse! Why do I rail on thee,
> Since thou, created to be awed by man,
> Wast born to bear?

ROBIN was a favorite sheep, killed by the wolf and mourned by the shepherd, in "The Shepherd and his Flock," one of the *Fables* of Jean de La Fontaine (1621–95). The shepherd recalled how Robin would follow him to town for a piece of bread, and would have followed him to the ends of the earth. Robin would listen when the shepherd piped a tune and knew his step from 100 yards away. Having finished his eulogy to poor Robin, the shepherd urged the flock to stay together to repel the wolf. The sheep agreed. They would avenge Robin. That night, the sheep thought they saw the wolf and scattered. It was not the wolf, but a shadow.

ROBINSON, wrote Beatrix Potter in *The Tale of Little Pig Robinson* (1930), was the " 'Piggy-wig . . . with a ring at the end of his nose' " in Edward Lear's poem "The Owl and the Pussy-Cat" (1867). In Potter's story, the pig went to town on errands for his aunts and was lured aboard the *Pound of Candles* by the ship's cook, to be fattened for the captain's birthday. The ship's cat was pining for her owl but arranged Robinson's escape in the jolly boat. The pig landed on the island of the Bong tree, where every food imaginable grew, including baked muffins. When the honeymooning cat and owl visited him 18 months later, Robinson was happily growing "fatter and more fatterer; and the ship's cook never found him."

ROB ROY was the new name Grace Coolidge gave a white collie named Oshkosh that was presented to President Calvin Coolidge in 1923. Coolidge enjoyed the dog, let him wander freely, and liked to show off his trick of nudging a piece of cake off the mantel, then catching it in mid-air. At a press conference one day, Rob Roy started whining. The President looked around, then snapped at the reporters to get their big feet off his dog's toes. Although Mrs. Coolidge had her own white collie, a bitch named Prudence Prim, she posed with Rob Roy for the portrait by Howard Chandler Christy that still hangs in the White House.

ROCINANTE, in Miguel Cervantes' *Don Quixote de la Mancha* (1605), was Don Quixote's horse, an "extremely consumptive-looking" old nag who was still enough of a stallion to trot up to a herd of Galician mares. They greeted him with kicks and bites, he lost his saddle, and their carters knocked him to the ground. Seeking vengeance, Don Quixote and his squire, Sancho Panza, were instead knocked flat too. But when the knight later took on twenty mounted men in the dark, Rocinante seemed to sprout wings, "so proud-stepping and light-footed did he show himself to be." The horse was rarely that active. When he and his close friend,

Sancho Panza's ass, were tired and their bellies full, Rocinante would drape his neck over the donkey's and the two of them would stand there, staring at the ground, for as long as three days.

ROCK-A-BYE-BEAR looked like a white TEDDY BEAR and sounded like the pulsing swoosh of blood through a mother's pelvic arteries that a fetus is capable of hearing for four months before birth. The bear was developed by two entrepreneurs, Bob Bissett and Marie Shields, and a Fort Lauderdale, Florida, obstetrician, Dr. William Eller, after they learned in 1975 that a Japanese doctor had found that wailing newborns could be soothed by the familiar intrauterine sounds. To record them, Eller inserted a tiny microphone through the dilated cervix and into the uterus of a cooperative patient going into labor. The recording was tested in the nursery of Fort Lauderdale's Holy Cross Hospital. "It's the most boring sound you've ever heard," said one nurse, but the babies calmed down immediately and usually dozed off within fifteen seconds. In 1979, the cuddly bear, containing a miniature circuit to reproduce the sound, was put on the market for $39.95. By mid-December, 25,000 had been sold.

ROCKY, the earnest squirrel in the television cartoon series "Rocky and His Friends," wears a pilot's helmet and goggles because he is a flying squirrel. He flies a lot in the course of rescuing BULLWINKLE the moose from the villainous Boris Badenov or from his own stupidity. Jay Ward Productions introduced the series in 1959.

RODILARD was the cat in two of the *Fables* of Jean de La Fontaine (1621–95).

In "The Rats in Council," the rats who had survived the cat's carnage met while Rodilard was off courting a tabby. The rats agreed that the only way to protect themselves was to tie a bell around his neck. Each one, however, had an excuse for not volunteering to bell the cat.

In "The Cat and the Old Rat," Rodilard, a four-legged Attila, strung himself up by his hind legs to dangle as though he were dead. When the mice emerged from their holes to celebrate, he pounced. As he crunched on the mice that he caught, Rodilard told the ones who escaped that he would get them too. And he did, by crouching in the kneading trough, completely covered by flour, until the greedy mice pattered in to their doom. But an old rat, who had lost part of his tail in an earlier battle, was suspicious of the floury shape and kept his distance, shouting that he knew Rodilard was there.

RODILARDUS (or GNAWBACON) was the huge, furry cat who frightened Panurge during the voyage in François Rabelais' *Gargantua and Pantagruel*, book IV (1535). When Pantagruel ordered the guns fired to salute the muses, his friend Panurge leaped out of the ship's storeroom like a startled goat, clutching the cat, who was wrapped in one of his stockings. He thought it was a little devil. The cat's name is from the Latin *rodo lardum*, which means "I gnaw bacon."

ROLAND was the durable horse ridden by the narrator in Robert Browning's "How They Brought the Good News from Ghent to Aix" (1843). Three messengers galloped abreast through the night, wordlessly keeping their pace. In the morning, one groaned as his mare collapsed. Within sight of Aix,* the second man's roan fell dead. And there was Roland:

> With his nostrils like pits full of blood
>   to the brim,
> And with circles of red for his eye-
>   sockets' rim.

Cheering him on, the narrator galloped into Aix, where all he could remember was sitting on the ground, hearing Roland praised, and pouring down the horse's throat the town's last measure of wine:

> Which (the burgesses voted by
>   common consent)
> Was no more than his due who
>   brought good news from Ghent.

RONALD was the chestnut charger that Maj. Gen. the Earl of Cardigan rode into the "Valley of Death" when he led the charge of the Light Brigade at Balaclava on October 25, 1854. Several lengths ahead of his troopers, Lord Cardigan was the first to gallop through murderous fire and to reach the battery of twelve Russian guns supported by thousands of cavalry. Then, having "led the Brigade and launched it with due impetus," as he later explained, and believing that it was "no part of a general's duty to fight the enemy among private soldiers," he turned Ronald around. Lord Cardigan rode slowly back down the valley alone, through shelling and sharpshooters' bullets. Neither he nor Ronald was touched.

THE ROOSEVELT BEARS appeared in a series of rhymed adventures by Seymour Eaton (Paul Piper) who was inspired by

---

*Aix is about 110 miles from Ghent. Browning did not say what the good news was.

THE ROOSEVELT BEARS

the popularity of THE TEDDY BEAR to create Teddy-B (for black) and Teddy-G (for gray), a pair of snappy dressers who have plenty of money and can read and write. In *The Roosevelt Bears* (1906), illustrated by V. Floyd Campbell, they head east from the mountains to see the world, leaving a trail of flabbergasted adults and delighted children from Kansas to New York. In Boston, the bears drive a car, land in jail for speeding, and receive degrees from Harvard, but their specialty is entertaining kids at circuses:

> Like heroes of a hundred fights
> The Roosevelt Bears in colored tights
> . . . took the stand to box a bout,
> But neither could knock the other out.

ROQUET was the faithful dog in legends about St. Roch, a fourteenth-century healer who was born in France and nursed the sick in northern Italy during a plague until he was stricken at Piacenza. Roch dragged himself into the woods to die, either willingly, to avoid infecting others, or because he was forced to. Tales vary but in most of them he was saved by a nobleman's dog

named Roquet who brought him a daily loaf of bread. Even after Roch was arrested as a spy and died in prison (ca. 1378), miraculous cures were attributed to him. To this day in some Roman Catholic parishes, dogs are blessed on August 16, the feast of St. Roch.

In another legend, St. Peter refused to admit Roquet to heaven with St. Roch. When the Lord intervened, St. Peter protested that he had never dreamed of bringing the cock who saved his soul. No sooner did the Lord say, "You may have him," than the other saints chimed in, wanting their animals. "Open the gates!" said the Lord, and a multitude of creatures entered, including the ox and ass from Bethlehem.

ROSABELLE, in *The Abbot* (1820) by Sir Walter Scott, was the palfrey that Douglas fetched from a guarded stable for Mary Queen of Scots after she fled Lochleven Castle. As soon as she was on the horse, the queen said, "I could almost swear I am at this moment mounted on my own favourite Rosabelle, who was never matched in Scotland for swiftness, for ease of motion and sureness of foot."

ROSWAL, the majestic hound who belonged to Sir Kenneth, the Scottish crusader, in *The Talisman* (1825) by Sir Walter Scott, was left to guard the banner of England when his master was lured away. The dog was nearly killed defending the flag but it vanished. The king of England, Richard Coeur-de-Lion, later arranged a procession of Christian troops past a new banner in order to give the Scottish knight and his dog, now healed, a chance to identify the assailant. As Conrade of Montferrat rode up, Roswal, "uttering a furious and savage yell, sprang forward, . . . leapt upon Conrade's noble charger, and seizing the Marquis by the throat, pulled him down from the saddle."

ROVER, the world's first canine movie star, made his debut in 1905 in *Rescued by Rover*, a seven-minute drama of a collie rescuing his master's baby from kidnappers. British film pioneer Cecil Hepworth produced the movie, featuring his wife, baby, and dog, whose real name was Blair. The demand for copies of the film was so great that Hepworth had to reshoot it twice because the negatives fell apart. Four successful sequels were made before Rover died in 1910.

ROWF, a large black mongrel who had barely survived submersion experiments at an animal laboratory, in *The Plague Dogs* (1978) by Richard Adams, was goaded into escaping by SNITTER, a fox terrier still bandaged after brain surgery. During their six weeks as fugitives in England's rugged Lake District, Rowf overcame his terror at the sight of water, protected Snitter, and learned to kill for food. As winter approached, however, they nearly starved and Rowf, cold and hungry, barked in rage at the snow-filled sky. After a false report circulated that the dogs were carriers of bubonic plague, the search for them intensified. It ended with the dogs swimming for their lives and being shot at when, incredibly, they were rescued.

ROWLF, a shaggy brown dog with floppy ears, was Jim Henson's first nationally known Muppet. Originally designed for dog food commercials, Rowlf was featured as a hound dog in "The Jimmy Dean Show"

on television in the 1960s, and then as a versatile pianist in "The Muppet Show," which began in 1976. As he told Victor Borge, a guest on the show, Rowlf played ragtime or Liszt, "but not Offenbach."

ROYAL GIFT, the first jackass to sire a mule in the United States, arrived in 1785. The gray Catalonian jack, 15 hands high, was sent by King Charles III of Spain, who made an exception to his law prohibiting export of breeding jacks, because George Washington wanted to breed draft animals at Mount Vernon. When the Marquis de Lafayette learned of Washington's project, he too sent a jack, the black Knight of Malta. With the two donkeys, and jennets also sent from Spain, Washington became the first breeder of American jacks as well as of American mules.

RUDOLPH, in Johnny Marks's song "Rudolph the Red-Nosed Reindeer" (1949), was shunned by his fellow reindeer because his nose glowed. But the glow made him a hero on a foggy Christmas Eve when Santa asked Rudolph to guide his sleigh by lighting the way. Robert L. May's story with the same title, published in a 1939 Montgomery Ward pamphlet, had inspired the song, which Gene Autry was persuaded (by his wife) to record. Autry also introduced it at a concert in New York City in September 1949. The song was an immediate hit. By 1982, it had been recorded more than 500 times and over 140 million records had been sold, a number surpassed only by Irving Berlin's "White Christmas" (1942). A television special animated with puppets, "The Story of Rudolph the Red-Nosed Reindeer," was presented in 1963 and has been shown every year since. (See also SANTA'S REINDEER.)

RUFF (1) is Dennis' big shaggy dog in *Dennis the Menace*, the cartoon panels by Hank Ketcham that first appeared in 1951 and were inspired by the antics of Ketcham's then 4-year-old son. Ruff does not do much except look stupid, but he does howl now and then if he's put out in the doghouse at night or hears someone practicing at a singing school.

RUFF (2), the Saint Bernard in *Tucker's Countryside* (1969) by George Selden, was an unwitting pawn in the "benign deception" that TUCKER MOUSE contrived to save the Old Meadow. HARRY CAT clawed the poor dog's nose, jumped on his back, still clawing, then raced for his life toward the orchard. Ruff chased him, of course, and landed, as planned, in the spot where Tucker wanted people to come. Ruff's barks brought them.

RUKENAW, the she-ape in the twelfth-century beast epic *Reynard the Fox*, defended her nephew REYNARD at court by reminding the king that the fox had once helped him. She also gathered forty beasts to support Reynard, including such former enemies as the beavers who "dared not gainsay Dame Rukenaw because they were afraid of her." The king was placated but ISEGRIM the wolf demanded a duel. To prepare Reynard, Rukenaw cropped his hair and gave him a slippery coating of olive oil. She told him to drink a lot and hold it so that he could piss on his tail and swat the wolf in the eyes with it to blind him. The fox should run from Isegrim too, kicking dust in his eyes and tiring him. "The

cunning goes before strength," she explained. Reynard won.

RUKSH, in Matthew Arnold's "Sohrab and Rustum" (1853), was Rustum's renowned "bright bay, with lofty crest." Sohrab, a young Tarter warrior in battle against the Persians, knew that the Persian lord, Rustum, was his father but had never seen him. Rustum, however, did not know he had a son. When a truce was called for Sohrab to challenge a Persian champion to single combat, it was Rustum who accepted. The two fought on until dusk as thunder rumbled, lightning flashed, and Ruksh "utter'd a dreadful cry . . . like the roar of some pain'd desert lion." Then Sohrab fell, Rustum's spear in his side. Only then did he learn that he had fought his father. The dying youth gave proof that he was Rustum's son and as the weeping Persian embraced him, Ruksh advanced "in mute woe," looking at the one and then the other:

> . . . and from his dark, compassionate
>   eyes,
> The big warm tears roll'd down, and
>   caked the sand.

(See RAKHSH.)

RUMPEL, a cat owned by Robert Southey (1774–1843), was formally named The Most Noble the Archduke Rumpelstizchen, Marquis Macbum, Earle Tomemange, Baron Raticide, Waowler, and Skaratchi. "After as long and happy a life as a cat could wish for," Rumpel died. Southey wrote, "We are each and all, servants included, more sorry for his loss, or rather, more affected by it, than any of us would like to confess."

RUPERT, the young bear who has been a favorite character in British comics since 1920, made his debut in the *Daily Express* in "The Adventures of a Little Lost Bear," a series of panels drawn by Mary Tourtel, with captions in verse by her husband, Herbert, an editor of the paper. Alfred Bestall took over the drawing in 1935 and was succeeded thirty years later by Alex Cubie. Rupert, who always wears a muffler and checked trousers, lives in Nutwood with Mummy and Daddy but is often away on fabulous adventures with Bill Badger, Edward Trunk the elephant, and other playmates. Since 1945, the stories about the popular little bear have been reprinted in strip form in color in the *Rupert Annual*, and a puppet film series for television was launched on Rupert's fiftieth anniversary in 1970.

RUSSEL, the fox in "The Nun's Priest's Tale" in *The Canterbury Tales* by Geoffrey Chaucer (ca. 1343–1400), was "ful of sly iniquitee." Chanticleer the rooster was inclined to flee when he saw the fox lurking in a bed of cabbages but Russel protested that he only wanted to hear the rooster sing. "Ravisshed with his flaterye," Chanticleer flapped his wings, stretched his neck, closed his eyes, and started to crow. At once, Russel seized him by the throat and hauled him on his back toward the woods. The barnyard hens set up a great cry and gave chase. So did the other animals, even the hogs. Chanticleer told Russel that if he were the fox, he would tell them all to go back, the fools. The instant Russel opened his mouth to reply, the rooster freed himself and flew up into a tree. Denying any wicked intent, the fox begged, "Com doun, and I shal telle yow what I mente." Chanticleer said he'd be damned if he would let Russel beguile him again, "for he that winketh whan he sholde see" deserved to have God forsake him. No, said the fox, God would punish the one who is so indiscreet that he jabbers when he should hold his peace.

SAEHRIMNIR, in Norse mythology, was the bountiful boar at Valhalla, where fallen Heroes chosen by Odin spent their days at battles and banquets. In the morning, they put on armor and killed each other. Then they all got up in perfect health to eat and drink together, the best of friends. Saehrimnir was served as dinner. Each day, the boar was boiled in a special kettle. Each night, he was alive and well again.

SAHA, the title character in Colette's *La Chatte* (1933), was so adored by Alain that when he married Camille, he took the cat from his mother's house to their small apartment. Resenting the rivalry of Alain's "hallowed animal," Camille pushed Saha off the railing of their ninth-floor balcony, but an awning broke her fall. Alain arrived and, because the cat screamed at Camille's touch and her claws were broken, he soon realized that Camille had pushed her. He went home, with Saha, to his mother. Overnight, the cat appeared to grow fat as she "sat and gazed at the garden with the eyes of a contented monarch." Admiring the way she fished for insects in the watering pot, Alain exclaimed, "Isn't she a wonder of a cat?" His mother sighed, "Yes, and she's your delusion—your chimera." Camille arrived, exchanged accusations with Alain, and, as she walked away, turned for a last look. Alain lolled in a chair while Saha, "on the watch, was following Camille's departure with the expression of a human being."

SALOME was Li'l Abner's beloved pig in Al Capp's saga of the hillbillies of Dogpatch, the comic strip *Li'l Abner* (1934–77).

SAM, Miss Chauncey's black cat in Walter de la Mare's "Broomsticks" from *Broomsticks and Other Tales* (1925), started to act strangely at the age of 7. After the new moon appeared, he sat staring out the window at dusk, making gestures with his forepaws. When he roamed the moor that night, Miss Chauncey heard a *whssh* sound in the sky, followed by Sam's caterwauling. She tried to keep him in but he escaped up the chimney. When she blocked the chimney the following night, he paced so restlessly, even parting the curtains to look out, that she let him go. Again she heard the *whssh*, and what sounded like a cackle of laughter. In the morning, she had to fight off a "rabblement" of cats chasing Sam home, and there were odd footprints and the mark of a crutch or a broomstick in the garden. With the full moon, the cat gradually reverted to being her pet but at the first sight of the crescent moon, the change began again: "He mouched about with a sly and furtive eye. And when he fawned on her, . . . the whole look of him was full of deceit."

SAMUEL WHISKERS, in Beatrix Potter's *The Roly-Poly Pudding* (1908), was a fat old rat in the attic who just sat watching and taking snuff while his skinny old wife ANNA MARIA tied up their prisoner, TOM KITTEN. When they heard a little dog coming to the rescue, Samuel Whiskers and his wife gathered whatever they could carry away in a stolen wheelbarrow and fled to Farmer Potatoes' barn, where they begat countless descendants.

SAMUEL WHISKERS

SAN DOMINGO, a mustang in Marguerite Henry's story *San Domingo* (1972), was foaled in the Nebraska Territory in 1857 and raised for two years by young Peter Lundy, until his father traded the colt for a Thoroughbred. In 1860, the boy was old enough to join the newly formed Pony Express, and in March 1861, he was reunited with Domingo. The pony, in superb condition, covered 39 miles in 2 hours and 33 minutes, in the urgent relay to California of President Abraham Lincoln's First Inaugural Address.

SANDY, a big mutt with one black ear and blank circles for eyes, had been Annie's companion in Harold Gray's comic strip *Little Orphan Annie* since its debut on August 5, 1924. As Annie's protector, the dog would bare his teeth and tree whoever meant to harm her. As her confidant, he grinned or drooped in whatever reaction was appropriate to what she told him. When he agreed with her, he said "Arf!" and when there was an emergency, he said "Arf! Arf!"

After Gray died in 1968, the efforts of other artists to continue *Little Orphan Annie* were so unsuccessful that in the 1970s his syndicate began to republish the original strip. *Annie*, a Broadway musical based on the strip, opened on April 21, 1977, with a live Sandy, trained by actor William Berloni, who had found the shaggy mutt at an animal shelter in Connecticut.

SANTA'S REINDEER, the original eight tiny ones, pulled St. Nick's miniature sleigh in Clement Moore's "A Visit from St. Nicholas":

More rapid than eagles his coursers
  they came,

And he whistled, and shouted, and
called them by name:
Now, *Dasher*! now, *Dancer*! now,
Prancer and *Vixen*!
On, *Comet*! on, *Cupid*! on, *Donner*
and *Blitzen*!

Professor Moore, a classical scholar renowned for *A Compendious Lexicon of the
Hebrew Language,* wrote the poem in 1822
as a present for his children. First published
anonymously and without his knowledge
in the Troy *Sentinel* in December 1823, the
poem soon became a classic, popularly
known as "The Night Before Christmas,"
but it was fifteen years before Dr. Moore
admitted that he had written it.

SARAH was the first chimpanzee to learn
a visual language invented in the late 1960s
by David Premack, a psychologist then at
the University of California at Santa
Barbara. For symbols, Premack used plastic
chips in various colors and shapes that
gave no clue to their meaning. Sarah
quickly learned that she would get a
banana, for example, when she picked the
symbol for it, a red square. After she acquired a number of words, Premack taught
her to "write" sentences like "Give Sarah
apple" by arranging the right chips verti-
cally on a magnetized board. By solving
multiple choice problems with a minimum
of choices and an edible reward, Sarah went
on to learn characteristics such as color and
shape, the concept of same or different, the
interrogative, and the negative. Her most
sophisticated accomplishment was to learn
the conditional "if–then" symbol. In a
typical pair of sentences, she would "read"
that if she took a banana she would not
get chocolate, and that if she took an apple,
she would. Sarah took the apple.

SARAH HUGGERSACK, a baby giant
anteater acquired by Gerald Durrell and his
wife, Jacquie, in Paraguay in 1954, had to
be bottle-fed. Jacquie observed in *Beasts in
My Bed* (1967) that Sarah's "idea of ecstasy
was to cling, with razor-like claws, either
to Gerry or me, or . . . a straw-filled sack."
Durrell adored Sarah, letting her share his
bed and "his every free moment." In England, after Sarah was placed in Paignton
Zoo, Durrell borrowed her for a lecture at
the Festival Hall in London. She "stole the
show, running along the stage, playing
with Gerry, and honking madly." The
stagestruck anteater did not want to get
back in her box.

SARAMA, a bitch in Hindu mythology,
was the great god Indra's watchdog and
messenger. When the evil Panis stole cattle
from the gods, Sarama took up the scent
and tracked the animals to the cave where
they were hidden. (See THE SARAMEYAU.)

THE SARAMEYAU, twin sons of the bitch
SARAMA in Hindu mythology, were savage,
four-eyed hounds who served Yama, the
god of death, by guiding the souls of the
dead to their final abode. The worthiest
went to Paradise. The most sinful, especially those who had killed dogs during
their lifetime, fell into a bottomless pit.

SARDAR, a handsome bay gelding, was
presented to Jacqueline Kennedy by President Mohammed Ayub Khan during her
1962 visit to Pakistan. The horse was flown
to Washington, D.C., in a Military Air
Transport Service plane, and to avert any
uproar reminiscent of the one over Elliott
Roosevelt's dog BLAZE, President John F.
Kennedy's press secretary, Pierre Salinger,

claimed that the plane was on a scheduled flight and had no other cargo.

SAUR I, in a legend similar to that of RAKKAE, was a dog chosen by the people of Norway as their king in the eleventh century. The hated King Eystein had agreed to abdicate only if they replaced him with a dog or a slave. "Signing" decrees with his paw, the dog-king reigned for three years, surrounded by courtiers who carried him in the rain lest he get wet. One day, Saur was dozing in a sheep meadow when a wolf attacked the nearest lamb. The dog jumped on the wolf, the courtiers did nothing, and the wolf killed the king.

SAVAGE SAM, the son of OLD YELLER in Fred Gipson's *Savage Sam* (1962), was a blue-tick trail hound who belonged to 6-year-old Little Arliss. When Arliss was captured by Apache horse thieves in Texas around 1871, the persistent dog trailed the boy's scent across country, surviving a tomahawk blow on his back and a fight with wolves. The pads of his feet wore so thin they oozed blood, but with his high, ringing cry, Sam led the boy's rescuers to the Indian encampment and killed the Apache who had tortured Arliss.

SCANNON, a black Newfoundland dog, was Meriwether Lewis' companion, watch-dog, and hunter on the Lewis and Clark expedition to explore the Louisiana Purchase. Geese and rabbits were easy game and he learned to catch antelope—"clumsy swimmers," noted Lewis—by overtaking them in the river and drowning them. In May 1805, Scannon tried the same stunt on a wounded beaver and nearly bled to death from a bite that cut an artery. Ten

days later, though, he was full of fight when "a large buffaloe Bull . . . ran up the bank in full speed . . . within a few inches of . . . the heads of the men as they lay sleeping." Lewis wrote, "My dog saved us by causing him to change his course." William Clark simply reported, "our Dog flew out." When Scannon was stolen by Indians in April 1806, Lewis sent three men after them with orders to shoot if there was any resistance. With satisfaction, he wrote in his journal that the thieves, sighting their pursuers 2 miles off, "left the dog and fled."

SCOOBY DOO, created in 1971 by Hanna-Barbera Productions for television cartoons, is a Great Dane who helps four high school students solve mysteries involving the supernatural all over the world, from the Bermuda Triangle to China. For a huge dog and a detective, Scooby has an unusual characteristic—the heart of a chicken. Faced with danger, he would rather turn his back and cower in a corner.

SCOUT was Tonto's horse in "The Lone Ranger" series created for radio in 1933. In the television series that began in 1949, Scout was a pinto. Tonto was played by Jay Silverheels, a Mohawk Indian.

SCRAPS, billed as a "thoroughbred mongrel," was Charlie Chaplin's co-star in *A Dog's Life* (1918), in which the tramp and the pooch scrounge for food, steal from thieves, and spread confusion until Charlie winds up with the girl, Scraps with a litter of puppies. Trainer Charles Gee, who had rescued the little white mutt from a dogcatcher, named him Brownie for the

SCRAPS

big patch over one eye and found him easy to train. Chaplin had rejected dozens of dogs before Brownie was brought to him, jumped on his lap, and got the part. After *A Dog's Life*, Brownie-Scraps starred in fifty two-reelers, often with Queenie, a trick horse. They specialized in rescuing children from burning buildings and dragging wounded heroes to safety.

SEBEK (or SOBK), a god of evil and death in Egyptian mythology, was represented as a crocodile, the dreaded animal who emerged from canals in time of drought to kill and eat other animals and people. At his temple in Fayum, sacred crocodiles adorned with jewels splashed around their own lake, which also provided holy water for Sebek's worshipers to drink.

[233]

SECRETARIAT became the first winner of American Thoroughbred racing's Triple Crown in twenty-five years when he won the Belmont by thirty-one lengths on June 9, 1973; in 1972, he had been the first 2-year-old ever named Horse of the Year. Affectionately known as "Big Red," the handsome chestnut had won the Kentucky Derby by 2½ lengths in record time for the mile and a quarter, 1:59 2/5, and the Preakness by 2½ lengths, but was denied a record there because the official clock was faulty. At Belmont, Secretariat reduced the record for the mile and a half by more than 2 seconds, finishing in 2:24, and was going so fast that even as jockey Ron Turcotte pulled him up, he set a world record for thirteen furlongs. The Triple Crown sweep convinced many racing experts that he was the greatest Thoroughbred that ever lived. He was retired in November 1973 because he had been syndicated for breeding shares worth a total of $6,080,000; but in his brief racing career—only sixteen months—Secretariat won sixteen of his twenty-one races, earned $1,316,808, and broke or equaled five track records.

THE SEIAN HORSE, a large bay of surpassing beauty, was not only fatal to his owners but also ruinous to their families and fortunes. Cneius Seius, his first owner, was put to death by Mark Antony. The horse's next owner, Cornelius Dolabella, ordered one of his own soldiers to kill him when his palace was subsequently captured by Caius Cassius in 43 B.C. Cassius next took possession of the horse and was killed by Octavian. The horse's fourth owner, Mark Antony, committed suicide. Consequently, *Ille homo habet equum Seianum* ("This man has a Seian horse") became a Latin expression for a man cursed with bad luck.

SELIMA, "demurest of the tabby kind," was Horace Walpole's cat, whose demise inspired Thomas Gray to write "Ode on the Death of a Favourite Cat Drowned in a Tub of Gold Fishes" (1748), after asking Walpole if he had the name right: "Selima, was it? or Fatima." In the poem, the cat gazed into the water, waving her tail, then stretched to reach one of the gliding forms:

> What female heart can gold despise?
> What Cat's averse to fish?

Selima fell in head first. She surfaced eight times, mewing "to ev'ry watry God" for help, but:

> . . . one false step is ne'er retriev'd . . .
> Not all that tempts your wand'ring
> eyes
> And heedless hearts, is lawful prize;
> Nor all, that glisters, gold.

SEMILLANTE, in Guy de Maupassant's story *"Une vendetta"* (1883), was a great, gaunt, long-haired dog whom the widow Saverini trained to avenge the death of her son. The old Corsican woman would keep Sémillante ("Sprightly") chained for days at a time, giving her only water, then turn her loose on a straw dummy with a sausage around its neck. At the end of three months, neither the chain nor the reward of food was needed to make Sémillante rip out the dummy's throat; the widow merely pointed to it and said, "Go!" The dog had not been fed for two days when she was taken across to Sardinia, where the son's murderer had fled. When the Widow Saverini found him, she cried, "Go, Go!

Eat him up!" and "Sémillante dug her fangs into his throat."

SEMINOLE SAM, the fast-talking fox in Walt Kelly's comic strip *Pogo*, convinced himself that "We're for Vice" could be the slogan for Pogo's second presidential campaign in 1956. Then he considered the candidate's image. "We're standing with our feet buttered on a pool of ball bearings," he brainstormed. "We need a new truth about Pogo—somethin' with a little jazz on it—even if we have to make it up."

SENSATION, a large lemon and white pointer, was 2½ years old and had won seven prizes in England when he was imported to America by the newly formed Westminster Kennel Club in 1877. His stud fee was only $35; in his first year in the United States, he also won $1,200 in prizes, on the bench and in the field. The club no longer has its own dogs and kennels, but an engraving of Sensation, its first dog, is still its emblem. The Best-in-Show award at the annual Westminster Dog Show, America's second oldest continuous sporting event (after the Kentucky Derby), is a sterling silver bowl etched with the figure of Sensation pointing.

SERGEANT MURPHY, a brown dog in Richard Scarry's picture books, is a police officer who rides his motorcycle around Busytown, unscrambling traffic, dispensing parking tickets, and keeping the peace. While chasing Bananas Gorilla, the compulsive banana thief, in *Richard Scarry's What Do People Do All Day?* (1968), Murphy lands on his head when the motorcycle slips on a banana peel. Saved by his crash helmet, he leads the handcuffed gorilla to the paddy wagon. At day's end, Sergeant Murphy goes home to Herself Murphy and their baby, Bridget.

SET, a violent and treacherous god in Egyptian mythology, was usually represented as a pig, which Egyptians hated, or a man with a pig's head. In a boat race with Horus for the throne of Egypt, Set turned himself into a hippopotamus and capsized his opponent's craft. But Horus won the throne and Set was relegated to howling in the sky as the god of storms.

SHADOW THE WEASEL, in the Thornton Burgess nature books, was a short-tempered, thieving scamp who usually sided with REDDY FOX and suffered for it. In *The Adventures of Peter Cottontail* (1914), Shadow was supposed to chase PETER RABBIT (2) out of the briar patch to the waiting Reddy but Peter maneuvered the weasel to a puddle, Shadow jumped— and fell in.

SHARATZ was the powerful mount of Marko Kraljevic, a fourteenth-century Serbian king who became a legendary hero celebrated in epic poems and folk songs. It was said that his piebald horse could leap forward the length of four lances and upward the length of three. In battle with the Turks, Sharatz would trample the cavalrymen into the ground, biting off the ears of their horses as he went along.

SHARDIK, in Richard Adams' *Shardik* (1974), was the ancient bear-god of the Ortelgans, a primitive tribe that once ruled a city and its empire but was now reduced to hunting for survival. When one of the hunters was saved from a leopard by a huge bear, more than twice as tall as a man, he believed he had seen the god Shardik incarnate and became the priest-king of the Ortelgans. Inspired by their worship of the live bear as their god, they regained their old empire, only to sink into the corruption of trading in child slaves to support it. Shardik, the live bear, was badly wounded by enemies but killed a slave trader before he died. The bear and a murdered child were placed on a pyre on a raft that was set ablaze and floated downstream. The cult of the bear survived, its worshipers dedicated to the well-being of children because Shardik died to save them.

SHASTA (1), imported from Mexico in 1947, was the first cougar mascot of the football team at the University of Houston, whose teams had been called Cougars since 1927. The first Shasta was retired in 1963; the fifth one, a 2-month-old cub, arrived at the university in 1980.

SHASTA (2), born May 6, 1948, at the Hogle Zoological Garden in Salt Lake City, Utah, was the first *liger* born in the United States to reach maturity. A *liger* is the hybrid product of a lion father and a tigress mother, a crossbreeding that would not occur outside of zoos because the natural ranges of these animals do not coincide. When a male tiger and a lioness breed, the result is a *tiglon*. In both cases, the offspring is sterile. Hogle Zoo keepers had arranged the mating of Daisy, the Bengal tiger, and Huey, the African lion, after five months' observation of their tractability while they were displayed in adjoining cages.

At birth, Shasta weighed only 12 ounces and was taken from her mother to be bottle-fed in a local household. Her name derived from people saying, "She 'hasta' have this, she 'hasta' have that." In three months, Shasta became a rambunctious 25-pounder and was returned to the zoo. Fully grown, she weighed 375 pounds. Her head was like a tiger's and her body had the shape of a large lioness and was lightly striped. She died in 1972 at the age of 24. In 1977, because of continued interest in this unique animal, the Hogle Zoo placed Shasta on permanent display as a mounted specimen.

SHERE KHAN, the lame tiger in Rudyard Kipling's *The Jungle Book* (1894), demanded the "man-cub," baby Mowgli, when the wolves took him into their cave. Raksha the Mother Wolf declared that she would raise the cub to hunt Shere Khan.

SHASTA (2)

The tiger backed off, growling, "The cub is mine, and to my teeth he will come in the end, O bushtailed thieves!" Ten years later, he again demanded the boy. Mowgli, who had been directed to bring fire from his people's village, grabbed the tiger by his chin whiskers and beat him on the head with a blazing branch. After his singed hair grew back, Shere Khan reappeared, determined to kill the boy, but was ambushed instead. While the tiger rested in a ravine, Mowgli sent a herd of bulls charging in from one side, the cows and calves from the other. Shere Khan was trampled to death.

SHIFT, an ugly old ape in C. S. Lewis' final Chronicle of Narnia, *The Last Battle* (1956), seized power by claiming to speak for ASLAN the Great Lion, whom he pretended to exhibit in brief displays of PUZZLE the ass, trussed up in a lion's hide. "True freedom means doing what I tell you," the despotic ape told his fellow beasts. But he soon took to drink, was forced to be the mouthpiece of invading soldiers he had let in, and died a horrible death.

SHOCK is the subject of "An Elegy on a Lap-Dog" (1720) by John Gay, who addresses the dog's mistress, Celia:

> No more thy hand shall smooth his
>   glossy hair,
> And comb the wavings of his pendent
>   ear.

Observing that "her torn fan gives real signs of grief," Gay implores Celia to stop crying:

> In man you'll find a more substantial
>   bliss,
> More grateful toying, and a sweeter
>   kiss. . . .

THE SHONY DOG, according to Cornish folklore, barks when a storm is coming, thus saving the fishermen from smashing their boats on the rocky shores.

SIAM, the first Siamese cat in the United States, was sent to President Rutherford B. Hayes's wife, Lucy, in November 1878 by the American consul in Bangkok. Siam was such a great favorite in the White House that when she died a year later, her body was stuffed.

SILVER and the Lone Ranger who rode him were created by George W. Trendle and Fran Striker for a radio series that began on January 30, 1933, and continued for over twenty years. The show spawned books, a comic strip (1938–71), comic books, movies, and a television series (1948–61). In the first book about the masked rider, *The Lone Ranger* (1938), Striker wrote that Silver, a 6-year-old wild stallion famous for saving his herd from Sioux horse hunters, had been injured in a buffalo stampede when the Ranger, who needed a mount, caught him. The Ranger gently broke the weakened horse to the saddle, then hobbled one of his forelegs before riding him out of the canyon. Once they reached the valley, the suspended forefoot was freed and the great horse raced across the land. From then on, the signal that the Lone Ranger was on his way was the sound of thundering hoofbeats and the cry of "Hi-Yo, Silver, Awa-a-ay!"

SILVER BLAZE, an undefeated 5-year-old bay of the Isonomy stock, was favored to win the Wessex Cup in Sir Arthur Conan Doyle's story "The Adventure of Silver Blaze" (1892). A week before the race, the horse disappeared and his trainer, John Straker, was found dead of a head injury, apparently murdered. The horse's owner, Colonel Ross, and Inspector Gregory of Scotland Yard invited Sherlock Holmes to join their investigation. He examined the contents of Straker's pockets and, with Dr. Watson, studied Silver Blaze's tracks. Four days later, Holmes and Watson joined Colonel Ross at the race, with Silver Blaze still missing. How the race comes out and justice is done—to Silver Blaze as well as to others—proves one of Holmes's best-known triumphs.

Controversy over Holmes's behavior persists. A number of writers, including the famous sports columnist Red Smith and Conan Doyle himself, have pointed out that Holmes committed several misdemeanors in his actions as investigator. The memory of Silver Blaze is untarnished, however. Every September since 1952, the Baker Street Irregulars have gathered at Belmont for the annual running of the Silver Blaze Handicap.

SILVERTAIL, a squirrel in Beatrix Potter's *The Tale of Timmy Tiptoes* (1911), could not remember where his nuts were buried, dug up some that belonged to another squirrel, and got in a fight. More squirrels joined the digging and fighting until they saw TIMMY TIPTOES innocently gathering his own nuts in a bag. They all converged on him and pushed him through a hole in a tree. Silvertail announced they would leave him there until he confessed.

SIMPKIN, the cat in Beatrix Potter's *The Tailor of Gloucester* (1903), hid the tailor's new thread when he discovered that his captive mice were gone. After the tailor,

who had to finish some work by noon on Christmas, went to bed with a fever, the famished cat, prowling the streets for food, found the mice working in the tailor's shop, but he could not get in. On Christmas morning, the tailor woke, his fever gone, to find the packet of thread on his bed and "the repentant Simpkin" offering breakfast. They hurried to the shop and as soon as the tailor unlocked the door, "Simpkin ran in, between his legs like a cat that expects something. . . . But there was no one there."

SIMPLE J. MALARKEY, a bobcat with an evil grin who looked and acted like Sen. Joseph R. McCarthy, turned up in Walt Kelly's comic strip *Pogo* in 1953, to investigate the inhabitants of the Okefenokee Swamp, and to tar and feather those who didn't look right. Malarkey was the first of a parade of animal caricatures of prominent political figures that endeared Kelly to many readers, and horrified others.

SINH, the sacred cat of Burma, belonged to Mun Ha, the high priest of a cult that worshiped Tsun Kyankze, a sapphire-eyed goddess who transmigrated the souls of dead priests into the bodies of sacred animals. Mun Ha spent his life in a temple on the side of a mountain, contemplating a statue of the goddess, his beloved cat at his side. One night, as enemies from Siam approached the temple, Mun Ha died. Instantly, the cat jumped up on his master's head. His yellow eyes turned as blue as the statue's and by staring at the south door of the temple, Sinh directed the priests to it to repel the invaders. For seven days, the cat sat gazing at the statue, then he died. Seven days after that, the priests convened to select Mun Ha's successor. The choice was made for them when a hundred blue-eyed cats, all looking exactly like Sinh, marched in to form a circle around the youngest priest.

SIR ISAAC NEWTON, the newt in Beatrix Potter's *The Tale of Mr. Jeremy Fisher* (1906), was invited to dinner by Mr. Jeremy Fisher the frog and arrived wearing his black and gold waistcoat.

SIR ORAN HAUT-TON, in Thomas Love Peacock's satirical novel *Melincourt* (1817), was an orangutan. Sylvan Forester, a young philosopher who believed that apes were members of the human family, had been able to teach him everything except speech and bought him a baronetcy and a seat in Parliament. Successfully launched in English society, Sir Oran Haut-ton was gallant and played the flute nicely, although he was inclined to jump out a window and head for the woods when he was in wine. His failing to speak in Parliament was respected as a sign that he was thinking instead. Peacock was inspired to create Sir Oran by James Burnett, Lord Monboddo (1714–99), a pioneer in anthropology who had proposed that an orangutan, able to play the flute but not to speak, was an example of "the infantine state of our species."

SIZI, the cat who belonged to Albert Schweitzer (1875–1965) while he was a medical missionary in Africa, was given the same consideration Mohammed gave his cat, Meuzza. Visitors to the clinic at Lambaréné would find the doctor writing prescriptions with his right hand because the cat had curled up in his left arm and gone to sleep, as had the arm.

SKINFAXI, the horse in Norse mythology whose name means "shining mane," was driven across the heavens by Dag (Day), the fair-complected son of Nott (Night), to brighten the earth and sky with the light from his mane.

SKIPPERDEE was Eloise's turtle in Kay Thompson's *Eloise* (1955), illustrated by Hilary Knight. Eloise was a resourceful 6-year-old who lived at the Plaza Hotel. Under a picture of her walking Skipperdee on a leash with a bow around his body, Eloise explained that the Plaza was the only hotel in New York that allowed you to have a turtle. Skipperdee wore sneakers and ate raisins, which Eloise ordered, usually one at a time, from room service. When she got up in the morning, Eloise would braid Skipperdee's ears because if she didn't, he would get cross and develop a rash. In the bathtub, he floated on her soap. Without his sneakers, he weighed nothing on the bathroom scales. With them, he weighed $1/2$ pound.

SKOLL was the wolf in Norse mythology who chased the sun across the sky while his brother wolf, Hati or Manigarm, pursued the moon. At the end of the world, Skoll swallowed the sun.

SLEEPY TOM was one of the original Big Four of pacing who appeared on the Grand Circuit of harness race tracks in 1878 and began to draw crowds with their strenuous five- and six-heat races. The most frequent winner was Sleepy Tom, billed as "the world's toughest piece of horseflesh." He was about 10 years old then, had been worked hard, and had been traded around to a variety of owners, once for a cheap watch, a bottle of whisky, and a 3-year-old colt. He was completely blind. His owner-driver in 1878, Stephen C. Phillips, guided him with a steady stream of talk. Once, when Phillips was thrown to the ground in a collision of sulkies, the pacer just stopped in his tracks and stood quietly until he heard his driver's voice again. In 1879, Sleepy Tom set a world record for pacing the mile, 2:12¾.

SLEIPNIR, Odin's magic steed in Norse mythology, was sired by Svadilfari, had eight legs, and could outrun the wind. When Odin's son Balder was killed, another son, Hermod, mounted Sleipnir and galloped to the kingdom of the dead in hope of retrieving him.

SLIPPERS, a gray, six-toed cat who belonged to President Theodore Roosevelt, had a habit of wandering off for days at a time and an unerring instinct for returning to the White House whenever a state dinner was scheduled. At one such affair for the diplomatic corps in 1906, the procession from the State Dining Room to the East Room, led by the President, who was escorting the wife of an important ambassador, came to a sudden stop in the corridor because Slippers was sprawled full-length in the middle of the rug. With a quick bow to the ambassador's wife, Roosevelt conducted her around the cat, and the line of glittering guests followed the leader.

SMOKEY BEAR has been both a symbolic and a real bear. The familiar poster figure with ranger hat, blue jeans, and shovel was created in 1944 by the U.S. Forest Service, with the help of The Advertising Council,

SMOKEY BEAR

Inc., to publicize its campaign to prevent forest fires. The real bear was a badly burned cub discovered in the Lincoln National Forest in New Mexico after a devastating five-day fire in 1950. Nursed back to health, he was adopted by the Forest Service and taken to Washington, D.C. As Smokey Bear, he became one of the most popular inhabitants of the National Zoo.

During the next twenty-five years, the mass media donated millions of dollars' worth of time and space to Smokey Bear and his message, "Only *you* can prevent forest fires!" Congress copyrighted Smokey's name and image in 1952 and by 1976 licensed products had earned more than $1.5 million in royalties for the Forest Service. And "Smokey" became the word for police in citizens' band radio jargon because the poster bear's hat was like those worn by state troopers.

The zoo Smokey, permanently stiff-legged from his burn injuries, grew to a height of 6 feet. He made celebrity appearances and acquired his own international fan club. Thousands of kids signed up as Junior Forest Rangers to receive a Ranger kit and "official" badge. Smokey died in 1976 and was buried at the Smokey Bear Historical Park in Capitan, New Mexico, near the spot where he had been found.

SMOKY (1), a bobcat, was one of hundreds of animals sent as gifts to President Calvin Coolidge. A few, like the dogs ROB ROY and LADDIE BUCK and the raccoon REBECCA, remained at the White House as pets. Others, including a pair of lion cubs, a wallaby, a pigmy hippopotamus, and a bear that liked marshmallows, were quickly forwarded to a zoo. Coolidge had no intention of keeping Smoky but was obliged to accept him graciously. In the Tennessee county where the animal was captured, 452 votes were cast in the 1924 presidential election —and 442 of them were for Coolidge.

SMOKY (2), the mouse-colored, blaze-faced, wild range pony in *Smoky* (1926) by Will James, was branded and gelded as a colt, then left free until he was a 4-year-old. Clint, the "bronco twister" for the ranch, broke him without breaking his spirit and rode him for five years until, because of his value as a cow horse, he was stolen. The thief rode him hundreds of miles south before Smoky finally threw the man and presumably killed him. The saddled horse turned up in the Arizona desert with dried blood on his jaws. Smoky became "The Cougar," a "fighting, man-hating, bucking outlaw," for six years a famous rodeo champion throughout the Southwest. When he began to fade, a livery stable paid $25 for him, changed his name to Cloudy, and hired him out as a saddle horse until he broke down and a truck farmer bought him for $3. The starved and mistreated old horse hauled the man's wagon into town one day when Clint happened to be there. He took Smoky home.

SNITTER, a black and white fox terrier who had been taken away from his master in *The Plague Dogs* (1978) by Richard Adams, had enough wits left after a drastic brain operation at an animal laboratory to recognize a chance to escape and to make ROWF, a large black mongrel, go with him. During their six weeks of wandering around England's Lake District, Snitter often hallucinated or raved irrationally, but he was sustained by the memory of his master.

SNOOPY, the omnipresent beagle, was created by Charles M. Schulz for his comic strip *Peanuts*, which made its debut on October 2, 1950. Nominally Charlie Brown's dog, Snoopy has a stomach clock that goes off at suppertime; he slathers kisses on pugnacious Lucy, and makes a hopeless shortstop. He does not speak but he has a teeming imagination. Walking upright, Snoopy becomes the world-famous quarterback hurling the bomb, the world-famous beagle scout leading a nature hike, or Joe Cool, hanging around in dark glasses. On top of his doghouse, he keeps neighbors awake with his typing, presents *War and Peace* at his Pawpet Theater, and in his greatest fantasy as the World War I ace in goggles and scarf, he takes his Sop-with Camel up to challenge the Red Baron in his Fokker triplane. As the Sopwith crashes to the ground, Snoopy lands in his supper dish: "How embarrassing! Curse you, Red Baron!"

The success of *Peanuts* has generated books, television specials, the musical comedy *You're a Good Man, Charlie Brown* (1967), and a huge assortment of licensed merchandise. With his image on everything from nightshirts to telephones to an 18-carat gold bank priced at $10,000, Snoopy is surely the most famous dog in the world. The model for him was Spike, a black and white dog who was given to Schulz when he was 13, but as Schulz says, "Snoopy is not a real dog. He is an image of what people would like a dog to be."

SNOWBALL was the honorable member of the trio of pigs who led the rebellion in George Orwell's *Animal Farm* (1946). "All animals are equal" was the slogan of the new society but SQUEALER was soon explaining why pigs deserved privileges while NAPOLEON (2) was preparing to seize power. Snowball alone worked for the common good. He led the fighting when Jones tried to recapture the farm and designed a windmill that the animals could build. They were ready to vote for the project when, at a signal from Napoleon, his dogs drove Snowball off the property. Snowball was never seen again and his memory was vilified.

SNOWBELL, in E. B. White's *Stuart Little* (1945), was a white cat who lived in New York City with STUART LITTLE, a mouse, and Stuart's human parents and brother. On the first night that a little bird named Margalo spent in the family's Boston fern, Snowbell was just about to pounce on her

when vigilant Stuart shot him in the ear with an arrow. The frustrated cat told a local angora how to climb into the house to eat the bird, but a pigeon who overheard the plot warned Margalo. She flew away. When Snowbell was questioned closely about Margalo's disappearance, he replied irritably: "I don't see why you have to make a pariah out of me just because that disagreeable little chippy flew the coop."

SNOWFLAKE, the world's first known albino gorilla, was discovered on October 1, 1966, in Rio Muni, a Spanish province in Africa now part of the Republic of Equatorial Guinea. The farmer who had just shot Snowflake's mother for raiding his banana grove was stunned to find the fuzzy white creature clinging to her body. A local naturalist bought Snowflake (*Copito de Nieve* in Spanish) for the Barcelona Zoo and set about taming him to prepare him for life in captivity. Snowflake weighed 19½ pounds and, judging by his teeth, was about 2 years old. His hair was completely white, his eyes blue, and his skin a light, pinkish, flesh color. His wrinkled face gave him the look of a sly old man with muttonchops and a crew cut. He drank milk right away, grew fond of cookies and baked ham, and detested his first bath. At the Barcelona Zoo, his appearance alone made him a star, but he also enjoyed clowning for the people.

SOLO, the female pup in Hugo van Lawick's television film *The Wild Dogs of Africa*, and his book *Solo* (1974), was the puniest member of a pack of African wild dogs roaming the Serengeti Plains in Tanzania. Havoc, the dominant bitch, had killed Solo's litter mates and ostracized

Solo's mother, depriving both mother and surviving pup of food. Savaged by Havoc's puppies, who were four weeks older, Solo soon lost the tips of her ears and was covered with puncture wounds. Only 8 weeks old when the pack began a 15-mile trek across the Serengeti in the dry season, Solo was too weak to keep up. One night, she lagged so far behind that a hyena closed in and van Lawick had to rescue her. After feeding her for a month, he intended to return her to her pack but could not locate it. He did, however, find a wild dog couple with five pups and, to his "intense relief," released Solo to live with them after the bitch gave her face a little lick.

SOUNDER, in William H. Armstrong's *Sounder* (1969), was part Georgia redbone hound and part bulldog, with a loud clear voice known all over the countryside. The hides of the coons and possums he caught for a black sharecropper brought cash, but one winter, the hunting was so bad that his master stole a ham to feed his family. When the man was taken away in chains, Sounder gave chase, was shot, and disappeared into the woods. Two months later, the dog turned up with one useless leg, one eye, and most of an ear missing. He was fed back to health but would not bark. Year after year, Sounder only whined when the sharecropper's son returned from searching for his father among the chain gangs. Then a distant figure appeared one day, approaching the cabin: "Suddenly the voice of the great coon hound broke the sultry August deadness. . . . The mighty voice rolled out upon the valley, . . . Sounder's master had come home."

SPARK PLUG, the racehorse draped in a patched blanket to hide his knock-knees, turned up in Billy de Beck's picaresque comic strip *Barney Google* in 1922. For the next twelve years, the top-hatted, bulb-nosed Barney made and lost fortunes with his nag. Sometimes he rode Sparky himself, once to beat the sheriff to the state line after not paying a hotel bill.

SPEEDY GONZALES, billed as "the fastest mouse in all Mexico," made his debut eluding SYLVESTER (1), the cat in the Academy Award-winning cartoon by Warner Brothers, *Speedy Gonzales* (1955). The little mouse in the big sombrero and red kerchief continued to zip around at great speed, toward a piece of cheese or away from the slow-moving Sylvester, in such films as *Here Today, Gone Tamale* (1959).

THE SPLIT ROCK WOLF was a predator said to have destroyed $10,000 worth of livestock in Wyoming before a professional hunter, H. P. Williams, tracked him down early in 1920. He made a scent from the wolf's carcass and took it to South Dakota in March when he joined dozens of bounty hunters going after the even more destructive CUSTER WOLF. Seven months later, that scent drew the Custer Wolf to the trap that finally caught him.

SPUMADOR was Prince Arthur's prancing Lybian steed in *The Faerie Queene* by Edmund Spenser (ca. 1552–99). In book II, canto XI, Arthur singlehandedly fought off the enemies of Alma, who were besieging her castle:

> And under neath him his courageous steed,
> The fierce Spumador, trode them down like docks;

The fierce Spumador borne of
 heavenly seed,
Such as Laomedon of Phaebus race did
 breed.

Spumador's name means "foaming one."

SQUEALER, a glib pig with a shrill voice
in George Orwell's *Animal Farm* (1946),
explained everything to the animals who
took over Mr. Jones's farm. According to
Squealer, pigs had privileges because they
were "brainworkers." SNOWBALL, the pig
who led the defense of the farm, was not a
hero but a traitor. Orders from NAPOLEON
(2), the boar who became dictator, were
not to be questioned because, said Squealer,
"Surely, comrades, you do not want Jones
back?" When rations were cut for all but
the pigs and the dogs who protected them,
Squealer spouted figures to "prove" that
the other animals were getting more food.
As usual, they believed every word.

SREDNI VASHTAR, in "Sredni Vashtar"
from *The Chronicles of Clovis* (1911) by
Saki (H. H. Munro), was a caged ferret
that Conradin, a lonely 10-year-old boy,
kept in the garden tool shed. He made up a
name for the beast, who he imagined was
a god, and worshiped him in elaborate
rituals. When Conradin's guardian, Mrs.
De Ropp, began to disapprove of his spending so much time in the shed, she inspected
it, found the locked hutch, then ransacked
his room for the key. As the boy watched
from the house, she reentered the shed.
Minutes passed, then out came the ferret,
"with eyes a-blink in the waning daylight,
and dark wet stains around the fur of jaw
and throat." He stopped to drink at a little
brook, then disappeared in the bushes. At

tea time, the maid went to the shed to
summon her mistress—and screamed in
horror. Conradin made himself another
piece of toast.

STASI was described by Konrad Lorenz
in *Man Meets Dog* (1953) as the most
faithful dog he ever knew. She was a cross-
breed who inherited sensitivity to human
feelings from her Alsatian great-grand-
mother TITO and "exclusive loyalty to the
pack-leader" from the dominant wolf-
strain of her chow forebears. When
Lorenz, home after a two-month absence,
departed a second time, the normally reti-
cent Stasi went on such a hen-killing rampage that she had to be penned in the yard.
At the first sight of Lorenz nine months
later, she rushed at him, barking and
growling, until she got his scent. She
stopped abruptly, stiffened, and raised her
head. "The mental torture of months found
outlet in the hair-raising yet beautiful tones
of a wolf's howl." Then she hurled herself
at him in exuberant affection and immediately resumed being a well-trained,
housebroken dog who "did not so much as
look at a hen."

STEAMBOAT was one of three favorite
horses that Daniel Webster buried at
Marshfield, his Massachusetts farm, with
what he called "the honors of war": standing upright, with halters and shoes on.
Since Steamboat was a fine roadster, a
monument was erected to him with a Latin
inscription noting that the *"equus cele-
berrimus"* died on November 3, 1838, and
concluding with the epitaph:

*SISTE, VIATOR, MAJOR TE
VIATOR HIC SISTIT!*

(Traveler, pause. A greater traveler
than you stops here!)

STEEL DUST, the first of the legendary
sires of the modern Quarter Horse, was
the fastest horse in the West in the 1850s,
when he beat every horse on the Texas
frontier and wrecked the economy of the
town of McKinney. Foaled in Kentucky in
1843 and taken to Lancaster, Texas, the
bay stallion developed into a powerful
sprinter, 15 hands high and weighing 1,200
pounds. In 1855, he was challenged to a
match race with Monmouth, an equally
well-known but larger horse in McKinney,
40 miles north. Although the town's population was only about 500, an estimated
10,000 people turned out for the race. At
the age of 12, Steel Dust was a gaunt,
sleepy-looking horse whose ribs showed,
which encouraged heavy wagering by the
locals, and the Lancaster delegation covered
every bet—money, land, livestock, anything. Steel Dust won by three lengths. A
later injury ended his racing career but he
was bred to many mares and his part-
thoroughbred lineage continues in several
important Quarter Horse families.

STORMY, Misty of Chincoteague's foal:
see MISTY.

STRAWBERRY was a tired old cab-horse
magically transported from London to
another world in *The Magician's Nephew*
(1955), the sixth Chronicle of Narnia by
C. S. Lewis. When ASLAN, the Great Lion,
created the idyllic land of Narnia, the horse
was given the power of speech. The lion
then gave the magician's nephew Digory a
mission and, to help him, transformed
Strawberry into a winged horse named

Fledge. Leaping 20 feet into the air for a
test flight, the horse neighed, curvetted,
then dropped back to earth "looking
awkward and surprised, but extremely
pleased."

STRIDER, in Leo Tolstoy's "Strider: The
Story of a Horse" (1886), was sired by a
Thoroughbred and gelded because he was
piebald. Given to the head groom, Strider
could not understand the idea of being
someone's property: "The words 'my horse'
applied to me, a live horse, seemed to me
as strange as to say 'my land,' 'my air,' or
'my water.' " His next owner, a profligate
prince, raced him against everything on the
road and always won, until the horse was
lamed by a 16-mile gallop after the prince's
mistress. Sold and resold, the formerly
majestic Strider wound up on a stud farm,
telling his story to the younger horses.
When a shabby old man visiting the farm
patted him and bragged about the great
piebald he had owned, Strider realized that
the visitor was his once brilliant and
wealthy prince. Before long, the Knacker
came to kill and flay the old gelding.
Dogs feasted on the carcass, a wolf picked
off the leavings for her cubs, and, a week
later, a peasant carried off the skull and
shoulder blades, all that remained. When
the prince died, "neither his skin, nor his
flesh, nor his bones, were of any use."

A musical based on the story was performed in Leningrad in 1976 and adapted
for production in New York City in 1979.

STRONGHEART, the first canine hero of
feature films, had been trained for police
work before screenwriter Jane Murfin and
her husband, director Larry Trimble, imported the 3-year-old German shepherd

from Germany in 1920. In *The Silent Call* (1921), the dog fought the villain, saved the heroine, and wrung the hearts of the audience when he returned to the cave where he had left his mate and puppies to find the entrance sealed by an explosion. Dropping the food he had brought, Strongheart sank to the ground and wept. The movie made him internationally famous. He starred in several more dramas and gave the first portrayal on screen of a guide dog for the blind before his early death.

STUART LITTLE, the debonair mouse in E. B. White's *Stuart Little* (1945), lived in New York City with his human parents and brother and SNOWBELL the cat. Stuart usually sported a hat and cane but changed to a sailor suit to take the helm of a model schooner in the Central Park pond. He was 7 years old when Margalo, a little bird staying with the family for a few days, became his dearest friend. When she flew away in the spring, the mouse was heartbroken; he obtained a miniature car and drove north to search for her. He stopped at a school that needed a substitute teacher, led discussions of ice cream and not being mean, then headed north again. At Ames' Crossing, he invited a tiny girl named Harriet Ames to go boating, but some big boys wrecked his little souvenir canoe and it started to rain. On his way again at dawn, Stuart encountered a telephone lineman at a fork in the road. Wishing him "fair skies and a tight grip," Stuart presented his card and asked the man to let him know if he ever saw Margalo on one of his poles. Then Stuart took the north fork. It seemed the right direction.

STUMPY, in Beatrix Potter's *The Tale of Little Pig Robinson* (1930), was a "large,

serious, well-behaved brown dog with a short tail." Since his late owner had left him 10 shillings a week for life, Stumpy lived comfortably with a retriever, a cat, and a housekeeper, and could afford to buy mutton chops for all of them. When ROBINSON came to town, Stumpy showed him around and later visited him on the isle of the Bong tree.

SUGAR, a cream-colored, part-Persian cat with a deformed left hip, was so terrified of riding in automobiles that his owners, Mr. and Mrs. Woods, gave him to neighbors in California before moving to a farm in Oklahoma in 1951. Fourteen months later, Mrs. Woods was in her barn with her back to the window when a cream-colored, part-Persian jumped through it onto her shoulder. As soon as she felt the cat's hip, she knew it was Sugar. The neighbors who had been given the cat later reported that Sugar had vanished two weeks after the Woodses left California.

Dr. J. B. Rhine, who had been investigating extrasensory perception in animals at Duke University, published a paper (with S. R. Feather) in the *Journal of Parapsychology* in 1962 citing Sugar's 1,500-mile trek as an example of "psi-trailing"— an animal following a departed companion with no sensory trail. "The distance being long enough," they wrote, "then the animal would have to be guided by a still unrecognized means of knowing."

SU-LIN, the first live giant panda seen in the Western world, arrived in San Francisco from China on December 18, 1936. Found in Szechuan in November by Mrs. William Harkness, he was 2 months old, weighed 5 pounds, and was thought to be a female. The public was enchanted, a panda craze developed (before Su-Lin's arrival, giant pandas had been considered game animals to be hunted and shot), and several more live pandas were imported. In February 1937, Su-Lin was placed in Chicago's Brookfield Zoo. His death in April 1938 was accidental—a piece of wood had stuck in his throat. The autopsy also revealed that he was a male.

SUN HOU-TZU, the "restless, cunning, indestructible" king of the monkeys in Chinese folklore, was released by the goddess of mercy from punishment for various misdeeds on condition that he be helpful to the pilgrim Tripitaka on his journey to India to study Buddhism. Hatched from a stone egg, Sun Hou-tzu lived on jade juice, could cover 30,000 miles in a single leap, and carried a magic rod that could be made infinitely large or as small as a needle. During the pilgrimage, he got Tripitaka in and out of all kinds of trouble, successfully overcame eighty-one tribulations, and finally, in his yearning for immortality, dedicated himself to Buddhism. As a reward, the monkey was named God of Victorious Strife and became the protective deity of travelers.

SURABHI, "the fragrant one" in Hindu mythology, was the cow of plenty who emerged from the Churning of the Ocean. Also called KAMADHENU, she had the power to fulfill every desire. In another legend, Prajapati, or Brahma, created Surabhi from his breath and was so pleased with her that he gave her a heaven of her own, accessible only to the most pious. NANDINI, "the cow of abundance," was one of her offspring.

SUSAN, the white cat in Beatrix Potter's *The Tale of Little Pig Robinson* (1930), belonged to Betsy, an old fisherman's wife who could hardly stand up because she had "rheumatics." When the fishing boats came in, the cat, wearing Betsy's bonnet and plaid shawl, was sent to the harbor to get herrings for supper.

SVADILFARI, a horse in Norse mythology, belonged to a giant who contracted with the gods to build a protective wall around Asgard, their home, in a year's time. The giant asked for the sun and the moon and the goddess Freya as payment, provided the work was completed by the first day of summer. Otherwise, he would get nothing. The gods agreed, confident that the giant wouldn't finish on time. Svadilfari was so powerful, however, that he pulled stones the size of mountains into place during the night, and the job was soon just three days short of being done. Loki, the trickster god who had arranged the deal, was forced to act—the uneasy gods were threatening to kill him. Transforming himself into a mare, Loki came whinnying out of the forest at dusk. The stallion dropped his work and followed the mare into the woods. The enraged giant was killed by Thor, the god of thunder. Svadilfari and Loki produced SLEIPNIR, who became the world's swiftest horse, perhaps because he had eight legs.

SYLVESTER (1), one of the great cats of animated cartoons, made his debut in *Life With Feathers* (1945), directed by Fritz Freleng for Warner Brothers. For fifteen years, the scrawny black and white cat with a red nose appeared with a variety of characters, including PORKY PIG, SPEEDY GONZALES, and Hippety Hopper, a baby kangaroo. His most frequent antagonist was Tweety Pie, the elusive little canary who never stopped chirping, "I taut I taw a puddy tat." They first tangled in *Tweetie Pie* (1947), which won an Academy Award. In *Birds Anonymous* (1957), which also won an Oscar, Sylvester vowed he would give up birds. He could not.

SYLVESTER (2), the donkey in William Steig's *Sylvester and the Magic Pebble* (1967), discovered a perfectly round red pebble one rainy day and as he held it, he wished the rain would stop. It did. Then he saw a hungry-looking lion staring at him. Too unnerved to think of wishing that the lion was a butterfly, Sylvester wished he was a rock and turned into one. Months later, when his parents set a picnic on the rock, his father picked up the magic pebble lying nearby and placed it on the rock, too. Sylvester wished himself restored.

SYLVIA, a well-bred young Englishwoman, had been married to Mr. Tebrick for a year when she suddenly changed into a fox, a small, pretty, red one, in *Lady into Fox* (1922) by David Garnett. Her loyal husband dismissed the servants, shot the dogs, and devoted himself to her care. Tebrick fed her, bathed her—"using scent very freely to hide somewhat her rank odour"—and, respecting her modesty, dressed her in a bed jacket. Since Sylvia could communicate with looks and gestures, they played cards and she chose music for him to play on the piano. Gradually, however, she changed. She killed and devoured a rabbit, tore off her clothes, and, in a struggle to get free, bit Tebrick. He let her go. Months later, Sylvia reappeared to show off her cubs. When Tebrick found her alone after the cubs had grown and gone, his vixen "at last sprang into his arms, flattened herself upon his breast, and kissed him gently, so that . . . he knew that she still loved him." But he could not save her from the hunters.

TABITHA TWITCHIT, a cat in several of Beatrix Potter's books, was a fretful mother and a sharp retailer. When her scrubbed and neatly dressed kittens—Mittens, Moppet, and Tom Kitten—lost their clothes while playing outdoors in *The Tale of Tom Kitten* (1907), she smacked them, sent them upstairs, and told her guests they were in bed with the measles. In *Ginger & Pickles* (1909), she refused to give credit in her shop. Ginger (1) and Pickles, who gave unlimited credit in theirs, ran out of money and had to close. "Tabitha Twitchit immediately raised the price of everything by a half-penny."

TAFFY, the cat observed in Christopher Morley's poem "In Honor of Taffy Topaz" (1929), thinks

> . . . chiefly of his meals.
> Asparagus, and cream, and fish,
> Are objects of his Freudian wish;
> What you don't give, he steals.

THE TAMMANY TIGER, Thomas Nast's symbol for Tammany Hall—New York City's corrupt Democratic organization run by William ("Boss") Tweed—appeared in the November 11, 1871, issue of *Harper's Weekly*, two days before the election. A dramatic cartoon that climaxed Nast's campaign against Tweed, "The Tammany Tiger Loose" is set in a Roman arena with an imperial Tweed and his cronies looking on as the vicious tiger, clawing a victim, glares at the reader. The picture's subtitle, "What are you going to do about it?" was a famous remark of Tweed's. Voters reacted, Democrats fared badly in the elections, and Tweed eventually went to jail. By an odd coincidence, the tiger symbol evolved from a tiger's head emblem painted on the Americus, or Big Six, Fire Company engine that Nast had admired as an immigrant boy when Tweed was the fire company's chief.

TANNGNOST and **TANNGRISNI:** see Thor's Goats.

TAO, the male Siamese cat in *The Incredible Journey* (1961) by Sheila Burnford, thrived during the trek through the wilder-

THE TAMMANY TIGER

ness with his two dog companions. He could easily catch his food—birds, chipmunks, etc.—or steal it by working a barn door latch to help himself to eggs. When old BODGER the bull terrier collapsed, the fearless cat attacked a bear cub and held off its mother with screams until LUATH (4), the young Labrador retriever, turned up. Then Tao revived Bodger with the smell of fresh meat by tearing at a carcass under his nose.

TARTAR, in *Shirley* (1849) by Charlotte Brontë, was Shirley Keeldar's dog, "of a breed between mastiff and bull-dog." Emily Brontë, Charlotte's sister, was the model for Shirley, and Emily's dog KEEPER was portrayed as Tartar, a dangerous dog who

would not tolerate being "struck or threatened by a stick." If that happened, warned Shirley, he would fly at the person's throat and not let go. Emily had a habit of reading by the hearth with her arm around Keeper. The fictional Shirley also liked to read, perched on a footstool or sitting on the rug, with Tartar stretched out beside her. She kept one hand on his head "because if she takes it away he groans and is discontented."

TARZAN, a beautiful palomino, was Ken Maynard's horse in western movies in the 1920s and 1930s. Maynard, an indifferent actor but a superb stunt rider, was a popular star at a time when the bashful hero of a western preferred to ride into the sunset with his horse rather than stay with the girl. To inject romance into the final fadeout, however, Tarzan had a trick of nudging his master into the arms of the leading lady.

THE TASMANIAN DEVIL, created for Warner Brothers cartoons by Robert McKimson, was a silly character with a maniacal grin who turned up to annoy Bugs Bunny in *Devil May Hare* (1953) and Daffy Duck in *Ducking the Devil* (1957). He bore only a slight resemblance, mostly dental, to the real Tasmanian devil, a ferocious little marsupial carnivore, *Sarcophilus harrisii*, whose ears turn red when he is disturbed.

THE TEDDY BEAR came into existence because President Theodore Roosevelt went hunting while he was in Mississippi to settle a boundary dispute in November 1902. When a little bear showed up in his camp, he refused to shoot it. Clifford Berryman's cartoon of the incident, "Drawing the Line in Mississippi," was published in the Washington *Star* on November 18, then widely reprinted.

When Morris Michtom, the owner of a small candy and toy store in Brooklyn, saw the cartoon, he and his wife made a stuffed brown plush bear with movable limbs and button eyes, labeled it "Teddy's Bear," and put it in the shop window with a copy of the cartoon. The bear was sold at once. So many more were ordered that Michtom soon founded the Ideal Toy Corporation. Coincidentally, in Germany the Steiff family exhibited their stuffed bear at the 1903 Leipzig toy fair. An American importer bought 3,000 of them. Teddy Bears became a national craze, celebrated in songs

THE TEDDY BEAR
The Teddy Bear sent to Theodore Roosevelt

like "The Teddy Bear's Picnic" (1907), which later became a favorite in England. Other companies began stuffing bears, circus clowns and chorus girls cavorted in Teddy Bear costumes, and in 1908, the Steiffs manufactured a million bears.

The craze subsided but not the bear's popularity. The Teddy Bear has become whatever its owner wants it to be. The one that Mrs. A. A. Milne bought in London for her son Christopher Robin in 1920 became Winnie-the-Pooh. In *The Teddy Bear Book* (1969), the British actor Peter Bull quoted people of all ages who had sent him their recollections of Teddy Bears as best friend, mascot, collector's treasure, therapeutic tool, etc. Some correspondents remembered the trauma of losing their beloved bears but the future poet laureate of England, Sir John Betjeman, still had his—Archibald Ormsby-Gore, a companion for sixty years. The original Teddy Bear that Morris Michtom sent to Theodore Roosevelt is now in "the nation's attic," the Smithsonian Institution in Washington, D.C.

TEDDY TAIL, "the Mouse that will make your children laugh," was the hero of *Teddy Tail*, the first daily comic strip in Great Britain. T.T., as he was called, was created by Charles Folkard in 1915; his adventures were continued by a series of artists who presented "the Mouse in your House" and his animal pals in strips and books until 1960.

TEEM was a little French dog who recounted his experiences in " 'Teem' A Treasure-Hunter" (1935), Rudyard Kipling's last story. A self-proclaimed artist at finding truffles, Teem explained: "From my Father I inherit my nose, and, perhaps, a touch of genius. From my Mother a practical philosophy without which even Genius is but a bird of one wing." Taken to England and stranded in the country after an automobile accident, Teem moved in with an old peasant and his invalid daughter. The dog soon discovered truffles in the area. "For, naturally, I followed my Art as every Artist must, even when it is misunderstood." It was. When he presented truffles to the couple, they "would throw—throw! —them for me to retrieve, as though they had been stones and I a puppy." But the fine lady at the nearby château not only bought the truffles, enabling the girl to have medical care, but also congratulated Teem in French.

TEMPLETON, the rat in *Charlotte's Web* (1952) by E. B. White, had "no milk of rodent kindness." When WILBUR, the young spring pig, wanted to play with him, Templeton snorted, "I am a glutton but not a merry-maker," and crept off to eat Wilbur's breakfast. The rat could not be bothered to help Charlotte the spider in her scheme to save Wilbur's life, until he was reminded that Wilbur was his meal ticket: no pig, no leftover slops. At the County Fair in the fall, Templeton had to be bribed for one last favor. Charlotte was dying and Wilbur wanted to take her egg sac back to the farm. The rat retrieved it for him in return for first dibs on Wilbur's every meal. In a few months, Templeton grew so fat that the old sheep advised him he would live longer if he ate less. "Who wants to live forever?" he sneered. "I am naturally a heavy eater and I get untold satisfaction from the pleasures of the feast."

TENCENDUR was Charlemagne's horse in *The Song of Roland*, the eleventh-century epic about the legendary hero of the battle at Roncevalles in 778. To avenge Roland's death, Charlemagne and his ten battalions fought the Saracens through the day. Toward evening, the emperor faced the pagans' leader, Balignant. As they clashed their saddles tipped, throwing them to the ground. They continued the fight on foot. A blow on the head stunned Charlemagne but he killed Balignant, and Duke Naimes rushed up to help the emperor back up on his horse.

THALES' MULE, in a story related by Michel de Montaigne in his *Essays*, II:12 (1580), was loaded with sacks of salt when he stumbled while fording a river. Realizing that the dissolving salt lightened his burden, the sly mule made a practice of falling into every stream he came to, until his master caught on to the trick and substituted a load of wool. Thales of Miletus (640–546 B.C.), the mule's master, was the Greek philosopher and sometime merchant who believed that the origin of all things was water.

THESEUS' HOUNDS are sent for in act 4, scene 1 of Shakespeare's *A Midsummer-Night's Dream* (1598) because Duke Theseus wants Hippolyta, his betrothed, to hear their music:

> My hounds are bred out of the Spartan
>   kind:
> So flewed, so sanded; and their heads
>   are hung
> With ears that sweep away the
>   morning dew—
> Crook-kneed, and dewlapped like
>   Thessalian bulls;
> Slow in pursuit; but matched in mouth
>   like bells,
> Each under each. A cry more tuneable
> Was never hollaed to, nor cheered
>   with horn,
> In Crete, in Sparta, nor in Thessaly.
> Judge when you hear.

THE THESPIAN LION, in Greek mythology, was devouring livestock around Mount Cithaeron when Heracles (Hercules), at the age of 17, killed a man and was sent by Amphytrion to a cattle farm in the area to learn to control his temper. Heracles, the son of Zeus by Amphytrion's wife, Alcmena, promptly killed the lion. From then on, in some accounts, Heracles wore the lion's hide like a cloak, with its head on his like a hood. In other tales, he wore the skin of THE NEMEAN LION, a trophy from the first of his twelve labors for King Eurystheus.

THIDWICK, in Dr. Seuss's *THIDWICK The Big-Hearted Moose* (1948), was helplessly hospitable. After he let a bug rest on his antlers, a spider hopped on, a bird built a nest, a squirrel hid nuts in holes that a woodpecker drilled, and a bobcat came aboard, followed by a turtle. Thidwick could do nothing: "For a host, above all must be nice to his guests." When winter came, his guests would not let him go south with his herd, and even invited more animals to make their home in his antlers. Hunters arrived with guns blazing. Thidwick could not run very fast with 500 pounds of company on his head, but a fact of nature saved his life: The time had come for his annual antler molt.

THOMASINA, the ginger cat in Paul Gallico's *Thomasina* (1957), belonged to young Mary Ruadh, whose father was a veterinarian. Suspecting a meningeal infection, he ordered that Thomasina be put down with chloroform and disposed of. But the comatose cat was taken in by a stranger and came to, convinced that she had been reincarnated as the Egyptian cat goddess Bast-Ra. Meanwhile, the heartbroken Mary went into a decline that threatened her life. Thomasina's mind cleared in time for her to race home through a storm to revive the dying child.

THOMASINA TITTLEMOUSE was a heroine in *The Tale of the Flopsy Bunnies* (1910) by Beatrix Potter. When Mr. McGregor tied the bunnies in a sack, she chewed a hole in the bottom of it to let them out. In *The Tale of Mrs. Tittlemouse* (1910), Thomasina was such a fussy housekeeper that she made her front door smaller to keep out MR. JACKSON, the fat toad who had cleared bees out of her storeroom and left a mess. At her party for mice friends only, he came to her window, was handed a drink, and drank to her health.

THOR'S GOATS, in Norse mythology, were Tanngnost (one who grinds his teeth) and Tanngrisni (one with gaps between his teeth, like a pig). They pulled Thor's chariot, which produced thunder as it rolled along. They also provided food. Thor could kill them, eat them, and then bring them back to life, as long as their bones and hides were saved.

One time, Thor and Loki the mischief maker drove off to the country with the goats. After arranging to spend the night at a farm, Thor proceeded to slaughter, flay, and cook his goats. He then invited the farmer and his family to share the meat. He asked that they put all the bones on the hides. They did, but Thjalfi, the farmer's son, had broken a thigh bone to get at the marrow. (Some say it was Loki who inveigled Thjalfi into breaking the bone.) The next day, Thor rose at dawn, dressed, and then raised his magic hammer to consecrate the goats' bones and hides. Instantly, the reassembled goats sprang to their feet, as lively as ever. But one of them limped, with a bad hind leg. Realizing that a bone had been broken, Thor was furious. The terrified family begged for mercy, offering him everything they owned. Thor settled for taking their son and Roskva, the daughter. Both stayed with him forever, and one goat limped forever.

"He got my goat" does not derive from this episode. The expression originated at American racetracks around the turn of the century, when a goat would be stabled with a Thoroughbred to keep it calm. If the goat was stolen the night before the race,

chances were the high-strung horse would be rattled and lose.

THE THREE BEARS were involuntary, absent hosts, but not to Goldilocks, when their story first appeared in *The Doctor* (1837) by Robert Southey, who recalled hearing the tale as a boy. The original ursine trio—Great, Huge Bear; Middle Bear; and Little, Small, Wee Bear—was all male, and the intruder was an impudent, little old woman who "said a bad word" each time she was displeased. When the bears came home to find her "ugly, dirty head" on the smallest bear's pillow, the sharp and shrill voice of Little, Small, Wee Bear woke her up. She escaped because "the Bears, like good, tidy Bears, as they were, always opened their bed-chamber window when they got up in the morning."

THREE TOES OF HARDING COUNTY was a famous outlaw wolf in South Dakota. He was said to have destroyed $50,000 worth of livestock while 150 hunters tried to catch him for thirteen years. A government hunter finally succeeded in 1925.

THUMPER the rabbit was Walt Disney's version of FRIEND HARE in the 1942 animated film of *Bambi* (1928) by Felix Salten. Like FLOWER the skunk, Thumper was a cute caricature, designed to amuse.

THUNDERHEAD, FLICKA's first foal in *Thunderhead* (1943) by Mary O'Hara, was an all-white throwback to the wild albino that had sired Flicka's dam. The colt took to wandering from the McLaughlins' Wyoming ranch to a valley deep in the Buckthorn hills, where the old albino kept a bunch of wild mares. Thunderhead always came home, but after he killed the albino to get his mares, he could not be allowed to return to an inevitable fight with the McLaughlins' thoroughbred stallion. Rather than sell or geld Thunderhead, young Ken McLaughlin left him with his mares and sealed the entrance to the valley.

THURBER'S DOGS, the ones he wrote about, were of many breeds. The ones he drew were bloodhoundish. Dorothy Parker said they looked like unbaked cookies.

The first short story James Thurber sold, "Josephine Has Her Day" (1923), was about a puny pup who inspired a fight that nearly demolished a general store. Josephine reappears in *Thurber's Dogs* (1955), the collection of thirty-two years of stories and drawings that also includes MUGGS, BARGE, and:

A Peke named Darien.

Feely, a 17-year-old Boston bull who was always carried under the arm of Emma Inch, a cook Thurber hired. Emma never cooked. Feely was never seen to walk.

Jeannie, Thurber's wandering Scotty who liked to mooch off other families.

Medve (Hungarian for "bear"), his first poodle, a champion black standard bitch who always threw up in the car because it might be taking her to a dog show, which she hated.

Cristabel, the poodle who grew old with Thurber and was sensitive to his loss of sight.

In a lifetime of observing dogs, Thurber never confused them with people. His feelings depended on the individual, of either species. "I am not a 'dog-lover,' " he wrote; "to me a dog-lover is a dog in love with another dog."

TIB was the farmyard tabby who helped locate the missing puppies in *The Hundred and One Dalmatians* (1956) by Dodie Smith. The cat's given name was Pussy Willow but "for playful moments" she liked Puss. PONGO, the sire of fifteen of the puppies, called her Mrs. Willow. COLONEL, the Sheepdog who organized the puppies' escape, addressed her as Lieutenant and complained that she had too many names. "I'm entitled to *nine* names as I've nine lives," she said.

TIBERT, the cat in the twelfth-century beast epic *Reynard the Fox,* was sent by the king to summon REYNARD to the court. On the way, the reluctant and superstitious cat saw a bird flying along on his left side and began to fear bad luck. At Reynard's house, the fox played on Tibert's passion for mice, saying the priest's barn was full of them. Reynard knew that after he had stolen a hen from the barn the night before, a trap had been set there. Tibert dived into the hole in the barn wall and yowled—the trap was sprung. The priest woke up and dashed to the barn, "all mother-naked." He beat Tibert with a stick, knocking out an eye, then reared back for the final blow. The desperate cat leaped between his legs and bit off a testicle. The priest's wife bemoaned her loss. Reynard nearly fell down laughing, but reminded her, "There is in this world many a chapel in which is rung but one bell." The fox went home believing Tibert was almost dead. But the cat struggled free and dragged himself back to the court. The king was furious and gathered his Council to advise him how to bring Reynard to justice.

T'IEN-KOW, in the mythology of ancient China, was the Celestial Dog "that howls in the sky." Since the people believed that his eating the sun or the moon caused an eclipse, they would beat drums and gongs during an eclipse in an effort to frighten him off. His master was Erh Lang, a nephew of the Jade Emperor, or Great Emperor of Heaven, and to protect the Emperor's palace from evil spirits, Erh Lang would sic T'ien-Kow on them to drive them away. This led to a tradition of protecting a cherished dog by placing an image of it on Erh Lang's altar.

TIGE, a talking bulldog with a ghastly grin, was first seen in 1897 in Richard Outcault's Sunday comic panel *The Yellow Kid*. Eying some urchins who had fallen into a snowbank, the ugly little dog remarked, "Snowed under." When Outcault launched the strip *Buster Brown* in 1902, Tige reappeared as Buster's dog. Buster, a mischievous boy in Little Lord Fauntleroy

TIGE

outfits, pulled outrageous pranks while Tige leered out at the reader, laughing, winking, standing on his head. The strip was so popular that boys were soon being dressed up like Buster Brown, all sorts of dogs were being named Tige, and in 1904, Outcault licensed more than forty manufacturers to sell Buster Brown products, including cigars and whisky. Although the strip ended in 1920, Buster and Tige live on in the trademarks of two companies: Buster Brown Textiles, Inc. (formerly Buster Brown Stocking Co.), which chose an American Staffordshire terrier in 1981 to tour as Tige and promote their children's wear; and Brown Shoe Company, which promoted Buster Brown shoes on children's television shows in the 1950s with a famous greeting from an animated version of Buster: "Hi, gang. I'm Buster Brown. I live in a shoe. This is my dog Tige. He lives there too."

TIGER (1), the cat, and KEEPER, the dog, were part of the family scene that Charlotte Brontë was homesick for while she was in Brussels in 1843. In a letter to her sister Emily on December 1, Charlotte wrote that she wanted "uncommonly" to be home, in the kitchen, with "you standing by, watching . . . that I save the best pieces of the leg of mutton for Tiger and Keeper, the first of which personages would be jumping about the dish and carving-knife, and the latter standing like a devouring flame on the kitchen-floor." A month later, Charlotte was home; she reported that the little cat had taken sick and died. "It is piteous to see even an animal lying lifeless," she told a friend.

TIGER (2), a gray-striped alley cat, turned up on the White House grounds and allowed President Calvin Coolidge (1923–1929) to adopt him. Coolidge liked to walk around with the cat draped around his neck, or sit on the porch with Tiger on his lap. The first time the cat took off, the President was so upset that he asked the local radio station to broadcast a description with an appeal for the cat's return. Tiger was found, eventually, in the Navy Building but strayed a second time and was never seen again.

TIGER TIM, a boyish tiger in a striped suit, is the oldest hero of British comics. Created in 1904 by Julius Stafford Baker, Tim and his mischievous pals—Willy Giraffe, Billy Bruin, Jacko the Monkey, et al.—made their debut in *Mrs. Hippo's Kindergarten*, the first newspaper strip in England. Later that year, Baker moved the strip to a magazine supplement with children's comics in color. The Hippo Boys, with Tiger Tim as ringleader, became famous as "The Bruin Boys" after they turned up at Mrs. Bruin's Boarding School in 1914. A new artist, Herbert Foxwell, made them the most popular characters in comics for the nursery set. The strip has appeared in comic periodicals ever since, most recently in Peter Woolcock's annual *Tiger Tim Fun Book*, begun in 1973.

TIGGER, "a Very Bouncy Animal, with a way of saying How-do-you-do, which always left your ears full of sand," suddenly showed up in the forest where the other animals lived in A. A. Milne's *The House at Pooh Corner* (1928). They liked him but RABBIT said, "There's too much of him," and conspired with PIGLET and WINNIE-THE-POOH to unbounce Tigger by losing him in the forest. Rabbit got lost

TIGGER

instead and was very glad to be found by the "Large and Helpful Tigger."

TIMBER DOODLE, a little white spaniel (whose name is an American term for the woodcock), was given to Charles Dickens in New York in 1842, delighted him, and was often mentioned in his letters. After returning to England, Dickens reported, "Little doggy now jumps over my stock at word of command," adding, "I have changed his name to Snittle Timbery as more sonorous and expressive." In 1844, the writer took his family to Genoa for a holiday but Timber had a terrible time. The Italian fleas were so ferocious that Dickens had to clip him: "He looks like the ghost of a drowned dog. . . . It is very awful to see him slide into a room. He knows the change upon him, and is always turning round and round to look for himself. I think he'll die of grief."

TIMMY TIPTOES, a fat gray squirrel in Beatrix Potter's *The Tale of Timmy Tiptoes* (1911), was stunned by a fall down the inside of a tree. CHIPPY HACKEE, the chipmunk who was already there, put him to bed and fed him nuts. Since that made the squirrel too fat to climb out through the woodpecker hole he had come in, the two friends stayed there, singing and cracking nuts, until a wind knocked over the top of the tree. Then Timmy Tiptoes went home to his wife, GOODY TIPTOES.

TIMMY WILLIE, the country mouse in Beatrix Potter's *The Tale of Johnny Town-mouse* (1913), did not enjoy his accidental visit to town, even with JOHNNY TOWN-MOUSE's fine hospitality. The noise kept him from sleeping and he lost weight because the food did not agree with him. When Johnny Town-mouse came to visit him, Timmy Willie was sure his friend would never want to live in town again after seeing the delights of country life. Timmy Willie was wrong.

TIMOTHY, a white cat who belonged to Dorothy L. Sayers (1893–1957), appeared in two of her poems. "For Timothy, in the Coinherence" is a reverent commendation to the Lord of "Thy servants' servant" who:

> . . . lived with Thy servants in the exchange
> Of affection.

"War Cat" is about a duel brought on by food shortages. Scorning the scraps in his dish, Timothy tells his mistress that since she no longer loves him, he will sit in a draft "on the stone floor and look miserable" until he dies of starvation "and a broken heart." She puts his food in a bowl for the chickens, tells him to stop crying, and dresses to go to the butcher. He gets on the table and licks the bowl clean:

> Is anything and everything attractive
> so long as it is got by stealing?
> Furtive and squalid cat,

she calls as he streaks out the door. But, she continues,

> . . . having put on my hat to go to the butcher's,
> I may as well go.

TIMOTHY MOUSE, in Walt Disney's animated feature *Dumbo* (1941), was a friend of DUMBO, the baby elephant with oversized ears. When Dumbo learned to fly by flapping them, he became the star of the circus and Timothy took over as his manager.

TIPKINS, a little dog in Beatrix Potter's *The Tale of Little Pig Robinson* (1930), stood on a stool behind the counter of Mr. Mumby's store, tying up groceries in blue paper bags. When ROBINSON settled on the island of the Bong tree, Tipkins and STUMPY, the big dog, went there to visit him.

TIPPIE was the frisky mutt in *Cap Stubbs and Tippie*, the easygoing comic strip about a boy, his dog, and his grandma that was created around 1921 by the great dog cartoonist, Edwina (Dumm). When Cap Stubbs, a cheerful, energetic kid, limped home from football scrimmage with torn clothes and a banged knee, the mournful Tippie followed, carrying his cap. When the boy started to play the piano, Tippie would leap onto Grandma Bailey's lap and howl. In the 1940s Tippie inspired several songs by the composer Helen Thomas that were published with illustrations by Edwina and recorded by Buffalo Bob Smith.

TITO, an Alsatian bitch who belonged to Konrad Lorenz, was so perceptive about her master's feelings that she would nip the bottom of anyone who got on his nerves. In *King Solomon's Ring* (1952) and *Man Meets Dog* (1953), Lorenz, a Nobel Laureate in 1973 for his studies of animal behavior, postulated that the golden jackal (*Canis aureus*) was the principal ancestor of domesticated dogs and that the wolf (*Canis lupus*) provided the dominant strain for only a few northern breeds, such as Eskimo dogs and chows. Tito, devoted and uninhibited, was a classic aureus dog, said Lorenz, while his wife's chow bitch, Pygi, was a typical lupus dog, aloof and independent. When a son of Tito unexpectedly mated Pygi, the resulting chow-Alsatian crossbreeds surprisingly inherited the best traits of both parents. Tito's legacy made the offspring "far more affectionate and much easier to train than pure-blooded chows."

TOAD of Toad Hall, in Kenneth Grahame's *The Wind in the Willows* (1908), took to the open road in a gypsy wagon after sailing, punting, and houseboating palled. When a motorcar knocked his wagon into a ditch, he found a new craze, motoring. He smashed six cars and was hospitalized three times before his friends RAT and MOLE confined him to his house to bring him to his senses. Tricky Toad got away but wound up in a distant dungeon with a twenty-year sentence for stealing a car and being cheeky to the police. Escaping in the washerwoman's clothes, bonnet and all, he made his way back to the Rat's home to boast of his adventures. Told he had made an ass of himself, Toad mumbled mutinously, "But it *was* fun, though!" Then he humbly agreed, "Yes, I've been a conceited old ass, I can quite see that."

TOBERMORY, in *The Chronicles of Clovis* (1911) by Saki (H. H. Munro), was the cat that Cornelius Appin, a guest at Lady Blemley's house party, claimed to have taught human speech. Sent to summon the cat, Sir Wilfred returned to report, "By Gad! he drawled out in a most horribly natural voice that he'd come when he dashed well pleased!" When Tobermory pleased to stroll in, he answered the guests' questions with devastating candor about who said what about whom, until, at the sight of the big yellow tom from the rectory, he vanished out the French window. The cat's dinner, seasoned with strychnine, was untouched that night, but Tobermory's corpse was found in the shrubbery the next morning. Marks on the body indicated that the tom was the killer. A few weeks later, someone read that an elephant in the Dresden Zoological Garden had killed an Englishman, Cornelius Oppin or Eppelin, "who had apparently been teasing it." Said Clovis, "If he was trying German irregular verbs on the poor beast, he deserved all he got."

TOBIT'S DOG, in Muslim legend, was one of the animals placed in heaven. In the Book of Tobit in the Apocrypha, the dog belonged to Tobit's son Tobias. He and the angel Raphael departed for Ecbatana, "the young man's dog with them." When they returned, "the dog went after them." Of all the books in the Bible, Tobit contains the only polite reference to a dog.

TOBY (1) is the dog in the Punch and Judy puppet shows. Originally a marionette, Punch and Punchinello first appeared in England in 1662 as an imported version of the buffoon Pulchinella of the Italian *Commedia dell'arte*. He acquired his wife, Judy, in the eighteenth century but Toby's origin is unknown. By the nineteenth century, the raucous, violent Punch and Judy shows had become popular street theater, with a real dog performing as Toby.

TOBY (2), in Thomas Hood's "The Lament of Toby, the Learned Pig" (1839), had been able to spell and read but his "intellect gets muddy," now that he has been retired from show business—"public fame's unstable" —to be fattened for the kill:

> Of all my literary kin
>   A farewell must be taken.
> Goodbye to the poetic Hogg!
>   The philosophic Bacon! . . .
> One thing I ask—when I am dead,
>   And past the Stygian ditches—
> And that is, let my schoolmaster
>   Have one of my two flitches.

TOBY (3), "an ugly, long-haired, lop-eared creature, half spaniel and half lurcher," in Sir Arthur Conan Doyle's *The Sign of Four* (1890), was sent for by Sherlock Holmes to track two men. At Pondicherry Lodge in Upper Norwood, Holmes dipped his handkerchief in the creosote that one of the fugitives had stepped in, and held it under the dog's nose. "With a most comical cock to its head, like a connoisseur sniffing the bouquet of a famous vintage," Toby got the scent and began leading Holmes and Dr. Watson toward London. At Knight's Place, the dog waddled around in circles, "one ear cocked and the other drooping," then dashed through a lumberyard, where, "with a triumphant yelp," he leaped on a barrel of creosote. Holmes and Watson "burst simultaneously into an uncontrollable fit of laughter." Taken back to his point of indecision, the dog darted off in a fresh direction. The trail ended on the bank of the Thames, where the fugitives had boarded a boat.

Watson returned Toby, with a half-sovereign, to his owner.

TOBY-CHIEN was the high-strung French bulldog in Colette's *Dialogues de bêtes* (1904), a series of conversations with Kiki-la-Doucette, a male angora cat, about themselves and "He" and "She," the people they live with. When dinner is late, Toby frets that there is no sound of plates, until aromas from the kitchen excite him into charging the cat. At each stop on a train ride, the dog panics at the noise, convinced there's a wreck. A thunderstorm sends him scooting under a bookcase: "I'd let my two ears be torn to ribbons before I'd come out of here." But Toby will submit to anything from Her—baths, medicine, teasing. He worships Her, "my sharp torment and my one sure refuge." The aloof Kiki remarks scornfully that when she throws an apple, Toby tears after it "as lost to all sense of decency as a mad thing."

TOM, the polo pony in "Jack and his Pony, Tom" from Hilaire Belloc's *New Cautionary Tales for Children* (1931), was fed sugar, hay, carrots, grass, greens, swedes, mangolds, beans, patent foods, bread, chocolate, and other things by Jack. Tom swelled. The "kindly boy" then gave him medicine, malted milk, and nutmeg ale. Tom staggered, fell, and could not get up. As Jack wept and prayed,

> The pony died, and as it died
> Kicked him severely in the side.

TOM and JERRY, the famous cat-and-mouse team in animated cartoons created for M-G-M by William Hanna and Joseph Barbera, made their debut in *Puss Gets the*

TOM AND JERRY
© 1940 Loew's Inc. Ren. 1967 MGM

Boot (1939). During the next eighteen years, seven of their fast-paced films won Academy Awards. The animals did not speak. Their actions were punctuated with music and sound effects. Most often, Tom chased the mouse. In *Kitty Foiled* (1947), he even managed to tie him to the tracks of a toy electric train. Jerry, as always, survived triumphant. In one of their greatest cartoons, *The Cat Concerto* (1946), Jerry skittered around inside a grand piano to disrupt Tom's rendering of the *Hungarian Rhapsody* by Franz Liszt. Their slapstick antics were seen in comic books for thirty years, starting in 1942. Tom and Jerry cartoons, made for M-G-M by Chuck Jones, began to appear on television in 1965. Hanna and Barbera had meanwhile estab-lished their own studio, and in 1975 they took over production of the cartoons.

TOM KITTEN, in Beatrix Potter's *The Tale of Tom Kitten* (1907), was so fat that his buttons popped and his clothes fell off when his mother, Tabitha Twitchit, put him in the garden with orders to stay clean until her guests arrived. Tom and his sisters Mittens and Moppet, who also lost their clothes, were smacked and sent up-stairs, where their racket "disturbed the dignity and repose" of Tabitha's tea party. In *The Roly-Poly Pudding* (1908), Tom was captured by two rats in the attic, Samuel Whiskers and Anna Maria. They coated him with butter and rolled him in dough to make a dumpling of him before he was rescued. From then on, Tom Kitten was afraid of anything bigger than a mouse.

TOMMY BROCK, the fat, dirty badger in Beatrix Potter's *The Tale of Mr. Tod* (1912), smelled so bad that he was easy to track to the house where MR. TOD the fox used to live. The badger had stolen BENJAMIN BUNNY's seven babies and parked them in the unlit oven while he went to sleep. Benjamin Bunny and PETER RABBIT (1) were burrowing under the house when Mr. Tod arrived, also drawn by the smell. The badger, with one eye "not perfectly shut," gave a virtuoso performance of snoring while the fox led a rope outside from a pail of water over the bed. The contraption drenched the bed but not Tommy. Dry and grinning, he was sipping tea in the kitchen when the fox finally found him.

TOM QUARTZ (1), Dick Baker's cat in Mark Twain's *Roughing It* (1872), "wouldn't let the Gov'ner of Californy be familiar with him. He never ketched a rat in his life—'peared to be above it." The cat knew more about mining than any man Dick ever saw. When Dick and his partner went prospecting for gold, Tom Quartz traipsed on home if he didn't like the spot they chose. If he did, he slept on their coats, snoring like a steamboat, until they struck a pocket. Then he would superintend. Tom Quartz "was *always* agin new fangled arrangements," but the men switched to quartz mining. One day, forgetting that the cat usually slept in the shaft, they set off a charge. Four million tons of rocks and dirt shot up a mile and a half in the air and "right in the dead center of it was old Tom Quartz a goin'

end over end." Two and a half minutes later, he landed 10 feet away. "The orneriest lookin' beast you ever saw" glared at the men, then marched home, "very prejudiced against quartz mining."

TOM QUARTZ (2), a real kitten that President Theodore Roosevelt named for Dick Baker's cat, TOM QUARTZ (1), lived in the White House and bedeviled young Quentin Roosevelt's little black terrier. In 1903, the President wrote to Quentin's brother Kermit about the end of a visit from the Speaker of the House, Joseph Cannon, "an exceedingly solemn, elderly gentleman . . . who certainly does not look to be of a playful nature." The departing Mr. Cannon was halfway down the stairs when the kitten saw him. Tom Quartz "jumped to the conclusion that he was a playmate escaping, and raced after him, suddenly grasping him by the leg . . . then loosening his hold he tore downstairs ahead of Mr. Cannon, who eyed him with iron calm and not one particle of surprise."

TOM THUMB and his wife, HUNCA MUNCA, were the mice who vandalized a doll's house in *The Tale of Two Bad Mice* (1904) by Beatrix Potter. Among other misdeeds, Tom pitched doll clothes out of the window and helped Hunca Munca drag some of the furniture to their hole, but he did have a conscience. He found a sixpence under the hearthrug and, on Christmas Eve, stuffed it in one of the doll's stockings to pay for the breakage.

TONTO was Harry Combes's 11-year-old cat in *Harry and Tonto* (1974) by Josh Greenfeld and Paul Mazursky. Harry, a 72-year-old retired teacher who lived in

Manhattan would talk to Tonto and interpret the cat's shake of the head or wave of the tail as responses. The big, ginger tabby slept with him, liked to jump onto his lap, and even submitted to a collar and leash for walks. When they were evicted because the apartment house was to be torn down, Harry's son on Long Island took them in but after a brief, miserable stay, Harry and his cat headed west in a secondhand car. By the time they reached California, Tonto had developed a taste for hero sandwiches and Harry had been involved with a variety of people, but he was still rootless. Then Tonto fell sick. The veterinarian said that it was a herpes virus to which an out-of-state cat would be particularly vulnerable. As Harry sat there, Tonto's eyes flickered briefly, then closed, and the cat rolled over, dead. " 'So long, kiddo,' said Harry, and closed his own eyes tightly."

TONY, Tom Mix's "Wonder Horse," was a sorrel with a blaze face and two white socks. Mix had been a spectacular rider in one- and two-reelers for the Selig Company, and when he began making feature films at the Fox Studios in 1917, he and Tony performed all their own stunts. The horse even ran through fire. The action-packed movies, often filmed in national parks, made Mix the biggest western star of all. To children, Tony was just as great a hero. Mix, devoted to his horse, made *Just Tony* (1922) in tribute to him. Tony was the first movie horse to have his own special van; music was played on the set to keep him from getting restless; and, between pictures, he and Mix toured Europe and the United States. They left Fox in 1927, having made more than sixty features that not only established the company but kept it solvent. (Years later, Twentieth Century-Fox Studios dedicated

TONY

one of its huge sound studios to the memory of Tom Mix and Tony.) The pair toured with a circus and made movies with other studios until 1932, when 23-year-old Tony was retired after being hurt in a fall. He died ten years later.

TOP CAT, the fast-talking alley cat created in 1961 by Hanna-Barbera Productions for the television cartoon series "Top Cat," shares a splendidly decorated garbage can in Manhattan with five other cats and concocts deals to raise their standard of living. T.C., as he is called, is so tricky he sometimes outwits himself. Decked out in a sheet to impersonate a rich maharajah, he meets the real one, who gives him a bag of rubies but, thinking they came from another imposter, Top Cat throws them away.

TOPPER was Hopalong Cassidy's horse. Clarence E. Mulford created Hopalong Cassidy as a raffish fellow in a series of western stories, but William Boyd, who played—some say, became—Hoppy in sixty-six movies between 1935 and 1948, made him a soft-spoken hero that children could idolize. In the movies, in the half-hour films made for the television series (1948–52), and in personal appearances as Hopalong Cassidy, Boyd always dressed in black. Topper was snow white.

TORNADO was the black stallion that Diego Vega, who was also Zorro, rode in the television series "Zorro" (1957–59), when he was not riding his white stallion, PHANTOM (2).

TOTO, Dorothy's little dog in L. Frank Baum's *The Wonderful Wizard of Oz*

TOTO

(1900), barked and snapped at the strange new creatures he encountered in Oz and hurt his teeth trying to bite the Tin Woodman. When Dorothy and her friends returned to the Wizard after the Wicked Witch was destroyed, a roar from THE COWARDLY LION jolted Toto into knocking over the screen that concealed the old humbug who called himself "Oz, the Great and Terrible." Oz and Dorothy were preparing to take off in a balloon that they hoped would return them to Kansas when Toto scooted into the crowd to bark at a kitten. Dorothy ran after him—and the balloon floated off without them. Eventually, they did get back to Kansas. As soon as they landed on Uncle Henry's farm, Toto ran to the barn, "barking joyously."

Since Toto was described as a "little black dog, with long, silky hair," the illustrator W. W. Denslow made him look like a disheveled terrier. Then Baum and Denslow had a falling out and subsequent Oz books were illustrated by John R. Neill, who redrew Toto as a Boston bull. In *The Road to Oz* (1909), Neill showed a prettier Dorothy and the new Toto gazing at statues of themselves drawn in Denslow's style, complete with the Denslow seahorse trademark.

TRAMP, the mutt in the Walt Disney Productions' cartoon feature *Lady and the Tramp* (1955), was a worldly stray who boasted that he wore "no man's collar." He adored LADY (2), a winsome cocker spaniel. When she was muzzled, Tramp routed attacking mastiffs, talked a beaver into chewing off the muzzle, and took Lady to an Italian restaurant. Then he persuaded her to join him in raiding a chicken house. She landed in the pound, where Tramp's old cronies told her what a bad character he was, but Tramp redeemed himself in a mighty battle with a rat threatening her owners' baby and settled into family life with Lady and their four puppies.

TRAVELER, the first of the white horse mascots of the Trojans, the football team of the University of Southern California, was part Tennessee Walking Horse, part Arabian, and had performed in movies. With his owner-rider Richard Saukko dressed as Tommy Trojan, an earlier mascot, Traveler appeared at the games from 1961 to 1966, rearing, bowing, and galloping around the stadium to celebrate touchdowns. He was retired at the age of 17. Traveler II was a Tennessee Walking Horse, and the current mascot, Traveler III, is an Arabian stallion who began training in 1975.

TRAVELER

TRAVELLER, a 4-year-old gray horse who had won prizes at county fairs, was called Jeff Davis when Confederate Gen. Robert E. Lee bought him in 1861. Lee soon changed his name to Traveller because he was such a good one—and used him almost daily for the rest of the Civil War. On April 9, 1865, Lee surrendered to Gen. Ulysses S. Grant at Appomattox Court House, Virginia, and then, with an audible sigh, mounted Traveller to ride back to his lines. Confederate soldiers lined his path, cheering, weeping, trying to touch him, and, failing that, patting his horse. Traveller reacted to the cheers the way he always did, by tossing his head. In September, when Lee became president of Washington College (now Washington and Lee University) in Lexington, Virginia, he used Traveller for the 108-mile journey there because, wrote Mrs. Lee, "He . . . does not like to part even for a time from his beloved steed." In Lexington, Traveller grazed on the Lees' front lawn. Although souvenir hunters plucking hairs from his mane and tail made the horse edgy with strangers, Lee rode him nearly every afternoon.

TRAY, BLANCHE, and SWEETHEART are mentioned but not seen in act 3, scene 6 of Shakespeare's *King Lear* (1608). In his madness, the distraught king says, "The little dogs and all, Tray, Blanche, and Sweetheart, see, they bark at me."

TREPP, a 66-pound golden retriever whose formal name is Intrepid, was 4 years old when his owner, Tom Kazo, began training him in 1974 to scent illegal drugs. Kazo, an expert dog-handler, was a police officer in Dade County, Florida, at the time. Two months later, Trepp sniffed out his first cache of narcotics, 1¼ tons of hashish stowed in the bulkheads of a sloop docked at Fort Lauderdale. At a Miami-area airport in 1975, Trepp caught a young girl getting off a plane: the doll she clutched was stuffed with cocaine. Once, when he and Kazo were strolling, Trepp started sniffing at a house. Kazo obtained a search warrant, and both marijuana and cocaine were found there. By 1979, Trepp had been credited with 100 arrests and the recovery of more than $63 million worth of narcotics. He also earned a listing as "the world's top police dog" in the 1978 edition of the *Guinness Book of World Records*, which noted that once when Trepp was set to detect ten hidden packets of drugs at a school demonstration, he found eleven.

TRICKI-WOO, a Pekingese in James Herriot's *All Creatures Great and Small* (1972), was "an outstandingly equable little creature, bursting with intelligence," but his owner, Mrs. Pumphrey, gave him twice the food he needed. Whenever the dog went "flop-bott," as she called it, Herriot, a young veterinarian, would arrive to clear Tricki's impacted anal glands and to give futile warnings against his gorging on sweets. Eventually, the bloated dog collapsed and Mrs. Pumphrey let Herriot hospitalize him. Two days with plenty of water but no food revived Tricki enough for him to start running around with the household dogs and in two weeks, with no medicine at all, he was "transformed into a lithe, hard-muscled animal." "Oh, Mr. Herriot," cried Mrs. Pumphrey, "how can I ever thank you? This is a triumph of surgery!"

TRIGGER, Roy Rogers' famous horse, was a gold palomino with white mane and tail, sired by a Thoroughbred out of a quarter-horse mare. Rogers bought the horse for $2,500 in 1938, when he began to star in musical westerns. Glen Randall, who had worked with show horses, helped train Trigger to do his own stunts but doubles were used for difficult or dangerous work after the horse became famous and valuable. Trigger's appearance in over 100 films contributed a great deal to the growing popularity of palominos. In the tradition of William S. Hart's tribute to FRITZ and Tom Mix's to TONY, Rogers made *My Pal Trigger* (1946) to honor his horse. The two of them also made countless public appearances and, in the late 1950s, began to appear regularly on television. Trigger died in 1965. His body was stuffed and placed on display at the Roy Rogers–Dale Evans Museum in Victorville, California, with Dale's horse, Buttermilk, and the family dog, BULLET, alongside.

THE TROJAN HORSE was built by the ancient Greeks to penetrate the walled city of Troy. In the story told by Vergil (70–19 B.C.) in the *Aeneid*, the Greeks spread word as they constructed the horse that it was an offering for their safe voyage home. Then they sailed away, only to hide on a nearby island while their best warriors, fully armed, were crammed into the huge hollow figure. The Trojans flocked out of their gates to marvel at the horse and, as Ulysses (Odysseus) had planned, a captured Greek straggler named Sinon convinced them that Minerva's favor would be transferred to them if they dragged the horse into their city. That night, Sinon let Ulysses and his men out of the horse. They opened the gates to admit the returned Greek army and, by dawn, Troy was in flames.

TROMPETTE, the new pit pony in Emile Zola's *Germinal* (1885), was a 3-year-old bay who lay dazed with fear after being lowered down the coal mine's shaft in a net. It took a lash of the whip to get him to his feet. The old horse, BATAILLE, gave him friendly snorts and nibbles when they met in the tunnels but Trompette "remained melancholy, with no taste for his task, as though tortured by regret for the light." Never acclimated, he sickened and died. Old Bataille had to haul his carcass back to the shaft.

TROTTER, an ARMY MULE mascot from 1957 to 1972, came from Fort Carson, Colorado, where he was famous as the only mule ever known to have mastered four gaits—walk, pace, canter, and trot—and to maintain a gait for eight hours, or about 50 miles. He was the last serial-numbered Army mule, with the number tatooed on his ear and on the inside of his lower lip. Retired from West Point to a farm in Otisville, New York, Trotter was about 51 years old when he died in December, 1981.

TRUFFLEHUNTER, the steadfast badger in *Prince Caspian* (1951), the second Chronicle of Narnia by C. S. Lewis, roused the other animals hiding in the woods to support Caspian against his uncle, who had usurped the throne: "This is the true King of Narnia we've got here." When, after a disastrous battle, the badger urged the prince to summon aid with his magic horn, help finally arrived in the form of Peter, the High King, who hugged the "best of badgers" for keeping faith. He deserved no special credit, said Trufflehunter. "I'm a beast and we don't change. I'm a badger, what's more, and we hold on."

TRUMP is the little dog sitting on his haunches in the foreground of William Hogarth's self-portrait, *The Painter and his Pug* (1745). The dog may not have been a purebred but the artist loved him dearly and, according to a contemporary, had "jocularly observed . . . a close resemblance between his own countenance and that of his favourite dog." The likeness was also noted by unfriendly caricaturists who dubbed Hogarth "Painter-Pugg." Trump was buried in the garden of his master's house at Chiswick in London.

TRUXTON was a bay stallion that Andrew Jackson bought in 1805 after seeing him lose a match race to a local champion named Greyhound. Jackson had resigned from the Tennessee superior court the year before and was deeply in debt. Gambling that with better training Truxton could win, he bet everything he could raise on a $5,000 match a few months later. Truxton won easily. The big bay son of DIOMED kept winning, and in his prime he was undefeated in 2-mile heats. Jackson wrote in *The American Farmer*: "His performances on the turf have surpassed those of any horse of his age that has ever been run in the Western country. . . . His speed is certainly known to all of those who have run against him." Truxton won over $20,000 and sired more than 400 colts, many of them winners.

He was also the indirect cause of a calamity. In 1806, Truxton was challenged to a $2,000 match race with another stallion, Ploughboy, who went lame in training. Ploughboy's owner had to forfeit $800 for postponing the race. When it was finally run before a huge gathering on April 3, Truxton was lame but won both heats handily. From the time of the forfeit, George Dickinson, the son-in-law of Ploughboy's owner, had been making scurrilous remarks about Mrs. Jackson and refused to stop, so Jackson challenged him to a duel. Dickinson was killed and Jackson was badly wounded.

TUCKER MOUSE, in three books by George Selden, shared a drainpipe in the Times Square subway station with HARRY CAT, who infuriated him by calling him "Mousiekins" but was his pal. The mouse lived well by scrounging—coins, scraps spilled from lunch counters, even ice cubes for soft drinks in paper cups. In *The Cricket in Times Square* (1960), Tucker and Harry befriended Chester, a musical cricket stranded in the station; in *Tucker's Countryside* (1969), the subway pair went to Connecticut to help Chester and his friends save a meadow from real estate developers. Tucker endured hay fever, insomnia, and a near-drowning, but his tricky scheme worked. In *Harry Cat's Pet Puppy* (1974), he took care of the stray that Harry dragged in, and when the pup outgrew the drainpipe, Tucker found a good home for him.

TUNIS was a big black gelding that Gen. Georges Boulanger, the French minister of war, bought specifically for his first Bastille Day review of the troops at Longchamp on July 14, 1886. His appointment as minister of war followed a conspicuously successful command of the army of occupation in the French protectorate of Tunis, for which he named the horse. Tunis' stylish prancing before 100,000 spectators at the review propelled Boulanger to national celebrity. The public adored him,

TRUMP

politicians from right to left supported him, and as Boulangism swept the land, he was elected to the Chamber of Deputies from the Nord.

In recollection of Boulanger's appearance at Longchamp, "The Man on Horseback" became the term for a military man who, anointed by destiny, comes forward to save his country by seizing power—even though Boulanger did not. He had the opportunity on January 27, 1889, when he was elected to the Chamber from Paris, but he refused to stage a *coup d'état* and soon left the country with his mistress and Tunis.

TUPPENNY, the guinea pig, "was a miserable object, because most of his hair had been pulled out," wrote Beatrix Potter in 1903 in *The Tale of Tuppeny*, published in 1971. His friends took up a collection to pay for a bottle of Quintessence of Abyssinian Artichoke concocted by the Barber, who claimed it could grow asparagus on a doorknob or even cure chicken pox. It took three bottles to get results. Then his hair grew so fast that Tuppenny spent all his money on haircuts. His family started cutting his hair and stuffing pincushions with it. He finally sold himself to a traveling circus and went on tour as TUPPENNY the HAIRY GUINEA-pig.

TWINKLEBERRY was one of the polite red squirrels in *The Tale of Squirrel Nutkin* (1903) by Beatrix Potter. Unlike his impudent brother NUTKIN, Twinkleberry and his cousins took gifts to Old Brown the owl and asked permission to gather nuts on his island.

TYRAS was the name of two of the many black Great Danes owned by Prince Otto von Bismarck during the course of his life (1815–98). "I love dogs," he wrote. "They never try to get even with you for having harmed them." The first Tyras accompanied young Otto to the University of Göttingen. When Bismarck was summoned to the rector's study for breaking a window, Tyras went too. The rector took one look at the huge dog, ducked behind a chair, and raised the fine.

The second Tyras was Bismarck's companion and bodyguard in his old age and the favorite of all his dogs. A Russian minister once made the mistake of waving his arms during an argument. Tyras knocked him to the floor. Household help had to be acceptable to the dog to be hired. At dinner, Bismarck would fling chunks of meat to Tyras. In 1888, Kaiser William II infuriated Bismarck by sending him a puny dog from a commercial kennel. Tyras had to be sent away lest he kill the newcomer.

UGA III, a white English bulldog, became the fifth bulldog mascot of the University of Georgia football team in 1973, succeeding his father UGA II and grandfather UGA I, whose graves under the scoreboard at Sanford Stadium are marked: NOT BAD FOR A DOG and DAMN GOOD DOG. The mascots' name derives from the school's abbreviated name, U of Ga.

UNC' BILLY POSSUM, in the Thornton Burgess nature books, came from Ol' Virginny and sounded like it. "What yo'all in such a right smart hurry fo'?" he exclaimed after PETER RABBIT (2) nearly collided with him. In *The Adventures of Peter Cottontail* (1914), the rabbit announced that he was going to hibernate like the other animals but as soon as he settled into his hole, Unc' Billy started barking like REDDY FOX while his pals made scratching and bumping noises. Peter fled to his briar patch and the possum laughed fit to kill.

VARAHA, Vishnu's third avatar in Hindu mythology, was the boar that Vishnu turned into when the earth was first covered by a flood, then captured by demons. The boar raced across the sky, dived into the water, and located the earth by its smell. After killing the leader of the demons holding it prisoner, Varaha used his powerful tusks to lift the earth back above the surface of the water.

VEILLANTIF was Roland's horse in *The Song of Roland,* the eleventh-century epic about the legendary hero of the battle at Roncevalles in A.D. 778. After Roland finally blew his horn to summon help from Charlemagne, the Saracens, hearing the trumpets of the approaching French, launched a last volley of spears and javelins. Spurring Veillantif, Roland charged again, but his horse, wounded in thirty places, was killed under him.

VERDUN BELLE, a mongrel bitch who attached herself to an American marine at Verdun in 1918, got lost when the regiment moved to Château-Thierry, then turned up at the field hospital where the young marine had sent her two puppies in the care of an ambulance driver. When the wounded began to arrive, Verdun Belle inspected each one, and before long, she found her marine. He came to while she was licking his face, and two cots were placed together so that she could look after him and the pups. Her story, written by (Sgt.) Alexander Woollcott, was published in the June 14, 1918, issue of *Stars and Stripes* and became a hardy perennial in his subsequent writings. After he retold it on his radio program "The Town Crier," his old *Stars and Stripes* editor, John T. Winterich, groaned in *Squads Write* (1931) that Verdun Belle had been supporting Woollcott since 1918 and that her story had appeared in "virtually every American periodical except *The Wall Street Journal* and the *Harvard Alumni Weekly.*"

THE WALRUS, in "The Walrus and the Carpenter" from Lewis Carroll's *Through the Looking-Glass, and What Alice Found There* (1871), walked along the shore with the Carpenter, the two of them weeping because there was so much sand and beseeching the Oysters to join them. Four little ones hurried up, more and more came hopping along, and after a mile or so, the Walrus and the Carpenter stopped to rest on a "conveniently low" rock:

"The time has come," the Walrus said,
  "To talk of many things:
Of shoes—and ships—and sealing
  wax—
  Of cabbages—and kings—
And why the sea is boiling hot—
  And whether pigs have wings."

The Oysters wanted to catch their breath. The Walrus said it was time to feed:

"But not on us!" the Oyster cried,
  Turning a little blue.

Wrong. The Walrus and the Carpenter ate them all.

Tweedledee recited the poem to Alice, who thought she liked the Walrus best "because he was a *little* sorry for the poor oysters." He ate more than the Carpenter, said Tweedledee, but the Carpenter ate as many as he could get, said Tweedledum. "Well, they were *both* very unpleasant characters," said Alice.

WASHOE, the first chimpanzee to communicate in words, was taught Ameslan (American Sign Language for the deaf) in a pioneer experiment devised by R. Allen and Beatrice Gardner, behavioral psychologists at the University of Nevada at Reno. Films of Keith Hayes's efforts to teach a chimpanzee named Vicki to speak, which failed because chimpanzees lack the necessary vocal apparatus, had nevertheless convinced the Gardners that chimpanzees have the mental capacity to learn a sign language. Ameslan was chosen in order to compare Washoe's development to that of deaf children.

Captured as an infant in Africa, Washoe was about a year old when the Gardners

THE WALRUS

acquired her in June 1966, named her for their Nevada county, and began raising her in a trailer. She was surrounded by toys but her trainers did not speak lest she be distracted. At first, the quickest way to teach her a sign was to show her an object and then arrange her hands into the configuration of its sign. Washoe soon learned to imitate her teachers' gestures. After three years of training, she could make 132 signs. She had also made 245 combinations of three or more of them, such as *you tickle me* and *hug me good.*

In 1971, Dr. Roger Fouts, the Gardners' former chief assistant, moved Washoe to the Institute for Primate Studies in Norman, Oklahoma, and for the first time since 1966, Washoe met other chimpanzees. She called them *black bugs.* When she saw her first swan, she signed *water bird.* In 1979, after twice giving birth to infants who died, Washoe adopted an 11-month-old male chimpanzee named Loulis and began teaching signs to him. Loulis learned so well that after a tantrum, he kept signing *hug* until she gave him one. "This will be the first case of cultural transmissions of a language between generations," said Fouts, "and it's going better than I expected."

WEBSTER, in P. G. Wodehouse's *The Story of Webster* (1932), was a large black cat that the Bishop of Bongo-Bongo left in the care of his nephew Lancelot, an artist in Chelsea. Intimidated by Webster's disapproving gaze, the nephew soon shaved daily, stopped smoking, dressed for dinner, and sold his ukulele. When Lancelot eventually poured himself a drink at the thought of marrying the girl Webster appeared to insist on, the cat's "familiar expression of quiet rebuke" made him drop the bottle, with astonishing results. Webster lapped up the whisky, his tongue "moving in and out like a piston," then started running around the room. After colliding with a footstool, he attacked it ferociously, "sparing neither tooth nor claw."

WEENIE was Eloise's dog in Kay Thompson's *Eloise* (1955), the story of a 6-year-old living at the Plaza Hotel in New York City.

Eloise thought he looked like a cat but Hilary Knight's illustrations made him look like a pug. Weenie would wake Eloise up with a lick on the face, and when her doll Saylor lost both arms, he comforted Saylor with a lick on the face.

WESSEX, a pedigreed, wirehaired terrier that belonged to Thomas Hardy's second wife, Florence, was the subject of three poems written by Hardy when he was in his eighties. "A Popular Personage at Home" is a soliloquy by the dog about his walks. Wessex visits a grave in "Why She Moved House," and in "Dead 'Wessex' the Dog to the Household" (he died in 1926 at the age of 13), he addresses the "Wistful ones" who miss him. In fact, only the childless writer and his wife did. The spoiled dog terrorized servants, bit postmen—in return, one kicked out two of his teeth—and at meals, he was allowed to walk around *on* the dining table. In 1921, Lady Cynthia Asquith endured his "contesting every single forkful" of her lunch and called him "the most despotic dog guests have ever suffered under." John Galsworthy was one of several who suffered ripped trousers. The only visitor Wessex never attacked was T. E. Lawrence.

WHITE FANG, the gray wolf born to KICHE in Jack London's *White Fang* (1906), fought and killed for survival as a cub in the wilderness, as a sled team leader for Indians, and, tormented into viciousness by a venal white man, as a killer of dogs in fights staged for gold rush gamblers in the Klondike. Weedon Scott, a mining expert appalled by the cruelty, bought White Fang. Recognizing the animal's intelligence, Scott patiently taught him to accept meat

from his hand and then to accept the touch of the hand. The wolf (who was one-fourth dog) grew to love the man and to accept his discipline.

THE WHITE HORSE OF UFFINGTON is a primitive figure, 374 feet long, that was etched on a hillside of White Horse Vale in Berkshire, England, by the removal of turf to reveal the white chalky soil underneath. Of seventeen white horses drawn on English hills, it is the oldest. From 1755 to 1859, festivals were held while vegetation was cleared from the outline, a procedure called "The Scouring of the White Horse." Some say it is a monument to King Alfred's victory over the Danes in 871; others link it to Hengist, the fifth-century Teutonic chieftain whose standard was a white horse; but the general belief is that it was there before the Roman invasion, a view shared by G. K. Chesterton (1874–1936) in his "Ballad of the White Horse":

> For the White Horse knew England
> When there was none to know;
> He saw the first oar break or bend,
> He saw heaven fall and the world end,
> O God, how long ago.

THE WHITE RABBIT, in *Alice's Adventures in Wonderland* (1865) by Lewis Carroll, was a snappy dresser and busy, busy. When Alice first saw him, he was whipping out his watch and muttering that he was late. Alice's curiosity about a rabbit having a waistcoat pocket and a watch to pull out of it led her to the rabbit-hole and down into it. He next appeared, "splendidly dressed," carrying white gloves and a large fan, and muttering about the Duchess, "Oh, *Wo'n't* she be savage if I've kept her waiting!" When Alice tried to speak to him,

THE WHITE RABBIT

he dropped his gloves and fan and scurried off. A while later, he trotted back to look for his things and, calling her Mary Ann, ordered her to fetch them. Said Alice to herself, "How queer it seems to be going messages for a rabbit!"

WHITE SURREY, in Shakespeare's *Richard III* (1593), is the doomed mount of King Richard. In act 5, scene 3, on the eve of the battle of Bosworth Field, Richard commands, "Saddle white Surrey for the field to-morrow." While Richard sleeps, the ghosts of his victims curse him. He wakes from his nightmare, pleading, "Give me another horse; bind up my wounds!" In scene 4, the battle is in progress. Sir William Catesby calls for help for the king: "His horse is slain and all on foot he fights." Richard appears, crying, "A horse! A horse! My kingdom for a horse!"

WILBUR, in *Charlotte's Web* (1952) by E. B. White, was a runt of a spring pig nursed to health by a little girl, then taken to be raised at her uncle's farm. Charlotte, a large gray spider, befriended the forlorn little pig, who thrived until he learned that he was being fattened for butchering. To save him, Charlotte rearranged her web to spell out, in letters glistening with dew, "SOME PIG!" People began to believe it and her second message, "TERRIFIC," inspired plans to take Wilbur to the County Fair. When she spun "RADIANT," the modest pig "did everything possible to make himself glow." At the fair, Wilbur won a special prize for attracting visitors, then fainted. But Charlotte, having laid her egg sac, was dying. Determined to take the sac home, Wilbur bribed TEMPLETON the rat to fetch it. The following spring, Charlotte's 514 babies hatched and Wilbur told the three that did not float away that he owed his life to their mother. The pig lived out his days in contentment, loving each new generation of spiders, but he never forgot Charlotte.

THE WILD BEAST OF GEVAUDAN killed at least sixty-four people, perhaps as many as a hundred, between 1764 and 1767 in the Cévennes Mountains of south-central France. It was said that he could leap high in the air, used his tail like a club, and had a nauseating stench. Some people thought he was a rabid wolf or a hyena or a panther. Others believed he was a warlock. In *Travels with a Donkey in the Cévennes* (1879), Robert Louis Stevenson called the Beast "the Napoléon Buonaparte of wolves" who "ate women and children and 'shepherdesses celebrated for their beauty,'" and chased armed horsemen, even on the king's highway. "M. Elie Berthet has made him the hero of a novel, which I have read, and do not want to read again."

In the April 1971 issue of *Natural History*, C. H. D. Clarke, a Canadian naturalist, reported that there were two Beasts. A 130-pound male, much bigger than any European wolf, was killed in 1766, and a smaller female was killed nine months later. Having found that most records of a wolf attacking a human being involved either a rabid wolf or a wolf-dog hybrid, Clarke concluded that the Beasts were hybrids since a wolf-dog cross can grow larger than either parent and is less afraid of men.

WILE E. COYOTE started chasing Road Runner in *Fast and Furry-ous* (1948), the first of a series of animated films that continued for fifteen years and can still be seen on television. Road Runner is a long-legged, ostrich-like bird based on the western cuckoo, *Geococcyx californianus*, who runs on the ground and is popularly called a road runner. The cartoon characters, created for Warner Brothers by Chuck Jones and Michael Maltese, have also appeared in comic books since 1958 and in the *Bugs Bunny/Road Runner Movie* (1979), which revived some of their great old chases. Wile E. has a magnificent obsession: to catch the speedy bird and eat him. The scrawny coyote sets crazy traps that don't work, or he gets caught in them. When he races after his prey across rugged landscape, a rock crushes him. Or he falls off a cliff. His ears droop in frustration and, again, Road Runner scoots away with a taunting "Beep Beep."

WILEY CATT, the shotgun-toting bobcat in Walt Kelly's comic strip *Pogo* (1948–75), was the reactionary of the Okefenokee Swamp. A threat to his ignorance was a threat to his country. Overhearing some small creatures adding one and one, then two and two, he bawled at them that one and one was eleven, two and two was twenty-two: "That's what we got schools for. What are you guys? Communists?"

WILL (GILLE) is the monkey who descends to earth, caduceus in hand, just as the elephant and the rhinoceros have arranged a duel in "The Elephant and Jupiter's Monkey," one of the *Fables* of Jean de La Fontaine (1621–95). The elephant is nonplused that the monkey does not know about the impending fight. "I am delighted to learn their names," says the haughty monkey. "We hardly concern ourselves with such matters in our vast halls." Why, then, has he come to earth, asks the embarrassed elephant. "To divide a blade of grass among some ants," Will replies. "We take care of everything. As for your case, the Council of Deities has heard nothing about it yet. The small and the great are equal in their eyes."

WILLIAM (1), the bright blue Egyptian faience hippopotamus at the Metropolitan Museum of Art in New York City, has become the museum's mascot. William was found in the Twelfth-Dynasty (ca. 1940 B.C.) tomb of a steward named Soneb, whose body was surrounded by figures of men and animals to do his work and to ensure good hunting in the next world. The hippo's name was given to him in England in the 1930s by Captain H. M. Raleigh, who reported in *Punch* that the animal had

WILLIAM (1)

become an "oracle" to the Raleigh family; by gazing at a color print of him, they could discern William's approval or disapproval of their plans, and they had learned from experience to heed his expression.

WILLIAM (2), a white cat that Charles Dickens (1812–70) was especially fond of, was renamed Williamina when her kittens were born. Not content with leaving them in the kitchen, she would carry them one by one to a corner in the writer's study. Dickens would evict them, she would persist in bringing them back, and he finally relented when she placed them at his feet.

After they grew too obstreperous, other homes were found for all but one, who became known as THE MASTER'S CAT.

WILLIAM (3), in James Thurber's "The Cat in the Lifeboat" from *Further Fables for Our Time* (1956), was so egotistical about being the only cat in town named William that he was convinced he was the "Will of Last Will and Testament, and the Willy of Willy Nilly." When he lost his job as a copy cat on the local paper, a "cat-crazy woman" took him on a voyage around the world. As the ship began to sink during a storm, he was certain he heard "William and children first!" and jumped into a lifeboat. A sailor threw him out, "like a long, incompleted forward pass." William had to swim to an island, an experience that produced traumatic amnesia. He could not remember his name.

WILLY was a yellow male cat whose selective sense of time was reported by the biologist Gustav Eckstein in *Everyday Miracle* (1948). Having heard that the cat came out of its house every Monday night at 7:45, Eckstein confirmed it three Mondays in a row, each time following Willy across the street, through a hedge, and onward to the window sill of a nurses' dining room where a well-attended Bingo game was in progress. "Oh yes, Willy knows Monday," said the ladies who kept him. Other nights, the cat went out earlier and came back as late as midnight for his supper but on Mondays, Willy ate promptly at 7:30 and came home at 9:45, when the Bingo game was finished. The ladies also told Eckstein that Willy knew 8:10 in the morning "exactly!" That was the time they went out, and he wanted to get in before the door was closed. If he was five minutes early, he would amble up the hill, maybe stopping to stretch in the sun, "but if he is late," they said, "—say 8 minutes after 8—he comes prancing."

WING COMMANDER, an American Saddle Horse bred by Dodge Stables, Castleton Farm, in Kentucky, was the world champion five-gaited horse for seven years in a row, from 1948 to 1954. Trained by Earl Teater, the liver-chestnut stallion drew ovations at horse shows when, at the command "Rack on!" he steadily increased his speed without changing the cadence of the four-beat gait. Retired to stud at Dodge Farms, Wing Commander was named the breed's leading sire for four straight years, starting in 1963.

WINKY, in *Pictures of the Floating World* (1919) by Amy Lowell, is the poet's cat. Miss Lowell remarks his inconsistencies in "To Winky." He is fussy about food but eats a bird and its feathers with no apparent injury. When he comes in wet, he fawns on her; but once dry, he departs with an impudent quirk of his tail:

> Cat,
> I am afraid of your poisonous beauty,
> I have seen you torturing a mouse.
> Yet when you lie purring in my lap
> I forget everything but how soft you
>   are. . . .
> Shall I choke you, Cat,
> Or kiss you?
> Really I do not know.

WINNIE, in R. D. Blackmore's *Lorna Doone* (1869), was the famous strawberry mare that belonged to the highwayman Tom Faggus. When young John Ridd, the story's narrator, insisted on riding her bareback, she reared, leaped over a gate, then a hedge, and rushed on until, at a whistle from her master, she sped home and dumped Ridd into the dunghill. Several years later, Ridd had to search for Faggus, now his brother-in-law, among the Duke of Monmouth's rebels. When he stopped on the battlefield to comfort a dying man, Ridd "felt warm lips laid against my cheek quite softly, and then a little push." It was Winnie. She would not let him mount her but as soon as he got on his own horse, KICKUMS, she darted off to lead him to her master. Ridd bound Faggus' wounds and tied him on Winnie. "I am safe," Faggus whispered. "Who can come near my Winnie mare?"

WINNIE-THE-POOH, the bear in A. A. Milne's *Winnie-the-Pooh* (1926) and *The House at Pooh Corner* (1928), was crazy about honey. He once ate so much on a visit to RABBIT that he got stuck going out the hole. Christopher Robin read to his north end and Rabbit hung wash on his south end for a week until he thinned down enough to be popped out like a cork. Pooh called himself a Bear of Little Brain but he invented the game of Poohsticks, which involved dropping sticks into a stream from one side of a bridge, then hanging over the other side to see whose stick floated by first. And he thought of using an upended umbrella for a boat to rescue PIGLET from a flood. As a poet, Pooh made up Hums, little verses punctuated with "Tiddely poms," and songs like "Sing Ho! for the life of a Bear!"

When Milne's young son, Christopher Robin, was given a TEDDY BEAR in 1920, he named it Winnie for a real bear in the London Zoo, and tacked on "the Pooh" for a swan he fed every morning. His father's books made Winnie-the-Pooh world-famous. In Russia, he is called *Vinni-Pukh*,

WINNIE-THE-POOH

a neat translation since *pukh* is Russian for swansdown. Pooh societies in several countries compose Hums or devise HEFFALUMP traps, and a group in New Zealand is said to play Poohsticks with people. Classicists everywhere welcomed *Winnie Ille Pu* (1961), Dr. Alexander Lennard's translation of the first Pooh book into Latin, hailed by the New York *Herald Tribune* as "the status book of the year."

WISHPOOSH was a monster beaver who snatched and drowned anyone who tried to fish in his lake in the northern Cascade Mountains, according to several American Indian tribes along the Columbia River. The Indians appealed for help to their trickster god COYOTE, who tied a spear to his wrist, went fishing, and, as soon as he was pulled under, stabbed the beaver. Their underwater thrashing was so violent that gorges opened and rivers widened as Wishpoosh, dragging Coyote along by the spear, struggled downstream to the Pacific. While the beaver swam out to eat whales to get his strength back, Coyote changed himself into a branch of a fir tree to float toward him. Wishpoosh swallowed the branch and was soon dead, butchered from within by the restored Coyote.

WITEZ II was a purebred Arabian stallion foaled in 1938 at the Janow Stud Farm in Poland. In 1943, the Janow stallions were dispersed to various farms in the region but the invading Germans recovered the horses and shipped them to a stud farm in Czechoslovakia. Toward the end of the war, the German veterinarian there managed to send word to the American forces, led by Gen. George S. Patton, that the approaching Russians were likely to slaughter the

WITEZ II

valuable Arabians for food. Patton immediately arranged their rescue. Witez II was sent to the former Kellogg Ranch in California, the most important breeding center for Arabian horses in the United States. Later, he was sold to E. E. Hurlbutt, the first president of the International Arabian Horse Association. In shows, Witez II won many awards and was twice grand champion. At stud, he produced two grand champion sons and countless other winners, male and female. Poland honored him in 1963 by including him in a set of postage stamps publicizing Polish horse breeding. Witez II, who died in 1965, is regarded as one of the great Arabian stallions of all time.

WOLF, Rip's dog in *Rip Van Winkle* (1820) by Washington Irving, was as henpecked by Dame Van Winkle as his master was. In the house, the dog "sneaked about with a gallows air . . . and at the least flourish of a broomstick . . . he would fly to the door with yelping precipitation." Escaping to the woods, Rip would assure Wolf that they would always be friends. The dog bristled and growled at the stranger they met in the Catskills but Rip drank some of the man's liquor and went to sleep. Wolf went home. Twenty years later, Rip returned to find a half-starved cur that looked like Wolf but snarled and showed his teeth when called by name. " 'My very dog,' sighed poor Rip, 'has forgotten me!' "

THE WOLF OF GUBBIO was terrorizing the people of the town of Gubbio at a time when St. Francis of Assisi (1182–1226) was preaching there, according to a famous legend in *The Little Flowers of St. Francis* (ca. 1380). When Francis learned that the people were afraid to go outside the town's gate, he walked out to meet the wolf, who rushed at him, jaws open wide. Making the sign of the cross, Francis said, "Come to me, Brother Wolf. In the name of Christ, I order you not to hurt me or anyone." The wolf lay down like a lamb. Francis then pledged that if the wolf promised never to hurt any animal or man, the townspeople would feed him and "neither man nor dogs will pursue you any more." The wolf wagged his tail, nodded, and gave a paw. They walked into the town together and Francis asked the wolf to repeat the promise in front of all the people. Again, the wolf wagged his tail and gave a paw. The wolf and the people kept the pact for two years, until the wolf died of old age. "And it is a striking fact that not a single dog ever barked at it."

XANTHIPPUS' DOG was so faithful to Xanthippus, the father of Pericles, that he swam alongside his master's galley to the island of Salamis when the Athenians had to evacuate their city in 480 B.C. Xanthippus buried the dog on a promontory known as Cynossema ("dog's grave").

XANTHUS and BALIUS, in the *Iliad* of Homer (eighth century B.C.), were Achilles' immortal horses. Zephyrus the west wind was their sire, and Podarge, a harpy, their dam. When Patroclus rode into battle wearing Achilles' armor to deceive the Trojans, Xanthus and Balius pulled the chariot. After Patroclus was killed, his comrade Automedon could not move the horses: "Hot tears fell from their eyes as they mourned the loss of their charioteer, and their noble manes drooped all wet from under the yoke-straps." But Zeus intervened to give them the strength and spirit to carry Automedon away. Enraged by Patroclus' death, Achilles donned new armor and leaped on the chariot, telling the horses to bring him back safely, not leave him dead as they had Patroclus. Xanthus bowed his head and, given the power of speech by Hera, said, "Dread Achilles, we will indeed save you now, but the day of your death is near, and the blame will not be ours." There was no need to foretell his death, Achilles replied, "For I well know that I am to fall here," and with a loud cry, he drove his horses forward to the front.

XANTHUS, PODARGUS, AETHON, and LAMPUS were Hector's horses in the *Iliad* of Homer (eighth century B.C.). Preparing to lead the Trojans against Diomed and Nestor, Hector addressed his horses: "Pay me for your keep now and for all the honey-sweet corn Andromache . . . has fed you and for the way she has mixed wine and water for you . . . before doing so even for me, her own husband." If the horses were swift enough for him to seize Nestor's shield and Diomed's armor, said Hector, the Greeks would sail away that same night. But that was not to happen. After many more battles, the *Iliad* ends with the funeral of Hector, "tamer of horses."

XENG-LI, the first giant panda born in captivity outside China, was born on August 10, 1980, at the Chapultepec Zoo in Mexico City. His father and mother, PE-PE and Ying-Ying, had been given to Mexico by the People's Republic of China in 1975, when they were both about 11 months old. Their ability to breed was attributed to their being raised together, to the altitude of Mexico City (7,500 feet, comparable to their native environment), to their special diet, and to luck. At birth, Xeng-Li (Chinese for "success") weighed just over 3 ounces and was 4 inches long. In one week, he doubled his weight but on the eighth day he died, apparently smothered by the 277-pound bulk of his mother.

Fortunately for the world's declining panda population, Pe-Pe and Ying-Ying bred successfully again. Their second baby was born in July 1981.

XOLOTL, in the mythology of the Nahuas and the Aztecs, was the twin of the god Quetzalcoatl. He often took the shape of a dog. To found a new human race when the present world was created, Xolotl the dog went to the underworld to fetch the bones of those who had lived before. The god of death chased Xolotl, who dropped the bones, shattering them. From each piece, a different tribe was born.

YERTLE THE TURTLE, in Dr. Seuss's *Yertle the Turtle and Other Stories* (1951), viewed his kingdom from a rock in a little pond until he decided he would be a greater king if he could see more. Perched on top of nine turtles stacked on the rock, he could see a mile. Ignoring complaints of back pains from Mack, the bottom turtle, Yertle ordered his throne raised. At the altitude of 200 turtles, he proclaimed himself King of the Birds and King of the Air. Then the moon rose above him. Furious, Yertle demanded 5,607 more turtles, Mack burped, the throne collapsed, and Yertle, dumped into the pond, became King of the Mud.

In 1979, Dr. Seuss (Theodore Seuss Geisel) told *Parents* magazine that Yertle, "a little domineering guy that pushes people around," was an intentional caricature of Adolf Hitler.

YOFUR, Mohammed's burro, was one of two admitted to the Moslem paradise, the Garden of Allah. BALAAM's ASS was the other.

YOGI BEAR, created by Hanna-Barbera Productions to co-star with HUCKLEBERRY HOUND in television cartoons, became so popular that his own series was launched in 1961. The amiable bear traipses around Jellystone Park with an insatiable appetite and larceny in his heart. At the sight of an unattended picnic basket, he cries, "I think I spy a Peezza Pie!" His best pal, a little bear named Boo-Boo, tries to make him obey park rules but Yogi, who proclaims himself "smarter than the average bear," delights in outwitting the Ranger. When the exasperated Ranger does grab him, Yogi protests haughtily, "I'll remind you, Sir—you're wrinkling my fur!"

YUANJING, the first giant panda bred by artificial insemination, was born at the Beijing (Peking) Zoo in the fall of 1978. She weighed a quarter of a pound and was said to look like a white hairless mouse; a twin died three days after birth. Within a month, Yuanjing weighed ten times as much as at birth, and at 8 months, she was a robust adolescent. A photograph of her

YERTLE THE TURTLE

being cuddled by her mother, Juanjuan, was so popular that figurines based on it were widely sold. The success of the artificial insemination also raised hopes that the procedure could work for other panda couples.

YUKI was a little white dog with a great grin whom President Lyndon B. Johnson adopted in November 1966, about six months after his beagle, Him, had been run over (see HIM AND HER). Johnson's daughter Luci had found the abandoned mutt at a gas station. The President loved all his dogs—the neurotic collie BLANCO as well as the countless beagle puppies—but Yuki (Japanese for "snow") quickly

became his favorite. They "sang" duets in melodious howls, traveled together, and often slept together.

YUKON KING, "swiftest and strongest lead dog in the Northwest," blazed the trail for Sergeant Preston of the Northwest Mounted Police, whose relentless pursuit of lawbreakers during the gold rush began in 1947 on the radio show "Challenge of the Yukon." The husky barked at the opening of each episode and became so prominent in the series—knocking down and disarming outlaws—that he became popularly known as Yukon King. In 1955, the show was successfully transferred to television as "Sergeant Preston of the Yukon."

ZAPAQUILDA was the female cat in *La Gatomaquaia* (*The Battle of the Cats*, 1634), Lope de Vega's epic poem, a parody of the literary epic, about a feline love triangle. The wicked cat Marramaquiz is determined to frustrate Micifuf, who is about to marry his beloved Zapaquilda. Marramaquiz ambushes their wedding party, abducts her to his castle, and keeps her there until Micifuf's friends surround the place.

ZEPHIR, the monkey in a black beret in Jean and Laurent de Brunhoff's books about BABAR the elephant, played the violin and went to school with cousin ARTHUR. In *Babar and His Children* (1938), when Babar's daughter Flora turned purple in her crib, the monkey reached down her throat to pull out the rattle she had swallowed. Zephir also got into mischief and, in *Babar the King* (1935), he got into a tub of vanilla cream.

ZERO was a shaggy mutt in *Little Annie Rooney*, the comic strip that first appeared on January 10, 1929, to compete with *Little Orphan Annie*. Brandon Walsh was the sole writer of the strip, but five different artists drew it at various times, including Darrell McClure, who drew the daily strip from 1930 until its end in 1966. Annie Rooney, a 12-year-old with black bangs, was resolutely cheerful in her efforts to elude her legal guardian, the terrible Mrs. Meany. Zero, Annie's faithful pal, mostly stood around listening to her monologues about her plight: "I get the wim-wams awful bad." But Annie appreciated him: "Gloryosky, Zero, you look grand! Honest, you do tricks like pooches in the circus!"

ZIRA, a female chimpanzee in *Planet of the Apes* (1964) by Pierre Boulle, is a scientist in a future world ruled by apes. In the film *Escape from the Planet of the Apes* (1971), a sequel to the 1968 movie version of the book, Zira and her mate CORNELIUS (2) travel two thousand years back to the present world. Cornelius warns Zira not to reveal her intelligence, but she becomes so exasperated by the psychiatrists who wonder why she won't eat a banana that she snaps, "Because I loathe bananas." After she admits that in her world apes use captive human beings for medical experiments, she and Cornelius become fugitives. They are killed, but not the future they represent: Zira had given birth and had left her baby with a sympathetic trainer at the circus.

ZLATEH, in Isaac Bashevis Singer's story "Zlateh the Goat" (1966), did not give much milk at the age of 12. Her owner, who needed money for Hanukkah, sent his son Aaron off with the trusting goat to sell her. Caught in a blizzard, the boy burrowed into a snow-covered haystack. He had some bread and cheese, Zlateh ate the hay, and, as her udder filled, he drank her milk. With comforting patience, the goat kept the boy warm and fed for three days, while he passed the time by talking to her. She would cock her ears to listen and then say, "Maaaa." When they finally made their way home, there was no more thought of selling Zlateh. Occasionally, Aaron would ask her if she remembered their time together: "And Zlateh would scratch her neck with a horn, shake her white bearded head and come out with the single sound which expressed all her thoughts, and all her love."

ZOMO, in the folklore of Hausaland (now part of northern Nigeria), was a hare who outsmarted bigger animals. In *Zomo, the Rabbit* (1966), Hugh Sturton translated and adapted the African versions of the animal stories told and retold by the Hausa people taken as slaves to America, where the hare became a rabbit and Zomo was turned into BRER RABBIT. In one tale, Zomo convinced

Damisa the leopard that another leopard, down in the well, had stolen his breakfast. Damisa roared at his reflection in the water and fell in. In another story, Zomo made a big bet that he could get a calabash of milk from the bush-cow. Flattered by the hare's saying she was so strong that she could split a tree, the cow pawed the ground, thundered toward the tree, and crashed into it, to be impaled by her horns. Zomo then helped himself to her milk.

ZORRO, a German shepherd-wolf, was in the Sierra Nevadas with his master, Mark Cooper of Orangevale, California, in November 1975, when Cooper lost his balance, fell 85 feet down a ravine into a creek, and was knocked unconscious. As he came to, Zorro was dragging him out of the water and up a steep, slag-rock bank. While friends went for help, Zorro slept on top of his master to keep him warm during the night. In the commotion of taking Cooper out by helicopter the next day, Zorro was left behind. Broadcast appeals brought volunteers to search for him and he was found a day later, guarding his master's backpack. In 1976, Zorro received a gold medal as the Ken-L-Ration Dog Hero of the Year.

ZSA ZSA, a rabbit who allegedly played a toy trumpet and drank beer, was sent to the White House during John F. Kennedy's presidency (1961–63). Reporters asked Press Secretary Pierre Salinger about the gift; he related the dialogue in his book *With Kennedy* (1966). The first question was, did Salinger know if the rabbit was a lush?

A. All I know about Zsa Zsa is that she's supposed to be able to play the first five bars of "The Star Spangled Banner" on a toy golden trumpet.

Q. Could we have the rabbit come over here and run through a couple of numbers for us?

A. I can ask her.

Q. Was the rabbit playing the trumpet as it came into the White House?

A. No, the trumpet came under separate cover and it will be sent to the orphanage with the rabbit. I don't think Zsa Zsa should be without her trumpet.

Q. You're not sending her to the orphanage?

A. Immediately.

SELECTED BIBLIOGRAPHY

ANIMALS IN GENERAL

Barloy, J. J. *Man and Animals*. Translation of *Les animaux domestiques* (1974). London: Gordon & Cremonesi, 1978.

Boudet, Jacques. *Man and Beast: A Visual History.* Translated from the French. New York: Golden Press, 1964.

Brewer, E. Cobham. *The Dictionary of Phrase and Fable* (1894). Reprinted New York: Avenel Books, 1978.

Carson, Gerald. *Men, Beasts, and Gods*. New York: Charles Scribner's Sons, 1972.

Clark, Kenneth. *Animals and Men*. New York: William Morrow, 1977; London: Thames and Hudson, 1977.

MYTHOLOGY, LEGEND, AND LORE

Bulfinch, Thomas. *The Age of Fable* (1855). New York: New American Library, Mentor Books, 1962.

————. *The Age of Chivalry* (1858) and *Legends of Charlemagne* (1862). New York: New American Library, Mentor Books, 1962.

Clark, Ella E. *Indian Legends from the Northern Rockies*. Norman: University of Oklahoma Press, 1966.

Cotterell, Arthur. *A Dictionary of World Mythology*. New York: G. P. Putnam's Sons, 1980; Toronto: Academic Press, 1980.

Crossley-Holland, Kevin. *The Norse Myths*. New York: Pantheon Books, 1980.

Funk & Wagnalls' *Standard Dictionary of Folklore, Mythology, and Legend*. 2 vols. New York: Funk & Wagnalls, 1951; London: The Mayflower Publishing Co., 1951.

Grimal, Pierre, ed. *Larousse World Mythology*. Middlesex, Eng.: Hamlyn, 1965.

Hamilton, Edith. *Mythology*. Boston: Little, Brown and Co., 1940.

Hoffman, Daniel. *Paul Bunyan: Last of the Frontier Demigods*. Philadelphia: Temple University Publications, distributed by Columbia University Press, 1952.

Mercatante, Anthony S. *Zoo of the Gods*. New York: Harper & Row, 1974.

Merwin, W. S., trans. *Medieval Epics*. New York: Modern Library, 1963.

Munch, Peter Andreas. *Norse Mythology*. The American-Scandinavian Foundation (1926). Reissued Detroit: Singing Tree Press, 1968.

Parker, Derek, and Parker, Julia. *The Immortals*. Exeter, Eng.: Webb & Bower, 1976.

Parrinder, Geoffrey. *A Dictionary of Non-Christian Religions*. Philadelphia: The Westminster Press, 1974. First published by Hulton Educational Publications, Ltd.

Rouse, W. H. D. *Gods, Heroes and Men*. London: John Murray Publishers Ltd., 1957; New York: New American Library, Signet Key Books, 1957.

Spence, Lewis. *Myths of the North American Indians*. London: George Harrap, 1914; Millwood, N.Y.: Kraus Reprint Co., 1972.

CATS

Fireman, Judy, ed. *Cat Catalog*. New York: Workman Publishing Co., 1976.

Kirk, Mildred. *The Everlasting Cat*. Woodstock, N.Y.: The Overlook Press, 1977.

Méry, Fernand. *The Life, History and Magic of the Cat*. Translation of *Le Chat* (1966) by Emma Street. London: Paul Hamlyn Ltd., 1967; New York: Grosset & Dunlap, 1968. First published in France as *Le Chat* by Editions Robert Laffont (1966).

Necker, Claire. *The Natural History of Cats*. Cranbury, N.J.: A. S. Barnes, 1970.

Van Vechten, Carl. *The Tiger in the House*. New York: Alfred A. Knopf, 1920, 1936.

DOGS

Denenberg, R. V., and Seidman, Eric. *Dog Catalog*. New York: Grosset & Dunlap, 1978.

Downey, Fairfax. *Great Dog Stories of All Time*. Garden City, N.Y.: Doubleday, 1962.

Loxton, Howard, ed. *Dogs*. London: Paul Hamlyn Ltd., 1962.

Méry, Fernand. *The Life, History and Magic of the Dog*. New York: Grosset & Dunlop, 1970; London: Cassell & Co. Ltd., 1970. First published in France as *Le Chien* by Editions Robert Laffont (1966).

Myrus, Don. *Dog Catalog*. New York: Macmillan, Collier Books, 1978; London: Collier Macmillan Publishers, 1978; Don Mills, Ont.: Collier Macmillan Canada, Ltd., 1978.

Ross, Estelle. *The Book of Noble Dogs*. New York and London: The Century Co., 1922.

HORSES

Alexander, David. *A Sound of Horses*. Indianapolis: Bobbs-Merrill Co., 1966.

Crowell, Pers. *Cavalcade of American Horses*. New York: McGraw-Hill, 1951.

Denhardt, Robert Moorman. *The Quarter Running Horse*. Norman: University of Oklahoma Press, 1979.

Livingston, Bernard. *Their Turf*. New York: Arbor House, 1973.

Longrigg, Roger. *The History of Horse Racing*. New York: Stein & Day, 1972.

Pines, Philip A. *The Complete Book of Harness Racing*. 3rd ed. New York: Arco Publishing Co., 1978.

Smith, Bradley. *The Horse in the West*. Cleveland: World, 1969.

Smith, Red. *Strawberries in the Wintertime*. New York: Quadrangle/ The New York Times Book Co., 1972.

Wiggins, Walt. *The Great American Speedhorse*. New York: Simon & Schuster, Sovereign Books, 1978.

OTHER SPECIES

Bourne, Geoffrey H., and Cohen, Maurey. *The Gentle Giants: The Gorilla Story*. New York: G. P. Putnam's Sons, 1975.

Brookshier, Frank. *The Burro*. Norman: University of Oklahoma Press, 1974.

Hedgepeth, William. *The Hog Book*. Garden City, N.Y.: Doubleday, 1978.

Linden, Eugene. *Apes, Men, and Language*. New York: Saturday Review Press/E. P. Dutton, 1975.

Lopez, Barry Holstun. *Of Wolves and Men.* New York: Charles Scribner's Sons, 1978.

Morris, Raymona, and Morris, Desmond. *Men and Apes.* New York: McGraw-Hill, 1966.

———. *Men and Pandas.* New York: McGraw-Hill, 1967.

Sebeok, Thomas A., and Umiker-Sebeok, Jean, eds. *Speaking of Apes.* New York: Plenum Publishing Co., 1980.

PERFORMING ANIMALS

Amaral, Anthony. *Movie Horses.* Indianapolis: Bobbs-Merrill Co., 1967,

Croft-Cooke, Rupert, and Cotes, Peter. *Circus: A World History.* New York: Macmillan, 1976.

Durant, John, and Durant, Alice. *Pictorial History of the American Circus.* Cranbury, N.J.: A. S. Barnes, Castle Books, 1957; London: Thomas Yoseloff, Ltd., 1957.

Fenin, George N., and Everson, William K. *The Western.* New York: Crown Publishers, Bonanza Books, 1962.

Fox, Charles Philip. *A Ticket to the Circus.* New York: Bramhall House, 1959.

Lee, Raymond. *Not So Dumb.* New York: A. S. Barnes, Castle Books, 1970.

Metz, Robert. *The Today Show.* New York: Playboy Press, 1977.

Rothel, David. *The Great Show Business Animals.* San Diego and New York: A. S. Barnes, 1980; London: The Tantivy Press, 1980.

Zinman, David H. *Saturday Afternoon at the Bijou.* New Rochelle, N.Y.: Arlington House, 1973.

COMIC STRIPS AND ANIMATED CARTOONS

Finch, Christopher. *The Art of Walt Disney.* New York: Harry N. Abrams, 1973.

Halas, John, and Rider, David. *The Great Movie Cartoon Parade.* New York: Crown Publishers, Bounty Books, 1976; United Kingdom: Triune Books, 1976.

Horn, Maurice, ed. *The World Encyclopedia of Comics.* New York: Chelsea House Publishers, 1976; London: New English Library Ltd., 1976.

Maltin, Leonard. *Of Mice and Magic.* New York: New American Library, 1980; Scarborough, Ont.: New American Library of Canada, 1980; London: New English Library Ltd., 1980.

Schickel, Richard. *The Disney Version.* New York: Simon & Schuster, 1968.

Terrace, Vincent. *The Complete Encyclopedia of Television Programs 1947–1979.* New York: A. S. Barnes, 1979; London: Thomas Yoseloff Ltd., 1979.

Thomas, Bob. *Walt Disney: Magician of the Movies.* New York: Grosset & Dunlap, 1966.

Waugh, Coulton. *The Comics.* New York: Macmillan, 1947.

MISCELLANEOUS SUBJECTS

Briggs, Hilton M., and Briggs, Dinus M. *Modern Breeds of Livestock.* 4th ed. New York: Macmillan, 1980.

Bryant, Traphes. *Dog Days at the White House.* New York: Macmillan, 1975.

Campbell, Hannah. *Why Did They Name It . . . ?* New York: Fleet Publishing Corp., 1964.

Hall, Angus. *Monsters and Mythic Beasts.* Garden City, N.Y.: Doubleday, 1976.

Kolatch, Alfred J. *Names for Pets.* Middle Village, N.Y.: Jonathan David, 1972.

Stern, Jane, and Stern, Michael. *Amazing America.* New York: Random House, 1977; Toronto: Random House of Canada Ltd., 1977.

Truman, Margaret. *White House Pets.* New York: David McKay Co., 1969.

Wels, Byron G. *Animal Heroes.* New York: Macmillan, 1979; Don Mills, Ont.: Collier Macmillan Canada Ltd., 1979; London: Collier Macmillan Publishers, 1979.

Wood, Gerald L. *The Guinness Book of Animal Facts and Feats.* Rev. ed. Enfield, Middlesex, Eng.: Guinness Superlatives Ltd., 1976; New York: Sterling Publishing Co., 1977.

PICTURE
CREDITS

With grateful thanks to the individuals and organizations who permitted use of their material.

ABDUL
The 50th Anniversary of Anzac stamp. The Australian Postal commission.
"The Man with the Donkey." The Victorian Government Tourist Authority.

ABLE AND BAKER
Alabama Space and Rocket Center, Huntsville, Alabama.

ALBERT
From *Ten Ever-Lovin' Blue-Eyed Years With Pogo* by Walt Kelly. Simon & Schuster, New York, 1959.

APIS
Apis bull, Egyptian Late Dynastic sculpture. The Metropolitan Museum of Art, Gift of Darius Ogden Mills, 1904.

ARGOS
"Ulysses & His Dog." Illustration by John Flaxman for Alexander Pope's *Homer's Odyssey*, 1793, reproduced in *Flaxman's Illustrations to Homer*. Dover Publications, Inc., New York, 1977.

BALAAM'S ASS
Engraving by J. A. Adams from *The Illuminated Bible*. Harper & Brothers, Publishers, New York, 1846.

BALTO
Courtesy New York City Parks and Recreation.

BAST
Bastet, Cat Goddess, Egyptian Late Dynastic to Early Ptolemaic Period, bronze with gold earring. The Metropolitan Museum of Art, Purchase, 1958, Funds from various donors.

BENJI
Photograph of Joe Camp's BENJI courtesy of Mulberry Square Productions, Inc.

BILL XXII
Courtesy the United States Naval Academy.

BILLY WHISKERS
Illustration by W. H. Fry from *Billy Whiskers: The Autobiography of a Goat* by Francis Trego Montgomery. Saalfied Publishing Company, Akron, Ohio, 1902. Reprinted by Dover Publications, Inc., New York, 1969.

BINGO
Courtesy Cracker Jack.

BLACK DIAMOND
Courtesy Manfra, Tordella and Brookes, Inc.

BOBBY COON
Illustration by Harrison Cady from *The Adventures of Unc' Billy Possum* by Thornton Burgess. Little, Brown and Company, Boston, 1914.

BRER RABBIT
BRER TARRYPIN
Illustrations by Arthur Burdette Frost from *Uncle Remus: His Songs and His Sayings* by Joel Chandler Harris. D. Appleton and Company, New York, 1896.

BUDDY
The Seeing Eye, Inc., Morristown, New Jersey.

BULL'S-EYE
"Sikes Attempting to Destroy his Dog." Illustration by George Cruikshank from *Oliver Twist* by Charles Dickens. Chapman and Hall, London; J. B. Lippincott & Co., Philadelphia, 1875.

THE CALYDONIAN BOAR
Meleager slays the Calydonian Boar. Detail of engraving after Johann Wilhelm Bauer (1600–42) for Ovid's *Metamorphoses* (Book 8). New York Public Library Picture Collection.

THE CHESHIRE CAT
Illustration by Sir John Tenniel from *Alice's Adventures in Wonderland* by Lewis Carroll, 1865.

CHESSIE
Courtesy The Chessie System.

CLAVILENO
Illustration by Gustave Doré from an 1863 French edition of *Don Quixote* by Miguel de Cervantes. Courtesy of The New York Public Library, Astor, Lenox and Tilden Foundations.

CORNPLANTER
"The Celebrated Cornplanter." Billy Rose Theatre Collection, The New York Public Library at Lincoln Center, Astor, Lenox and Tilden Foundations.

THE COWARDLY LION
Illustration by W. W. Denslow from *The Wonderful Wizard of Oz* by L. Frank Baum. George M. Hill Company, Chicago and New York, 1900. Reprinted by Dover Publications, Inc., New York, 1960.

CUWART
Illustration by Wilhelm von Kaulbach from *Reineke Fuchs* (*Reynard the Fox*) by Johann von Goethe, Stuttgart, 1846. Print Collection, The New York Public Library, Astor, Lenox and Tilden Foundations.

THE DEMOCRATIC DONKEY
"FINE-ASS COMMITTEE." Cartoon by Thomas Nast, 1873, from *Th. Nast: His Period and His Pictures* by Albert Bigelow Paine. The Macmillan Company, New York and London, 1904. Reprinted by The Pyne Press, Princeton, N.J., 1974.

DICK WHITTINGTON'S CAT
The Whittington Stone, Highgate Hill, London. British Tourist Authority photograph.

EEYORE
Illustration by Ernest H. Shepard from *Winnie-the-Pooh* by A. A. Milne. E. P. Dutton & Co., Inc., New York, 1926.

ERSWIND
Woodcut from a Latin edition of *Reynard the Fox*, Frankfurt, Germany, 1584. Rare Books and Manuscript Division, The New York Public Library, Astor, Lenox and Tilden Foundations.

FLORA TEMPLE
Courtesy the Hall of Fame of the Trotter, Goshen, New York.

FOSS
Later editions of the Nonsense Books by Edward Lear.

FRITZ
Movie Star News, New York.

GARGANTUA
Billy Rose Theatre Collection, The New York Public Library at Lincoln Center, Astor, Lenox and Tilden Foundations.

GERTIE
Museum of Modern Art/Film Stills Archive, New York.

THE GODOLPHIN ARABIAN
Engraving by George Townley Stubbs, 1794, after a painting by George Stubbs. Art, Prints and Photographs Division, The New York Public Library, Astor, Lenox and Tilden Foundations.

GREYFRIARS BOBBY
Courtesy the British Tourist Authority.

GRIMBERT
Woodcut attributed to Erhart Altdorfer. From a Danish edition of *Reynard the Fox*, Lybeck, 1555. Spencer Collection, The New York Public Library, Astor, Lenox and Tilden Foundations.

GRIZZLE

"Doctor Syntax Sketching the Lake." Illustration by Thomas Rowlandson from *Tour of Dr. Syntax* by William Combe, 1812–21. Print Collection, The New York Public Library, Astor, Lenox and Tilden Foundations.

HAM

Ham being unzipped from his space suit. Alabama Space and Rocket Center, Huntsville, Alabama.

HAMBLETONIAN

"Rysdyk's Hambletonian." Lithograph by Nathaniel Currier and James Ives, after J. H. Wright, 1865. Courtesy the Hall of Fame of the Trotter, Goshen, New York.

HSING-HSING AND LING-LING

Jessie Cohen, National Zoological Park, Smithsonian Institution.

JACK (1)

David Barritt, Muldersdrift, South Africa.

JIP (1)

"Our Housekeeping." Illustration by H. K. Browne from *David Copperfield* by Charles Dickens. Chapman and Hall, London; J. B. Lippincott & Co., Philadelphia, 1875.

JUMBO (1)

"What a Trifle May Embroil Nations!" The British Lion says to the American Eagle, "In the name of Queen Victoria, the Royal Family and over a million children, I demand his release." Cartoon by Thomas Nast, 1882. The Library of Congress.

JUSTIN MORGAN

University of Vermont Morgan Horse Farm, Middlebury, Vermont.

KEEPER

Drawing by Emily Brontë of her dog, Keeper. Reproduced by permission of the Brontë Society, Brontë Parsonage, Haworth, Yorkshire, England.

KOSHIN

Author's photograph.

LASSIE (2)
The boy (played by Roddy McDowell) has just learned that Lassie must be sold. Still photograph from the MGM release *LASSIE COME HOME.* © 1943 Loew's Inc. Ren. 1970 MGM.

LELAPS
"A Mythological Subject" (The Death of Procris) by Piero di Cosimo (1462–1521). Reproduced by courtesy of the Trustees, The National Gallery, London.

THE LION OF LUCERNE
Swiss National Tourist Office.

LUCY, THE MARGATE ELEPHANT
Copyrighted photograph courtesy of The Save Lucy Committee, Inc., P.O. Box 3000, Margate, N.J. 08402.

THE MACK BULLDOG
Courtesy Mack Trucks, Inc.

MANEKI NEKO
Author's photograph.

MAN O' WAR
New York Racing Association.

MAROCCO
English woodcut, 1595, reproduced in *Book of Days* by Robert Chambers. Originally published 1862–64 in England; republished by J. B. Lippincott, Philadelphia, 1891.

mehitabel
"what have i done to deserve all these kittens." Drawing by George Herriman from *The Lives and Times of Archy and Mehitabel* by Don Marquis. Doubleday & Company, Inc., Garden City, New York, 1933.

MISS BIANCA
Illustration by Garth Williams from *The Rescuers* by Margery Sharp. Little, Brown and Co., Boston, 1959.

MR. JEREMY FISHER
Illustration from *The Tale of Mr. Jeremy Fisher* by Beatrix Potter.
Frederick Warne & Co., London, 1904.

MRS. TIGGY-WINKLE
Illustration from *The Tale of Mrs. Tiggy-Winkle* by Beatrix Potter.
Frederick Warne & Co., London, 1905.

MOUFLAR
Woodcut from *Fables choisies* by Jean de La Fontaine, Paris, 1787.
Courtesy of The New York Public Library, Astor, Lenox and Tilden
Foundations.

NANDI
Nandi the Sacred Bull. Indian, XII–XIII Century. The Metropolitan
Museum of Art, Rogers Fund, 1946.

THE NEMEAN LION
Greek vase, terracotta, about 560 B.C. The Metropolitan Museum of
Art, Fletcher Fund, 1940.

THE NITTANY LION
The Pennsylvania State University.

OLD JOE
Photograph and drawing courtesy R. J. Reynolds Tobacco Co.

OLD MR. BENJAMIN BUNNY
Illustration from *The Tale of Mr. Benjamin Bunny* by Beatrix Potter.
Frederick Warne & Co., London, 1904.

OLD WHITEY
The Library of Congress.

PATIENCE AND FORTITUDE
Author's photographs.

PAUL PRY
"A Distinguished Member of the Humane Society" by Sir Edwin
Landseer. The Tate Gallery, London.

POGO
Drawing from *Ten Ever-Lovin' Blue-Eyed Years with Pogo* by Walt Kelly. Simon & Schuster, New York, 1959.

PONTO
"The Sagacious Dog." Illustration by Robert Seymour from *The Pickwick Papers* by Charles Dickens. Chapman and Hall, London; J. B. Lippincott & Co., Philadelphia, 1873.

PUSS IN BOOTS
Illustration by Gustave Doré from *Les Contes de Perrault, dessins par Gustave Doré*. Originally published by J. Hetzel, Libraire-Editeur, Paris, 1867. Reprinted in *Perrault's Fairy Tales*, translated by A. E. Johnson. Dover Publications, Inc., New York, 1969.

RA
The cat Ra slaying Apep the snake by the Persea Tree. Egyptian manuscript ca. 2000 B.C. Reproduced by permission of The Board of Trinity College, Dublin.

RAMINAGROBIS
"*Le Chat, La Belette, et Le Petit Lapin.*" Illustration by J. J. Grandville from *The Fables of La Fontaine* (translated from the French by Elizur Wright). Boston, 1841. General Research Division, The New York Public Library, Astor, Lenox and Tilden Foundations.

RATON (1)
Illustration by K. Girardet from *Fables de La Fontaine* by Jean de La Fontaine. Tours, 1866. General Research Division, The New York Public Library, Astor, Lenox and Tilden Foundations.

THE REPUBLICAN ELEPHANT
"SAVED (?)" Cartoon by Thomas Nast, 1877, from *Th. Nast: His Period and His Pictures* by Albert Bigelow Paine. The Macmillan Company, New York and London, 1904. Reprinted by The Pyne Press, Princeton, N.J., 1974.

REYNARD
"The Fox's Arrival at Court." Etching by Aldert van Everdingen (1621–75) from *The Pleasant History of Reynard the Fox* (Felix Summerly, ed.). London, 1843. Courtesy of The New York Public Library, Astor, Lenox and Tilden Foundations.

RIN TIN TIN
Movie Star News, New York.

THE ROOSEVELT BEARS
Illustration by V. Floyd Campbell from *The Roosevelt Bears* by Seymour Eaton (Paul Piper). Edward Stern & Company, Inc., Philadelphia, 1906. Reprinted by Dover Publications, Inc., New York, 1979.

SAMUEL WHISKERS
Cover illustration from *The Roly-Poly Pudding* by Beatrix Potter. Frederick Warne & Co., London, 1908.

SCRAPS
Museum of Modern Art/Film Stills Archive, New York.

SHASTA (2)
Courtesy Hogle Zoological Garden, Salt Lake City, Utah.

SMOKEY BEAR
Courtesy United States Department of Agriculture–Forest Service.

THE TAMMANY TIGER
"THE TAMMANY TIGER LOOSE.—'What are you going to do about it?'" Cartoon by Thomas Nast, November 11, 1871, from *Th. Nast: His Period and His Pictures* by Albert Bigelow Paine. The Macmillan Company, New York and London, 1904. Reprinted by The Pyne Press, Princeton, N.J., 1974.

THE TEDDY BEAR
Smithsonian Institution Photo No. 74–797.

TIGE
Buster Brown and Tige. A portion of a comic strip by Richard Outcault from a collection in the book *Buster Brown and His Resolutions*. Frederick A. Stokes Company, New York, ca. 1904. Reprinted by Dover Publications, Inc., New York, 1974.

TIGGER
From *The House at Pooh Corner* by A. A. Milne, illustrated by Ernest H. Shepard. E. P. Dutton & Co., Inc., New York, 1928.

TOM AND JERRY
Still photograph from the MGM cartoon *TOM AND JERRY*. ©
1940. Loew's Inc. Ren. 1967 MGM.

TONY
Movie Star News, New York.

TOTO
Illustration by W. W. Denslow from *The Wonderful Wizard of Oz*
by L. Frank Baum. George M. Hill Company, Chicago and New
York, 1900. Reprinted by Dover Publications Inc., New York, 1960.

TRAVELER
Courtesy USC Sports Information Office.

TRUMP
"The Artist and His Dog" by William Hogarth. The Tate Gallery,
London.

THE WALRUS
"The Walrus and the Carpenter." Illustration by Sir John Tenniel
from *Through the Looking-Glass, and What Alice Found There* by
Lewis Carroll, 1871.

THE WHITE RABBIT
Illustration by Sir John Tenniel from *Alice's Adventures in Wonderland* by Lewis Carroll, 1865.

WILLIAM (1)
Egyptian, XII Dynasty, about 1940 B.C. The Metropolitan Museum of
Art, Gift of Edward S. Harkness, 1917.

WINNIE-THE-POOH
From *Winnie-the-Pooh* by A. A. Milne, illustrated by Ernest H.
Shepard. E. P. Dutton & Co., Inc., New York, 1926.

WITEZ II
Courtesy Roman J. Burkiewicz, Frisco, Colorado.

YERTLE THE TURTLE
Part of an illustration from the book *YERTLE the TURTLE and Other
Stories* by Dr. Seuss. Random House, Inc., New York, 1958.

INDEX

Note: Numbers in italic refer to illustrations.